The
Psychoanalytic
Study
of the Child

VOLUME FIFTY-SIX

Kindly submit seven copies of new manuscripts to

Albert J. Solnit, M.D.
Yale Child Study Center
230 South Frontage Road
P.O. Box 207900
New Haven, CT 06520-7900
Phone: (203) 785-2518

The Psychoanalytic Study of the Child

VOLUME FIFTY-SIX

New Haven and London
Yale University Press
2001

Designed by Sally Harris
and set in Baskerville type.
Printed in the United States of America by
Vail-Ballou Press, Inc., Binghamton, N.Y.

Library of Congress catalog card number: 45-11304
International standard book number: 0-300-08989-9
A catalogue record for this book is available from the British Library.

The paper in this book meets the guidelines for
permanence and durability of the Committee on
Production Guidelines for Book Longevity of the
Council on Library Resources.
2 4 6 8 10 9 7 5 3 1

Contents

SPECIAL SECTION ON
CHANGES IN TECHNIQUE IN
CHILD PSYCHOANALYSIS
SINCE THE PUBLICATION OF
*NORMALITY AND PATHOLOGY
IN CHILDHOOD*
BY ANNA FREUD

Introduction and Historical Perspective

ALBERT J. SOLNIT, M.D.

ON 11 MARCH 2000 THE PSYCHOANALYTIC RESEARCH AND DEVELOP-
ment Fund and *The Psychoanalytic Study of the Child,* with the support
of the Child Study Center, Yale University School of Medicine,
cosponsored a clinical scientific meeting—Symposium on Changes
in the Technique of Child Psychoanalysis since the Publication of
Anna Freud's *Normality and Pathology in Childhood* (1965)—to reflect
on changes in the technique of child psychoanalysis since the publication of Anna Freud's classic work. The nine papers that follow in
this special section were presented at that meeting, and in two cases
we include the discussions as well. The following excerpt from a 1961
paper by Peter Neubauer, a pioneer in child analysis, will set the historical perspective for these papers.

> The scientific study of child development did not begin until the
> twentieth century, which has been called, among other things, the
> Century of the Child. If it is to live up to this label, we must make bet-
> ter use of the next forty years than we have of the past sixty. But the
> revolution in child psychiatry is still relatively young, and I will begin
> by trying to sketch the somewhat erratic course it has taken so far.
> If I dwell on the thought and influence of [Sigmund] Freud, it is
> because I speak as a child psychiatrist and psychoanalyst. . . . Freud
> was the first to attempt to give us a body of scientific knowledge that
> would lead to a general psychology of man. The anthropologists, ap-
> plying this knowledge to the study of culture and society, found that
> child-rearing processes furnished illuminating clues to an under-

Sterling Professor Emeritus of Pediatrics and Psychiatry and senior research scientist at Yale University School of Medicine and Child Study Center; former commis-
sioner, Department of Mental Health and Addiction Services, State of Connecticut.

The Psychoanalytic Study of the Child 56, ed. Albert J. Solnit, Peter B. Neubauer, Samuel
Abrams, and A. Scott Dowling (Yale University Press, copyright © 2001 by Albert J.
Solnit, Peter B. Neubauer, Samuel Abrams, and A. Scott Dowling).

standing of people and their institutions. The pediatricians learned to connect physical growth with emotional development, and the way was paved for Dr. Spock to write his bible on the subject of infant care. Whichever way we turn, we detect the seminal influence of Freud's discoveries.

Unfortunately, it must be added that Freud's theories have also been widely misunderstood. For one thing, they have often been taken to mean that discipline should be suspended, controls eliminated—in sum, that the child should be continuously gratified. Freud, on the contrary, pointed out that denial and conflict were as essential a part of the process of growth as gratification, and he never minimized the child's need for direction.

In fact, Freudian psychology does not, as some people apparently imagine, provide a set of ready-made prescriptions for the rearing of children. It has forced us to take into account not only what the mother or teacher does to a child, but also how it is done; not only whether the mother nurses the baby and spends much time with him, but also whether she is able to give him gratification and support his strivings for mastery. The complexity of the interactions between mother and child cannot be reduced to rigid formulas. Love and understanding cannot be prescribed, and if they are not genuinely manifested, the most enlightened efforts to do what is best for the child may not be effective.

Freud's investigations into the neuroses of adults forced him to reconstruct their early childhoods and provided clinical support for the old belief that "the child is father of the man." His findings led him to frame not only a psychology of man but also laws of human development, and his contributions have completely changed our image of childhood. Gone is the sentimental view that childhood is an era of innocence and the belief that an innate process of development continuously unfolds along more or less immutable lines. Freud suggested that, from birth on, the child's development proceeds in a succession of well-defined stages, each with its own distinctive psychic organization, and that at each stage environmental factors can foster health and achievement or bring about lasting retardation and pathology. . . . The whole of Freud's contribution points up the complexity of human nature and the intricacy of the laws which govern the early phases of development. Whoever has understood a single page of Freud knows that he never dealt in facile prescriptions.[1]

This symposium probably should have been called "Techniques in Child Psychoanalysis since the publication of Anna Freud's *The Ego*

1. Peter Neubauer, The Century of the Child, *The Atlantic*, Special Supplement on "Psychiatry in American Life," July 1961, pp. 84–87.

and the Mechanisms of Defense" in 1936. In her foreword to the revised edition of that work, published in 1966, Anna Freud stated,

> Much has changed in this respect in the thirty years which have elapsed since then until, by now, the ego as a psychic structure has become a legitimate object of psychoanalytic study. If, in 1936, it was sufficient to enumerate and illustrate ego mechanisms, to inquire into their chronology, and to assess the role of the defense organization as a whole for the maintenance of health or illness, this can no longer be done today without relating the ego's defensive achievements to its other aspects—i.e., to its primary deficiencies, its apparatuses and functions, its autonomies, etc. . . . [It] was decided to leave the original text intact, and to relegate more recent thinking to a further volume (1965) in which the aspects of *Normality and Pathology in Childhood* are pursued, especially with regard to their developmental and diagnostic implications.[2]

In this same volume, Anna Freud, after describing and discussing the ego as observer, states,

> Again, the technique of child analysis which I myself have advocated (1926–1927) is a good example of the dangers of one-sidedness. If we must give up free association, make but a sparing use of the interpretation of symbols, and begin to interpret the transference only at an advanced stage in the treatment, three important avenues to the discovery of id contents and ego activities are closed to us. The question then arises which I propose to answer in the next chapter: how can we make good these deficiencies and, in spite of all, pass beyond the superficial strata of psychic life?[3]

Historical Perspective

In conducting a child psychoanalytic treatment, to what extent do we respond to the dynamics of new knowledge about child development? And how does our increasing experience in child psychoanalysis, with the "widening scope" of psychoanalysis, stimulate a refinement and elaboration of our theory and technique in analytic work with children and adolescents?

Two major currents of dialogue and questions are apparent in the literature and in the three substantive papers that follow. The questions and the dialogues are focused on:

2. Anna Freud, The Ego and the Mechanisms of Defense, *The Writings of Anna Freud*, Vol. II, Rev. Ed. (New York: International Universities Press, 1966).
3. Ibid., p. 27.

(1) How the changing conditions of life, culture, and society are experienced by children and their parents (caregivers); and

(2) How the refinements and elaborations of our knowledge, presumptions, and theory-building regarding how children mature and develop have become applied and useful to child analysts and their patients.

These two currents converge when child analysts widen the scope of their clinical work and apply the best available knowledge about the maturing, developing child in their analytic work. The widening scope of analytic work with children confronts obstacles to healthy or sound development ranging from inborn maturational difficulties (e.g., autism, Tourette's syndrome, blindness, deafness, early-onset pervasive developmental disorders) to developmental difficulties that originate in internally bound harsh, disorganizing, traumatic and/or deprivational social and environmental environments (e.g., juvenile delinquency, traumatic brain injuries, alcoholism and substance abuse).

Of course, it is not an either/or situation; often an inborn difficulty is a magnet for a traumatic/depriving environment; and conversely the damaging environment often favors what is weak in the child and hinders the child's use of his or her development-promoting resources.

Each author in this seminar has implicitly indicated an awareness of endowment and experience in his technical management of the analysis.

In *Normality and Pathology in Childhood,* Anna Freud stated, "In a psychoanalytic clinic for children, the whole range of childhood disorders comes up for diagnosis, with a demand for treatment, beginning at one extreme end with the most common developmental difficulties, the educational failures and upsets, the delays and arrests in mental growth, and leading by way of traumatized and seduced cases and the infantile neurosis proper to the other extreme of atypical grave ego defects, grave libido defects, borderline disturbances, autistic and psychotic states, delinquent or near-schizophrenic adolescents, etc." (p. 213).

Historically and today, we have emphasized play as our medium for communication with younger children. (Play includes games, art activities, certain physical activities, etc.) With child analytic patients who are older, we use both play and conversation as the media for becoming aware of the inner life of the child and how it relates to the child's behaviors, attitudes, and motivations.

Unlike the Kleinians, we have been unwilling to make adultamorphic interpretations (directly from the play and words of children), insisting that we try to put ourselves into the skin of the child in order to make inferences and interpretations that are as close as is feasible to the child's cognitive and emotional capacities and experiences. We do not discount the extent to which play continuity or disruption (see Erik Erikson) can approximate a quick view of the child's inner life—i.e., can be compared to free association. But the child's immature cognitive, emotional, and self-observing capacities do not enable the child or the analyst to go beyond speculation in considering play themes, sequences, and affective contents in the manner that free association is used in the psychoanalytic treatment of adults.

The analyst who imagines how the analysand is feeling, thinking, expecting, and tolerating pretending has a more apt approximation when working with adults than when playing with a child. With children, especially younger ones, play includes motor activity and pretend or fantasy themes with less self-observing verbal communications than characterize adult analysis.

This is not a new insight, but in reviewing the changes in the technique of child analysis since 1965, it is useful to factor in how the analyst is a significant adult in the present, albeit a playing, observing, listening, talking person for the child. Therefore, technically, how much weight should the child analyst today give to the real as compared to what is transferred from the present and the past? In putting himself or herself "into the skin" of the child, to what extent, technically and theoretically, does the analyst use interpretation (verbal or in play exchanges) for clarification and insight? To what extent is it allowed to interfere with or discourage or distort play experiences as development-promoting?

If the child analyst is a playing, listening, observing, talking adult friend of the child, to what extent are verbalizations, clarifications, and interpretations a dilution and interference with the personal, development-promoting relationship between the child and the analyst as an adult relating to the child as a friendly, guiding, protecting, stimulating, educating, safeguarding person whom the child views as his grown-up friend.

In the increased attention to and weight of this personal relationship between child and adult, what theoretical and technical changes and advances have been made and documented?

Ironically, the literature reflects this view but to my mind has added little or nothing to Anna Freud's contributions between 1936 ("The Ego and the Mechanisms of Defense") and 1965 (*Normality and Pathology in Childhood*). This is indicated by the following quotations from Anna Freud:

In her Preface to that work, Anna Freud says:

> It is no easy matter . . . to fashion a technique which complies with the main demands of classical psychoanalysis—to interpret resistance and transference phenomena; to undo repressions and regressions and to substitute sophisticated, adaptive measures for primitive, pathogenic mechanisms of defense; and generally to strengthen the ego functions and widen the area in the mind over which the ego can exert control.
>
> So far, the various child analytic centers have come up with their own solutions of these difficulties, varying widely with regard to the materials offered to the child as a substitute for verbal communication, the depth of interpretation aimed at, the amount of permitted gratification or implied frustration of wishes, and the inclusion or exclusion of the parents. . . .
>
> There is no absolute psychoanalytic technique for use with children, but rather a set of analytic principles which have to be adapted to specific cases. Variations in technique represent appropriate specific adaptations of the basic set of analytic principles rather than deviations from standard technique. . . .
>
> Child analysts do not really know at present which cases need variations from and additions to the analytic technique that has been developed. Analysts are interested in the limits within which analysis is the method of choice, and this is the question we have pursued over the years at the Hampstead Clinic. Full internalization of conflict does not occur for many years, and the child may need help with the environment. Therefore, in child analysis, assistance from both sides is needed—internal help for the method of coping, but external help for undue pressures on the child. These questions are especially relevant for the youngest age group, for whom the conflicts with the environment are so important.[4]

I have concentrated on Anna Freud's contributions as the basis for a historical perspective—hers is the most lucid and articulate—though other pioneers, especially Hug-Hellmuth, Steffi and Berta Bornstein, Anny Katan, Marianne Kris, and Margaret Mahler are vital contributors to that historical view of technique in child analysis.

---

4. *The Technique of Child Psychoanalysis: Discussions with Anna Freud, Joseph Sandler, Hansi Kennedy, and Robert L. Tyson* (Cambridge, Mass.: Harvard University Press, 1980), pp. ix, 199, 268.

Opening of Discussion

ALICE B. COLONNA, M.A.

DR. SOLNIT POINTS TO A NUMBER OF CENTRAL QUESTIONS AND CUR-
rents that are important in assessing technical changes in child psychoanalysis since Anna Freud wrote "Normality and Pathology in
Childhood" in 1965. He also refers to changes in the lives of families
and their impact on the early experiences of children. He suggests
that the tension between the environmental and the innate has been
part of the productive aspect of psychoanalytic theory and technique.

In considering changes since 1965 it seems useful to survey how
the technique of child psychoanalysis evolved during Anna Freud's
life since it was so closely bound up with her own clinical and scientific development. Anna Freud's leadership was so central to the history of child psychoanalysis that one can follow the parallel in theory
and technique as she conceptualized them when she was a young
teacher in Vienna and consulting with a group of teachers. While engaged in this work she was deeply involved in the psychoanalytic
world at a most dynamic and formative period. She has described the
seminars in which both candidates and graduates participated; previously there had been no seminars for candidates for there were only
candidates being analyzed by Freud and therefore no teachers. Aichhorn's work with delinquent adolescents influenced some of Anna
Freud's discoveries about adolescence; this was important for technique since she had to devise innovative ways to broaden the base of
child analysis to include these children, previously considered un-
suitable for psychoanalysis. At the same time she learned about early
development from the Edith Jackson nursery, which served some of

Assistant professor at the Yale Child Study Center; child analysis faculty at the Western New England Institute for Psychoanalysis; graduate, Anna Freud Centre.

The Psychoanalytic Study of the Child 56, ed. Albert J. Solnit, Peter B. Neubauer, Samuel
Abrams, and A. Scott Dowling (Yale University Press, copyright © 2001 by Albert J.
Solnit, Peter B. Neubauer, Samuel Abrams, and A. Scott Dowling).

Vienna's poorest (often homeless) families and young children. She was particularly interested in feeding disturbances and was innovative in the way feeding was carried out in this nursery.

The early combination of very intensive work with children and theoretical and clinical exposure to the group of pioneers who gathered around Freud was certainly formative for her later work. She retained great respect for the experiences children have on a daily basis, whether at home, in schools, hospitals, neighborhood, etc. She always gave great weight to the capacity of the child's ego to benefit from caregivers, teachers, and peers and never recommended child analysis as appropriate for everybody. She developed her skills in integrating the innate, the environmental, and the unknown gradually, over many years of moving between the theoretical issues and the very practical problems facing families and other caregivers. This ability to move freely between the most abstract and theoretical and the most concrete and immediate, in discussions with those who were working directly with children at every level, was a quality unique to her.

Soon after her arrival in England it became apparent that the Kleinian group of psychoanalysts who preceded her had already become established. Many British psychoanalysts were intrigued by Melanie Klein's imaginative and, in their view, innovative formulations of theory and technique. Finding that Klein's views differed profoundly from hers, Anna Freud decided to move ahead in her own independent manner. However, in the developmental lines she acknowledged the contribution Klein had made to her thinking about early infancy. This capacity to go her own way would become a characteristic way of working for Anna Freud, in many ways not unlike the stand her father had taken in earlier years in Vienna.

Later, during wartime, extensive observations made by the young child-care workers in the nurseries she directed became the basis for many changes in the care of the children evacuated from London who lived in the nurseries maintained by Anna Freud and Dorothy Burlingham. Much was learned about attachment and loss that assisted Anna Freud in developing her theory and technique of child psychoanalysis. Later the study of six children flown to England from the concentration camps revealed Anna Freud's remarkable ability to make inferences about the way early deprivations and important deficiencies had affected their development. In the absence of a close relationship to a mother or consistent substitute they turned to each other (Freud & Dann, 1951). Careful observations by their devoted caregivers, Sophie and Gertrude Dann, formed the basis of this study. The group of orphaned children were wild and unruly. They were housed together, apart from the older children who had come from the camps to the UK to be adopted by English families. These young children were given a year to prepare to separate from each other and live in orderly adoptive English families. The achievement of this task in the short span of one year is described through many vignettes.

Anna Freud showed the breadth of her interest in personality development in the face of deprivation and loss. (see Downey, "Early Object Relations into New Objects," this volume). Her capacity to modify and alter technique according to the growing knowledge about children and families was a part of Anna Freud's genius. All her life she greeted new insight and knowledge with enthusiasm and enjoyment. She welcomed the need to reformulate and resynthesize what she had learned from the constantly changing practice of psychoanalysis during her lifetime. Later, after the establishment of the Hampstead Clinic, Anna Freud encouraged others to develop their ideas and welcomed differences.

The evolution of her technique had a dynamic quality from the beginning and could never be reduced to a simplistic set of formula or rules. Technique in her view was a way of thinking and applying theoretical principles. In the profile and developmental lines Anna Freud refocused the current diagnostic view, pointing to the return to normal development as the aim of analysis for children. Thus she brought about a major reorientation in diagnostic thinking. Previously psychiatrists had been accustomed to focusing upon the deviant or neurotic symptomatology and often had insufficient experience with the many healthy children who functioned well in their families and schools. They rarely looked at the "whole" child until the profile. The changes in the clinic itself were monumental. In diagnostic meetings, clinicians were forced to examine and think about other questions and hypotheses that could be confirmed or rejected as the analysis progressed. In a sense analysis could be thought of as an extended evaluation in which change took place as modifications were brought about in the personality. This way of organizing material about a patient had important effects on technique as it evolved, paralleling the move from the momentous discoveries of the id and the power of the unconscious to an appreciation of the role of the ego. The widening scope of child psychoanalysis accompanied changes in family life and in the experiences of children that result. Families with more perplexing and complex problems appeared at the clinic for help.

Looked at from this perspective, the profile and developmental lines complement each other, resulting in a formulation of the technique the therapist would use in the application of theory. The profile is a metapsychological set of hypotheses, a cross-section of the personality. The developmental lines rely more on the clinician's ability to extrapolate the child's inner levels of development from observations of his behavior in a variety of settings. This makes them useful and creative, encompassing ways of viewing and assessing children who are difficult to understand in the more traditional formulations. The unevenness of development provided a helpful framework for clarification and planning.

Anna Freud also clarified many of the differences in technique between adult and child analysis and therapy. Her primary interest was in offering the patient tools to use in working with the self—that is, for the patient to take an assertive stance toward his own difficulties. Technique involved finding the right way to help the patient engage actively. This position has been important in clarifying goals and the extent to which they are those of the patient or of the analyst. Anna Freud's concern was to learn from her patients and to make use of what she had learned in theory and technique. That children are brought by a parent and do not choose when to begin, continue, or terminate treatment has had a major impact on technique. Anna Freud saw child analysis as the most important though not the only way to learn about the inner life of the child. Later she also thought of it as a way to reject or confirm initial hypotheses. She insisted that trainees observe children in many different settings in order to develop a sense of the strength of the their egos and their capacity to progress toward normality. She stressed that the observer needed time to learn to look and listen in a new way, regardless of any expertise he or she might bring.

In the late 1950s, she expanded her interests and activities into community outreaches that combined to form a picture of many aspects of development. These included observations in the baby clinic, toddler group, nursery school, and a school for blind and outreaches in the in-home care of families of the blind. These were important for the child analyst in learning to put himself into the skin of the child.

The question of how change takes place in personality and character development always intrigued her, as is evident from the following comment: "Where are finished or developing character structures open to influence? We know they are open to many influences, because there are many people who never have therapy and who still undergo quite extraordinary personality changes during their life-time, according to experience in relationships . . . sometimes experience through frustration, sometimes through satisfaction, sometimes through a new world opening up to them. And this is largely an unexplored field, but very worthwhile to explore from what we see happen in child analysis" (quoted by Penman, 1995, in A. Hurry, 1998, p. 32.)

With the establishment of the Hampstead Child-Therapy Course and Clinic in 1947, Anna Freud was able to study the wide range of problems faced by families after the war and to offer a variety of methods and appropriate techniques. A large number of children in intensive psychoanalysis provided the core of the learning experience. In addition, weekly therapy and mother guidance sessions were studied. The baby clinic, toddler groups, and two nursery schools provided scope for the observation and study of children in and out of analytic treatment. Case material was studied exhaustively through profiles, developmental lines, and the Psa index. Thus the formulations in the 1960s themselves represented the fruition of many years of study of observational data.

CHANGES IN THE TECHNIQUE OF CHILD ANALYSIS SINCE 1965

For Anna Freud technique was individualized—she used whatever aspects of theory helped her to understand the case. There was a personalized quality to the way she worked. In nursery school weekly meetings the formulations that led to the developmental lines were slowly evolved as was the profile. These were discussed in many meetings and study groups. The developmental lines initially were based on the nursery teachers' intuitive awareness of when the child was ready to benefit from some hours away from home. The notion of developmental help began when Anna Freud encouraged and guided trainees in the nursery to offer special support and guidance to children experiencing difficulties. Blind children were all given an hour a day of individual "special help" away from the group. In this work the developmental lines provided a most useful framework for understanding the child as he or she functioned in the group environment. The therapist often engaged the child in the classroom or, if further intervention was required, in the treatment room. Educational methods as well as psychoanalysis might be utilized.

This developmental help was viewed as different from psychoanalytic treatment, which was intended to "interpret resistance and transference phenomena; undo repressions and regressions and to substitute sophisticated, adaptive measures for primitive, pathogenic mechanisms of defense; and generally to strengthen the ego functions and widen the area in the mind over which the ego can exert control" (Anna Freud, quoted in Sandler et al. 1980).

Developmental help as it was conceptualized in later years had to do partly with the changing nature of pathology and the widening scope of child psychoanalysis. These brought into focus many new technical possibilities to be considered. In the 1970s Anna Freud was concerned with the lives of more disturbed children who were referred for treatment. The families who came were increasingly stressed and under pressures related to their work lives, the difficulties of finding reliable help at home, and the problems of child care.

SUMMARY

The history of technique in child analysis has clearly been an outcome of Anna Freud's work over the years, which in many ways culminated in 1980.

BIBLIOGRAPHY

COHLER, B., & ZIMMERMAN, P. (1997). Youth in residential care: From war nursery to therapeutic milieu. *Psychoanal. Study Child.* 52:359–386.

COLONNA, A. (1996). Observation and development, *Psychoanal. Study Child.* 51:217–234.

EDGCUMBE, ROSE (2000). *Anna Freud: A view of development, disturbance and therapeutic technique.* London: Routledge.

FREUD, ANNA (1960b). Entry into nursery school: The psychological pre-requisites, in *The Writings Anna Freud,* 5:281–300. New York: International Universities Press.

——— (1962a). The concept of developmental lines, *Psychoanal. Study Child.* 18:245–265.

——— (1965a). Normality and pathology: The case for and against residential nurseries, in *Infants without Families and Reports on the Hampstead Nurseries 1939–1945,* in *Childhood: Assessments of Development,* London: Karnak 1989.

FREUD, A., & BURLINGHAM, D. (1944). *Infants without families.* London: Hogarth.

FREUD, A., & DANN, S. (1951). An Experiment in Group Upbringings. *The Writings of Anna Freud,* vol. 4, New York: International Universities Press.

HURRY, A. (ED.) (1998). *Psychoanalysis and Developmental Therapy,* London: Karnac.

NEUBAUER, P. B. (1984). Anna Freud's concept of developmental lines, *Psychoanal. Study Child.* 39:15–27.

SANDLER, J., KENNEDY, H., & TYSON, R. L. (1980). *The Technique of Child Psychoanalysis.* London: Karnac.

SOLNIT, A. J., & NEWMAN, L. M. (1984). Anna Freud: The child expert, *Psychoanal. Study Child.* 39:45–63.

WALLERSTEIN, R. S. (1984). Anna Freud: Radical innovator and staunch conservative, *Psychoanal. Study Child.* 39:65–80.

YORKE, C. (1983). Anna Freud's contributions to our knowledge of child development, *Psychoanal. Study Child.* 51:7–24.

EMERGING ISSUES
Some Observations about Changes in Technique in Child Analysis

PETER B. NEUBAUER, M.D.

CHANGE CAN BEST BE ASSESSED, AND THEN WITH ONLY LIMITED ACCU-racy, from a historical point of view. When one is part of the Zeitgeist, one's vision will be blurred, and thus one will not be able to predict which advances will be enduring. It will be difficult to foresee the measure of overextension that accompanies the arrival of new ideas or to determine how much of the past has been inappropriately discarded. It is even more difficult to evaluate the changes in psychoanalytic technique, for there are no singular rules that guide it.

In order to avoid overemphasizing new theories on some aspects of psychic life to the neglect of others, Anna Freud introduced the metapsychological profile and explored the interaction of the developmental lines. Only their complex relationship can explain developmental progression, deviation, or transition.

Anna Freud's *Normality and Pathology in Childhood* (1965) is a book that reconfirms for us basic child-analytic propositions, explores the multitude of pathological conditions, and proposes a significant new direction for studying normality and pathology by declaring that "the child analyst, who sees progressive *development* as the most *essential* function of the immature, is deeply and centrally involved with the

Clinical professor of psychiatry at New York University, supervising and training analyst at Columbia University and Psychoanalytic Institute, New York University; past president of the Association for Child Psychoanalysis.

The Psychoanalytic Study of the Child 56, ed. Albert J. Solnit, Peter B. Neubauer, Samuel Abrams, and A. Scott Dowling (Yale University Press, copyright © 2001 by Albert J. Solnit, Peter B. Neubauer, Samuel Abrams, and A. Scott Dowling).

intactness or disturbance—i.e., the normality or abnormality—of this vital process." This formulation has elevated development to metapsychological dimensions. Reconstruction and the genetic point of view are often regarded as part of a developmental approach. Adult analysts have not as yet fully accepted the developmental point of view. The reason, Anna Freud suggested, rests on the assumption that "psychoanalysis with adults owes its therapeutic successes to the liberation of particular forces which are present normally within the structure of the personality and work spontaneously in the direction of the cure. These curative tendencies . . . , if assisted by treatment, are harnessed to analytic aim. They are represented by the patient's innate urges to complete development. . . . The adult's tendency to repeat is . . . complicated in the child by his hunger for new experience and new objects."

These propositions deserve extensive discussion, for they lead directly to the significance of the developmental point of view for psychoanalytic technique.

There is Anna Freud's view that the liberation of developmental forces will work spontaneously in favor of cure. This follows the expectation that the removal of unconscious conflicts, repressions, and fixations will free the ego to "do its work." At the same time, there is the proposal that the curative tendencies, *assisted* by treatment, will support the analytic aim. In the past it was believed that any alliance with the patient's ego could violate the requirement of analytic neutrality, of an equidistant position from the superego, ego, and id. Is this also true for the assistance of developmental progression?

To offer technical "assistance" as part of the therapeutic intervention appears to many analysts to be outside the psychoanalytic tradition; they believe that it belongs to the non-analytic instruments of psychotherapy. We should therefore remind ourselves that support of the ego or of development differs from the technique of resolving neurotic conflicts. We must bear in mind that strengthening the ego or developmental reorganization will affect the dynamics of the patient's conflicts, defenses, and compromise formation. Does therapeutic assistance inevitably lead to dilution of or deviation from a more analytic intervention? We assume that developmental assistance not only may strengthen the child-analytic intervention but, with certain modifications, may be equally useful in the analysis of adults.

Anna Freud (1965) proposed the developmental lines to "represent the results of interaction between drive and ego-superego development and their reaction to environmental influences, i.e., between maturation, adaptation and structuralization." Thus the concept of developmental lines refers to the complex interaction of multiple factors which express the process of developmental progression.

These are historical realities that inform us of the child's achievement or failures in development. Anna Freud's prototype of a developmental line is from dependency to emotional self-reliance and adult object relationships. Other lines are from suckling to rational eating, from the baby to the toy, and from play to work. The line must encompass all three psychic structures, plus maturation and adaptation. Clearly, a line of lying or temper tantrums or rivalry would not fulfill this requirement. Anna Freud expected that her proposal and her outline of some of the developmental lines would enable us to fill in the details in each sequence. But this has not yet taken place, except in the area of early object relations.

This is similar to Hartmann's comments on the multiple functions of the ego apparatus and other ego functions and the failure of child analysts to study memory, language, and motility more thoroughly. One common explanation is that psychoanalytic technique is designed to gain access to the preconscious and unconscious but is not equally useful for studying the components of the ego. The early proposals of libidinal sequences were not matched by an equal knowledge of ego stages or of the maturational timetable. The psychoanalyst has to rely on other disciplines to furnish the information required to complete these lines of development. The psychoanalyst feels more secure in reconstructing the past to signify the developmental interferences (such as repression, fixation, or deviation from the developmental path) than in trying to predict the result of the interlocking forces that will come into play. "The indications which emerge are more useful for the diagnosis of pathology and a revelation of the past than they are for deciding issues which concern the normal or the outlook for the future." (A. Freud, 1965).

Has this emphasis on the developmental point of view contributed to our understanding of therapeutic change? What are the basic factors that facilitate and create the change from pathology to normality?

Anna Freud's emphasis on the tendency to repeat, to establish transference, leads in the adult to assimilation and integration. "In fact, child analysis would receive very little help from the curative forces if it were not for one exception which restores the balance. . . . By definition, and owing to the process of maturation, the urge to *complete development* is immeasurably stronger in the immature than it can ever be in later life" (1965). This proposition implies, among other things, that the power of development is strongest in childhood: thus it challenges the position of those who assert that development continues throughout life.

In adult analysis the focus is on pathological conflicts, but the child analyst is asked to "include" in his work an alliance with the power of the developmental process—the need to complete, to undo fixations and regressions. It is therefore logical for the child analyst to use the urge for developmental progression to complement his psychoanalytic technique. According to the findings of our study group on Development and Technique, coordinating the developmental and psychoanalytic processes is a significant application of Anna Freud's original propositions. It indicates how much time passed to explore the full implications of the developmental point of view and its influence on the therapeutic interventions. It seems that to support the child's developmental forces, which anticipate and form the future, creates resistances among some child analysts, as if this could derail the psychoanalytic task. Since the findings have been published in the *Psychoanalytic Study of the Child* (1999), it is not necessary to document here that such concerns can be proved to be unwarranted.

Anna Freud refers to assimilation and integration as the working-through of conflicts in adults. Indeed, the psychoanalyst relies on the synthetic (Nunberg) or integrative (Hartmann) function of the ego to achieve a new psychic structure. It is not yet clear how this process of integration or ego synthesis takes place. In addition, the organizational function of development does not refer to new structure formation alone; not all changes serve development. The shifts in drive expressions, superego formations, and adaptation should lead to a new organization with new mental hierarchies and discontinuities of earlier developmental organization.

There is an effort to further define the action of the developmental forces. I shall refer to two studies in order to see whether these new developmental propositions offer changes in the technique of child analysis.

In "Clocks, Engines and Quarks—Love, Dreams and Genes: What Makes Development Happen?" (1999), Linda C. Mayes states that "to know that development happens is a different matter from knowing how it is regulated, timed, what are the implications of mistrust or failed events, and what is the room for error or normal variation in this time-process." Reviewing contemporary models of development, Mayes finds:

1. "Current models of gene-environment interaction emphasize a dialectic between genetically timed events with environment. . . . In

the context of the multilevel interactions, . . . there are constant processes of loss. . . . Reorganization of functions leads to the emergence
of psychological properties that have not clear antecedents."

2. There is a tension between linear progressive processes and interactive ones. Mayes refers to the notion that development is a
staged, linear process, not interactive, and partly predictable. This reminds us of Freud:

> So long as we trace the chain of development from the final outcome
> backwards, the chain of events appears continuous, and we feel we
> have gained insight that is completely satisfactory or even exhaustive.
> But if we proceed in the reverse way, if we start from the premises in-
> ferred from the analysis and try to follow these up to the final result,
> then we no longer get the impression of an inevitable sequence of
> events which could not have been otherwise determined. . . . We
> never know beforehand which of the determining factors will prove
> the weaker or the stronger. We only say at the end that those which
> succeeded must have been stronger. Hence, the chain of causation
> can always be recognized with certainty if we follow the line of analy-
> sis, whereas to predict it along the one of synthesis is impossible
> (1920).

3. The fantasies people have about development allow each of us
to deny the basic biology at times—to live in fantasy outside the body
and to deny our own responsibility. Here, Mayes speaks of resistances
to accepting the factors that contribute to the changes built into the
developmental blueprint. The position Mayes prefers is based on her
notion of imbalance between developmental linear channels. She assumes that periods of imbalance may provide an impetus to move development along. It is this model that makes her suggest that "efforts
toward adaptation and reaching equilibrium among lines of development are . . . part of the fuel that pushes development on."

According to Mayes, development happens through

1. gene-environment interaction; loss-discontinuity; new organization without antecedents

2. linear process and interactive ones.

3. fantasies about development; basic biological blueprint. Imbalance provides impetus for development.

Thus Mayes continues to explore Anna Freud's propositions about
development and adds her own. She attempts to explain the forces
that strive to complete development by suggesting that "it is the imbalances between developmental linear channels which contribute
to the completion. This is an important notion for therapeutic inter-

vention. How do we know when imbalances burden or interfere with development and when they become the fuel for continuation of development?" Mayes refers to those tensions beyond conflict in the usual dynamic sense.

Mayes also addresses the nature–nurture issue, in two ways. First, she says that nature, maturational forces, leads to loss. I assume that she refers here to developmental discontinuities. And she speaks of the general fantasies about development which then deny the significance of the developmental blueprint, which contributes to change and serves to diminish the need for the powerful parental influences.

That new organization can emerge without antecedents needs further clarification. We have accepted the notion that unresolved conflicts in one stage of development will be carried into the next stage in a state of transformation without resolution or co-existence with previous conflicts in a new organization.

In which area can we expect the shifts from one stage to the next—beyond developmental fixation or regression—and in which will new organizations, new psychic hierarchies emerge? What can and what cannot be predicted? This question is linked to the remarks by Sigmund Freud (1920) quoted above.

Moreover, Mayes introduces, or reintroduces, the concept of adaptation. Her concept differs from that of Hartmann, who positioned adaptation as a characteristic of the ego. Mayes ascribes to adaptation the faculty to increase the individual's chance of proceeding with development. This raises the question of whether what is adaptive for one developmental phase may become maladaptive later. What are the differences between compromise formation and adaptation as Mayes defines it? Adaptation in a conventional sense refers to the capacity for reality testing or, better, reality formation. It can imply the ability to create a "selective environment"—that is, to respond to those external conditions that suit the ego and the internal demands. Is adaptation supported by the maturational forces, language, motor control, memory, etc?

Clearly, Mayes confirms Anna Freud's developmental investigation. She offers new concepts and thereby new questions.

To summarize: Mayes's proposition that imbalance among developmental lines contributes to the completion of development and promotes integration and developmental progression is an interesting and useful extension of Anna Freud's work. In addition, Mayes views development in the broadest context, from gene-environmental interaction to the adaptational forces that foster progression. This reminds us of the role of Anna Freud's profile.

There are in her paper other notions, such as the emergence of new organizations without antecedents, which demand further clarification. There are hierarchies based on new organizations and on developmental discontinuities. There are also phase reorganizations evolving new primacies by transferring earlier developmental modes into new maturational sequences. Libidinal-phase progressions are not mirrored by those that follow object relations. Mahler could not integrate her separation-individuation steps with the libidinal-aggressive phase progressions. The structural layers of the mind do not seem to follow the same developmental timetable and sequences.

Mayes's paper raises significant issues as new aspects of development are brought into focus.

I shall now refer to propositions influenced by the object relations point of view. I am citing the findings of the Boston Process of Change Study Group, published "Non-Interpretative Mechanisms in Psychoanalytic Therapy" in the *International Journal of Psycho-Analysis* (1998). The article explores how psychoanalytic therapies bring about change. The authors state that more than interpretation is necessary to bring about change, that "more resides in interactional, intersubjective processes that give rise to implicit relational knowing." They found that these experiences bring about new organization or reorganization and the knowledge of ways of being with others.

Their approach is based on the model of mother–infant interaction and non-linear dynamic systems. I shall discuss their findings and apply them to the technique of child analysis. They declare that "treatment has taken the form of psychological acts versus psychological words." This appears to be close to the characterization of play in child analysis.

This study proposes that there are special "moments of authentic person-to-person connection with the therapist that alter the relationship with him and thereby the patient's sense of himself." It suggests that many therapies fail or are terminated, not because of incorrect or unaccepted interpretations, "but because of missed opportunities for meaningful connection between two people." This emphasis on intersubjective experiences does not minimize the role of interpretation. The article outlines the declarative or conscious verbal domain and the implicit procedural or relational domain. It postulates that there are two kinds of knowledge, two kinds of representation, and two kinds of memory, correlated with developmental sequences. Thus psychic function appears to overstress the significance of multiple internalization, object representation, and the regulatory function of affect as part of the internal balance.

The authors state that there is a moment of recognition for both analyst and patient. "A major subjective feature of a shift in implicit relational knowing is that it will feel like a sudden qualitative change." For them these concepts provide the best models to capture the process of "moving along" based on the nature of specific moments of meeting.

The proposal of the Boston study group differs markedly from Anna Freud's work. It shifts the pivotal psychic components to the object interactive domain. While it addresses child analytic technique, its relation to their concepts of development is clear. Interobject knowing facilitates therapeutic change, therefore the pivotal technique is reduced to the act of experience.

Kris's "good hour" and "Aha" experience are understood to be based not on the recovery of unconscious wishes and fears but rather on the moment of recognition and implicit relational knowing. Thus, the effective healing experience must be object related; in a sense it is beyond the repetition inherent in the transference experience.

The "moving along" is not related to the processes of maturation or to the factors that seek the completion of development. It is the result of "specific moments of meeting." Thus, the authors maintain that the pivotal factor in resolving conflicts lies in the interrelationship of patient and therapist, not of significant objects of the developmental unfolding. It is not suprising that there are, then, two kinds of knowledge, representation and memory. This division raises many questions.

This work highlights the new emphasis on what is curative. It may be a useful addition to our psychoanalytic awareness of the factors that contribute to therapeutic effectiveness. It leads to a substitution of all other intervention strategies for it rests on a mother–infant model. Thus, these studies not only expand awareness of object relations experiences, affectively based knowing, but also significantly reduce the range of pathologies and therefore intervention strategies. The conflicts that emerge during development, the transformation of symptoms, and the emergent maturational capacities are thereby given insufficient weight. The complexity of developmental reorganization, the succeeding stages of development, are neglected in favor of the healing role of the sharing experience between therapist and patient. Thus the development processes are inadequately explored.

I have selected some of the proposals that affect changes in technique: the technique of developmental assistance, alliance with the development forces that strive for the completion of development, the function of adaptation, and the stresses based on incongruency between developmental lines demanding developmental solutions. The object relations approach offers new explorations of the power of object interaction between patient and analyst. Some colleagues propose the model of mother-infant relations for therapeutic intervention.

What about Anna Freud's view of object relations? She stated that the dependency of the child on the parent, due to immaturity, affects transference experiences in child analysis. She also suggested that "lack of introspection is a general ego attitude, characteristic of childhood and adhered to by the child as an effective deterrent against mental pain. It is only in identification with a trusted adult and in alliance with him that it is given up and reluctantly replaced by a more honest viewing of the inner world" (1965). Here identification and alliance will achieve the analytic aim. This formulation appears to be close to those that rely on the early object relations model of therapy, but it is important to note that Anna Freud employed this alliance and identification in order to arrive at a more honest view of the inner life.

The role of play in child analysis may offer another mode of intervention. Playing rests on the ability to displace conflict from primary objects to toys, animals, friends, to search for the resolution of conflicts in relationships with others rather than with primary objects, for these conflicts are too painful to face. Resolution of conflicts by the interpretation of these conflicts does not demand that within the dynamics of the play manifest and latent story are possible. One does not demand that the child face the original conflicts with the parents. There needs to be first an alliance and identification with the therapist. This constitutes a basic difference between child and adult analysis. Play shifts the relationship—the intersubjectivity—to the field of action in fantasy, creating new perspectives on the inner world.

A considerable cross-section of the psychoanalytic community today pins its faith on analysis of the first years of life, with the purpose of therapeutically modifying the impact of the earliest experiences.

Freud's discovery that every neurosis of the adult is preceded by an infantile neurosis and that the latter has to be analyzed before the former can be reached is paraphrased today by some analysts as follows: every infantile neurosis in the oedipal period is preceded by fateful interactions between infant and mother in the very first days and months of life, and it is the archaic preverbal phase that has to be revived in the transference and analyzed before the later infantile neurosis can be approached effectively.

It is obvious that different methods are needed for approaching the earliest and later phases. Lampl de Groot mentions "nonverbal modes of communication." Others speak of "silent communication" between analyst and patient to stress the need for the analyst's intuitive understanding of the patient's signs and signals. There is no doubt that neither memory nor verbal recall reaches into the depths of postnatal, preverbal experience. Therefore, "remembering yields its place to repetition, verbal communication to reenactment." (A. Freud, 1971). "The difference between transference in children and in adults is that what the adult transfers and revives in the transference neurosis are object relationships of the past and relationships to a fantasy object, whereas the child, even in matters of the past, has the past relationship or fantasy firmly fixed to the person of the parent" (A. Freud, 1980). The new object relations propositions challenge this assumption.

I have quoted extensively from Anna Freud in order to illustrate how much of her thought still guides the work of child analysis. The history of psychoanalysis clearly reveals the shifting attention from one to another factor that constitutes the work of the mind. The early study of the role of trauma and the drives was followed by a change from topography to the psychic structure, with the focus on the ego and the analysis of the defenses. Now the weight is on object relations, the study of the therapist as an object, and intersubjectivity as the significant therapeutic modality. As new discoveries emerge, it seems unreasonable to expect that one can maintain a position equidistant from all mental agencies. The use of Anna Freud's metapsychological profile avoids a one-sided approach in the exploration of the function of the mind.

The Psychoanalytic Research and Development Study Group on Play has demonstrated that playing is more than the child's expression of free association, and more than an entrance to pre- and unconscious fears and wishes. In analysis it allows us to resolve past and present conflicts, prepares us to understand the future, and thereby maintains a developmental point of view. It provides child analysts with the opportunity to facilitate and to ally with the forces which strive for the completion of development.

It seems that some propositions, however useful when appropriately targeted, neglect other propositions that have been found useful for many forms of pathology in the past. For example, some of the new concepts make no reference to drive expressions or to the dynamics of the interstructural relationships. Affect regulation has, so it seems, substituted or replace drive expressions.

Anna Freud's *Normality and Pathology in Childhood* continues to guide us in maintaining a sound basis for the advance of psychoanalysis.

BIBLIOGRAPHY

ABRAMS, S., NEUBAUER, P. B., & SOLNIT, A. J. (1999). *The Psychoanalytic Study of the Child.* New Haven: Yale Univ. Press, 54:87–90.

FREUD, A. (1965). *Normality and Pathology in Childhood.* New York: Int. Univ. Press.

———— (1971). *The Writings of Anna Freud.* Cambridge, Mass.: Harvard Univ. Press.

FREUD, S. (1920). Psychoanalytic case of homosexuality in a woman. *S.E.* 20:248–258, 167–168.

MAYES, L. C. (1999). Clocks, engines, quarks—Love, dreams, and genes. *Psychoanal. Study of the Child,* 54:169–190.

SANDLER, J., KENNEDY, H., & TYSON, R. (1980). *The Technique of Child Analysis. Discussion with Anna Freud.* Cambridge, Mass.: Harvard Univ. Press. p. 92.

STERN, D., SANDER, L., NAHUM, J., & HARRISON, A. (1998). Process of Change. *Int. Jrnl. of Psychoanal.* p. 7903.

The Work of Transformation

Changes in Technique since Anna Freud's
Normality and Pathology in Childhood

STEVEN LURIA ABLON, M.D.

> Psychoanalysis aims to restore the artist in the pa-
> tient, the part of the person that makes interest de-
> spite, or whatever, the early environment. At its most
> extreme, for the artist her own life, it is not so much
> a question of what she has been given (no one
> chooses their parents, but everyone invents them,
> makes what they can of them). The psychoanalytic
> model here is the dream, or the child's infantile sex-
> ual theory, in which so-called reality functions more
> like a hint than an instruction, setting the dreamer
> and child off on the work of transformation (Phil-
> lips, 1998, pp. 4–5).

NORMALITY AND PATHOLOGY IN CHILDHOOD IS A BRILLIANT, COMPREHEN-
sive, complex, and pioneering book. It is not possible in this limited
discussion to do justice to Anna Freud's monumental work. In 1965 a
powerful factor affecting technique in child analysis was an effort to
legitimize child analysis by making it more congruent with views of
adult analysis. According to Anna Freud (1965): "Although the differences between child analysis and adult analysis came in focus grad-

Training and supervising adult and child analyst, Boston Psychoanalytic Institute;
associate clinical professor of psychiatry, Harvard University Medical School, Massa-
chusetts General Hospital.

I would like to express my appreciation to Gridth Ablon, Arthur Valenstein, and
The Center for Advanced Psychoanalytic Studies, Group 2, for their help in developing these ideas.

The Psychoanalytic Study of the Child 56, ed. Albert J. Solnit, Peter B. Neubauer, Samuel
Abrams, and A. Scott Dowling (Yale University Press, copyright © 2001 by Albert J.
Solnit, Peter B. Neubauer, Samuel Abrams, and A. Scott Dowling).

ually, the child analysts themselves were in no hurry to proclaim the independence of their procedure from classical technique. On the contrary, the tendency was definitely to emphasize the similarity or near-identity of the two processes" (p. 25).

Over the ensuing 35 years technique in child analysis came to diverge from technique in classical adult analysis in many ways, stimulated by efforts to respond to the developmental needs of children at different ages. In addition to treating children with largely neurotic difficulties, child analysts explored ways of treating children with more severe developmental problems. They responded to what children in analysis seemed to indicate was helpful technically and what characterized therapeutic action in child analysis. Rather than trying to conform to adult analytic technique, child analytic approaches began to be incorporated increasingly in features of adult analytic technique. These features include greater awareness of object relations, identifications, introjects, and relational and interpersonal factors. In addition, technical considerations involving enactment and action, preoedipal foci, affect, uses of the countertransference, and the therapeutic action of play have become important considerations first in child analysis and subsequently also in adult analytic technique. Many of these developments are present in the work of Anna Freud and were subsequently extended and elaborated. For example, Anna Freud's focus on developmental lines and developmental energies can be related to the way such concepts as the therapeutic action of play and object relations facilitate new organizations and actualize developmental progression, bringing into awareness new therapeutic possibilities.

I will explore the topic of changes in child analytic technique by examining an hour in the analysis of a six-and-a-half-year-old girl. This session is from the middle of a three-year analysis.

Emma was five when she was brought for four-days-a-week analysis because of compulsive masturbating and withholding her stools. Her symptoms began when she was four and her brother, Scott, was born. At one year Emma was weaned from the bottle over a five-week period, with one bottle being eliminated each week. Toilet training started when she was two. Emma was resistant. Then her mother became pregnant, had a miscarriage, and abandoned her struggles with Emma. Toilet training was complete at around age three. From the time when Emma was three months old until she was three and a half her mother was preoccupied with her father's (Emma's grandfather's) battle with cancer. Emma's mother said that she fully experienced her sadness about the death of her father only after Scott's birth.

When Scott was born, Emma did not show any anger or jealousy but began to withhold her stools. She would refuse to go to the bathroom, look uncomfortable, and strain. Her mother gave her raisins, prunes, and laxatives. She was not given enemas or suppositories. Emma began to say that she was afraid to have a bowel movement and told her mother a baby would come out if she did. She changed her underwear frequently, worrying that there was a stain of stool or a drop of urine in it. She would sit on the toilet for long periods of time wiping herself, saying that she was not dry yet and masturbating. Emma's father was a supportive husband and an involved father but at that time was preoccupied with starting a business.

ANALYTIC HOUR

It is a Thursday in January. Emma comes into the office reluctantly. This is unusual for her, she is generally eager and energetic. (I wonder to myself why she is different and whether she is struggling with something). She throws her coat and boots on the floor and says she is angry that Will (an elderly family friend) died. She says that now her mother has to go away until next Tuesday night at 11:15. She gives me sign language for Oreo cookies. (I keep cookies in a drawer in the office and produce them if a child asks for something to eat. I am thinking that Emma misses her mother and is hungry for her. I think how in Emma's early years her mother was sad and preoccupied with her father's dying.) Emma says that her Oma (her mother's mother) will be taking care of her. She explains that her grandmother is from Holland and that's why they call her Oma. She adds that her Oma has wrinkles on her chin and looks older that her other grandmother but is really younger. Emma says, "You have wrinkles on your chin; how old are you?" (I find myself thinking that I wished I did not have wrinkles on my chin. Even now, when my mother has wrinkles, her face is as smooth and beautiful in my mind as it was when I was a young child.) I ask her what she thinks and she says, "Forty." (I think that this must seem old to Emma and I wonder if she thinks of me as her grandparents' age.) She says that she does not have wrinkles. Emma then shows me a scrape on her knee and says she hurt it. (Is she communicating about injuries, getting older, and death? I do not want to foreclose the many possible bifurcations of the material. I wait, letting her know by my expression that I am interested in her continuing.) Sounding sad, Emma says, "I miss my Zayde" (grandfather). I say, "Emma, you sound sad." Emma replies, "My mother lied and told me he died of old age, but he died of cancer and they couldn't help him. My mother was afraid I would worry that if you get sick, you die."

At this point Emma splits the cookie in half and scrapes out the white frosting in the middle. She tells it, "Don't hide, go with your friends into my tummy." She pretends several times to be dead and then alive. I say, "Maybe you wish your Zayde could be dead and then alive again." Emma says, "My Zayde was so nice." Then she plays hide and seek in the office for a while. (I think she is continuing to communicate about losing people—her mother, Zayde, and me at the end of the hours and in the transference. I decide to let her play at this.) Emma sings, "I got the whole world in my arms, I got the little bitty babies in my arms. I got the whole wide world in my arms, I have the little bitty babies in my arms." Lying down on the couch, Emma directs me to cover her with a blanket. She seems sad and lonely. She says, "I need shelter and food. I have been left in the cold snow." I reply, "You seem sad and lonely like when Zayde was sick and died and now when your mother will be away." Emma responds by asking me, "Do you know what I want the most in the world?" (I am thinking primarily about nurturance, but also about a baby and a penis.) Emma then sits up on the couch and cuts the cookie with a plastic playdough knife, almost hurting herself. (I sense that this could involve many possibilities such as guilt, self-punitiveness, loss, separation, and castration.) She says, "I want four, four, four." (I am unsure about the meaning of this. I wait for her to communicate more about what she wants the most in the world.) Emma then lies down on the couch again, looks upset, and says, "My leg hurts. I pulled a muscle yesterday. Do you know what I want the next most?" Then forcefully she adds, "I want your pen." In an adamant tone of voice she says, "And I am going to keep it." I say, "Maybe you are upset about being hurt and want something from me to make you feel better." (I think she is talking about a comforting connection both to me and to my penis. I also think Emma is talking about having exciting life-affirming feelings instead of sad lonely feelings about coldness and death.) Emma points to her pubic area. After that she points to my pubic area and asks what is she pointing to. I ask, "Is it my penis?" Emma excitedly says, "Yes!" In a passionate tone she asks me, "What do boys want the most?" I ask, what? With gusto she says, "Vagina!" Emma says, "I know it will be time to leave soon and I don't want leave." I say, "I know you don't." She insists, "I want to keep your pen and your blanket!" I say,

"You want something to remember me by, a comforting blankie, a baby, and a penis." She asks, "Do you know what dumb means?" I say, "Maybe it means you think what I said was dumb." Forcefully but also a little shyly Emma says, "It means I love you."

DISCUSSION

I will review Emma's hour highlighting some of the changes in child analytic technique since *Normality and Pathology in Childhood*. To begin with I describe my reactions, associations, and thinking during the hour, which reflects my focus on a two-person psychology. Attention to my experience, and my flow of association is part of a focus on my experience as more than countertransference in the narrow sense. I view my reactions as likely to be informative based on a mix of components such as projective identification, resonance with Emma's affect, non-verbal cues, and the use of my preconscious (Blos 1999). For instance, when Emma talks about wrinkles, I find myself wishing that I did not have wrinkles on my chin and thinking that my mother's face was smooth and beautiful in my mind even after she had grown older and wrinkled. This reminds me that despite the focus on nurturing there may be a powerful affective oedipal current in the hour. I am aware that the constant conversation in my mind and my particular choice of interventions have to do with my sensibility and understandings, which underscores the current thinking about the analytic experience as cocreated.

Immersed in the spirit of her time, Anna Freud's writings nevertheless contained elements that foreshadow current changes in technique. For example, her sense of co-creation:

> Just as "no two analysts would ever give precisely the same interpretations," we find on closer examination that no two of a given analyst's patients are ever handled by him in precisely the same manner. With some patients we remain deadly serious. With others, humor or even jokes, may play a part. With some the terms in which interpretations are couched have to be literal ones; others find it easier to accept the same content when given in the form of similes and analogies. There are differences in the ways in which we receive and send off patients, and in the degree to which we permit a real relationship to the patient to coexist with the transferred, fantasied one. There is, even within the strictness of the analytic setting, a varying amount of ease felt by the analyst and patient (1954, pp. 359–360)

Emma asks me for cookies, which she knows I keep in the office. This represents a change in technique from an earlier time, when lack of gratification was stringently stressed. The idea was that a scrupulous avoidance of gratification helped increase the anxiety necessary for the analytic work and brought the transference more into focus. In Emma's case I approach the cookie as part of the associations, the play, and informative enactments that I use to understand Emma's struggles. In the hour I use it to explore Emma's hunger for nurturance from her mother and from me in the mother transference. I think about the cookies as babies in her body and the connection between babies and feces. (This is explored in subsequent hours.) In addition, I think it supports an alliance that is needed to supply a sense of safety so that the highly charged oedipal and preoedipal issues in the transference can be approached. This resonates with what Anna Freud described as the "double relationship" and unique balance with each patient in which the analyst is both transference object and new object.

I want to emphasize that the technical issues are discussed in general terms but they are always modified to fit the unique domain of each child. In addition, I am concerned that because of efforts toward conciseness and clarity, discussing the technical differences in Emma's hour presents a falsely simplified contrast rather than a more accurate and inevitable overlap and spectrum. When Emma eats the cookies and says, "Don't hide, go with your friends into my tummy," she is taking in good things, her Zayde and what she gets from me. This relative shift in technical thinking in terms of the importance of object relations, introjects, and identifications (Sabot 1980) was anticipated by Anna Freud (in 1965),

> All individuals, as they develop and mature, have a hunger for *new experience* which is as strong as the urge to *repeat*. The former is an important part of the child's normal equipment; nevertheless, neurotic development tips the balance in favor of the latter. The child who enters analysis sees in the analyst a new object and treats him as such, so far as he has a healthy part to his personality. He uses the analyst for repetition—i.e., transference—so far as his neurosis or other disturbance comes into question. The double relationship is not easily handled by the analyst (p. 38).

When Emma shows me a scrape on her knee and says it hurts I let her know by my expression that I am interested, concerned, and following her. This reflects a change in technical considerations in child analysis, giving non-verbal aspects of treatment more weight as communications and interventions. When Emma and I are talking about wishing her Zayde could be alive again Emma plays hide and seek. I think she is saying, will you be my Zayde and replace my losses—including that of her mother grieving for her father? I think she is communicating about death, separation, loss, and reunion in relation to her Zayde, her mother, and me in the transference, but rather than verbalize this I decide to let her play it out. I do this a number of times in the hour. This is a shift in terms of recognizing that change can come about through other than the verbal intellectual channel. This emphasizes the area of learning through interaction and relating. It also includes learning not only through cognition but also through action—that is, procedural learning, like learning to ride a bike (The Process of Change Study Group, 1998). Some of these ideas formulated from infant observation are applied to technical considerations in child analysis. Not surprisingly, Anna Freud strongly endorsed the value of infant observation (1953), an area of study that has blossomed in the past few decades and has greatly influenced our ideas about development and technique.

In recent years the therapeutic action of play has been increasingly recognized (Waelder 1933; Huizinga 1938; Winnicott 1971; Erikson 1972; Loewald 1987; Cohen and Solnit 1993; Solnit, Cohen, and Neubauer 1993; Frankel, 1998). From a neuroscience perspective, Panksepp (1998) observes that there is an innate adaptive capacity to play: "A great deal of joy arises from the arousal of play circuits with the brain. Although this is a reasonable assertion, it can only be supposition until the identity of play circuits had been more completely revealed by brain research. That play is a primary emotional function of the mammalian brain was not recognized until recently, but now the existence of such brain systems is a certainty" (p. 281).

An important technical aspect of my work with Emma flows from my impression that Emma and perhaps most children have an inborn capacity to enter into analytic work as enthusiastic partners. This is based on their non-verbal awareness of the therapeutic action of play and their natural energy directed toward developmental progression. Children see as a great and sometimes life transforming opportunity the chance to work in the intermediate play space with an emphatic player who is willing to accompany them wherever their analytic voyage takes them and who will try to understand the nature of the voyage. These factors contribute to a strong and growing alliance between the child and the analyst from very early in an analysis. While Anna Freud wrote, "The urge to complete development is immeasurably stronger in the immature than it can ever be in later life" (1965, p. 28), she was influenced by the perspective of the therapeutic alliance in adult analysis. Children, she said, "do not develop the same wish to get well and the same type of treatment alliance. . . . Altogether, the child analyst is faced by many difficult treatment situations which tax his skill. What he feels most acutely is the fact that for long stretches of the analysis he has to manage without a therapeutic alliance with his patient." (pp. 28, 36).

As the hour continues, Emma sings, "I have the whole world in my arm, I have the little bitty baby in my arms" and lies down on the couch saying that she needs food and shelter. Emma moves freely between words, action, and play. Although it is not the same as verbal free association in adults, this movement between words, action, and play in my experience can be considered the child's equivalent of free association. The technical ramifications of this are that in Emma's hour I take her words, actions and play as highly informative. This is in contrast to Anna Freud's view that

> Play with toys, drawing, painting, staging of fantasy games, acting in the transference have been introduced and accepted in place of free association, and *faute de mieux,* child analysts have tried to convince themselves that they are valid substitutes for it. In truth, they are nothing of the kind. It is one disadvantage that some of these modes of behavior produce mainly symbolic material and that this introduces into child analysis the element of doubt, uncertainty, arbitrariness which are inseparable from symbolic interpretation in general. Another disadvantage lies in the fact that under pressure of the unconscious the child acts instead of talking, and this unfortunately introduces limits in to the analytic situation" (pp. 29–30).

Doubt and uncertainty are part of the mystery, surprise, and discovery of the analytic interaction. It is largely our discomfort with doubt and uncertainty (Jacob 1995) that leads to premature closure and arbitrariness. Historically Anna Freud's point of view about free association and play related to the technical viewpoint that in adult analysis it is important for the analyst to be minimally active and directive so as not to interfere with free association. The child analyst has to be more actively involved with the child, and this would interfere with free association. My impression is that words are only one form of symbolic expression and, in fact, often not the most eloquent or direct form of communication (Stern 1985). Association through play, action, and symbols in addition to words is perhaps the most comprehensive form of expression in adults as well as children.

In Emma's hour there is a mix of play and verbalization, and my approach is less dominated by an emphasis on verbalization and interpretation than might have been the case for Anna Freud. Emma's play with the cookies, with hide and seek, with the blanket, with being hurt is substantially free association. In fact, I believe that play is the language *par excellence* of children and that we adults have lost much of our awareness of this earlier state and fail to fully explore this mode of communication with themselves and others. Likewise, as adults we are partially unaware of the greater directness and immediacy of play than of the sometimes elegant, affectively diluted uses of word symbols. It often seems that the action and symbolic expression of play gives children a stronger purchase on their fantasies, conflicts, and feelings and therefore more accessibility to therapeutic gain.

The technique of using children's play as equivalent to free association was pioneered by Hug-Helmuth (1919, 1991 {Mclean and Rappen}) and extended in the work of Melanie Klein. Klein wrote: "For play is the child's most important medium of expression. If we make use of this play technique we soon find that the child brings as many associations to the separate elements of its play as adults do to the separate elements of their dreams. These separate play-elements are indications to the trained observer; and as it plays, the child talks as well, and says all sorts of things which have the value of genuine associations" (1975, p. 8).

An aspect of play as a transformative communication is expressed by Schimek: "The different levels at which a concrete experience or object can be represented must not be viewed as merely different codes, different systems of labels attached to the same object. Each level of symbolic representation changes the experience of the object represented, its meaning, function, and relationship to other objects" (1975, p. 185). Erikson, in his writings about play in analysis, seemed to be aware of the continuity of free association and play: "Freud, in freeing the neurotics of his repressed era from the onus of degeneracy, invented a method of playful communication called 'free association' which has taught man (way beyond the clinical setting) to play back and forth between what is most conscious to him and what has remained unverbalized or become repressed. And he has taught man to give freer play to fantasies and impulses which, if not realized in sexual foreplay or 'sublimated' in actuality, help only to narrow his *Spielraum* to the point of explosions in symptomatic actions" (1972, 335).

When Emma is playing being left in the cold snow, I say, "You seem sad and lonely like when Zayde was sick and died and now when your mother will be away." I offer a construction for Emma to consider, but I focus on the verbalization of affect in addition to insight and cognitive expansion. When Emma responds by asking me if I know what she wants most in the world, although I am thinking primarily about nurturance but also about a baby and a penis, I leave it open to avoid foreclosing other possible communications. This is also technically consistent with Anna Freud's approach of letting the transference evolve and not heating it up by interventions. It seems to me that Emma turns to sexuality as a way of dealing with loss. Sexuality is affirmative of life in contrast to death, and sexuality makes vital the loss, coldness, and sadness of Zayde's being dead, her mother's being away and perhaps her loneliness during the period of her mother's grief. At this point I do not interpret this to Emma. Although generally I help her put her feelings and fantasies into words, here I think that she needs more time to express these issues in her play. A week later Emma and I talk about how these exciting sexual feelings help her feel less sad about missing her Zayde, her mother and father, and me.

A year earlier in the analysis Emma had insisted that she wanted me to take my clothes off and that she would show me her bottom. She had grown greatly in her ability to bear these exciting sexual feelings and express them in play and in words. My awareness of and capacity to tolerate the highly erotic nature of the transference have facilitated my leaving it open for her to continue in her format. Emma forcefully asks me if I know what she wants the next most, and in an adamant tone of voice says she wants my pen. When she says she is going to keep it, I say that she is upset about being hurt and wants something from me to make her feel better. Although I think she is talking about my penis, I think she is also talking about a comforting connection to me. My intervention is at the preoedipal as well as the oedipal level. Anna Freud might emphasize the oedipal level more. When Emma points to my pubic area and asks what she is pointing to I decide to ask, "Is it a penis?" At this point I have in mind letting her know that I am prepared to permit her to elaborate these charged feelings. I could have helped her work with the protective efforts by saying something like, "Emma, you point and ask me to guess, perhaps this is something that is hard to speak about?" or "Sometimes when kids are excited it is hard to say what they want." I took her a step further with my comment, which runs the risk of being overstimulating, but I anticipate that Emma can manage this and further elaborate her feelings, conflicts, and fantasies and the many layers involved in her assertion.

When Emma says she misses her Zayde she sounds sad. This is one of many places where, in addition to drive and defense, I try to follow the affect in the hour. When I say, "Emma, you sound sad," I help her put words to her feelings—something both Anny Katan (1961) and

Anna Freud (1965) emphasized. Anna Freud wrote: "The ego of the young child has the developmental task to master on the one hand orientation in the external world and on the other hand the chaotic emotional states which exist within himself. It gains its victories and advances whenever such impressions are grasped, put into thoughts or words, and submitted to the secondary process" (p. 32).

At the end of the hour, when Emma says she does not want to leave, and I say, "I know you don't," technically this is more in the realm of the container of affect and the holding environment (Bion 1962; Winnicott 1965). Emma gains in her capacity to not only to contain but also to regulate affect, and observes how I handle my feelings. At the end of the hour, when Emma says, "It means I love you," in the transference I am the blanket mother and the penis father. She feels safe and nurtured, and this frees her to tell me that what I said was dumb and also to play the Oedipus with gusto. This reflects the relational and cocreated nature of the analysis. In Anna Freud's developmental lines, there is no line of development for object relations and the consolidation of the self, although these are implicit. These areas have developed with a technical focus on introjects, implicit relational learning, and the transference-countertransference matrix in both adult and child analysis. I am not proposing a dichotomy between what might be called classical aspects of technique and newer modifications. I believe such aspects as the therapeutic action of play, relational forces, the centrality of affect, and the two-person psychology as well as conflict, drive, and defense and verbalized insight are all useful as adapted to the clinical situation and the unique psychology of each patient.

BIBLIOGRAPHY

BION, W. R. (1962). *Learning From Experience*. London: Heinemann.
BLOS, P. (1999). The Affective Experience of the Child Analyst and the Concept of Countertransference. Marianne Kris Lecture at the 1999 Annual Meeting of the Association for Child Psychoanalysis. Seattle, WA.
COHEN, P. M., & SOLNIT, A. J. (1993). Play and Therapeutic Action. *Psychoanalytic Study Child*. 48:49–63.
ERIKSON, E. H. (1972). Play and Actuality in Erik H. Erikson, *A Way of Looking at Things. Selected Papers from 1930 to 1980*. S. Schlein, ed. New York: W.W. Norton. 1987.
FRENKEL, J. B. (1998). "The Play's the Thing: How the Essential Processes of Therapy Are Seen Most Clearly in Child Therapy." *Psychoanalytic Dialogues*. 8:1,149–182.

FREUD, A. (1953). Some Remarks on Infant Observation. In *The Writings of Anna Freud*. Vol. IV, 1945–1956, New York: International Universities Press.

FREUD, A. (1954). The Widening Scope of Indications for Psychoanalysis: Discussion. In *The Writings of Anna Freud*, Vol. IV, 1945–1956, New York: International Universities Press.

FREUD, A. (1965). "Normality and Pathology in Childhood: Assessments of Development" in *The Writings of Anna Freud*, Vol. VI, New York: International Universities Press.

HUG-HELLMUTH, H. VON. (1919). *A Study of the Mental Life of the Child*. Washington, D.C.: Nervous and Mental Diseases Publishing Co.

HUIZINGA, J. (1938). *Homo Ludens: A Study of the Play Element in Culture*. Boston: Beacon Press, 1955.

JACOB, F. (1995). *The Statue Within*. Plainview, NY: Cold Spring Harbor Laboratory Press.

KATAN, A. (1961). Some Thoughts about the Role of Verbalization in Early Childhood. *Psychoanal. Study of the Child* 16:184–188.

KLEIN, M. (1975). *The Psychoanalysis of Children*. New York: Delacorte. (1932).

LOEWALD, E. L. (1987). Therapeutic play in space and time. *Psychoanal. Study Child*, 42:173–192.

MACLEAN, G., & RAPPEN, U. (1991). *Hermine Hug-Hellmuth, Her Life and Work*. New York and London: Routledge.

PANKSEPP, J. (1998). *Affective Neuroscience*. New York: Oxford University Press.

PHILLIPS, A. (1998). *The Beast in the Nursery*. New York: Vintage Books.

THE PROCESS OF CHANGE STUDY GROUP. (1998). *Infant Mental Health Journal*. 19:3,277–353.

SABOT, L. M. (1980). Conceptualizing the Nature of the Therapeutic Action of Child Analysis, A Panel Report. *J. Am Psa.* 28:1,161–180.

SCHIMEK, J. (1975). A critical re-examination of Freud's concept of mental representation. *Int. J. Psychoanalysis*, 2:171–187.

SOLNIT, A. J., COHEN, D. J., & NEUBAUER, P. B. (1993). *The Many Meanings of Play*. New Haven: Yale Univ. Press.

STERN, D. N. (1985). *The Interpersonal World of the Infant. A View from Psychoanalysis and Developmental Psychology*. New York: Basic Books.

WAELDER, R. (1933). The Psychoanalytic Theory of Play. *Psa. Quart.*, 2:208–224.

WINNICOTT, D. W. (1971). *Playing and Reality*. New York: Basic Books.

——— (1965). *The Maturational Processes and the Facilitating Environment*. London: Hogarth.

Early Object Relations
into New Objects

T. WAYNE DOWNEY, M.D.

THE SUBJECT OF THIS SYMPOSIUM, CHANGES IN CHILD-ANALYTIC technique since the publication in 1965 of Anna Freud's *Normality and Pathology in Childhood,* invites all sorts of responses. It might be fitting to use an earlier paper by Anna Freud and Sophie Dann (1951) as a benchmark to demonstrate changes in our theoretical understanding and their impact on technique over the past 35 years. I focus on this earlier publication because it stands out in the psychoanalytic literature as a testimony to qualities of the ego that press toward completion of development, qualities that have tended to be obscured by technical emphases on resistance to recovery and defenses against psychological growth.

The Freud-Dann paper, "An Experiment in Group Upbringing," is a report on a group of six children who had been interred for three years in the concentration camp at Terezin, Czechoslovakia, and who, in October of 1945, were brought to Bulldogs Bank in England for resuscitation from war trauma. The report on their recovery as studied by Freud and Dann helps us to address the fundamental question of how maturation and development interact in the context of normal growth and analytic reconstitution. How is the internal biological reality of temperament made manifest in the psyche, and how are the developmental influences of social reality internalized

Clinical professor of psychiatry and child psychiatry, Yale School of Medicine and Yale Child Study Center; training and supervising analyst, The Western New England Institute For Psychoanalysis, New Haven, Connecticut.

I would like to express my gratitude to Alice B. Colonna, M.A., for both calling John's autobiography to my attention and critiquing an earlier version of this paper.

The Psychoanalytic Study of the Child 56, ed. Albert J. Solnit, Peter B. Neubauer, Samuel Abrams, and A. Scott Dowling (Yale University Press, copyright © 2001 by Albert J. Solnit, Peter B. Neubauer, Samuel Abrams, and A. Scott Dowling).

(Hartmann and Kris, 1945)? Anna Freud wrote extensively on the technique of child analysis from the viewpoints of play, internalization, and verbalization. Her paper about the Thereisenstadt war orphans suggests another dimension for understanding recovery, both analytic recovery and the recovery of most individuals through the opportunities of everyday life. Somewhat by implication, it emphasizes the possibilities for the resumption of psychological growth through the provision of a proper holding environment rather than through the usual analytic mode of verbalization and interpretation.

The Children's Group at Bulldogs Bank

The Freud-Dann paper provides the descriptive data needed to frame our questions and to further our explorations of self/object development and developmental objects. It helps us understand more about the conditions for developmental growth and the consummation of development. Its dense and precise detail and typically understated arguments are characteristic of Anna Freud's genius for simultaneously applying and deriving psychoanalytic principles from analytically informed child observation. The "experiment within the experiment," as it seems to have evolved, was to extend the findings beyond what was wrong with each of the children to consider the more basic question of how these six youngsters could have substituted the group as love object in place of a parent.

The experiment at Bulldogs Bank was intended to determine what could be done for these orphans, using contemporary psychoanalytic precepts to reverse the depredations of fate and restore them to a normal developmental track, with particular emphasis on object relations. Implicit in this, the work separates out the developmental factors from the traumatic factors. It clarifies how therapeutic interventions may emphasize the resumption of maturational growth, on the one hand, and how such a resumption of growth may differ from the therapeutic action commonly associated with developmental growth, on the other. One of the major questions confronting Freud-Dann was whether the libidinal and aggressive bonding that formed such an extreme adaptation for the group could give way to a more fluid adaptable sense of individuality within a safer community. The pieces of the puzzle of the war waifs who so captured their attention reassemble in novel ways as current concepts and older underutilized theoretical ideas add richness to their previous findings. I will reconsider this paper in light of certain theoretical concepts that were not in vogue at the time, such as Hartmann's (1939) ideas about adaptation and the conflict-free sphere of ego functioning. It also seems to me that Winnicott's (1953) concepts of the transitional object and transitional phenomena and Loewald's (1961) persuasive metaphors about the infant as agent in the mother–infant dual unit add further dimension to the findings. Loewald's paper complements Hartmann's notion of more and less object-related and more and less conflicted spheres of ego functioning—that is, the Loewaldian infant as more or less active and interactive in relation to the mother devoted to its development. Hartmann's (1952) concept of object constancy also adds significance to these observations as does Spitz's (1946) theory of anaclitic depression. By and large I have not used other sources on the "experiment" except for the descriptions of Theresienstadt in the works of Berkley (1993) and Volovkova (1993).

Berkely (1993) provides a detailed history of "Theresienstadt." The Terezin concentration camp, where the children struggled to live for three years, was originally a barrack town inhabited by fewer than 8,000 soldiers and citizens. In October of 1941 it was converted into a ghetto for "special" Jews, those who had been of outstanding civic, military, or artistic service to Germany. Administered by the SS and overseen by a Jewish Council of Elders, it was intended as a model camp, a place to demonstrate the good care the Jews were receiving at the hands of the Nazis.

By the time Terezin was liberated by the Russian army, in May of 1945, 141,000 Jews from all over Europe had been processed through it. At any given time its population ranged from 40,000 to 60,000. It has been calculated that there were 1.6 square meters of space for each inhabitant. Inhabitants were forced to work 80–100 hours per week. Deaths occurred at the rate of 100 to 150 each day. During the three and a half years of the camp's existence, 88,000 persons were shipped out to death camps in the East while 33,000 died at Terezin. On December 31, 1943, there were 3,367 children in the camp. Either through death or transfer to the death camps, by December 31, 1944, there were only 819 children.

At war's end, in the summer of 1945, three girls, Ruth, Miriam, and Leah, and three boys, John, Paul, and Peter, all in their fourth year, were rescued from the Tereszin camp. (While all the children were Jewish, for unknown reasons in this report all the boys were accorded New Testament names.) They were taken first to a Czech castle, where they were overfed and overstimulated relative to the barren circumstances of their lives at Tereszin. After a month they were flown to a reception station at Windemere, England. The waifs remained there for two months before making the third and last move of their fourth year. On October 15, 1945, they were taken into a makeshift nursery at "Bulldogs Bank," a country house in West Hoathly, Sussex, where for the next 12 months they were to be studied by Miss Freud and cared for by Sophie Dann and her sister Gertrud.

All of these children had been reared without a significant parent since midway through their first year of life. Thus they grew up "without an early mother or father image in their unconscious minds to which their earliest libidinal strivings might have been attached" (p. 166). Anna Freud makes the important point that these children had not been actively rejected by their mothers but were passively rejected according to cruel and atrocious circumstance.

All six of the children had passed through innumerable anonymous hands in the first year of their lives. At Tereszin they were tended on the Ward for Motherless Children by a succession of women inmates including Martha Wenger who had been in charge of the ward and wrote to Anna Freud about life in the camp. During their second and third years they eked out an existence as a peer group in an atmosphere of ongoing terror and loss at Tereszin, where they were cared for at starvation-level circumstances (they all seemed to have presented later with signs of protein deficiency). They suffered general deprivation in the areas of nutriment, mother love, and the oral gratifications and self/object development that go with both. Paradoxically, they existed in the camp "in an abundance of community influence" in an interpersonal field of unstable relationships and muted passivity at the very edge of life.

Miss Freud emphasizes that over time in Tereszin the children had formed into an "age group". As with most orphans, even those adopted immediately at birth, there are many historical blind spots that can never be filled. One such blind spot in the account has to do with the formation of the group and its membership when it finally arrived at Bulldogs Bank. What distinguished this group from the other 1,000 concentration camp children to enter England at the same time? What made them stand out in such a way that they were given the special circumstances, financial support, and experimental conditions of Bulldogs Bank? Was it always a group of just six of the youngest at Tereszin or were there others who were lost to disease and extermination? Some of the behaviors described later in the Freud-Dann paper, such as the children's restless exchange of seats at meals, suggest that there may have been other members of the group at an earlier time. Conceivably, older children may have been a factor in consolidating the group. They may be remembered only in the group's reactions to outsiders, outside threats, and the availability of help.

The "experiment in group upbringing" was in many ways an attempt to see what could be done to reverse group process in a group that had ostensibly brought itself up. Because of their age and the extremity of their early childhood circumstances, they were survivors of a horror that they readily and unconsciously dramatized in their infantile gang terrorism. Its name and full meaning were buried in a complex of infantile amnesia and traumatically induced repression. The "experiment" at Bulldogs Bank tested the extent to which the privations these children were subjected to in the concentration camp resulted in maturational delay as opposed to the more readily understood and accepted notion of traumatic arrest in their psychic growth. This hypothesized delay was then countered by Miss Freud's provision of stable living circumstances in the company of constant, compassionate, and energetic caretakers. The children's living situation at Bulldogs Bank attempted to measure in a qualitative rather than a quantitative manner whether and how much their delay could be reversed by a developmentally oriented psychoanalytic program. Implicit in this approach is the emphasis on "living through" on the basis of a therapeutic milieu rather than 'working through' by the medium of therapeutic interpretation; providing conditions of love, loving, and safe aggressive containment rather than interpreting the wishes and resistances involved with such libidinal and aggressive energies.

To a surprising extent, the experiment was successful. Through the construction of a compassionate environment, the ego, drive, and object-related development of these war-torn children was considerably enhanced. Maturation picked up where it had been blocked by harsh circumstances. The unmanageable traumatic pain that necessarily underwent repression would have to await other measures.

The implicit emphasis on therapeutic milieu as opposed to the therapeutic action of interpretation allows us to conceptualize how children may recover from developmental delay and yet still experience considerable ongoing internal conflict. As I understand it, interpretation then is called for to help traumatized individuals grasp unconscious unassimilatable fear, pain, and rage and the accompanying shards of memory subsequent to their camp exposure and nomadic non-dyadic lives. The Freud-Dann approach to these children demonstrated what can be accomplished in the way of developmental remediation in the less object-tied, less inter- and intrapsychically conflicted areas of childhood ego functioning without invoking a mutative interpretive relationship.

GROUP FORMATION

There is a vivid description of the group's cohesiveness at the beginning of their stay at Bulldogs Bank. Feelings of warmth, love, and affection were shared only among members of the group; they were angry, cheerless, and harshly manipulative toward "outsiders." They used grownups to meet immediate needs that they could not somehow manage to meet themselves. When need satisfaction had been accomplished, they would again ignore the adults. They were always on the alert for danger from without and always ready to attack.

In keeping with the wartime psychological climate and the developmental emphases of the time, Anna Freud was preoccupied with the dominant question of how the infant is acted upon by the environment and environmental agents. Her emphasis was on the "combination of fateful outside circumstances" that conspired to create children with a group-related psychology in which dyadic mother–child dynamics seemed to be denied, replaced by an interdependence in which the group was more than the sum of its individual egos. On closer viewing, we perceive that the group functioned in what seems to be a protean maternal fashion. It may be that, as Miss Freud says, while the unconscious imago of a parental representation is virtually absent in children who have had little or no experience with parents, there persists a pre-programmed tendency to contact or form an entity with analogous functions. The manner in which the group's director changed according to the group's changing needs is an aspect of this protean group character. The group was apparently leaderless, with each member possessing the potential for temporarily directing the group in relation to certain functions. For instance, John would preside at mealtimes, Miriam would fulfill the occasional group need for somebody to be pampered as a queen bee, and Peter came to the fore when a gamesman was needed to invent and direct play activities. Thus the group seemed to function in a manner consonant with the anaclitic dynamics described by Spitz. At times it represented an early mother–child unit composed of confused and shifting part and whole objects where instinctual need and object are interchangeable.

Functionally as well as on an unconscious level among its members, the group represented a mother substitute. It was protector and guardian, auxiliary ego, regulator of love within the group, and projector of hate to the outside. On one level a dominant metaphor of child rearing in which a dyadically related individual psychology emerges from the active reciprocity of the "mother-child dual-unit" (Loewald, 1961) seemed to be breached. On another level the group can be viewed as forming a nurturing and protective libidinally fused and aggressively demarcated body. To put it in another way, this peer group can be conceptualized as anaclitically interdependent. It will not go forward in time or space without its six component parts. It walks with Ruth, not ahead of her. It takes up with Miriam where it left off with her before she was separated by quarantine. It reasserts its disavowal of the shifts toward a dyadic economy that have occurred in her absence. We might wonder, again, if the group once had more parts that in Tereszin were distilled to six. Did the unarticulated experience of group attrition and depressive loss serve as the anaclitic glue that kept the group centered? The constant haggling of the members in the absence of serious physical hostilities seems to be more in the service of maintaining aggressively driven, object-seeking contact and aliveness with each other rather than inflicting psychological damage. Perhaps silence was equated with abandonment and death.

Anna Freud assumed that restitution of ego capacities for relatedness in these traumatized children would come from either returning them to a nurturing dyadic relation if that had been repressed, or stimulating the emergence of such a relation if the arrest was of a pre-dyadic nature. Providing oral libidinal compensations and options had the effect of both loosening the group libidinal glue and directing the group members to people who might help them overcome their emotional and physical starvation.

At this juncture we might speculate that part of the cost of group formation in the absence of the one significant other is the development of an early neurotic symptom, a dyadic phobia. Because it occurs early in development, fear and symbol blend together. Fear of another easily becomes fear of all others in a one-to-one situation. This can lead to a generalized avoidance of dyads and an overdetermined predilection for groups. It can explain why these children erupted in rage at being offered a helping hand in getting off a bus. The children had had, after all, a certain subsistence level of nurture and care in the camp. In the midst of physical and emotional deprivation and developmental understimulation there was also a degree of libidinal stimulation and gratification—enough, I would speculate, to make the children wary and avoidant of the pain associated with such unsatisfying and suboptimal relations. The net effect was to increase the potential for group bonding. Potential relationships with adults remained at a level that probably also reflected the anxious despair of the doomed. Given the constant threat of separation and death, a full dyadic personal relationship would be construed as potentially pain ridden, too threatening to risk. At a level only slightly beyond psychological and physical starvation, adults were failing them at every moment.

It speaks to both the latent needs of the children for close personal relationships with adults and the canny social engineering of the Freud-Dann "experiment" that within a few months the children's investment in group function had started to give way to more differentiated dyadic dynamics. Not surprisingly, they proved to be quite variable in their dyadic potentials. Ruth exhibited the greatest affinity for dyadic engagement. Of all the children, she had the longest history of a one-to-one relationship; as noted earlier, her connection with Martha Wenger went all the way back to Tereszin. At the Windemere reception camp it was Ruth who established the first individual contact by a group member in England. She responded electrically to being serenaded by Alice Goldberger's harmonica playing. After that initial engagement she would dance for and cling to Alice whenever they met.

ADAPTATION AND MALADAPTATION

In this classic work of child observation the individual child's subjugation of individual identity for group identity in the interests of adaptation and survival was accepted and understood as a developmental anomaly (as it was, but only in part). There was, after all, some safety in numbers. However, understanding of the children's aggressive affinity for "peer groupness" as well as their other disturbed behaviors benefits from being subjected to the analytic standards proffered by Hartmann (1939). Using Hartmann's ideas about the role of adaptation in development, we can now understand that the unrelenting, potentially blighting impact of environment on these young children was buffered by gains in the conflict-free sphere of ego functioning. What increase in understanding comes if we think of the child's ego as actively engaging, fashioning, and internalizing stressors? The blank masks of trauma that the Bulldogs Bank children wore on their faces no doubt reflected defensive detachment, but they may also have reflected identification with the affective stringencies of their environment and a necessary concealment of their highly activated and alerted ego state. Their guarded behavior and facial expression could signify an adaptation to what they had internalized and shaped from the surround.

We are confronted with a model of ego functioning that extends beyond its theoretical submission to the drives and beyond its executive functions in maintaining psychic harmony and minimizing anxiety in relation to environmental dangers. The data of this paper suggest that the ego can sponsor progressive energies in the service of cognitive and perceptual growth in children raised in minimal conditions for survival. The point is not that they will succumb to marasmus or emerge unscathed from such early experiences but that they do emerge with surprising amounts of the psychological equipment ready to kick in given the availability of a supportive environment. Their developed intelligence (except perhaps for Miriam) in the service of group adaptation and their facility with languages point to areas of ego that may in some individuals and some circumstances be less object- and field-dependent than is usually thought to be the case for optimal development.

Despite the cruel and rigid routines of Tereszin, these children possessed the ego resiliency and behavioral determination of survivors. They had a knack for the active that they also employed in adapting to the demands of Bulldogs Bank. Indeed, their hyperactivity and ceaseless moving of the furniture, as well as their use of sugar as salt to accommodate a shift from bland to seasoned foods, are ways in which the children attempted to adapt to an overrich, overstimulating new environment. Their motor play dramatized their many moves and their constant investment in attempts to shift their adaptation from the silence and passivity of the camp to the enunciated activity of the Banks. In contemporary terms they may be viewed, yet again, as agents vis-à-vis mother or world rather than as merely passive recipients or victims of fate.

Their capacities for speech survived intact. They were all well-spoken and used speech to communicate in the group idiom for ongoing orientation to their surroundings as well as to ward off intrusions from the outside world. The children's use of "stupid" in German or English to insult or chastise a grownup is one example (p. 142). Another is their ability to pick up a second language, English, within four or five months of coming to Bulldogs Bank. German was extinguished from their lexicon after ten months there. It seems paradoxical and yet maturationally apt that certain ego functions such as speech and motility may emerge largely independent of direct object relations. As I mentioned earlier, expanding upon Hartmann and

Kris, maturation does not occur in some interpersonal vacuum. There must be some exposure to objects and some space to be motile in. Beyond that, functions tend to emerge in a conflict-free manner unless object relations are directly noxious to the child. This is like walking. Having walking loved ones around all the time tends to have no effect on the timing of the onset of walking by the infant unless the developmental circumstances are overwhelmingly interfering.

Resilience is a function of adaptability, and, as Hartman has noted, the ego is the organ of adaptation. Our capacity for adaptation may be enhanced or diminished by experience, but, like talent and temperament, it is an aspect of ego functioning that the individual is born with and practices. Their resilience permitted these children to extract nurture at whatever level it was available and to potentiate it psychologically far beyond what was actually there. It enabled them to gather the shards of need satisfaction from many doomed nurturers at Tereszin and to bring them together in their own group experiment in constructing the anaclitically available mother substitute that was the group. This group formation demonstrated the capacity to inform minimal maternal experience from an early level of object relatedness with a shared fantasy. It is in this construction of a fantasy that is shared by the group, a fantasy of hope, protection and sustenance, that the ego is able to act as agent in circumstances that seem, on the surface, to offer overwhelming possibilities for trauma and psychic damage.

The fantasy emerges in the mind more as a response to the psychobiology of the body than to the stimuli of experience. An adaptation emerges in the group hyperrelatedness and finally group invention by the children in the grim circumstances of object estrangement and libidinal deficit that the Tereszin concentration camp provided. Abject passivity as viewed from the perspective of the outside observer was transformed into action through the children's aggressive and libidinal interplay with each other! From a slightly different perspective, we might speculate that positive sibling dynamics, which usually remain in the background in the well functioning nuclear family, where the dominance of ties to the parents is assured, emerged in full force in the Bulldogs Bank children. Where conflicts over status and competition are the norm for "family" children, for these waifs the other side of the sibling coin, cooperation became the currency of their transactions. Rather than refining their libidinal capacities with their parents and honing their aggression with their siblings, they became, at one level, sibling collaborators and cooperators. This is often the natural history of sibships after parents have become aged or have died.

In the abundant material and psychological circumstances of Bulldogs Bank, what might initially have been read as maladaptation could be understood as a quite successful adaptation in children whose only consistent world had been that of the concentration camp. Following this line of thought, the description of the meaning and usage of spoons (p. 152) seems to suggest some further conceptualizations. Freud and Dann report the interesting phenomenon that group identity regularly broke down when it came time for each child to select a spoon of his or her own. Then, individual hostility and aggressive self-assertion would regularly take over. In striking contrast to their usual militaristic emphasis on group cohesion, at least three times a day the group collapsed into a chaotic mass of warring individuals who were surprisingly uninhibited in attempting to get their own needs met first and best. It developed that in Tereszin a spoon was each child's only constant possession and mark of identity. For the children, the "little things" therefore were "symbols of their otherwise forgotten past." We can speculate that the "forgotten past" also extends into the maternal haze of earliest infancy, when anaclitic phenomena abound, at a time before true object differentiation and separation could develop and occur. As part of the meaning attached to that earlier epoch, "little things" could also signify a time when the children themselves were the little things in the exclusive, transient, or perhaps only wished-for care of their mothers or substitute mothers. "Forgotten" because memory, unlike language and motility, is so truculent in the early years and so reflective of affective experiences of object constancy or inconstancy. Lost objects easily succumb to the state of inconstant memory and infantile amnesia.

In the meaning of the "little things" we can discern some of the qualities of the transitional object as put forth by Winnicott (1953). This object should symbolize the soothing and continuous aspect of the relationship between child and mother, whether in wish or fact or some combination. At the least we can imagine that the quest for uniqueness and oneness with another has pre-adaptive developmental possibilities that will get expressed in some form or other and in some degree with little regard for the libidinal soil in which the child is raised. The spoons, the little things, then can come to stand in a

vestigial manner for both the absent or lost dyad and its long hoped-
for rediscovery in a new object relation. The spoons are magnified in
importance because they carry such transitional meanings. At mealtimes the anxiety, rage, and shifting positions in regard to need satisfaction at the table all probably acted out in quite intense and vivid
detail the children's latent wish to be found and considered special
by the nurturing other. Transitional phenomena invested the spoons
as emblematic of this quest. In this perspective, the group was merely
the holding environment for a deeper, more precious wish, that a stable object would come and break through the obdurate adaptation
of the Group-together and help each of them to Oneness with some
Other.

A lurking question remains. How far down the road of sibling-
group formation may a child go before the road becomes a one-way
street? What cost becomes associated with dismantling group supports and replacing them with dyadic dynamics when the group has
carried with it for so long the deepest of the individual's emotional
realities? How far in terms of time and experience before the oneness of the group cannot be satisfactorily translated into the otherness of individual selves? These are questions for which there are no
clear answers. They are pertinent to the current tendency to place
siblings who have lost family coherence in separate foster-care situations.

The spoons are a significant example of the way in which the children could turn maturational opportunities into a more complex developmental event of self-definition and self-protection. Other examples arise from conceptualizations of the aggressive drive, which
Anna Freud (1972) had a major role in defining both before and after this paper. The aggressive drive per se obviously was a central
force in ensuring the children's survival. It established a projective
and introjective hostile boundary around the group within which the
libidinal energies of each individual flowed interpsychically in the
constant creation and rediscovery of the "group as mother." A bond
of hateful passion, directed predominantly outward (except, as already noted, at mealtimes), replaced libidinal energies for which
there had been only unavailable and unsatisfactory objects. Libidinal
energies were withdrawn from their usual dyadic aims. The long-
standing object relation of Ruth and Martha Wenger that was established when Martha was superintendent of the Ward for Motherless
Children. is the exception to this group rule of libidinal economy.
Love between generations was put on hold, so to speak. Libidinal energies bound the group membership together while hostile aggres-

sion kept dangerous others and paranoid energies at bay (Downey, 1984).

Another of Anna Freud's concepts that can be invoked in this context is identification with the aggressor. It is hardly a stretch to think of the children's constant hostile litany of "bloder," "aunt," or "fool" directed toward themselves at times and rather constantly toward their adult servants as having arisen from identification with the insults of the guards at Tereszin. Identification with the aggressor, as a mechanism of both ego-defense and id-expression, has typically janusian characteristics. In addition to its hostile identification, it is a projection of the child's inferior, weak status onto someone else. One face of the mechanism is the victim; the other is identification with the victimizer—passivity versus activity, vulnerability versus power. So, on the one hand the children, who had been exposed to the brutality of the guards and their dogs, were frantically fearful of any dog. On the other hand, as a group they were capable of themselves becoming a growling, biting, warring watchdog!

Object constancy is another concept that Anna Freud, along with Hartmann (1952), was instrumental in elucidating and establishing over the fifteen years after publishing this paper. Given the developmental needs of the surviving self to come up with a constant and enduring other (or, in this case, others) to play off of, it is notable that in the harsh circumstances of these children group constancy took the place of the constant object. The group became the new object. In the underworld of transience and disappearances that constituted the concentration camp, peers, or at least some peers, were always there.

THE CHILDREN

It is also instructive to cull the descriptions of the various children scattered throughout the text and develop pictures of them as individuals. Thus Ruth and Paul were described as the most disturbed children in the group. Ruth expressed her rage through spitting. She had difficulties falling asleep and was a thumbsucker. Freud-Dann describes her as the only child of the group to choose a real mother substitute, Gertrud. The substitute relationship Ruth had established in Tereszin plus her subsequent attempts to attach herself to constant maternal objects left her in a turmoil; she attempted to assert her importance to the mother-figure and to take possession of her at the same time that she anxiously worried about being lost and left. "And Ruth? And Ruth?" was her insecure plaint to Gertrud (p. 146). Ruth did not like walks and exercised her power in the group by refusing to go on them, lagging behind, or calling the other group members to fall in with her, which they did! There is every reason the think that if we had the requisite historical data we would find that, as in the case of the spoons, this is an enactment of a very specific memory, a highly overdetermined repetition of things past. Perhaps we would find that Ruth's resistance to walks had in it important meanings and experiences of separation or death. There is a sense, though, in which the group meant less to Ruth than to any of the others. She helped Leah out of a sense of obligation to a fellow group member rather than out of friendship. She was the one most prepared to break ranks and display overt sibling-rivalrous dynamics. Ruth was the most openly jealous, possessive, envious, and competitive. She constantly attacked other children, behaving in a sadistic manner towards them and breaking their toys and possessions.

The episode of October 1945 in which Ruth gathered and lost her acorns stands out. Ruth gets Gertrud to fill her basket with acorns. Peter knocks into her, apparently accidentally, and spills them. Ruth responds by stealing the contents of Miriam's basket. She fights with John when she attempts to do the same with him. The episode ends with Paul's pleasantly conceding the contents of his basket to Ruth. We might say that Ruth developed the furthest of the children in terms of object relatedness and ambivalence. Her construction of a constant representation of self and other is still remarkably insecure and shaky. She has gained the most from "mothers" so she can appreciate more than the other children how much she has to lose. Her groupness easily succumbs to projected hostility when she feels and fears that she might be displaced or replaced with regard to a significant other. She will commit crimes and steal to protect what she deems hers alone. At those times individual attacks quickly supplant her uneasy sense of group cohesion.

Miriam lost her mother at birth. Bulldogs Bank was her fifth move in just over three years of life. She soothed herself by sucking her tongue. She developed special relations with the boys in the group, from whom she expected and received all sorts of help. This seemed to serve to maintain group cohesion. For instance, she would repeatedly summon the boys to pick up flowers that she had intentionally dropped. She was the first member of the group to openly appropriate an adult, saying in October 1945 "Sophie, my Sophie." At times she was remarkable for helping out with chores or aiding the adults. Interestingly, she was the one member of the group to possess a transitional object, a doll, and would allow only Paul to hold it. She helps us to understand the link between construction of the transitional object and the acquisition of a new object. In November she generously attempted to give the doll to Paul, only to find that she could not live without it.

We tend to think of the construction of the transitional object as Winnicott did, as "invented" out of the space of the mother–child relationship and existing as a replacement for that relationship. However, here we are faced with the paradox of Miriam's having constructed a transitional object in the absence of a deep maternal attachment. We can perhaps explain this on the basis that Miriam's capacity for relatedness, while more delayed than Ruth's emerged relatively intact in the conflict-free sphere of her ego functioning. She seemed to require very little experience of object nurture to "invent" and maintain a hopeful transitional object fantasy of an enduring relation with another. For Miriam that "other" was a man, Mr. E. (Often orphans will be more attracted to men as their memories of relations to women tend to be connected to the pain and deprivation they have experienced at the hands of women in orphanages and other institutions.) Early in 1946, Miriam formed a passionate attachment, first to Mr. E's picture book and then to his fatherly person. When he left the village she converted a postcard from him into an object with transitional qualities that went everywhere with her even though finally "it was no more than a grubby piece of paper" (p. 147). Miriam's inherent capacities in the transitional realm permitted her to smooth over Mr. E's leaving and to deal with his absence without ostensible resentment or feelings of rejection. Ruth's object experience had caused her to identify absence with conflict and trouble. Miriam possessed a built-in mechanism, refined by experience, for coping with object loss less conflictually and more realistically. For her, it need not be the end of the world as it threatened to be for Ruth.

Leah arrived at Bulldogs Bank in December 1945, after six weeks of quarantine. The five other members had started to crack the group shell and let some glimmers of meaningful adult relationships into their lives. With Leah's arrival the group reverted to its original stance of warding off the outside adult world. Leah is described as the most ordinary of the six children as well as the slowest. She, too, was a thumbsucker. When compared to the other children, with their active, hostile, and aggressive stances, Leah appears to have a much more passive bent. We cannot tell how much her passivity was a temperamental given. In terms of the environment a contribution also could come from her internalization of the deadly starvation-based

inactivity of everyone in the Ward for Motherless Children. Her passivity could be the outcome of living in a world where the first and almost only imperative was the conservation of energy through inactivity. She showed little overt aggression. She was subservient to Ruth,
"My Ruth." Ruth capitalized on Leah's passive dependency in one
episode that also involved Paul. Paul took Ruth's doll. She cried for
its return. Leah retrieved it from Paul and returned it to Ruth. Ruth
then meanly rejected Leah's charitable act by returning the doll to
Paul and continuing to cry!

Leah, however, did develop a relationship to "her Judith." There is
mention that while passive, she managed to be aggressively noisy. But
when Judith was tired, Leah generally tried to reign in her loudness
out of consideration for her. Leah showed the object-searching behavior and object promiscuity so often noted in children who survive
sparse affective circumstances. She grabbed for any potential relationship. Judith meant something to her but not so much that Leah
in her passive clinging way did not force herself upon the visitors she
encountered in her travels. For Leah indiscriminate need satisfaction
by someone, anyone, was not supplanted by the higher-order need
for gratification in the context of an exclusive relationship with a significant other.

Peter was the youngest of the group. In contrast to Leah, he is described as appealing. His qualities of being "engaging, fearless, and
naughty" bespeak an imagination, a charm, and a capacity for engagement that would seem to belie the fact that Bulldogs Bank was
the sixth move of his young life. His oral and phallic aggression was
quite available to him. He was a thumbsucker, a biter, and a spitter.
When enraged he would urinate on things. He too had a sleep disturbance. Early on he showed an attachment to Gertrud, about one
month after Miriam expressed her attachment to Sophie. He was the
second of the group to signal the development of a relationship with
an adult. He was also somewhat possessive of Sophie. Indeed, Peter
made a point of running to get Sophie a piece of candy to replace
one she had lost—another example of an empathic, charitable identification with someone who has lost something important! In spite
of his own fear of waves and water, he rescued Ruth from being
touched by an incoming wave at the beach. As mentioned earlier, his
rich imagination contributed to his being the group's gamesmaster.

Paul receives much mention throughout the paper because of the
ongoing high level of his very public disturbance and also his capacity to engage so many individuals in so many ways. He was a chronic,
compulsive, and open masturbator. He tended to express his con-

classmate. From his immediate grasp of the bitter truth of
hate's words it is obvious that he had some inkling that this
ase. While he was amnesic for Tereszin and most of the pe-
re his adoption, he did have vague memories of living with a
children at some early point. The fact of his adoption also
nse in confirming a vague and persistent sense that he was
v "different" from the rest of his family. Parenthetically, we
der if this sense that many adopted children have of being
nt" (whether or not they know of their adoption) does not
m some genetic "charm" in that their resonances are not
someone with chromosomal contributions from each par-

's adoptive parents, particularly his mother, had a deep narcis-
vestment in keeping his origins secret, so deep that it seemed
e these otherwise sensitive people unable to attend to any as-
John's inner life, as though addressing any of his inner expe-
would inevitably lead back to the secret. Indeed, while he had
me so much in an environment that sponsored conflict-free
pment, John still had much to overcome in the form of inner
and depressive pain stored deep in the halls of his memory.
arents' attitude toward his adoption paradoxically increased his
ct about fitting into their family group or going off on his own.
ritings attest to the guilt, self-blame, and depression he suf-
, in common with other survivors of extreme circumstances,
o his belief that these feelings were intensified by his family ex-
nce.

hn had two recurrent dreams that seemed to emanate from the
before his adoption. In one repeated dream he is in a big house
a racetrack. The house is surrounded by tall trees. In the second
m he is looking down on hills and "pretty lights." When he told
mother about the dreams she was curtly dismissive, telling him to
et about them, that everyone had such meaningless dreams! She
ed upon learning that John had found out (through his adoptive
ndmother) that he was born in Austria.

finally, in deep conflict about disobeying his parents' wishes by dif-
entiating himself from them, John began to research his origins.
is research commenced in earnest in his late teens. He had fallen
love and was engaged to be married. His new wife would become
rough his development the representation of a new object, re-
cting in one person the best of the protective libidinal energies of
e original group. In order to be married in a synagogue, he needed
nfirmation that his natural mother was Jewish. In the course of his

flicts and yearnings in more directly sexual terms than the other children. He showed Leah his penis several times and was quite explicit
in his wish that Gertrud attend to it. Interestingly enough, Paul was
also a budding altruist. He was not aggressive. He spent much of his
time immersed in masturbation or thumbsucking but could interrupt these activities to come to the rescue of another child or to help
adults serve a meal. He protected John at one point. He shared his
chocolate, leftover cake crumbs, and his Care Package from America
with the other children. He stepped on a nettle so that John could finally get a ladybird. He was very fond of Miriam. The two of them
pitched a violent tantrum in apparent protest of the attempt of a bus
conductor to help the children off the bus against their stated desires.

Paul exhibited fetishistic behavior dramatically by rhythmically
rubbing a bib against his nose while sucking his thumb. In the absence of this new object substitute he would anticipate returning to
its gratifying, food-smeared, smelly presence. He had many food fads
and aversions. He loved corn flakes and starchy foods. Miss Freud's
voice comes through clearly when she remarks: "The feeder fetish,
together with these regressive spells and the ambivalence to food,
may hint at the continued action of some (satisfying or distressing)
experience on the oral level to which the child is fixed and which he
reactivates compulsively to the overt accompaniment of a autoerotic
practice" (p. 150).

Paul's use of adults seems more complex than most of the other
children's. When Miriam hits Sophie in the eye and causes it to water,
Miriam looks concerned about what she has done to Sophie. Paul intervenes and insults Sophie as though it was her fault that she has
gotten hurt. Then he goes to comfort Miriam! It is as though in making Sophie responsible for being hurt by Miriam, Paul is, as a victim,
projecting onto the adult his own passive, guilt-laden experience.

Paul expressed his wishes to Gertrud that she kiss, suck, or fondle
his penis. In his doll play he manipulated the doll's arms to depict
it masturbating. Such a vivid, explicit, distinctly non-playlike action
suggests that Paul was attempting to overcome an overstimulating
and overwhelming sexual experience with an older child or adult.
He seems to be compulsively attempting to turn passive trauma and
excitement into active mastery. As we see nowadays with children
who have been sexually violated, Paul seems to have been acting out
an actual sexual victimization by publicly flaunting his masturbation
and attempting to draw others into his sexual world. It may be that
he was merely converting imagination into compulsive energy in or-

der to fill a void in his experiences of gratification, but it seems more likely that Paul was communicating in the best developmental language at his command that he had been sexually traumatized. As a possible remedy he attempted to turn Miriam's doll into an object with enduring and soothing transitional qualities. Over a period of ten weeks he partially succeeded before he lost the doll.

It would seem that Paul lacked the history and perspective of a special trusting relationship with an adult that would sustain the magical wish for mother–infant unity and differentiation. Otherwise the doll would not have been lost and he would have been successful in converting it into the hopeful vessel of a doll with transitional qualities. Fate and adults had not been kind enough to Paul (or disinterested enough) to permit such a transitional development.

In the spectrum of disorders of the Bulldogs Bank children we have Ruth at one extreme. She was predominantly developmentally delayed. She knew what she was missing, wishing for, and unable to have by way of a maternal relationship, and she was disturbed and suffering because of her hunger for a new object. At the other extreme is Paul, maturationally stunted, overwhelmed, traumatized, and neuroticized by overstimulation and probable injury at the hands of an adult.

JOHN'S SEARCH

John was the oldest of the children, aged three years and ten months when he reached Bulldogs Bank. It was thought that he might have had a substantial relationship with his mother, perhaps until the end of his first year. Subsequent data from his autobiography pin his age at the time of her loss to three and a half months. Like the other children, he had disturbances of isolation, soothing, and body competence. He was a notable thumbsucker and a bedwetter. John was the group director at mealtimes: when he pushed away his plate everybody else would also stop eating. Perhaps this role was connected with his being the oldest. He was capable of great anger. Throughout the narrative there are scattered references to his rages. Early in his time at Bulldogs Bank it is noted that John spit at and hit adults. In November 1945 he refused to get out of bed, lying there kicking and screaming. Another time he demanded seconds on cake; Ruth and Miriam obliged him by giving him theirs. Later in the year he had a tantrum when a "ladybird" flew away from him. We can speculate that this event was freighted by affect related to his vanished mother and other losses. John was also notably charitable. When Paul was

sick, John gave him a piece of bu
protector and (as the libidinal
become more prominent) his a
"little thing," the spoon, seeme
vested in dim memories of or fo
one point it is recorded that he hi
participated vigorously in a charac
tachments, John in December 194
fering her a piece of candy. John's
in April 1946 is moving and poign
clitic depression that lasted over a
children he had the warmest relatic
course of their year at Bulldogs Ba
none of the children developed a re
more than lukewarm compared to t
fought his way out of the depressior
dren and their toys. His loss of a new
his "siblings" as objects of hostility in
ment and failure. It was four weeks be
acceptance of Maureen's departure.

As John entered his forties, he grew
his origins and began a series of writing
and identity. In this endeavor he was obs
and outside of him but he was greatly aic
years. John entitled his clutch of reminis
researching his past *Lost and Waiting To*
1982 and has distributed them freely at
poignant story we get a sense of the quali
him to be among the less than 100 childr
out of Tereszin alive, as Weil (Volavkova) es

After the year at Bulldogs Bank, John an
brought to another English manor house,
stayed for about six months, until he was ad
tremely warm, caring English couple. In hi
them numerous times for pampering and
seems likely that this dose of love, which migh
another child, was necessary for John in pr
mate for potentiating recovery from developn
him to become a loving and working family
The downside of his parents' attentions was
bring themselves to tell him about his adopti
When he was ten the fact of his adoption was sa

him by a
his classn
was the
riod befo
group o
made se
someho
may wo
"differe
stem fr
those
ent.

John
sistic ir
to mak
pect o
rience
overco
devel
arrest
His p
confl
His
fered
and
perio

Jo
time
near
drea
his
for
rag
gra

fer
Th
in
th
fl
th
c

research he learned his real name and that of his mother as well. He also learned that he had been in Tereszin, was brought to England in a bomber, and was adopted from a manor house in Lingfield. He traveled to Lingfield, which is the site of a racetrack, and found the house in his first dream, Weir Courtenay, where the Dann sisters and Alice Goldberger had presided over his adoption. He soon confirmed that the beautiful dream of looking down at the lights captured quite specifically the evening view from Bulldogs Bank, where he had spent such a momentous year.

It is notable that these "screen dreams" continually pressed his past into his consciousness but apparently on the condition that the people who shared his life at those times remained invisible. Those early relationships, surrounded by pain and loss, remained unassimilated, irretrievable, and confined to John's neurotic core. Certainly the experience of loss recurred at Bulldogs Bank: Sophie Dann was away for two months, Maureen left for good, and Mr. E. also departed the scene. While John or Miriam or Ruth may have resonated more openly with one absence or another, the group as a whole, existing as it did to deny meaningful adult relationships, would have experienced paroxysms of the pain of separation and loss, new versions of the everyday concentration camp experience. Finally there was the loss of the group as it was disarticulated and its former members were adopted into different families around the globe.

Following these startling dream developments there was a lapse of 17 years in John's search. This may reflect his absorption in family life with a wife and two daughters. It may also express his conflict over completing his search. Finally he was contacted by the Dann sisters. A reunion of sorts ensued later when his wife recognized Alice Goldberger, "the matron of Weir Courtenay," on the television program "This Is Your Life." John was reunited with her and some of the other members of the group, but the details of the meeting remain vague in John's report. He came across a further measure of the intensity of his parents' resolve to insulate him from knowledge of his adoption when he learned that for years while he was growing up Alice Goldberger lived around the corner from him. His mother had resisted Alice's efforts to continue contact with John.

Slowly but steadily, over the years John made his way into the Holocaust experience which in some ways he lived every day but could not recall. He recovered largely through group and new object means in a manner that was beyond insight. He attended survivors meetings in England and Israel. He spoke and communicated with survivors and others with a specialized interest in the Holocaust and its aftermath.

He visited Tereszin and felt that a weight had been lifted from his psyche. At the same time the guilt at being a survivor and the mystery of what it was supposed to mean that he was so 'special' and yet so un-acknowledged in the world (he sported no camp tattoo) tormented him. He became depressed. Perhaps it would be more accurate to say that as his self-knowledge of his origins mounted and his obsession with the Holocaust asserted itself in a more and more unbridled fash-ion, John's childhood anaclitic depression resurfaced. He was then able to feel more "empty and miserable" about all that was missing and all that he had missed.

In a final section, written by his wife, we learn of John's discovery that Maly Trostenets, a camp near Minsk, was the final resting-place of his murdered mother. Another measure of his pent-up grief and depression is released on his visit to the camp as he stands by the monument to the 200,000 people killed there and tells his mother, Elsa, of his life.

In reading the Freud-Dann work and John's account of his subse-quent life we receive vivid and moving confirmation of the critical importance of personal history to one's sense of identity and of the human conflict around knowing and not knowing that history. In the process of escaping seemingly intolerable pain by the not knowing of repression, the individual becomes confined to a less meaningful, emptier sense of self, cut off from the affect and the self-knowledge that accompany it. This is an enormous price to pay. In John's in-stance the inner state of acceptance of pain and loss was waiting to be found.

SUMMARY

Two strands of change are suggested by this review, one matura-tional, the other therapeutic or developmental (Hartmann and Kris, 1945). By "maturational" I mean to suggest energies that infuse the individual from earliest life in a manner that includes object rela-tions, but for the healthy exercise of which object relations per se need not be of central and crucial importance. Within wide limits such energies may be delayed until growth conditions prevail without significant distortion of certain of the organism's ego functions. Therapeutic change is analogous to developmental change in that both involve the crucial presence of another to release energies. In therapeutic change these are energies that have been repressed be-yond the reach of developmental dynamics. In everyday development crisis and synthesis alternate in conjunction with new and emerging objects to add to the psychological structures brought to the fore by maturation.

In many instances, as we see with John, over time and in a less focussed manner, developmental changes can approximate therapeutic change and visa versa. Freud-Dann in their "experiment" pursued one line, in which the equipmental delay brought on by extremely adverse living circumstances was redressed by providing an interpersonally enriching, loving, developmentally facilitating milieu. The sketches of individual children and John's subsequent story provide a perspective into what becomes the stuff of growth and what remains the stuff of neurosis. The developmental reserves and ego resilience of these children were impressive but probably not extraordinary. Usual growth ensued as soon as they were provided with the rich soil of Bulldogs Bank instead of the desert sand of the Tereszin concentration camp. However, no one can escape such adverse circumstances without having taken in the stuff of neurosis. Affects and percepts that were not assimilatable or even available to consciousness at the time remain buried in the unconscious. Pain deprived of meaning is buried as neurosis. As we see in John's story, experience that cannot be integrated at the time is locked away from whatever developmental progression has occurred. Intolerable affects and ideas require particular circumstances of object relation and verbalization such as are found in the context of psychoanalysis and arrived at through psychoanalytic interpretation. Or, as in John's case, they may give way only slowly and irregularly over long stretches of time, when subjected to life experiences in the company of new object relations.

Broadly stated, the Freud-Dann paper helps us to appreciate that there are several pathways of protection and growth in the ego that involve the discovery or construction of new objects. Family-romance fantasies are a common manifestation of new-object phenomena. Transitional object phenomena are also related. For some individuals at a particular time or over a span of time, providing the right circumstances for the resumption of maturational and developmental growth is all it takes to make them whole. Changes in the adaptive ego are sufficient to alleviate the conflicts stemming from the neurotic ego. For others, depending upon the degree of their neurotic impairment, or for the same individual under other circumstances, therapeutic change in the deepest sense demands the relatively unconditional presence of the interactive and interpreting other. Children of the storm who come in for shelter and warmth may thrive, but they also require a means of getting at the storm in their core that has been internalized as part of the ego's survival mechanism.

What can be extracted from the poignant story of the Bulldogs Bank children about current child-analytic technique? The psychoanalytic piano now may be more formally conceptualized as having white as well as black keys. Most analyses, adult and child, have been conducted as though the "black keys"—pressure to mastery through repetition and its subsequent interpretation in relation to the transference—were the sole agents of therapeutic change. Reviewing maturation and development in relation to the resumption of psychological growth suggests that the provision of a beneficent environment, the "white keys," may lead to the resumption of maturational growth and change. The difference between the two modalities would be in the relative need for a significant other to bring about such change.

Expanding on Hartmann and Kris, we can say that maturation requires a certain level of human stimulation and a supportive environment to unfold. At times in our work we encounter a psychoanalysis of and about maturation rather than primarily transference and interpretation. By and large the structure and functions of the ego that have been impeded in their exercise by traumatic circumstances in the environment are reactivated by a generalized holding environment rather than a relationship. In the practice of psychoanalysis this means that the child analyst may be more relaxed about the nonverbal play and relational aspects of the work; he need not fear that dynamics not captured in secondary process are lost to change. To the extent that the analysis provides an opportunity for maturational expression, growth will occur. When growth has been impeded by direct and significant interpersonal factors, the standard interpretative clarifications of defense, drive, and object relations in the context of removing the transference distortions regarding the analyst (and the world) are essential for recovery. Where the sequence of repetition through practice to mastery has become frozen by thwarting and stunting relationships, these potentially dead-end examples of neurotic object constancy must be played out on the "black keys." The amalgamation of the black of transference developments and the white of maturational emergence is paradigmatic for the discovery of new objects and new senses of self. In everyday life and analysis, maturation may lead to dramatic change that has hitherto been poorly identified and conceptualized.

In child analysis, play is the medium for picking the lock of both arrested maturation and stultified development. Realizing that should flicts and yearnings in more directly sexual terms than the other children. He showed Leah his penis several times and was quite explicit in his wish that Gertrud attend to it. Interestingly enough, Paul was also a budding altruist. He was not aggressive. He spent much of his time immersed in masturbation or thumbsucking but could interrupt these activities to come to the rescue of another child or to help adults serve a meal. He protected John at one point. He shared his chocolate, leftover cake crumbs, and his Care Package from America with the other children. He stepped on a nettle so that John could finally get a ladybird. He was very fond of Miriam. The two of them pitched a violent tantrum in apparent protest of the attempt of a bus conductor to help the children off the bus against their stated desires.

Paul exhibited fetishistic behavior dramatically by rhythmically rubbing a bib against his nose while sucking his thumb. In the absence of this new object substitute he would anticipate returning to its gratifying, food-smeared, smelly presence. He had many food fads and aversions. He loved corn flakes and starchy foods. Miss Freud's voice comes through clearly when she remarks: "The feeder fetish, together with these regressive spells and the ambivalence to food, may hint at the continued action of some (satisfying or distressing) experience on the oral level to which the child is fixed and which he reactivates compulsively to the overt accompaniment of a autoerotic practice" (p. 150).

Paul's use of adults seems more complex than most of the other children's. When Miriam hits Sophie in the eye and causes it to water, Miriam looks concerned about what she has done to Sophie. Paul intervenes and insults Sophie as though it was her fault that she has gotten hurt. Then he goes to comfort Miriam! It is as though in making Sophie responsible for being hurt by Miriam, Paul is, as a victim, projecting onto the adult his own passive, guilt-laden experience.

Paul expressed his wishes to Gertrud that she kiss, suck, or fondle his penis. In his doll play he manipulated the doll's arms to depict it masturbating. Such a vivid, explicit, distinctly non-playlike action suggests that Paul was attempting to overcome an overstimulating and overwhelming sexual experience with an older child or adult. He seems to be compulsively attempting to turn passive trauma and excitement into active mastery. As we see nowadays with children who have been sexually violated, Paul seems to have been acting out an actual sexual victimization by publicly flaunting his masturbation and attempting to draw others into his sexual world. It may be that he was merely converting imagination into compulsive energy in order to fill a void in his experiences of gratification, but it seems more likely that Paul was communicating in the best developmental language at his command that he had been sexually traumatized. As a possible remedy he attempted to turn Miriam's doll into an object with enduring and soothing transitional qualities. Over a period of ten weeks he partially succeeded before he lost the doll.

It would seem that Paul lacked the history and perspective of a special trusting relationship with an adult that would sustain the magical wish for mother–infant unity and differentiation. Otherwise the doll would not have been lost and he would have been successful in converting it into the hopeful vessel of a doll with transitional qualities. Fate and adults had not been kind enough to Paul (or disinterested enough) to permit such a transitional development.

In the spectrum of disorders of the Bulldogs Bank children we have Ruth at one extreme. She was predominantly developmentally delayed. She knew what she was missing, wishing for, and unable to have by way of a maternal relationship, and she was disturbed and suffering because of her hunger for a new object. At the other extreme is Paul, maturationally stunted, overwhelmed, traumatized, and neuroticized by overstimulation and probable injury at the hands of an adult.

JOHN'S SEARCH

John was the oldest of the children, aged three years and ten months when he reached Bulldogs Bank. It was thought that he might have had a substantial relationship with his mother, perhaps until the end of his first year. Subsequent data from his autobiography pin his age at the time of her loss to three and a half months. Like the other children, he had disturbances of isolation, soothing, and body competence. He was a notable thumbsucker and a bedwetter. John was the group director at mealtimes: when he pushed away his plate everybody else would also stop eating. Perhaps this role was connected with his being the oldest. He was capable of great anger. Throughout the narrative there are scattered references to his rages. Early in his time at Bulldogs Bank it is noted that John spit at and hit adults. In November 1945 he refused to get out of bed, lying there kicking and screaming. Another time he demanded seconds on cake; Ruth and Miriam obliged him by giving him theirs. Later in the year he had a tantrum when a "ladybird" flew away from him. We can speculate that this event was freighted by affect related to his vanished mother and other losses. John was also notably charitable. When Paul was sick, John gave him a piece of bun. Leah was at various times both his protector and (as the libidinal connections with adults heat up and become more prominent) his attacker. For John in particular, the "little thing," the spoon, seemed to have unconscious meanings vested in dim memories of or fond hopes for a maternal object. At one point it is recorded that he hid his spoon on his person and then participated vigorously in a charade to find it. In the realm of real attachments, John in December 1945 made an overture to Sophie, offering her a piece of candy. John's reaction to Maureen's departure in April 1946 is moving and poignant. He sunk into a marked anaclitic depression that lasted over a period of twelve days. Of all the children he had the warmest relationship with Maureen. (Over the course of their year at Bulldogs Bank, though, it is reported that none of the children developed a relationship with an adult that was more than lukewarm compared to their love for each other.) As he fought his way out of the depression John attacked the other children and their toys. His loss of a new object parent figure reinstated his "siblings" as objects of hostility in the face of parental abandonment and failure. It was four weeks before he began to show a quiet acceptance of Maureen's departure.

As John entered his forties, he grew increasingly troubled about his origins and began a series of writings about his search for solace and identity. In this endeavor he was obstructed by forces both within and outside of him but he was greatly aided by Lita, his wife of twenty years. John entitled his clutch of reminiscences and this chronicle of researching his past *Lost and Waiting To Be Found*. He began them in 1982 and has distributed them freely at intervals since then. In his poignant story we get a sense of the qualities that may have enabled him to be among the less than 100 children out of 15,000 to come out of Tereszin alive, as Weil (Volavkova) estimated.

After the year at Bulldogs Bank, John and the other children were brought to another English manor house, Weir Courtenay, where he stayed for about six months, until he was adopted at age five by an extremely warm, caring English couple. In his writings, John rebukes them numerous times for pampering and overprotecting him. It seems likely that this dose of love, which might have led to spoiling in another child, was necessary for John in providing the proper climate for potentiating recovery from developmental delay. It enabled him to become a loving and working family man in his own right. The downside of his parents' attentions was that they could never bring themselves to tell him about his adoption and his early life. When he was ten the fact of his adoption was sadistically disclosed to him by a classmate. From his immediate grasp of the bitter truth of his classmate's words it is obvious that he had some inkling that this was the case. While he was amnesic for Tereszin and most of the period before his adoption, he did have vague memories of living with a group of children at some early point. The fact of his adoption also made sense in confirming a vague and persistent sense that he was somehow "different" from the rest of his family. Parenthetically, we may wonder if this sense that many adopted children have of being "different" (whether or not they know of their adoption) does not stem from some genetic "charm" in that their resonances are not those of someone with chromosomal contributions from each parent.

John's adoptive parents, particularly his mother, had a deep narcissistic investment in keeping his origins secret, so deep that it seemed to make these otherwise sensitive people unable to attend to any aspect of John's inner life, as though addressing any of his inner experience would inevitably lead back to the secret. Indeed, while he had overcome so much in an environment that sponsored conflict-free development, John still had much to overcome in the form of inner arrest and depressive pain stored deep in the halls of his memory. His parents' attitude toward his adoption paradoxically increased his conflict about fitting into their family group or going off on his own. His writings attest to the guilt, self-blame, and depression he suffered, in common with other survivors of extreme circumstances, and to his belief that these feelings were intensified by his family experience.

John had two recurrent dreams that seemed to emanate from the time before his adoption. In one repeated dream he is in a big house near a racetrack. The house is surrounded by tall trees. In the second dream he is looking down on hills and "pretty lights." When he told his mother about the dreams she was curtly dismissive, telling him to forget about them, that everyone had such meaningless dreams! She raged upon learning that John had found out (through his adoptive grandmother) that he was born in Austria.

Finally, in deep conflict about disobeying his parents' wishes by differentiating himself from them, John began to research his origins. This research commenced in earnest in his late teens. He had fallen in love and was engaged to be married. His new wife would become through his development the representation of a new object, reflecting in one person the best of the protective libidinal energies of the original group. In order to be married in a synagogue, he needed confirmation that his natural mother was Jewish. In the course of his

research he learned his real name and that of his mother as well. He also learned that he had been in Tereszin, was brought to England in a bomber, and was adopted from a manor house in Lingfield. He traveled to Lingfield, which is the site of a racetrack, and found the house in his first dream, Weir Courtenay, where the Dann sisters and Alice Goldberger had presided over his adoption. He soon confirmed that the beautiful dream of looking down at the lights captured quite specifically the evening view from Bulldogs Bank, where he had spent such a momentous year.

It is notable that these "screen dreams" continually pressed his past into his consciousness but apparently on the condition that the people who shared his life at those times remained invisible. Those early relationships, surrounded by pain and loss, remained unassimilated, irretrievable, and confined to John's neurotic core. Certainly the experience of loss recurred at Bulldogs Bank: Sophie Dann was away for two months, Maureen left for good, and Mr. E. also departed the scene. While John or Miriam or Ruth may have resonated more openly with one absence or another, the group as a whole, existing as it did to deny meaningful adult relationships, would have experienced paroxysms of the pain of separation and loss, new versions of the everyday concentration camp experience. Finally there was the loss of the group as it was disarticulated and its former members were adopted into different families around the globe.

Following these startling dream developments there was a lapse of 17 years in John's search. This may reflect his absorption in family life with a wife and two daughters. It may also express his conflict over completing his search. Finally he was contacted by the Dann sisters. A reunion of sorts ensued later when his wife recognized Alice Goldberger, "the matron of Weir Courtenay," on the television program "This Is Your Life." John was reunited with her and some of the other members of the group, but the details of the meeting remain vague in John's report. He came across a further measure of the intensity of his parents' resolve to insulate him from knowledge of his adoption when he learned that for years while he was growing up Alice Goldberger lived around the corner from him. His mother had resisted Alice's efforts to continue contact with John.

Slowly but steadily, over the years John made his way into the Holocaust experience which in some ways he lived every day but could not recall. He recovered largely through group and new object means in a manner that was beyond insight. He attended survivors meetings in England and Israel. He spoke and communicated with survivors and others with a specialized interest in the Holocaust and its aftermath.

He visited Tereszin and felt that a weight had been lifted from his psyche. At the same time the guilt at being a survivor and the mystery of what it was supposed to mean that he was so 'special' and yet so un-acknowledged in the world (he sported no camp tattoo) tormented him. He became depressed. Perhaps it would be more accurate to say that as his self-knowledge of his origins mounted and his obsession with the Holocaust asserted itself in a more and more unbridled fash-ion, John's childhood anaclitic depression resurfaced. He was then able to feel more "empty and miserable" about all that was missing and all that he had missed.

In a final section, written by his wife, we learn of John's discovery that Maly Trostenets, a camp near Minsk, was the final resting-place of his murdered mother. Another measure of his pent-up grief and depression is released on his visit to the camp as he stands by the monument to the 200,000 people killed there and tells his mother, Elsa, of his life.

In reading the Freud-Dann work and John's account of his subse-quent life we receive vivid and moving confirmation of the critical importance of personal history to one's sense of identity and of the human conflict around knowing and not knowing that history. In the process of escaping seemingly intolerable pain by the not knowing of repression, the individual becomes confined to a less meaningful, emptier sense of self, cut off from the affect and the self-knowledge that accompany it. This is an enormous price to pay. In John's in-stance the inner state of acceptance of pain and loss was waiting to be found.

SUMMARY

Two strands of change are suggested by this review, one matura-tional, the other therapeutic or developmental (Hartmann and Kris, 1945). By "maturational" I mean to suggest energies that infuse the individual from earliest life in a manner that includes object rela-tions, but for the healthy exercise of which object relations per se need not be of central and crucial importance. Within wide limits such energies may be delayed until growth conditions prevail without significant distortion of certain of the organism's ego functions. Therapeutic change is analogous to developmental change in that both involve the crucial presence of another to release energies. In therapeutic change these are energies that have been repressed be-yond the reach of developmental dynamics. In everyday develop-

ment crisis and synthesis alternate in conjunction with new and emerging objects to add to the psychological structures brought to the fore by maturation.

In many instances, as we see with John, over time and in a less focussed manner, developmental changes can approximate therapeutic change and visa versa. Freud-Dann in their "experiment" pursued one line, in which the equipmental delay brought on by extremely adverse living circumstances was redressed by providing an interpersonally enriching, loving, developmentally facilitating milieu. The sketches of individual children and John's subsequent story provide a perspective into what becomes the stuff of growth and what remains the stuff of neurosis. The developmental reserves and ego resilience of these children were impressive but probably not extraordinary. Usual growth ensued as soon as they were provided with the rich soil of Bulldogs Bank instead of the desert sand of the Tereszin concentration camp. However, no one can escape such adverse circumstances without having taken in the stuff of neurosis. Affects and percepts that were not assimilatable or even available to consciousness at the time remain buried in the unconscious. Pain deprived of meaning is buried as neurosis. As we see in John's story, experience that cannot be integrated at the time is locked away from whatever developmental progression has occurred. Intolerable affects and ideas require particular circumstances of object relation and verbalization such as are found in the context of psychoanalysis and arrived at through psychoanalytic interpretation. Or, as in John's case, they may give way only slowly and irregularly over long stretches of time, when subjected to life experiences in the company of new object relations.

Broadly stated, the Freud-Dann paper helps us to appreciate that there are several pathways of protection and growth in the ego that involve the discovery or construction of new objects. Family-romance fantasies are a common manifestation of new-object phenomena. Transitional object phenomena are also related. For some individuals at a particular time or over a span of time, providing the right circumstances for the resumption of maturational and developmental growth is all it takes to make them whole. Changes in the adaptive ego are sufficient to alleviate the conflicts stemming from the neurotic ego. For others, depending upon the degree of their neurotic impairment, or for the same individual under other circumstances, therapeutic change in the deepest sense demands the relatively unconditional presence of the interactive and interpreting other. Children of the storm who come in for shelter and warmth may thrive, but they also require a means of getting at the storm in their core that has been internalized as part of the ego's survival mechanism.

What can be extracted from the poignant story of the Bulldogs Bank children about current child-analytic technique? The psycho-analytic piano now may be more formally conceptualized as having white as well as black keys. Most analyses, adult and child, have been conducted as though the "black keys"—pressure to mastery through repetition and its subsequent interpretation in relation to the trans-ference—were the sole agents of therapeutic change. Reviewing mat-uration and development in relation to the resumption of psycholog-ical growth suggests that the provision of a beneficent environment, the "white keys," may lead to the resumption of maturational growth and change. The difference between the two modalities would be in the relative need for a significant other to bring about such change.

Expanding on Hartmann and Kris, we can say that maturation re-quires a certain level of human stimulation and a supportive environ-ment to unfold. At times in our work we encounter a psychoanalysis of and about maturation rather than primarily transference and in-terpretation. By and large the structure and functions of the ego that have been impeded in their exercise by traumatic circumstances in the environment are reactivated by a generalized holding environ-ment rather than a relationship. In the practice of psychoanalysis this means that the child analyst may be more relaxed about the nonver-bal play and relational aspects of the work; he need not fear that dy-namics not captured in secondary process are lost to change. To the extent that the analysis provides an opportunity for maturational ex-pression, growth will occur. When growth has been impeded by di-rect and significant interpersonal factors, the standard interpretative clarifications of defense, drive, and object relations in the context of removing the transference distortions regarding the analyst (and the world) are essential for recovery. Where the sequence of repetition through practice to mastery has become frozen by thwarting and stunting relationships, these potentially dead-end examples of neu-rotic object constancy must be played out on the "black keys." The amalgamation of the black of transference developments and the white of maturational emergence is paradigmatic for the discovery of new objects and new senses of self. In everyday life and analysis, mat-uration may lead to dramatic change that has hitherto been poorly identified and conceptualized.

In child analysis, play is the medium for picking the lock of both arrested maturation and stultified development. Realizing that should

permit the child analyst to engage more freely with the child in their own style of play without being overly concerned about the presence or absence of relational dynamic material. Non-dynamic play may not usually be defensive play, though it has often been misinterpreted as such. It may represent activity supporting renewed maturation—practice play in the service of memory, motility, or small or large motor function rather than in the service of the playful, repetitive externalization of threatening introjects. Dynamic play highlights the stagnant or emerging functions of the ego with regard to defense and affect management, which may then be interpreted using the play as key or using words as key to unlock the troubled relationship that is being dramatized. The analyst remains in a non-defensive stance, assigned by the analysand as audience or benign participant.

Similarly, in adult analyses some individuals come pre-programmed not so much for interpretation as to discover the analyst as new object. They are in search of near psychobiological maturational closure on an object, already constituted in fantasy, that is respectful, attentive, objective, interested, and sometimes enlightening in their attempts at analytic understanding and developmental homeostasis. This phenomenon is akin to love at first sight, though without the flagrant libidinal romantic element. It occurs as the analytic narrative unfolds and the patient comes to a new sense of self, often around some developmental role or mix of roles, such as spouse, lover, mother, student, sibling, or worker. The point is that playing on the black and white keys of development and maturation leads to the appreciation of a psychoanalytic instrument that is at once more complex and yet easier to get music out of. And development continues from early objects to new objects.

New and renewed understandings of analytic events necessarily guide the analyst in the timing of his traditional activities of attending, listening, talking, and relating. A contemporary surge of clinical understanding has led to a more active and informed relatedness on the part of the analyst that allows for a more compassionate approach to verbalization, whether with adults or children. We now know that not every word and every dynamic needs to be funneled through interpretation. The spontaneous powers for recovery that are stimulated by the analytic ground and the analytic process may come to be more accepted as a component of therapeutic gain. Appreciation of the balance of power between the verbal and nonverbal aspects of the analytic process in bringing about therapeutic change has increased. This has led to a greater parity of power and responsibility in the therapeutic alliance. The idea of a "tilted partnership" in which both members work for or against the powerful forces of the analytic process, or of a reciprocal relationship between analyst and analysand has become available to replace the former emphasis on the "tilted relationship." The analyst need no longer be so much in charge of the proceedings whether through deep interpretations of the unconscious or by obsessive attention to associational detail.

The ongoing process of developing a body of theoretical and technical understanding that is both reliable and plastic demands an openness that at times flies in the face of the imperative needs of our patients and our profession for clinical confidence and certainty. The analytic clinician, part artist and part scientist, is forever struggling to balance the interminable task of culling new understanding from experience while imposing previously derived understandings that while sure are yet subject to changes stimulated by analytic experience. The Freud-Dann study and this report may help us to be both more stalwart and more humble in our approach to our ambitious analytic task.

In the analytic context increasing differentiation of self and object worlds has come to inform the therapeutic actions of the analyst and provide a better contemporary map of the growth and development of object relations. The question addressed then becomes, "How do we understand the process of maturation of (part) object relations as it brings about the development (and invention) of new objects?" This question also attempts to address the central yet illusive phenomenon of object reconstitution and redefinition, which bridges both everyday and analytic life. Over the past 35 years there has been a movement towards increased differentiation of the object world in terms of both older and newer concepts. Now we can commence to speak more clearly about transference objects, developmental objects, old objects, new objects, transitional objects, abstinent objects, gratifying objects, and the like. We can articulate their meanings as both theoretical entities and contributors to larger aspects of self/ object life as they relate to current issues of technique and change.

If growth and maturation give way in a proper fashion to development object relation becomes appended upon object relation, preparing the way for new object dynamics and object representations of new levels of maturity and complexity. Development is used here in two ways, both as a process of growth and change and as the outcome of that process. It is not that we are ever without a primitive yearning for oneness with mother, for this is both a primary object experience of perpetual longing and the foundation of ever more complex object relations. However, the contemporary impracticalities and unreality of such a "mother–infant dual unit" (Loewald, 1961) lead paradoxically through mourning to the substitution of an object relation that is more enduringly gratifying and internally structured, if less ecstatic. An object relation is internalized that is more tempered by the realities of two psychologies rather than the infant assertions of one. If this were not the case there would be little incentive for maturation to lead to development and for increasingly complex and sublimated developmental sequences to subsume more drive-dominated relations. Here we might think of the child's calling, singing, or whistling to attract mother's attention and presence rather than the peri-verbal toddler's whining. As we see in our contemporary review of the Bulldogs Bank children, in some circumstances it is the maturational drive to establish a comforting object context that is key. For these children, lacking an ongoing continuous experience with one mothering agent, minimal amounts of intense but virtually anonymous nurturing experience sufficed to generate deep sibling caring and love.

Anna Freud (1965) has written about the "new object," the establishment of a new sense of self and other through the largely unconscious processes of a developing and finally relatively developed object constancy, in relation to child psychoanalysis, and Hans Loewald (1965) has done so in relation to psychoanalysis proper. The establishment of the new object can be conceptualized as a driving force for psychological growth that acts both in and apart from psychoanalysis. The urge to find a new object, a novel source of relatedness in everyday life and in psychoanalysis, leads to the individual's striving against often nearly overwhelming odds to complete development. This is development that, as we age, is ever more object related and less "maturational" in the earlier sense in which the word was used. It is not that development within the life cycle is ever complete per se, but in the face of changes in drive, structure, and object over a lifetime, development continues to search out the most parsimonious subliminatory and adaptive solutions. As life advances these are almost always tied to object relations.

The new object is an internal construct of wished-for change and transference wishes. As such it is a theoretical bridging construct. It is a synthesis of the transference object, with its emphasis on mastery through repetition, and the developmental object that arises out of pressures for innovation and novelty. The novel elements may be apart from transference or they may include new editions of transference elements. The "invention" of the new object implies that the individual has taken on a new relation to his sense of self as well. It involves an external object but it is not that "object," just as a transitional object involves an external object but is not that object. As Anna Freud has pointed out, this is particularly true of the developing child but it also applies to development throughout the life cycle. As she put it, "Owing to the process of maturation, the urge to complete development is immeasurably stronger in the immature than it ever will be in later life" (p. 28). It is an ongoing challenge to attempt to delineate the implications of this 'urge to complete development' for psychoanalytic theory and technique. But in the child the tension between new object and old object in the person of the analyst is because of the maturational pressures that intensify the more general developmental trends.

How does the analyst lend himself to the inherent conflict between new and old object relations, between respecting the need for newness and novelty and the forces that press for transference repetition? How can one respect the unconscious growth of the former while stimulating, through the interpretation of drive, object, and defense, the increasingly conscious presence in self-understanding of the latter? These are central technical questions in psychoanalysis as it relates to development. Even raising these questions in this manner points to significant changes in analytic understanding and technique that have developed over the last generation of analysts.

BIBLIOGRAPHY

BERKLEY, G. (1993). *Hitler's Gift: The Study of Tereseinstadt.* Boston, Mass.: Branden Books.
DOWNEY, T. (1984). Within the pleasure principle. *Psychoanal. Study Child,* 39:101–136.
FREUD, A. (1965). *Normality and Pathology in Childhood.*
——— (1972). Comments on aggression. *Int. J. Psychoanal.,* 53:163–171.
——— & BURLINGHAM, D. (1943). *War and Children.* New York: Medical War Books.
FREUD, A., & DANN, S. (1951). An experiment in group upbringing. *Psychoanal. Study Child,* 6:127–168.
HARTMANN, H. (1939). *Ego Psychology and the Problem of Adaptation.* New York: International Universities Press.
——— (1952). Mutual influences in the development of the ego and the id. *Psychoanal. Study Child,* 7:9–30.
——— & KRIS, E. The genetic approach in psychoanalysis. *Psychoanal. Study Child,* 1:11–30.
KRIS, E. (1956). The personal myth. *J. Amer. Psychoanal. Assn.,* 4:653–681.

LOEWALD, H. (1961). On the therapeuticaction of psychoanalysis. *Int. J. Psychoanal.*, 41:16–33.

SPITZ, R. (1946). Anaclitic depression. *Psychoanal. Study Child*, 2:313–342.

WINNICOTT, D. (1953). Transitional objects and transitional phenomenan. *Int. J. Psychoanal.*, 34:89–97.

VOLOVKOVA, E., ED. (1993). . . . *I Never Saw Another Butterfly* . . . New York: Schocken.

YOUNG, J. (1982-). *Lost and Waiting to Be Found.* Unpublished Autobiography.

Discussion of "Early Object Relations into New Objects"

A. SCOTT DOWLING, M.D.

OF THE RANGE OF TOPICS DISCUSSED IN DR. DOWNEY'S PAPER, "EARLY
Object Relations into New Objects," I will consider only one: a comparison of environmental influences with therapeutic influences in
creating psychological change in children. Anna Freud considered
this topic briefly in *Normality and Pathology of Childhood* (1965) and, by
implication, in "An Experiment in Group Upbringing" (1951). She
also included discussion of the issue in several subsequent papers as
well. (A. Freud, 1974, 1976, 1978)

"An Experiment in Group Upbringing" is unusual in the writings
of Anna Freud in its demonstration of the possibility of personality
change under the influence of a caring milieu. Though not the intention of the paper, it does, by implication, open a window to the
therapeutic possibilities of non-interpretive environmental interventions. "Environment" is, of course, a term which is understood here
and in "An Experiment in Group Upbringing" as encompassing not
only the material aspects of life—food, shelter, safety, recreation and
so on—but also, and primarily, the provision of interested, responsive, committed and consistent persons. The issue raised by Anna
Freud and expanded upon and discussed by Dr. Downey concerns
the therapeutic potential of such care and the evidence of its effects
on the concentration camp children cared for at Bulldogs Banks.
There is no question about the necessity of such care for normal development; normality depends upon the ongoing provision of age
appropriate caretaking as is available in the lives of most healthy chil-

Training and supervising analyst, Cleveland Psychoanalytic Institute, Cleveland,
Ohio.

The Psychoanalytic Study of the Child 56, ed. Albert J. Solnit, Peter B. Neubauer, Samuel
Abrams, and A. Scott Dowling (Yale University Press, copyright © 2001 by Albert J.
Solnit, Peter B. Neubauer, Samuel Abrams, and A. Scott Dowling).

dren. What is at issue is the therapeutic potential and the capacity of devoted caretaking to undo fixations, alter defensive patterns, and contribute to structure building with adaptive, age appropriate modification of the personality.

In *Normality and Pathology of Childhood,* Anna Freud's states: "the ego of the young child has the developmental task to master on the one hand orientation in the external world and on the other hand the chaotic emotional states which exist within himself. It gains its victories and advances whenever such impressions are grasped, put into thoughts or words, and submitted to the secondary process." (p. 32).

She goes on: "For a variety of reasons, young children come into analytic treatment with this development delayed or uncompleted. With them, the process of interpretation proper goes hand in hand with verbalizing numerous strivings which as such are not incapable of consciousness (i.e. under primary repression) but have not yet succeeded in achieving ego status, consciousness, and secondary elaboration." (p. 32).

When these victories and advances are achieved, the result is that the domain of the ego is widened. The area of life experience firmly within the range of balanced ego assessment and adaptive response is increased. Correspondingly there is a reduction of the area of life experience which is subject to the control of unrecognized needs, affects, and goals or is subsumed to the requirements of repetition. Examples include: an unconscious need for nourishment experienced as a compulsive need to eat; unconscious fear experienced as touchy aggressiveness; unconscious beating fantasies expressed in altruistic surrender; and scenes of violence, repressed and unknown to the conscious mind, endlessly repeated in a variety of forms which dominate work, play, and relationships. These unconscious contents and their various forms of expression in consciousness and in action are the stuff of neurosis. Can they also be the stuff of developmental "living through," to use Dr. Downey's term? Components of the personality, constricted by the forms dictated by immaturity and by traumatic fixation, can, we know, be freed for renewed developmental progress by therapeutic interpretive intervention. To what degree can the same be achieved by "living through"?

Can we delineate the similarities of therapeutic intervention and a caring milieu by which a child's "orientation in the external world" and "chaotic emotional states" are "grasped, put into thoughts or words and submitted to the secondary process"? It seems likely that Anna Freud would have been open to consideration of ways other than being "put into thoughts and words" by which orientation to the world occurs and chaotic emotional states are quieted and ordered. These additional ways would include preverbal processes leading to strengthening of the "foundations of the personality" and which provide the psychological conditions which make motor learning possible. They would include object related affective and communicative processes which proceed wholly or in part outside of verbal interaction, e.g., mother–infant attunement, non-verbal reciprocity and communication with an other, and empathy. Here, and in personality change in older children, interpersonal empathy which supports, anticipates, and sometimes leads the child forward into new, more complex or more adaptive modes of behavior and thought are crucial both for progressive development and for undoing the effects of conflict and trauma. Both the loving and effective caretaker and the loving and effective therapist has the child's past in mind, shapes responses (whether through interpretation of milieu planning and response) that keep that past in mind and are consonant with the affective and cognitive state of the particular child. Although detailed interaction of the Danns or others with the children of Bulldog Banks is not described, the individual portraits of the children make it clear that careful attention to those differences guided their care. Although the methods are not detailed, "An Experiment in Group Upbringing" is an outstanding example of the power of the milieu to effect decisive change in the lives and personalities of children.

In spite of the implied evidence of this paper, Anna Freud did not consider external change as sufficient to undo neurotic structures or to reverse traumatic fixations:

> But in spite of accumulated evidence that adverse environmental circumstances have pathological results, nothing should convince the child analyst that alterations in external reality can work cures, except perhaps in earliest infancy. Such a belief would imply that external factors alone can be pathogenic agents and that their interactions with internal ones can be taken lightly. Such an assumption runs counter to the experience of the analyst. Every psychoanalytic investigation shows that pathogenic factors are operative on both sides and once they are intertwined, pathology becomes ingrained in the structure of the personality and is removed only by therapeutic measures which affect the structure. . . . External factors . . . achieve their pathological significance by way of interaction with the innate disposition and with acquired, internalized libidinal and ego attitudes. (1965, pp. 51–52).

It seems clear that the children of Terezsin present the possibility for dramatic change, if not cure, through the effects of the milieu.

These infants grew up together in an environment barren of consistent, nurturing, interpersonal contact with adults but with the support of a peer group that took on elements of maternal functions. An expectation of human relations and support could and did develop between these toddlers, drastically distorted from what we ordinarily mean by such terms in adult–infant interactions. Living in an environment of personal concern by caring adults, Sophie and Gertrud Dann, and others, such as Mr. E., changes of relationship and structure occurred in less than a year, a dramatically short period of time.

Bulldogs Bank provided conditions of love, loving, and safe aggressive containment. The program worked, "ego, drive and object relationship development was boosted." Development could pick up where it left off, though still with a heavy burden of traumatic and repressed pain.

Though beyond the purpose of this discussion, a study of the mutuality of milieu and therapeutic processes would be of benefit to an understanding of both. It might even provide a glimpse of a more fundamental unifying structure common to both. "An Experiment in Group Upbringing" and Dr. Downey's paper provide direct and indirect contributions to such a study.

In our clinical work, whether in private office, public clinic, hospital or school, our interventions, in every instance, with every child, deal with the mutual interaction of inner life with the nature and effects of the external world. The two are ultimately inextricable within the mind of the individual and, in that inextricability, have a complementary and indivisible influence. Two simple instances will illustrate. A child of six who had been physically and psychologically injured by her parents regularly reacts with hyperexcitability, verbal defiance, and physical anger when asked to clean her room and join with others in washing dishes in her foster home. The foster mother responds to these repeated reactions with her continuing supportive presence; verbal and, if necessary, physical containment and control; expression of confidence in the child's ability to do the assigned tasks; participation in the task with the child; and appreciation when the tasks are completed. She does not provide interpretations of unconscious meaning nor does she reconstruct unconscious fantasies or repressed events though she may intuitively acknowledge preconscious awareness by her child. This foster mother provides a "therapeutic milieu" which makes use of a positive object relationship as the vehicle through which fears can be quieted, constructive actions and attitudes can be fostered, retaliative concerns can be altered, defensive aggressive attitudes can be set aside, and enjoyment of participation with others in a constructive task achieved. Such developmental "living through" is a daily occurrence, multiplied many times over, in many foster homes and other therapeutic milieus of our modern society, such as long-term residential treatment centers. Unfortunately, planful "living through" is not characteristic of all or, probably, a majority of foster homes or milieus for parentless children. As a parallel example, we can envision the effective analytic therapist of a similarly afflicted foster child. He will provide far more verbal, *interpretive* understanding of affect, moods, actions, and attitudes but, in addition, he will (like the foster mother) assist the child in achieving verbalization of affects, moods and intentions, and in gaining a concept of time, of cause and effect and, of special importance, of the possibilities of object relationship.

These two modes of assistance, via life experience (e.g., foster or residential care with therapeutic intent) and in analytic therapy, differ outwardly most dramatically in the relationship of child and adult. In the former there is a 24-hour commitment (in residential care, an eight-hour commitment) with a caring adult and engagement in the "real" activities, relationships, and consequences of daily life; in the latter there is a limited time commitment, at most five hours a week, more likely less than that; provision of a space in which past and present are expected to coexist and be understood; and a relationship in which there is a possibility of expression of wish and fantasy and of interpretive response which would be incompatible with ordinary daily living between parent and child. Each mode of interaction is distinct, yet there is extensive overlap and similarities of each with the other, especially in the goals and intentions of the work and in the ego strengthening aspects of the work.

"An Experiment in Group Upbringing" presents one example of the effects of "milieu work" and of "living through." Of the six children, "four lost their mothers at birth or immediately afterward; one before the age of twelve months, one at an unspecified date." "All of the children wandered for some time from one place to another, with several complete changes of adult environment." "None of the children had known any other circumstances of life than those of a group setting. They were ignorant of the meaning of a 'family.'" "None of the children had experience of normal life outside a camp or big institution." The challenge to the value of "milieu work" could only be greater if there had been no persons in the child's life or if that relationship had been deeply ambivalent.

The basis of the adaptation to life of these six children at the time of their arrival at Bulldogs Bank was their exclusive centering on the group, insisting on being together in almost all circumstances and showing separation concerns whenever this was not possible. They were unremittingly aggressive to adult, more accurately to the environment which they "experienced as strange, hostile and interfering." Gradually this hostility gave way to interest in the adults, making them a part of the group in taking turns, being possessive, accepting care and assistance. The children were functioning at a two-year-old level in a number of ways: in modes of thinking, in attitudes to adults outside their home, and in much of their emotional development. Although they were "hypersensitive, restless, aggressive and difficult to handle . . . and showed a heightened autoerotism . . . they were neither deficient, delinquent nor psychotic." (Freud and Dann, p. 168) Their libidinization of the group, comparable in some respects to the unique relationship of twins and quite unlike the usual relationship of siblings, served as a basis from which ego development could proceed.

Dr. Downey describes the movement of these children from an exclusive focus on the group with associated severe developmental delays or blocks to a capacity, one year later, for individual relationships, renewed ego development in learning, object relationships, containment of fears, play activities and the acquisition of a new language. It is a reasonable inference that not only a capacity for individual relationship with adults but a modification of defense, of conscience and of desire had occurred during their year long stay at Bulldogs Banks.

Freud and Dann do not spell out the specific aspects of the environment which they believe were crucial in effecting that change. It is not their purpose to explore this issue; they do not describe the mode of care, the routine, the verbal interventions, the planful use of relationships, activity, learning opportunities, or other aspects of the material or personal environment at Bulldogs Banks in any detail. We know only that the personnel of the home and the individual care they provided was the basis for the children's gradual movement toward relinquishment of the group as the center of the libidinal lives and toward vastly different patterns of personality expression. It is not Anna Freud's interest to present a mode of milieu care that can effect structural change although it is, I think, fair for us to depict the dissolution of developmental blocks, the reduction of the effects of horrific and long continued traumatic conditions, and the movement from a lifelong absence of adult focused, singular object relationships toward a capacity for such relationships as structural change that resulted from the emotional nutriments of that environment. Nor does Anna Freud consider the effects of the termination of the Bulldogs Banks experiment after a year. There was, after all, renewed loss at that point as the children were removed from Bulldogs Banks and from each other. The tragedy of loss and lack of continuity is tragically emphasized by Dr. Downey's account of Paul's unending confusion and search in later life. It is important to that later life and to his eventual partial peace of mind in finding the death place of his mother, that Paul had the companionship and love of a devoted wife whom he was able to love as well.

In what ways are developmental delay and traumatic fixation different? A developmental delay occurs when some factor, either external or internal, does not sustain and support progression of development. Temporary and inconsequential delays occur in all children due to fluctuating levels of psychological readiness for the next movement toward greater autonomy or when the meaning of progress provokes conflict. Interferences with developmental progression may also occur due to illness, disappointments, or object loss. Psychological trauma has been defined in a variety of ways. In structural terms it is considered an "overwhelming of the ego." In experiential terms, psychological trauma can be defined as an experience of intense helplessness. It is an inability to respond to a threat, associated with intense affective helplessness. Delay or block implies a less severe, more easily reversible process; "arrest" suggests a more fundamental and intransigent state. In practical situations it can be difficult to draw a line between the two conditions. The child faced with the challenge of school entrance may feel utterly helpless but neither the intensity nor the impact of that challenge is usually of sufficient severity to merit the label of trauma. On the other hand, a seemingly minor developmental interference may, with time, be recognized as an intransigent trauma due to the special meaning of the event to the child.

We enter here into a complex set of questions and considerations, beyond the purpose or competence of this discussion. The "urge to complete development" and "the balance of progressive and regressive forces" need to be considered in detail. A more complete discussion of the nature of psychological trauma and of the rhythms and individual variations in development and of susceptibility to delay would be helpful. Whatever additional understanding may be added by fuller discussion of these points, the fact remains that planful, consistent, object oriented care in a living environment can work wonders, both in altering overt behavior and, more importantly, in effecting structural changes in the personality.

Psychoanalysis, in its recognition of the value of individual psycho-analyses, has made important contributions to an understanding of personality change through living. Aichhorn's contributions (1948) are well known and have been extended by numbers of not so well-known contributors to this subject. (Redl and Wineman, 1951; Mayer and Blum, 1971) In our present extremity of social upheaval, poverty, disease, and the seemingly unending trauma of war and genocide, it is relevant to devote renewed energies to a better understanding of how psychoanalytically informed care, both in foster or adoptive families and in group settings, can undo repressions, heal traumatically frozen personalities, and help set children on the path of progressive development. Such therapeutic care needs to be seen as the companion clinical method, distinct yet powerful in its own right, of individual therapy.

BIBLIOGRAPHY

AICHHORN, A. (1948). *Wayward Youth*. New York: Viking Press.

FREUD, A. (1965). *Normality and Pathology of Childhood*. New York: International Universities Press.

FREUD, A., & DANN, S. (1951). An experiment in group upbringing. *Psychoanal. Study Child* 6:127–168.

FREUD, A. (1974). A psychoanalytic view of developmental psychopathology. *Journal of the Philadelphia Association for Psychoanalysis* Vol. 1:7–17.

——— (1978). The principal task of child analysis. *Bulletin of the Hampstead Clinic*. Vol. 1:11–16.

——— (1976). Changes in psychoanalytic practice and experience. *International Journal of Psychoanalysis* 57:257–260.

MAYER, M., & BLUM, A. (1971). *Healing Through Living: A Symposium on Residential Treatment*. Springfield, Ill.: Charles C. Thomas.

REDL, F., & WINEMAN, D. (1951). *Children Who Hate: The Disorganization and Breakdown of Behavioral Controls*. Glencoe, Ill.: Free Press.

Anna Freud and the Evolution
of Psychoanalytic Technique

EUGENE J. MAHON, M.D.

THE FOCUS OF THIS PAPER IS ON THE EVOLUTION OF CHILD PSYCHOAN-
alytic technique and the contributions of Anna Freud's book on normality and pathology to this evolution. I will argue that two concepts
in particular in that seminal work have influenced technique subtly
and profoundly. I believe that the concept of developmental lines
and the outline of a metapsychological profile force the analyst into a
state of therapeutic readiness whereby he is always assessing developmental and dynamic considerations that lead to changes in technique and guard against complacency and involutional therapeutic
tendencies. If there is a complementary series of incremental nodal
points that construct the components of pathology, one could argue
that normality is constructed similarly, as epigenetic developmental
strata and lines become more advanced, coherent, and integrated.
The developmentally informed analyst is always assessing the normality and pathology of clinical process: his technique is constantly being influenced consciously and preconsciously by Anna Freudian insights about developmental lines and metapsychological assessments.

How the normal and the pathological interweave to form the complexity of human psychology has been the subject matter of psychoanalysis since Freud first cracked the code of hysterical symptomatology, only to discover that the enigmatic secret language that
informed symptoms was not fundamentally different from the psychological and semiotic principles that gave dreams, parapraxes, and

Supervising and training analyst, Columbia College of Physicians and Surgeons,
Psychoanalytic Center for Training and Research; private practitioner of adult and
child psychoanalysis.

The Psychoanalytic Study of the Child 56, ed. Albert J. Solnit, Peter B. Neubauer, Samuel
Abrams, and A. Scott Dowling (Yale University Press, copyright © 2001 by Albert J.
Solnit, Peter B. Neubauer, Samuel Abrams, and A. Scott Dowling).

character their shape and structure. The world has never forgiven Freud for suggesting that madness and sanity had a common symbolic ancestry. Even as astute an observer of the human condition as James Joyce, ranting against the generalizations of psychology, exclaimed, "Psychologist! What can each man know but what passes through his mind?" (Ellmann 1982).

Anna Freud spent a lifetime studying "what passes through the minds" of children and adults, forever alert to the mysterious complexities of pathology but equally alert to the mysterious complexities of normality. For Anna Freud, normality was to be defined not in the negative, as the absence of pathology, but as an organic developmental complexity whose components would not reveal themselves unless subjected to subtle and intense psychoanalytic scrutiny.

How do Anna Freud's ideas in general and particularly the ideas of *Normality and Pathology* influence technique? By making normality and its developmental lines as significant a point of entry into the study of the mind as the earlier approach through pathology and its apertures of investigation (the hysterical symptom, the obsessional symptom, to take two obvious examples). In the tradition of Sigmund Freud, Anna Freud made the totality of the human mind the subject matter of psychoanalysis and not the diminished scope the concept of psychopathlogy alone would imply. One could argue that this point of view is as old as the concept of free association. Analysands do not confine themselves to certain free-associative paths in their zeal to track down the pathological. The fundamental rule is to thwart the one-track mind and the relentless repetition compulsions of pathology. In streams of consciousness and unconsciousness the normal and the pathological are invited to bathe together. No prejudicial manifestos, no off-limit zones, no psychological ghettos. The concept of free association, an attempt to weigh pathology in the same scales as normality, is psychologically democratic. "I am a man. Nothing human is alien to me:" Anna and Sigmund Freud were indebted not only to Sophocles but also to Protagoras for the ancient modernity of their ideas.

If Sigmund Freud's concept of free association started this democratic line of psychological thought, Anna Freud's ideas on normality and pathology spell it out more clearly, more practically. The mind can be conceptualized as a potential space into which developmental lines of achievement are constantly flowing. The mind, of course, can also be depicted as a breeding ground of conflict and a brokerage house of compromise and resolution, unconscious civil wars that lead to ententes and détentes, adaptive or maladaptive treaties, depending on an unconscious intrigue of multiple determinants. Cross-sections of the mind at any given psychological moment would presumably show conflict pathology, normality, and development in a great flux of dynamic complexity.

Psychoanalytic technique is an attempt to gauge this complexity and influence it. The essence of psychoanalytic technique suggests that influence that doesn't come from empathic understanding is at best suggestion, at worst coercion. In a sense psychoanalytic technique is the deconstruction of influence, the laying bare for the analysand of the multiplicity of developmental and conflictual influences that shape or misshape him, out of his awareness. If normalities and pathologies are the result of birthright, constitution, development, and experience, predestination doesn't have to be the outcome if awareness can influence the architect as he designs his blueprints.

I would like the present the analysis of Adam from the ages of 4 to 6 and again when he turned 11. One could argue that there is a hiatus of normality from 6 to 11, and yet, guided by Anna Freudian developmental and metapsychological ideas, such statements would seem to conceal more meaning than they deliver. Under the normalities of latency, are manifestations of pathology far from the surface? If conflict resolution is seen as an ongoing adjudication of adaptive vs. maladaptive possibilities, normality can hardly ever be considered absolute any more than pathology can. By focusing on a single line of development, I attempt to show how the mind is the constant inventor of its own normalities and pathologies and that the task of analysis is to assist the inventor in his conscious and unconscious workshops. I am borrowing the word "invention" from Harold Bloom and Tom Stoppard, but I am using it in my own idiosyncratic psychoanalytic way. Harold Bloom (1998) credits Shakespeare with "the invention of the human," suggesting that one literary mind and its "inventiveness" can have a profound effect on culture and history and can influence the psychology of all future generations as literary ideals become social realities. If this is hyperbole on Bloom's part, it seems to me that a grain of truth can be extracted from it: the invention of the human is an ongoing process, from the caves of Lascaux to the consulting rooms of Freud's Vienna. In a similar vein, Tom Stoppard (1997) has recently written a dramatic treatise on "the invention of love" in which he argues that romantic love, like "clocks, trousers and algebra," had to be invented and was in fact invented by Catullus in first-century Rome in his love poems! If this Stoppardian hyperbole is a match for Bloom's, I still believe there is also a kernel of truth that can be extracted from it: human affects, like love and hatred, have been *cultivated* by thousands of years of psychological and social experience. From a psychoanalytic point of view, we could say that they are invented, re-invented, and modified by the ego—a statement of Freudian agency that Bloom and Stoppard might reject. However, it is this concept of the agency of the ego in the invention and modulation of affect that informs normal and pathological aspects of development.

I want to focus on one developmental line only as I chart Adam's development through normal and pathological waters. I will call this developmental line "the invention of hatred," Stoppardian in derivation but essentially Freudian in the way I will develop it. I will suggest that there is a line from seemingly thoughtless, impulsive aggression to thoughtful, rational, assertive action and that Adam needed analysis to get the hang of it. I will attempt to show that the invention of hatred as I am defining it is unthinkable without its developmental counterpart, the invention of love.

ADAM'S ANALYSIS: TWO PHASES IN THE EVOLUTION OF TECHNIQUE

At age 4 Adam had developed a symptom that puzzled and alarmed his parents and seemed to bewilder him as well. A personable and playful boy, he would occasionally lash out unexpectedly at children in his vicinity. Precipitating events, either current or genetic, seemed elusive. The parents, sensitive, responsible overseers of the child's development, entered into a cooperative, non-defensive alliance with the analyst in the service of understanding and correcting what had gone awry. The only developmental incident that seemed to have etiological significance was the dismissal of a nanny who may have "accidentally" spilled some tea on Adam's head. The parents were unsure how much significance to assign to this event, and had Adam not developed his "aggressive" symptom at age 4, the nanny's behavior might well have been forgotten. The nanny's unusual name, Grasiena (Siena for short), would reveal its significance not in the first installment of analysis but in the second, when Adam was 11.

Phase I: I will summarize the first "phase" of analysis briefly as a backdrop for the subsequent analytic process. Adam's symptom (impulsive aggression toward his peers in kindergarten) made its appearance slowly in the analytic process and in a very disguised and sublimated manner. With great oedipal glee, he would enter the playroom, run ahead of the analyst, and "steal" his chair. This theft of the analyst's chair became part of an elaborate play sequence that spanned months, revealing many facets of Adam's oedipal conflicts. Having stolen the chair, he would return it to the analyst and then go into hiding behind the chair. From his hide-out he would knock on the "door" of the analyst's head to announce his emergence. He enjoyed the characterization of this play as his assumption of the role of head knocker. Perhaps the nanny's assault on his head with her tea spilling was being reversed in these episodes, now in an oedipal context and with more sublimated expression.

The oedipal context seemed obvious from the rest of his associative activities and analytic process. For instance, the head knocker was also a sculptor, a draughtsman, and a joke teller, the unconscious just barely concealed by these inchoate defensive strategies. As draughtsman he would sometimes write his father's initials, erase them, and replace them with his own. When his oedipal wishes became too transparent in play, he would relieve his anxiety by leaving the playroom to refuel briefly with his mother in the waiting room and then return to the analytic process, reassured that "reality" was not as fragile a concept as play, imagination, and transference had momentarily suggested. A piece of humor and a piece of sculpture were even more dramatic indications of unconscious conflicts struggling to reveal themselves and conceal themselves all at once. The diurnal theft of the analyst's chair seemed to trigger the memory of a nocturnal theft that occurred in a dream. The dream seemed like a joke to Adam, and indeed it was first presented as such.

Question: Why did the chicken steal the bagpipes?
Answer: Because he wanted to have a perfect house.

When the jokester returned for subsequent analysis at age 11, this joke became the subject of a much more elaborate and sophisticated analytic process, highlighting the amazing difference between animistic pre-operational cognitive analytic process and the "formal" cognitive properties of early adolescence. But for the moment let us follow the analytic process sequentially and return to the first rendition of the dream/joke. Clues to its meaning came in the form of sculpture and play. As plasticine was manipulated into a representation of "bagpipes," it became clear that the dream image was not merely a musical reference but a phallic one as well, since scrotum and penis seemed much more discernible than the bag or pipes associated with the Scottish musical instrument. In subsequent play, an elephant that bore a strong associative resemblance to the bag/pipes/scrotum/penis/sculpture, with its central body from which limbs, tail, and trunk protrude, was dismembered with totemic primitive zeal. The animal can rise again, phoenix-like, out of its own ashes, given the plasticity of play and sublimatory resourcefulness, just as transference can quickly shift from knocking on the door of the analyst's head to fixing his shoes with pretend nails and hammer, aggression threatened by anxiety seeking redress in reaction formations and acts of social reparation.

A final comment about the outcome of the first phase of treatment. The symptom of impulsive aggression gradually diminished and eventually vanished altogether, its energies undoubtedly rechanneled into the transference and sublimatory manifestations of analytic process. The analysand's intellectual potential, always impressive, was now soaring, given its new freedom from neurotic harassment. The Oedipus complex having bequeathed most of its resources to its heir, the superego, through the usual processes of identification, repression and infantile amnesia had paved the way for a latency of incredible potential and Eriksonian industry. Some practical issues (geographic distance, financial considerations) influenced the mostly developmental psychoanalytic factors that informed the decision to terminate or at least interrupt analysis at this stage. Parents and analysand were completely comfortable with the notion of resumption of analysis should the need arise. The subsequent analysis would suggest that not all of the aggression had been rerouted into channels of ego mastery but that one of the heirs of the Oedipus complex, the superego, may have made off with more resources that it was supposed to and that its embezzlement of developmental funds was not always in the service of adaptation. Demoralization was being proposed and perpetuated rather than an age-appropriate enlightened sense of morality. It was in this demoralized state that Adam returned to analysis at age 11, puzzled by the unconscious forces that seemed suddenly to have impinged on his psychological process.

Phase II: The five-year interval between the two phases of Adam's analysis, while seemingly "latent," was nonetheless packed with existential incident and psychological achievement and struggle. At the end of the first phase, Adam presented me with a parting gift: a drawing, a child's-eye view of the universe, one could call it perhaps, in which an impressionistic distribution of the world's oceans and land masses was captured with grace and simplicity. It was a psychological as well as a geographic statement, perhaps Adam's view of an expanded internal world as well as its objective correlative in the external world of reality. (In any case, Adam's drawing adorns the shelf of my consulting room, a silent witness to one episode in the never-ending story of analytic process.) Adam wrote to me analyst a few times about his progress and about his missing the analytic relationship. I responded to these communications. When his grandfather died, Adam wrote about his love for the man and the sadness of his loss. Much moved by this letter, I replied in a letter that contained the idea that "love is the great wheel that turns the universe" even when sadness and loss darken its contours for a while.

After that communication, I didn't hear from Adam until his parents, sensing that he needed to return to analysis, called for a consultation. Subsequently I learned that Adam had had a very difficult time with his grief over his grandfather's death but that he wanted to deal with it "on his own." He eventually gave up grieving when a boy whose father had died managed to get over his grief and resume his academic progress: Adam, in a seemingly competitive, comparative attitude, decided that if his peer could handle an even greater loss, he should pull himself together and get on with his development. This was the non-empathic "stiff upper lip" state of his psychology when he returned to analysis. He also felt harassed by increasing academic pressures; and the exercise of his unusual intellectual endowment, once a matter of pride and pleasure, was fast becoming a chore.

In the first session he described his sense of academic ennui, which he knew was only the tip of an iceberg of a deeper psychological suffering—i.e., his shattered sense of self-esteem. Recently he had told his parents about his diminished self-worth. The parents felt partially reassured when Adam expressed confidence in his ability to redress that state of affairs with another bout of analysis. The academic ennui was perhaps an easier point of entry into a resumption of analytic collaboration, and that was where we started. Reflecting on his recent academic slump, he complained that his teacher, Mrs. Swift, favored the other children and seemed to be unappreciative of his efforts while praising those of his peers. Not having seen Adam for a few years, I proposed a trial interpretation to test the current developmental state of his psychological mindedness.

"Do you suppose that there might be a Mrs. Swift inside you as well as outside?"

"You mean the problem is inside me but it colors what's outside? But why would that be?"

He clearly had come back prepared to work, and I told him we would figure it out together. He said, "It's not as if we're starting from scratch. We've done a lot of work already."

I agreed. As if seeking a genetic answer to his earlier question, he began to talk about his best friend, a boy in early latency who had abandoned him and taken up with a new clique of friends. Adam felt unworthy, betrayed, and hurt, but the anger was not accessible. "Where did it go?" I asked. "You mean it went inside, don't you? I am very mean to myself inside instead of being mean to Jimmy outside."

He went on to describe the interior of his mind as a kind of Supreme Court ruled by a triumvirate—Boss One, Boss Two, Boss Three. Boss One was severe, totalitarian, unrelenting; Boss Two was empathic, decent, fair; Boss Three, instead of being cruel inside like Boss One, was cruel to others. "But Boss One and Boss Three work together," Adam asserted knowingly. He wished he could be rid of both of them and be guided only by Boss Two.

I was very impressed with Adam's capacity to reflect on the workings of his mind; it was clearly a continuation of our earlier work but in a new, more mature developmental key. A major portion of he ensuing analysis would be an elaboration of the pedigree of Boss One and a redistribution of energy between the three psychological power brokers.

Two parapraxes from the early phase of the analysis highlight the way in which conflict was represented and interpreted. Discussing the triumvirate of Boss One, Boss Two, Boss Three, Adam, intending to say, "I want Boss Two to comfort me," actually said, "I want Boss Two to confront me." He could not immediately understand the function of the psychological mischief that turned "comfort" into "confrontation," but when the analyst suggested that Boss One seemed to have usurped Boss Two's agenda—putting words in his mouth, so to speak—Adam was amazed at this notion. "Boss One is sneaky and speedy," he acknowledged soberly. "And he seems to think you shouldn't be comforted," I suggested, trying to make the conflict more obvious.

Another parapraxis began to convince Adam that unconscious influence behind the scenes could upstage the conscious narrative when it was least expected. Meaning to describe the new covenant between him and his teacher, he said "convent," suggesting that he saw the teacher as an authoritarian nun rather than as a human role model with whom he could forge an alliance. Adam saw both of these parapraxes as evidence of the spin Boss One could put on things from his unconscious power base behind the scenes.

Adam became more and more fascinated by the concept of who was the real boss in his mind, himself or some hidden aspect of himself. He would often return to Jimmy, the boy who had betrayed him, but he slowly began to realize that he had betrayed himself when instead of standing up to Jimmy he had swallowed his anger and began to berate himself in the privacy of his own imagination. Jimmy "is only a red herring," Adam would say in his most Sherlock Holmesian manner, insight never too far from humor in his quick-witted analytic mind. As he began to talk about his competitive rivalry with his father, the "red herring's" reason to shift the emphasis became more transparent. Playing chess with his father, Adam would bristle when father, instead of playing "for real," would patronize him. "If you were to make this move instead of that, you would gain such and such advantage," was a remark by his father that pushed oedipal buttons of near-lethal potential in a pre-adolescent whose hormones were plotting the permanent de-stabilization of whatever vestiges of latency remained intact at this transitional stage of development. A dream brought these issues into sharper focus.

"I am in a grungy room. The wall paint is peeling. It's a motel called The Sands of Time. There's a centipede in the bed clothes. I try to smash it. The softness of the mattress seems to shield it. I tip it onto the floor the better to smash it against the hard surface of the floor boards." His associations at first led backward in time to a centipede on his wall when he was 5 years of age. He awakened and called his father. Then the associations led to current events: a friend teasing him with a rubber snake, like a centipede with jaws. He was angry not with his friend but at the centipede. "Anti-centipede, anti-Semitism," he mused enjoying his mastery over these "big" words. He knocked the head off his friend's rubber centipede and then began to reflect on Boss One. Could Boss One be anti-centipede, anti-temper? It was temper that first brought him to analysis. He could reflect on the components of that temper more insightfully than ever. Not only had tea been spilled on his head, but the family had moved from a beloved home to one that took time to get used to. The idea that his phallic strivings and the loss of nanny and home might be used against him by Boss One in one of his many insinuations was not accessible to interpretation at this point. Centipede = penis was flatly rejected, Adam insisting that right now his interest was still much more in teddy bears than in sexual exploration. In less than a few months of analytic process the centipede's obvious sexual symbolism would no longer need to be denied.

The analysis of dreams seemed to be stirring up genetic memories. A complex dream led to many new insights.

"A nuclear power plant. About to blow up. Trying to keep the lid on. Hitler, Mussolini dividing up the spoils of Italy. I let them have the country but not Venice, Milan, Siena. In the cabin of the train where negotiations are going on a guard has a gun but it's pointing toward the ground."

This dream was not only analyzed immediately but returned to over many months as the associative process reviewed its contents again and again. In the immediate analysis, Hitler and Mussolini seemed like obvious stand-ins for Boss One, the ego, uncomfortable with its explosive power plants and conflicted downward-pointing guns, trying to at least hold onto some psychological territories. In subsequent analyses of this same dream, Adam would associate Siena with the nanny Grasiena, wondering if he had felt guilty that she was fired on his account. Maybe he loved her and wanted her back. Maybe she was a symbol of childhood, a respite from he future with all its aggressive and phallic implications. In this context he remembered another dream from the third grade: "A large number 6 is chasing me around. I'm running away from large numbers."

Among the many associations he had to this dream, six = sex was the most humorous. But the topic was no longer off limits. He had seen a movie in school of a baby being born ("a bloody thing coming out of a swollen hole"), and he had discussed erections with his father. He had thought they (erections) were signs of disease and that menstruation was "peeing blood." He was quickly relieved. His mind began to wander. He did humorous imitations of a Chinese man and of Ghandi. He realized that he was putting great distance between the sexual topic and himself, as if Boss One were saying, "Don't think these dirty thoughts in the USA." His humor reminded me of the joke he had told me many years ago.

Question: Why did the chicken steal the bagpipes?
Answer: Because he wanted to have a perfect house.

When I told him the joke, he was amused, saying, "But that joke doesn't have a punch line." He immediately supplied two witty punch lines.

Question: Why did the chicken steal the bagpipes?
Answer: Because he wanted to sing and be supper!
Answer: Because he wanted to research his Scottish origins.

The gulf between a five-year-old's understanding of humor and a twelve-year-old's is nicely illustrated here, but more importantly, when I asked Adam if our recent understandings could shed any new light on the five-year-old's joke, he immediately and enthusiastically replied," "Yes, oh yes. If Boss One insists that the dirty sexual stuff has no place in an American mind (a perfect house), then he would have to hire a chicken to steal the dirty stuff (bagpipes = 5 little pipes sticking out of a big bag, get it?) and make off with it to keep the house picture perfect!" In a sense, Adam had been tricked and bushwhacked by a one and a five and a six but he was beginning to turn the tables on Boss One and retrieve his libidinal and aggressive development from a bad joke certain unconscious numbers had been playing on him.

Adam's aggression, relatively free of Boss One's tyranny, began to make its appearance socially and also in the transference. Adam was shedding some of his timidity with his peers. His aggression would take an intellectual form, of course, his superior intellect being an assault weapon when he felt the need to turn it on his friends. He would sneer at their excessive boasting when they flaunted their knowledge, a sign of inferiority, as Adam well knew with his astute and developing psychological-mindedness. But he was not reluctant to bring the haughty down by exposing their lack of knowledge of a word like "caduceus," whose meaning and etymology he could then explain to his vanquished foe. In the transference he could be sarcastic, witty, and contradictory when the need arose.

A dream that stumped both of us with its minimalism he eventually figured out. The dream depicted the color green followed by the color black. The two colors kept replacing each other sequentially throughout the dream. That was the total content. This dream followed a much more elaborate and more accessible dream, and our first interpretation addressed the resistance that gave us so little to work with, as if the mind were sorry it had revealed so much in previous dreams. But Adam stumbled on a clue that made the dream less impregnable. The chair the analyst sits in is green. Perhaps the green represents his alliance with the analyst against the dark forces (black) of Boss One. Then Adam turned the tables: "Of course it could be that I'm on the side of blackness, destroying your chair, the seat of power, stealing it like in the old days." On another occasion he felt comfortable enough to ridicule my analytic curiosity. He remembered a dream he had at age 7. "I woke up in a dream. The dream was about the tale of two cities. 'It was the worst of times, it was the best of times.' I tore out the last pages of the book." The analyst, betraying his own interest in dreams within dreams perhaps more than his responsibility first and foremost to analyze the dreamer, suggested that if the dreamer woke up in the dream, then the rest of the dream must have been a dream within a dream. Adam pounced, ridiculing my philosophical pedantry: "Oh, you mean it could be a dream within a dream and right now what's happening might not be happening? Is reality reality or is existence a dream?" Trying to recover, I said: "I guess my leg was asking to be pulled and you couldn't resist it." We both had a good laugh. I had temporarily lost sight of my patient and gotten what I deserved!

Adam's burgeoning capacity to compete academically and socially with his peers led to the recovery of an important memory: a song he had made up when he was three. The words were: "You just can't wake up the sponge." Adam had been talking about how he stumped his classmate Stanley by reciting the Russian alphabet. Stanley had been bragging about his French, and his ignorance of Russian brought him down a peg. Adam's satisfaction was palpable, yet his memory from age three illustrated how quickly aggressive and competitive thoughts could lead to associations that implied the censure of Boss One. It was clear to Adam that the sponge, like the bagpipes, was a reference to the penis. He talked about an expression four-year-olds use when talking about the penis: "Sometimes my eleventh finger points." The analyst offered a tentative formulation. "So could Boss One be the singer of the song 'Don't wake up the sponge'? Would you buy that?" "Yes, I would," Adam declared emphatically and exploded with a salesman's voice in a most humorous riff: "But the real question is: would you buy the knife that can cut through aluminum?"

Adam immediately commented on his humor as his anti-Boss One side. "Boss One is anti-sex. Humor tries to play with it." He became philosophical, talking about light. "We don't see things. We see light bouncing off things. So in the dark there's nothing there." "Where did thoughts about light come from?" I ask. "I was reading that patterns of colors cause epileptic seizures. I was thinking it's light bouncing off colors that cause epileptic seizures." "These are amazing ideas," I say admiringly. He goes on to talk about rods and cones and color blindness. "Tiny cells in the retina determine what we see," Adam says philosophically. "Now you're able to think philosophically. How do these grand thoughts feel?" I inquire. "Feels good. The average human uses 8 percent of his brain." Adam says, but quickly turns the tables on himself in a delightful piece of self-mockery: "I use 9 percent!" We both laugh. But I underline the positive aggressive forward momentum: "Now you are not afraid to wake up the sponge of your mind." "Funny you should say that. Sponge of the mind reminds me of Bovine Spongioform Encephalitis. I remember my father talking about it when I was little. But I didn't understand the meaning. Just the words. The sponge of my mind was not yet old enough to soak up all the information until I grew up." "So you feel your development was not complete yet?" I remark. "Yes, I remember my father singing, 'Nutri Grain, my little son, makes you grow up big and strong.' That was an indicator that I would grow. The idea was planted in my head."

Adam's impressive analytic work on waking up the sponge of his mind exposed more and more of the unconscious superego pathology that second-guessed his developmental progress. Curiously enough, this alone did not lead to immediate academic or other developmental momentum. This puzzled Adam. He had convinced himself that Boss One's control had been diminished and that consequently his academic "joie" had returned. But his grades did not comply with this wishful thinking. Adam was fooling himself, but he was totally unaware of it, a clinical fact that eventually forced him to acknowledge his impressive capacity for denial. This could not be worked through until Adam recognized his identification with Puck in *A Midsummer Night's Dream*. This represented his wish to be infantile and magical forever and to overthrow Boss One in fantasy without having to develop a hard working ego that could replace Boss One's power through the reality of insight rather than through the self-deception of denial. As Adam began to learn that Puck and Boss One colluded in their attempts to hoodwink a hardworking, maturing, but anxious ego, he could observe that the light at the end of the tunnel of neurosis was switch-operated rather than controlled by external random forces. Locating the switch and the complex functioning is the continuing enterprise of a work in progress. The analysis is obviously not over, but Adam, with his new "formal" cognitive potential and his free-associative skills, has learned how to put sexuality, aggression, censorship, and humor on the analytic table, the better to free his mind from neurotic shackles and to reap the benefits as well as weather the impending storms of adolescence.

DISCUSSION

In the first phase of analysis, Adam was helped to express his symptom in the transference, where it could be studied most directly. Humor, play, language, drawings, sculpture, and transference of course assisted him in his efforts to transform what once was the specific content of his symptoms into the current content of a psychoanalytic process that would help him untie the knots of neurosis. Technique, in a nutshell, was the grease that facilitated the momentum of that transformation. An analyst who felt that his chair was a great symbol of authority that should never be relinquished to an impudent child would obviously not be able to foster the playful climate in which oedipal usurpation and mischief could be enacted, the better to expose the components of conflict and analyze them. Similarly, an analyst who felt that "head knocking" was a violation of his personal space would not be facilitating the entry of the genetic material about Grasiena's "assault" on Adam's head into the transference. It is in this clinical context that the concept of developmental lines becomes crucial, especially the line I am calling the invention of hatred.

Adam's symptom of impulsive aggression against his unwitting peers was an alarming example of a developmental line gone awry. A sensitive, intelligent, endearing little boy would suddenly lash out at an unsuspecting peer, as if "possessed" by some unconscious genetic force that, without provocation, seemed to demand, even command expression. Psychoanalytic reconstruction, in an attempt to make sense of this seemingly senseless act of aggression, would suggest that Adam was reenacting a traumatic memory, this time Adam playing all the parts: the unsuspecting victim of Adam's aggression is of course a depiction of Adam himself, shocked and surprised when Grasiena spilled the tea on his head; Adam, the aggressor is his own assumption of Grasiena's role in hurting him. (In phase two of the analysis), Adam's understanding of the meaning of his multidetermined identification with Grasiena will become clearer and more "workable." In the first phase, it seemed crucial that the aggression should find an outlet (or is it an inlet?) into the playground of transference so that the developmental line and its malformation could be studied and modified. In more psychoanalytic terminology, the ego needed to play with the aggression and find sublimatory channels for it rather than repress it too quickly or transform it into reaction formations or restrictive character traits. If the superego has harnessed too much of this aggressive energy to its own sadistic purposes, a way has to be found to represent and expose this aspect of the tyrannical conscience in the playfulness of the clinical process. Phase two hindsight suggests that the therapeutic process in phase one may not have addressed this issue sufficiently to allow the developmental line to advance throughout latency and adolescence without further analytic intervention. This is debatable, of course, when we consider that successful entry into latency can hardly be accomplished without some relative "dissolution" or at least repression of the Oedipus complex, which is inconcievable without the establishment of the superego.

If identification and repression transform the drama of the Oedipus complex into the relative quiscence of latency, the developmental line I am calling the invention of hatred reflects the multidetermined regressive and progressive forces that impinge on it at this ambiguous, conflicted, yet seemingly latent period of development. In this period, the hatred (aggression) seems to find expression not only in what Erikson has called "industry" but also in what I have elsewhere called the normal chauvinism of latency (Mahon, 1986). (I am referring to the gender exclusivity of latency, when boys and girls seem to keep the Oedipus complex "repressed" and at bay by having little to do with each other, a kind of "offensive" defensive contempt for each other that highlights the repressed sexual energy it pretends to conceal.) Adam was not in treatment throughout this phase even though his grief after his grandfather's death may have warranted it. When preadolescence brought some new urgencies into the developmental picture, the progressive invention of hatred seemed unmanageable without further analysis, and phase two was ready to be initiated.

Phase two made it immediately clear that if self-sabotage on the academic front was symptomatically prominent, Adam's developmental lines of insight, intelligence, and humor had been far from arrested. (The developmental line that involves the invention of hatred may have regressed, to be sure, and will be our main focus presently: at this point I am merely stressing that Adam's impressive psychological-mindedness had grown apace.)

When two parapraxes were brought to Adam's attention, he quickly seemed to accept the implication that there is an unconscious "that shapes our ends, rough-hew them how we may." (Shakespeare may forgive me for misquoting him slightly to make a Freudian point.) Had the unconscious been prepared perhaps by the previous analysis, or was this the developmental expansion of his own impressive endowment? In any case, technique is influenced by these considerations. Adam's response to the unconscious "secret" that had been blurted out inadvertently by the parapraxes was not defensive. He did not feel a narcissistic injury that forced him to deny that his verbally expressive "house" was ever other than perfect. He did not feel invaded or corrected by the alertness of the analyst who brought the error to his attention in the first place. In fact he seemed genuinely curious about the workings of his psyche and the complexity of all the preconscious and unconscious corridors in the labyrinth of his mind. Metapsychological assessment at this phase of analysis would suggest that even if Adam had a byzantine superego that confounded him, he also had a resourceful ego that knew how to revive the alliance with his analyst in the service of correcting his developmental quandaries and regressions. It is the analyst's appreciation of this ego's conflicts, sensitivities, resiliencies, not to mention courage, that will allow the alliance to challenge the intimidating power of the superego and free the developmental line under consideration and promote the invention of hatred.

For instance, when the analyst suggested prematurely that the centipede in Adam's dream could be a symbolic representation of the penis in particular or sexuality in general, Adam rejected the idea out of hand, protesting that he was more interested in transitional objects than penises at this stage of his development. The analyst's technique became "transitional" at this clinical juncture, "holding" the analysand's need to insist on his preoedipal dependencies rather than highlighting the flight from the sexual mandates of impending adolescence. Ironically, by taking the regression seriously, the analyst prepares the psychological ground for progression. This fundamental understanding of a developmental line's progressive and regressive oscillations (a quintessential Anna Freudian insight) informs technique throughout all the stops and starts, advances and detours, motions and contrary motions of dynamic process. Is it not amazing (unless one has become too clinically jaded or complacent to appreciate it) to consider that Adam only a month or two later will be able to talk so freely about his sexual conflicts?

Metapsychological assessment at the beginning of phase two throws the wisdom of termination or interruption of analysis at the end of phase one into question. Can interruption or termination be considered an aspect of technique? Termination certainly, interruption probably, might be the most honest answer. At the end of phase one, Adam's social and academic life were sources of great pleasure to him and his impulsive aggressive behavior seemed to be behind him. His parents were ecstatic about the treatment result, and it was with great gratitude and tears in their eyes that they broached the subject of termination. The Oedipus complex seemed to be repressed, latency was beginning to assert its dominion over the industrious "operational" faculties of Adam's cognitive world, and all seemed for the best in this best of all possible developmental worlds. Was there, however, a harsh but hidden totalitarian superego presid-

ing too absolutely over this normality or pseudonormality? Perhaps
yes. Or perhaps the death of grandfather and other unpredictable
traumas overburdened latency's adaptive capacities, and superego regression became mandatory to keep the psychological house in order.

If our speculations about latency have to be retrospective, the
treatment from age 11 on, which we now turn to again, can continue
to be reviewed prospectively. At the beginning of phase two, Adam's
immediate readiness to "hear" an interpretation and use it productively to advance his own understanding was impressive. If his first inclination was to blame his academic problems on Mrs. Swift and his
social timidity of Jimmy, the analyst's suggestive implication of an in-
teriority that informs the external world was immediately embraced
and transformed into his own language. "You mean the problem is
inside me, but it colors what's outside. But why would that be?" He
recognizes the internal nature of his dilemmas, he senses that an internal lens can bend the light of reality to its own neurotic viewpoint,
but he is puzzled by the insight and curious. This remarkable capacity for puzzlement and curiosity leads him to his formulation about
the triumvirate of bosses that rule his mind, an insight that became
so crucial to our understanding of his conflicts with the invention of
hatred. The interpretation of the parapraxis comfort-confront gave
him access to the notion that unconsciously he might believe that he
does not deserve to be comforted. Later, of course, through the interpretation of the Mussolini-Hitler-Siena dream he came to realize
that he had struck a pact with his fascist superego: Leave Siena to me,
and you can keep the rest of my development, "Siena" meaning that
he yearned to hold onto the childhood love that he believes he lost
by having aggressive-phallic developmental instincts that ruined his
perfect house.

In terms of technique, it is important to stress that Adam's insight
into his conflicted relationship with his own phallic/aggressive development took many months of analytic process to unfold. I believe it
is the technique of defense analysis (often attributed to the joint clinical labors of Berta Bornstein and Anna Freud) that makes insightful
progress possible. This is not the place to review all that is meant by
the concept "defense analysis," but since the philosophy is very relevant to my discussion I must stress that an analysis that creates a psychological climate in which the ego is encouraged to review its strate-
gic options by flinging the free-associative nets as far and wide as
anxiety and courage will allow is different from an analysis in which
the ego is bombarded or overwhelmed by the analyst's intrusive clev-
erness, however well meaning this kind of exhibitionistic brilliance

may purport to be. In other words, when Adam first presented the "Siena" dream, even though its meaning seemed obvious to the analyst, Anna Freudian technique insists that Adam's free-associative musings about his dreams and his jokes and his memories are the only royal roads that will eventually lead him to full possession of all his mind's potential. I think the clinical material speaks for itself in that regard: Adam, having first rejected the centipede's sexual meaning, eventually embraces the sexuality of the sponge and bagpipes; "symbols" that were once "desexualized" in screen memory and humor are now "resexualized" in the clinical alchemy of free-associative process. This is development in a psychoanalytic key, the invention of love, the invention of hatred approaching the vineyards of adolescence free-associative step by step. There is even a place for humility in this brave new world of free-associative possibility: when Adam realised that his insights into the machinations of Boss One's fascist police state did not lead to an immediate new psychological democracy and the end of Boss One's autocracy, sadness, deflation, and disappointment dampened his enthusiasm for analytic process until he was able to make something new out of his own self-deception. Suddenly he realized his identification with Puck in *A Midsummer Night's Dream,* and a new analytic chapter in self-understanding had begun. Boss One did not work alone: in collusion with Puck, who had one foot in the ego and one foot in the id, the irrational could run off with the seemingly rational structures of the mind in such a variety of directions that it would take a very nimble-footed technique indeed to keep up with it!

I have suggested that technique in this case has been influenced by development. If technique is essentially a product of psychoanalytic evenly hovering attention and empathic listening, development is a crucial variable as one assesses what can and cannot be processed at different stages of the life cycle. The developmental line I am proposing as an organizing lens through which to view much of Adam's psychoanalytic process makes it quite clear that the concept of aggression is fundamentally different to a four-year-old than to an 11-year-old. In fact it is the advancing structural maturity implicit in the concept that makes its complexity an object of self-scrutiny at all. Larcenous chicken, pilfered bagpipes, and perfect house may have been minted by the four-year-old wordsmith, but deconstruction would have to wait for what Piaget has called "formal" properties of thought and psychoanalysis would call a nascent free-associative capacity.

If psychoanalytic technique is born of a complex compendium of ideas about free association, transference, countertransference, defense, instinct, psychic structure, and topography, to name a few, the normalities of developmental lines add a distinctly Anna Freudian component to the topic. Technique without a developmental component is unthinkable in Adam's case. In Freud's celebrated Dora case history (Freud, 1905), psychoanalytic hindsight suggests that the lack of a developmental point of view was perhaps the Achilles heel of Freud's countertransference that led to the ultimate loss of contact with his analysand. Is it possible that adults older than Dora have hidden developmental issues, less obvious than Adam's or Dora's, that could use additional developmental sensibility to augment "classical" technique? Are issues of tact and timing not always informed by developmental as well as dynamic considerations?

I have argued that the mind is the inventor of its own normalities and pathologies, its hatreds and its loves. I don't know if Anna Freud would endorse my notion of the mind as inventor, but I do believe that the propositions of developmental lines called the invention of hatred and the invention of love are essentially extensions of her ideas.

In 1965 Anna Freud wrote:

> Aggression becomes a menace to social adaptation only when it appears in pure culture, either unfused with libido or defused from it. The cause of this usually lies not in the aggressive drive itself but in the libidinal processes which may not have developed sufficiently for the task of toning down and binding aggression or which lose that capacity at some point during the child's development owing to disappointments in object love, imagined or real rejections, object loss, etc. A special danger point for defusion is the anal-sadistic phase during which aggression reaches a normal peak and its social usefulness is especially dependent on its close association with equal amounts of libido. Any emotional upset at this time frees the child's normal sadism of its libidinal admixtures so that it becomes pure destructiveness and, as such, turns against animate and inanimate objects as well as against the self. What happens then is that the half-playful, provoking, self-willed attitudes of the toddler become fixed in the personality as quarrelsomeness, ruthless acquisitiveness, and a preference for hostile rather than friendly relations with fellow beings. More important still, aggression in this defused form is not controllable, either externally by the parents or internally by ego and superego. If fusion is not re-established through strengthening of the libidinal processes and new object attachments, the destructive tendencies become a major cause for delinquency and criminality.

I am suggesting that this is a reference to what I'm calling the invention of hatred/the invention of love in different language. If

Adam began his inventive psychological life imagining that he could sever hatred from love and lash out indiscriminately, the invention of hatred and the complementary invention of love led him, under psychoanalytic surveillance, toward the invention of the human, an ideal that should keep him busy for the rest of his life.

BIBLIOGRAPHY

BLOOM, H. (1998). *Shakespeare. The Invention of the Human.* New York: Riverhead Books.

ELLMANN, R. (1982). *James Joyce.* New York, Oxford, and Toronto: Oxford University Press.

FREUD, A. (1965). Normality and Pathology in Childhood: Assessments of Development. *The Writings of Anna Freud,* Vol. VI. New York: International Universities Press.

FREUD, S. (1905). Fragment of an Analysis of a Case of Hysteria. *Standard Edition.* 7:1–112.

MAHON, E. (1986). The Contribution of Adolescence to Male Psychology. In *The Psychology of Men,* eds. G. I. Fogel, F. M. Lane, and R. S. Liebert. New York: Basic Books.

STOPPARD, T. (1997). *The Invention of Love.* New York: Grove Press.

Discussion of "Anna Freud and the Evolution of Psychoanalytic Technique"

ANTON O. KRIS, M.D.

IT IS A PARTICULAR HONOR TO BE SELECTED THE SOLE INVITED MEM-
ber of this meeting who is *not* a child analyst, though I may perhaps
claim the longest personal association with child analysis of any of
the participants. After brief consideration, however, I have concluded that my early experience, by which I first imagined I might establish a place for myself at this rich table of child analysts, does not
enter into the scope of today's topic. I recognized that I could not escape the plain fact that my experience in treating children was confined to one year of psychiatric residency training, prior to 1965. Although I have had a good deal of experience with adolescents in
psychotherapy, my experience as an analyst is entirely with adults. I
cannot, from my own knowledge, say much about the current state
or recent developments in child psychoanalysis. So I have elected to
focus on the *differences* between adult analysis and what I have read
and heard of child analysis.

In the years up to 1950 little attention was paid to issues of separation, either in the analysis of adults or in child analysis, although the
theoretical basis for paying attention to early separations had been
established in the 1920s, and Anna Freud's studies in the 1940s were
known to many, if not all, analysts. An enormous upsurge of interest
in separation and in the development of object relations in the 1950s

Training and supervising analyst at the Boston Psychoanalytic Society and Institute;
clinical professor of psychiatry at Harvard Medical School.

The Psychoanalytic Study of the Child 56, ed. Albert J. Solnit, Peter B. Neubauer, Samuel
Abrams, and A. Scott Dowling (Yale University Press, copyright © 2001 by Albert J.
Solnit, Peter B. Neubauer, Samuel Abrams, and A. Scott Dowling).

and 1960s dramatically changed psychoanalytic practice. Young North American psychoanalysts were still virtually forbidden to pay attention to the work of Melanie Klein and her students, but the writings of Balint and Winnicott, who were seen as friends, slowly entered our curricula. Certainly, *Normality and Pathology in Childhood,* which was the single most influential book for me in my analytic training, devotes considerable attention to issues of separation.

Dr. Ablon, in his paper (p. 27), draws attention to Anna Freud's remarkable emphasis on the differences between child analysis and adult analysis, especially "the absence of free association" (p. 29) in child analysis, which comes as a bit of a showstopper in *Normality and Pathology in Childhood:* "To my mind, no remedy for this lack has been discovered over the years. Play with toys, drawing, painting, staging of fantasy games, acting in the transference have been introduced and accepted in place of free association and, *faute de mieux,* child analysts have tried to convince themselves that they are valid substitutes for it. In truth, they are nothing of the kind" (p. 29).

Dr. Ablon does not share Anna Freud's view that the absence of free association is a significant difference between child analysis and adult analysis. He attributes her view to an adherence to the policy of minimal interventions by adult analysts. He would surely agree that Anna Freud's view also derives from her recognition that introspection and insight in children are very different from introspection and insight in adults. The 1978 Hampstead Clinic Colloquium papers, of which Peter Neubauer's (1979) contribution was particularly important to me, discuss this point extensively.

I shall approach this remarkable difference of opinion by looking at what it ells us of the psychoanalysis of adults. I want to suggest that Anna Freud's approach to child analysis was in the conceptual lead and that her emphasis on the difference between adult and child analysis can be taken not only as a discourse on the limitations of child analysis but also as *commentary on adult analysis,* although it was surely not consciously intended to be so. To forestall misunderstanding, my aim is not to propose that Anna Freud was wrong in her view that there are differences between child analysis and adult analysis. My interest, in fact, is not in those differences that still seem relevant. Some of the differences that she discussed, however, represent aspects of adult psychoanalysis that have been modified in the direction of their child-analytic counterparts. Those are the ones I shall address.

In addition to the absence of free association, Anna Freud particularly stressed differences in regard to *action* and to the nature of the *transferences*. Apart from Hans Loewald (e.g., 1960), few adult analysts in 1965 would have written about new object relationships in analysis, as Anna Freud did (p. 38). And the shibboleth of the invariably intense transference neurosis in adult analysis had not yet yielded to the view of a variety of transference manifestations, in a multitude of shapes and sizes, that most of us would speak of today. Yet there they are in Anna Freud's account, though presented as differences from the adult.

Anna Freud drew a distinction between the adult patient's cooperative engagement in free association and the child's limitations in suspending censorship. We may read her discussion of the differences—profitably, I believe—as a hint that any analytic technique that relies too heavily on conscious cooperation is likely to produce compliance rather than liberation. I believe that Anna Freud greatly overestimated the value of conscious commitment of adult patients to their analytic work; its role in the method of free association seems to me far less, even in adults, than she believed. That is, I suppose that in both adults and children the most important driving forces of analysis are only modestly under conscious control.

To choose another area, we have come to recognize the vital place of action in adult analysis. The adult psychoanalysis of the 1950s placed unnecessary restrictions on the expression of memory and feeling in action, limiting the scope and depth of psychoanalytic work. Anna Freud deplored "the fact that under the pressure of the unconscious the child *acts* instead of talking, and this unfortunately introduces limits into the analytic situation" (p. 30). She pointed out, also, that *aggressive* action, particularly, appeared in the treatment. Her aim was not to discourage child analysts, however, but to draw their attention to the special tasks and developmental conditions of working with children. "The difference between the two techniques lies not in the aim but in the type of material that comes up to be interpreted" (p. 31). The analysis of adults, I believe, has similarly come to new ways of coping with material that previously required exclusion by fiat. The treatment of the pre-oedipal and non-verbal have found a salutary place in adult analytic technique.

The child analysis described in *Normality and Pathology* is far livelier than the adult psychoanalysis of the same period. Freud's determination to have psychoanalysis accepted as science—objective science—had prevented the full investigation and use of countertransference and the analyst's personality (Kris, 1994). Consequently, adult analysis had developed a desiccated, antiseptic cast. Steven Ablon (pp. 27–38) summarizes the kinds of change we have seen in adult analysis in the past 35 years, especially in our views of transference and countertransference and in our view of action, though he presents them as changes in *child* analysis. I believe that the changes are in the child *analysts,* whose analytic outlook is no longer required to be split, as was Anna Freud's.

So, in sum, I understand Anna Freud's emphasis on the differences between adult and child analysis as a twofold statement: of the prevailing developmental conditions of the child patients, on the one hand, and of the prevailing conceptual conditions of adult analysts, on the other.

I should now like to approach Eugene Mahon's beautiful account of his work with Adam, taking the views I have just expressed as a hypothesis. However much he feels indebted to Anna Freud for her ideas about developmental lines, including especially her views on the ubiquity of regression and her formulation of the metapsychological profiles, I want to ask whether Dr. Mahon's clinical presentation allows us to conclude that child analysis has advanced since the publication of *Normality and Pathology.*

To begin with, Dr. Mahon shows plainly enough that he does not concern himself with the idea that in doing child analysis he is breaking the rules of adult analysis. He is "into" the engagement with Adam, and that is that. I do believe that this is an advance from 1965. I agree with Dr. Mahon's view that an "analyst who felt that his chair was a great symbol of authority that should never be relinquished to an impudent child would obviously not be able to foster the playful climate in which oedipal usurpation and mischief could be enacted, the better to expose the components of conflict and analyze them" (p. 89). The spirit of Winnicott has fused with the intellect of Anna Freud in Eugene Mahon's child analysis.

We hear, in the radically abbreviated account of the first phase of the analysis, how Adam expressed his concerns, in play, in drawing, in sculpture, in jokes, and in a dream. He also expressed his anxieties about the analytic experience by running to his mother. We hear nothing of how or whether Dr. Mahon conveyed his own understanding to Adam. What was the connection between Adam's sudden outbursts and the oedipal anxieties? He tells us that the outbursts vanished and Adam's intellect soared. He believes that a rechannelling of energies and a transformation of the Oedipus complex via identification and superego formation account for the change. I think these useful formulations are, despite their value, a bit of a throwback. I would have liked to hear something about the influence of Dr. Mahon as new object and why he was needed. Is the report limited by the requirements of discretion? I wondered whether the role of the nanny was a convenient family fiction (not contradicted by the

Siena of the second analysis or the theory of the traumatic event of tea being spilled on Adam's head)—a fiction employed to cover the problem of parental deficiencies. The head-knocking game made me wonder whether the father was a colleague—a humorless one, at that ... but I had better break off these speculations and return to my task.

The second phase of the analysis, which shows an older child, who comes pretty close, indeed, to using free association, displays again the wonderful involvement of analyst and patient. For my purposes, I want to single out the "dream within a dream" sequence, which shows Dr. Mahon to be very comfortable about acknowledging an error. In 1965, shame and defenses against it would have been the response of many adult analysts and, I suppose, many child analysts as well. Both child analysis and adult analysis have been advanced by a greater tolerance of ambiguity, paradox, and uncertainty, and an awareness of the analyst's fallibility.

I share with Dr. Mahon the view that Anna Freud's understanding of regression has enormously influenced analysts of children and adults and led to a general advance. It certainly influenced my own work. "Ironically," he writes, "by taking the regression seriously the analyst prepares the psychological ground for progression." I agree with him, too, when he sums up the treatment as: "development in a psychoanalytic key, the invention of love, the invention of hatred approaching the vineyards of adolescence free-associative step by step." As I understand his focus on developmental lines and the metapsychological profile, Dr. Mahon concludes that Anna Freud's ideas contributed enormously to the establishment of a developmental point of view, which has transformed child analysis in the years that followed their introduction.

Silently, in the background, a host of complementary changes in adult analysis have freed child analysts from a sense that they diverge from "true" psychoanalysis.

BIBLIOGRAPHY

FREUD, A. (1965). *Normality and Pathology in Childhood. W.* 6.

KRIS, A. O. (1994). Freud's treatment of a narcissistic patient. *Int. J. Psychoanal.,* 75:649–664.

LOEWALD, H. (1960). On the therapeutic action of psycho-analysis. *Int. J. Psychoanal.,* 41:16–33.

NEUBAUER, P. (1979). The role of insight in psychoanalysis. *JAPA,* 27, Suppl. 29–40.

REMARKS OF MODERATOR
Recognizing Mood Regulation in Psychoanalytic Therapy

MORTIMER OSTOW, M.D., MED.SC.D.

I SHOULD LIKE TO SUGGEST THAT MORE ATTENTION NEEDS TO BE GIVEN to the issue of mood regulation in an effort to improve our understanding of mental illness from a psychoanalytic point of view. I believe that mood is a centrally important component of each analytic session, as it is at almost every moment of life. While mood is obviously influenced by current experience, it is also true that mood influences content, thoughts, interests, free associations, and, of course, dreams. In fact, dreams are transparent windows onto mood and its regulation. Every dream interpretation must necessarily take note of mood and allow for it in an interpreting content. Moreover, in every psychoanalytic session we must take note of mood at the outset and follow its vicissitudes.

We hear a good deal of discussion currently about affect regulation. Let me try to make this concept more precise and more useful. I believe that affect is best understood as an aspect of instinct. That connection becomes more relevant if we employ the ethologic concept of instinct rather than the classical psychoanalytic concept. In other words, I suggest here a taxonomy of affect based upon instinct.

We can recognize at least three different qualities of affect in association with each of the instincts with which we work. The appetitive

Emeritus Professor of Pastoral Psychiatry, Jewish Theological Seminary of America; President, Psychoanalytic Research and Development Fund.

Read at the conference on Child Psychoanalysis, New Haven, Connecticut, March 10–11, 2000.

The Psychoanalytic Study of the Child 56, ed. Albert J. Solnit, Peter B. Neubauer, Samuel Abrams, and A. Scott Dowling (Yale University Press, copyright © 2001 by Albert J. Solnit, Peter B. Neubauer, Samuel Abrams, and A. Scott Dowling).

or conative phase of instinctual behavior is associated with an affect
specific to that phase and that instinct. For example, the eager anticipation of sexual gratification is accompanied by a specific affect that
is universally recognized and enjoyed. Arbitrarily, and for convenience, I refer to the appetitive affect as an emotion. The consumma-
tory phase of instinctual behavior is accompanied by its own affect,
which, again arbitrarily and for convenience, I refer to simply as a
feeling. The consummation of the instinct is followed by a phase of
relief—literally or figuratively, detumescence. Freud spoke of gratification associated with the relief of tension. Although these propositions invite a good deal of discussion, that would not be appropriate
on this occasion.

I bring up the subject of the taxonomy of affect to distinguish between those affects associated with a specific instinct and the affect
associated with readiness to activate an instinct, any instinct—that is,
readiness to respond instinctually to whatever internal needs may
arise or whatever opportunities or dangers may be encountered in
the outside world. That affect I call mood. It corresponds, I believe,
to the affect generated by the dopaminergic system that Panksepp
(1998) calls the seeking system. This is the system that motivates enterprise and provides for the activation of instinct on appropriate occasion.

I have been arguing for some time that mood varies cyclically, as
does attentiveness. There are obvious circadian cycles and probably
also cycles of minutes to hours, perhaps corresponding to the REM
cycles of sleep—e.g., about 90 minutes with 45-minute harmonics,
corresponding to academic and psychoanalytic hours. We see mood
fluctuations during the dreams of patients with affect disease, each
phase lasting no more than a few moments. But if we inspect tran-
scripts of psychoanalytic sessions of 45–50 minutes, we often find de-
tectable mood swings of a period corresponding to the length of the
session.

Let us look at the case Steve Ablon describes. At the beginning
of the session reported, Emma is unhappy and angry about her
mother's departure and Will's death. She asks for cookies from Steve
to sustain her against her unhappiness. We are concerned then with
wrinkles, old age, disease, and death, referring to her grandmother,
to Steve, and to Zayde; that is, she reverts to her sad, perhaps depressive mood. She then tries to revive by engaging in games of death and
recovery, and hide and seek. "I've got the little bitty babies in my
arms." One wonders whether she is identifying with the mother god
or the helpless infant. She ends up identifying with the baby, hungry

and cold, when the attempt to recover fails. She recovers to joyous excitement in sexual attachment to Steve. In other words, we recognize here three cycles of sadness followed by attempts to recover. Steve gives us his reactions; they shadow the patient's moods.

This type of analysis does not preempt content and genetic analysis but it does demonstrate the structure of the session—it is the mood structure that determines which aspect of content comes to the fore at each moment in behavior and in thought. In a sense the mood fluctuations may be thought of as an affective conflict resolved not by compromise but by alternation.

In adults with mood disease, these swings may be fairly pronounced and more frequent. They appear in most of their dreams. Without mood disease, the mood oscillations may be narrower in amplitude and less extreme. In children and adolescents, mood swings come about as result of the early phases of mood disease including ADD, but they also may be merely manifestations of the normal process of development of the capacity for mood regulation.

Let's see how this applies to Gene Mahon's case. We do not have any full sessions so we cannot examine for intrasession mood fluctuation. But Gene has given us data about mood, which he has recognized and emphasized. Adam's primary symptom is aggressive behavior, seemingly without provocation. In the context of mood regulation, episodic aggressive behavior is used as a defensive measure against a depressive mood. The chair stealing and the head knocking represent Promethean challenges to authority, the father, each followed by guilty and anxious hiding: think about Adam and Eve in the garden. Similarly, replacing father's initials with his own produces anxiety. These episodes of anxiety require repair by contact with mother. With psychoanalytic treatment and further maturation, the aggression subsided.

During the second phase of analysis, starting at eleven, the patient describes three "bosses"—which I believe are based upon three states of minds or moods; in fact they are projected sources of these moods. The severe boss elicits depression. The empathic boss elicits euthymia. The cruel boss is the source of his defensive hostility. Aggression returns in dreams: the anti-centipede, anti-Semitism complex; the nuclear power plant threatening to blow up while Adam tries to keep the lid on. The dream of the alternation of green and black (green is the color of rebirth—see Psalm 23; black is the color of death) expresses the feeling of the alternation of death and rebirth. (cf. Emma's alternation of being dead and being alive). The identification with Puck signifies the wish to avoid adult responsibility (note the dream about the motel labeled The Sands of Time). Such concerns are usually associated with low self-esteem, which is an issue with Adam and is often associated with difficulty in studying though there seems to be no difficulty in learning here. I have tried to show that a number of Adam's presenting complaints, fantasies, and dreams are determined by mood and its vicissitudes.

A sensitivity to mood and its fluctuations during the analytic session—and in dreams—makes us aware of a force that determines the selection and procession of dynamically determined instinctual tendencies, and the fantasies, wishes, and behavior to which they give rise.

BIBLIOGRAPHY

PANKSEPP, J. (1998). *Affective Neuroscience.* Oxford: New York.

SUMMATION
Unrealized Possibilities

Comments on Anna Freud's
Normality and Pathology in Childhood

SAMUEL ABRAMS, M.D.

ANNA FREUD'S *NORMALITY AND PATHOLOGY IN CHILDHOOD* PROPOSED radical approaches to the treatment of children. Since its publication in 1965 there have been important changes in the way in which analysts address their child patients. For example, they have moved away from autocracy and toward responsive interaction. However, it remains unclear whether those changes were derived principally from Anna Freud's radical proposals or, indeed, exactly what those proposals were.

This discussion is in three sections: (1) What did Anna Freud say? (2) What obstacles exist to implementing what she said? (3) What can be done about it?

WHAT DID SHE SAY?

Ms. Freud was both a conserver and an innovator, often a very difficult straddle. Sometimes these traits have been interpreted as reflecting an ambivalence to her father, at other times as an extraordinary feature of her personality (Wallerstein, 1984, Ekins and Freeman, 1998, Kris, 2000).

Clinical professor, the Psychoanalytic Institute at the New York University School of Medicine.

The Psychoanalytic Study of the Child 56, ed. Albert J. Solnit, Peter B. Neubauer, Samuel Abrams, and A. Scott Dowling (Yale University Press, copyright © 2001 by Albert J. Solnit, Peter B. Neubauer, Samuel Abrams, and A. Scott Dowling).

In her book, Ms. Freud affirmed her conservatism in a variety of ways—for example, by emphasizing the diagnostic usefulness of the metapsychological profile and by underscoring the value of interpretation when addressing neurotic disorders. Furthermore, in a real testament to tradition, she insisted on a specific meaning of the transference. She defined it as a revived past object, a relationship to the analyst that is gradually differentiated from other relationships after considerable effort, not something that is a formidable presence at the outset, and certainly not just any feeling the patient might have for the analyst (pp. 36–7). Hers is a differentiated as well as a conservative definition, not a global or an elastic one. One might gauge the influence of her book by determining how successful she was at perpetuating the traditional perspectives and technical tools invented in adult analysis, but that would not track her innovations.

In any case, it is her innovative side that is far more dominant in the volume. "Innovative" may be too weak a word. In what amounts to a clarion call, she proposed that child analysts ought to be "adventurous," even "revolutionary" (p. 110).

The book's influence on contemporary child-analytic technique might best be determined by assessing the success of her revolutionary proposals. Four interweaving adventuresome areas can be delineated: (a) her view of new diagnostic and therapeutic possibilities; (b) her introduction of the role of developmental *discontinuities;* (c) her consideration of a special set of *continuities* in development; and (d) her attempts to differentiate and integrate different sources of data.

New Diagnostic and Therapeutic Possibilities. As a conserver, Ms. Freud urged child analysts to continue to appreciate the significance of neurotic disorders in childhood, recognizing the centrality of the infantile neurosis in such disorders and the therapeutic value of attending to transference (past object), resistance, and interpretation. The usefulness of accessing unconscious conflicts with suitable child patients is easily illustrated (e.g., Mahon, 2001).

As an innovator, Ms. Freud stressed that child patients also experience their analysts as new objects, externalized objects, or objects of drives. By asserting the existence of such differentiated phenomena, which are ordinarily veiled by the global term "transference," she opened up the opportunity of discovering different forms of therapeutic action. Not only could this illuminate different ways of getting better, but it might lead to the discovery of different disorders to get better from.

What she meant by a *new* object may at first glance appear ambiguous. The confusion is most easily addressed with this question: is the "new" evoked by special distinguishing features of the treating person, or does it arise out of the progressive internal structuralization only to become actualized upon the treating person? That is, is it a response to the outside, or does it arise from the inside? *The Many Meanings of Play,* a collection edited by Dr. Solnit and others (1993) helps to illuminate and clarify such clinical dilemmas. Individual articles describe how play can be developmentally promoted by providing new experiences to actualize the inherent developmental potential. In other instances play can be relationally enhancing and can symbolically represent unconscious conflicts as well, but play as promoting development proves a worthy fresh exploration. Newly arising organizations search for circumstances and people to be actualized. A child's use of an analyst in just such a service was Anna Freud's meaning of a *new* object.

She suggested that the therapeutic situation—in addition to many other things—provides a setting in which to search for such *new* objects and experiences. This is a reflection of a "hunger" in children that is as powerful as the need to repeat past experiences in adults (A. Freud, 1965, p. 38). New objects and new experiences assist in actualizing the developmental potential in each fresh level.

It is useful to distinguish the yield of relationships with *new* objects from the yield of relationships with *real* objects. Real object relationships involve concrete actual characteristics such as warmth, empathy, affect-tolerance, authenticity, curiosity—features that are regularly provided by therapists. These traits may promote mutuality and identification and hence may facilitate growth in patients (at any age), especially children. They yield positive therapeutic results through the mutative consequences of a felicitous interactive exchange (e.g., Ablon, 2001). However, unlike the felicitous consequences of the real, new object experiences yield positive therapeutic results by promoting the transformational potential of each developmental organization.

Ms. Freud's discovery of the existence of such distinctions as old, new, real, and externalized objects led her to the recognition that different forms of therapeutic action may be tapped from such encounters. This makes it incumbent upon child analysts to carefully differentiate the nature of the sought-for interaction in the children they treat and not to confuse one for the other. Among other things, such differentiation can help in distinguishing neurotic from non-neurotic disturbances and may open up new therapeutic possibilities other than those arising from insight or corrective emotional experiences. Overlap, of course, is common. Downey has (2001) provided an especially rich paper that attends to the significance of the complexities of object interaction, suggesting that the new can modulate the backwards pull of the old. The new can be tapped to assist children in overcoming certain developmental limitations. He cites the Bulldog's Bank children, but it is obvious that there are therapeutic possibilities in his descriptions that may be applicable to many other youngsters in addition to those who have been victimized by unusually severe trauma. Downey describes this as "developmental remediation."

His perspective can be contrasted with that of clinicians who regard the "new" object as an expression of the real qualities of the analyst, qualities that provide sources of identification and authentic mutuality. Unlike Downey's, this form of growth-promoting relies on a real reciprocal transaction, not necessarily on tapping the possibilities inherent in the progressive internal structuralization.

Ms. Freud further suggested that new therapeutic possibilities be subordinated to a new primary goal in the treatment of children. If the adult model stressed the resolution of intrapsychic conflicts and a resulting reorganization of existing structures, the child analyst would be expected to shift attention to the restoration of normal development—specifically, the assurance that the potential for future new organizations will be sustained. There is only one factor to consider in evaluating children, Miss Freud noted as she embarked on her radical departure, "the child's capacity to move forward in progressive steps until maturation, development in all areas of the personality, and adaptation to the social community have been completed. . . . Upsets . . . have to be taken seriously as soon as development itself is affected, whether slowed up, reversed, or brought to a standstill altogether" (p. 123).

However, if recognizing the impediments to development was to be the new benchmark for child analysts, they would be required to become knowledgeable about more than structures in conflict. They would need to have a conceptual grasp of the *developmental process* and recognize the empirical markers that affirm the competence of the progression.

The developmental process, Ms. Freud noted, is co-determined by endowment, the environment, and the rate of internal structuralization (p. 64; see also A. Freud, 1974, p. 150). Intrapsychic conflict, however important it is for the neuroses, is not the sole engine that drives growth and development. If that is true, then new modes of treatment action lie in devising ways to resolve the impediments to development arising from sources other than conflict.

Discovering those new modes depends on acquiring enhanced diagnostic skills that go beyond the metapsychological profile. Ms. Freud provided a new evaluative instrument, the developmental profile, that rested on her expanded theory. The profile has sometimes been described as too difficult to implement, operationally mundane, and somewhat uneven in its levels of abstraction. Whatever the truth of those allegations, in order to make a definite diagnosis of distressed children, Ms. Freud suggested that child analysts would henceforth be expected to find and coordinate useful features of this new instrument in order to promote their work with children.

The influence of discontinuities. The developmental profile was an empirical template informed by a complex conceptual theory. The theory stressed a *discontinuous* progression rather than a linear one. Regrettably, there were and are so many "developmental" theories around that it is important to underscore the particular features that characterized Ms. Freud's so that it will not be confused with the others.

Her theory was anchored in biology. Consequently, she focused first on a biological determinant, a inherent, maturationally informed program that encodes a blueprinted sequence of anticipated developmental plateaus or organizations. The rate of this process of internally derived structuralization varies in different children. The engine that drives it all is an additional inherent feature. These new plateaus or organizations feature phase-specific tasks and new ways of thinking, feeling, and behaving. Each organization effectively transforms antecedent structures and functions as well as ushering in new ones.

A second determinant of the progression resides in the object-interaction system. Children actively search for new objects to help actualize the emerging developmental organizations. Consequently, the success of the progression is also influenced by the availability of new objects and the characteristics of the new experiences they provide. "What the environment is expected to contribute," Ms. Freud wrote, "are the provisions of appropriate human objects, their accepting, promoting, stimulating and controlling attitudes toward the child." (1974, p. 135).

In short, Ms. Freud's epigenetically bound theory stressed maturational anlagen, object-seeking and developmental hierarchies. She argued that child analysts would be handicapped without a background in developmental timetables and the complexities of the developmental process (1965, p. 114). How could they possibly introduce new modes of therapeutic action to assist developmentally derived disorders without a firm grounding in the developmental process itself and the ways in which it might go awry?

Ms. Freud may have hoped that her developmental theory would prevail and that her initial proposals might be augmented through further research. Regrettably, that hope has been realized in only a modest way. Have an adventuresome new breed of child analysts studied inherent variations in internal structuralization? Have there been clinical papers on the effects of variations in the pull forward, the impetus that drives the progression? Are there many publications demonstrating the analyst as a new object to assist in actualizing an emerging new hierarchy? I cannot think of more than a few clinicians concerned with such issues, and they were principally stimulated directly or indirectly by the work of Peter Neubauer in the New York area or the Child Study Center at Yale.

Her attention to discontinuities led Ms. Freud to recognize that the ensuing program might also be subject to *unevenness* or *disharmony;* that is, one developmental line might be accelerated or retarded compared to the others. What kinds of disorder arose from such disparities? How might the object interaction augment or reduce these disparities? Would diagnostic refinements add to our ability to distinguish such nuances so that we might introduce techniques to limit the burden of such disparities? How can an analyst actively help to rectify such unevenness, assuming it has been recognized? As far as I know there have been very few attempts to raise these questions, much less provide answers.

The role of continuities. In addition to understanding the discontinuities in development derived from a hierarchically ordered sequence, Ms. Freud suggested that there were other aberrant constitutional givens that could exert a *continuous* impact throughout all periods of growth. For example, children born with low frustration tolerance, excessive anxiety states, unusual progressive-regressive balances burden the integrity of all their new plateaus as well as the quality of their object-relations. How far would child analysts go in attempting to pick up those constitutional limitations and begin to think of ways of helping those children or their parents reduce the impact upon subsequent growth? And what about other features of endowment—special talents, for example, that might ease the turbulence of development? Could we learn to tap such abilities and leverage them against delays and conflicts? Currently, there is a wide interest in constitutional givens as determinants in the psychoses, autistic disorders, dyslexia, ADD, Aspergers, and Tourettes as well as endogenous depressions. Approaches have been devised to deal with these disorders, although they do not especially rely upon the use of psychological interventions. Few recognize that such contemporary interests are related to Anna Freud's innovative ideas of 1965 regarding variations in endowment.

Differentiation and integration of different sources of data. Ms. Freud dealt with data derived from child analysis and adult analysis, on the one hand, and the analytic process and the developmental process, on the other. She hoped to conserve the yield of clinical research in adulthood, with its focus on intrapsychic conflicts. However, she distinguished this from the approach in child analysis which required monitoring a much wider intrapsychic domain, precisely because children were driven by different engines than adults. The scope in child analysis would be wider because the child's mind is in the throes of a forward and backward movements, of transformations derived from newly emerging organizations, and because variations in endowment and the object-interactional system could have completely unexpected impacts on the emerging mind. The adult mind is in throes of its own since it must deal with all sorts of residual undercurrents derived from childhood. However, the throes are different so that the approach to relief requires different techniques.

For those who endorse Anna Freud's emphasis on differences, the question becomes, how would the distinguishing of differences affect the way analysts work with children as contrasted with adults? For Ms. Freud child analysis and adult analysis are different, the metapsychological profile and developmental profile are different, the psychoanalytic process and the developmental process are different, the diagnostic possibilities and the modes of therapeutic action are different. How difficult would it be to coordinate such differences between some of the established features of analysis learned from adults and the new discoveries gleaned from development? And as far as children were concerned, could the analytic process be coordinated with the developmental process in treatment?

Ablon (2001) and Mahon (2001) succeed in coordinating development and analysis, but they each emphasize different aspects of both processes. Ablon underscores a strong interactive presence to facilitate therapeutic action through identifications and growth-promoting experiences that arise from the jointly created enterprise. The engine that runs his "developmental" is based on the proposition that in open systems, complexity by itself moves development forward. The complexity, as he sees it, derives from the intersubjective exchange. He traces this emphasis on two-person psychology to some of Ms. Freud's comments about verbalization and the use of play. He perceives the contributions of interpersonal psychology as important factors in contemporary analysis and sees less difficulty in coordinating adult and child analysis because for him there are few salient differences.

Mahon coordinates developmental lines and metapsychology and sees his task as promoting maximal insight. He emphasizes analysis as a work of discovery, the discovery of unconscious conflicts, the discovery of normal responses such as grief, and the discovery of talents that can be used to promote the treatment. He also views the mode of therapeutic action as insight for both children and adults, so, at least in that sense, he perceives little difference between child and adult work. Ablon co-invents, and Mahon co-discovers. Ablon applies responsive interaction, Mahon applies insight. Both analysts are talented and both therapies yield positive results, but the mode of therapeutic action is different for each analyst, and neither mode is especially what Anna Freud proposed when she extended her views about assistance to impediments in development.

This problem of coordinating analysis and development—of coordinating modes of therapeutic action that rely on insight or the relational exchange with therapeutic actions that rely on assists to the development program—has been addressed in both general and specific terms by two recent study groups sponsored by the Psychoanalytic Research and Development Fund. The first yielded a book, *The Many Meanings of Play* (Solnit, Cohen, and Neubauer, 1993). The second, a study group engaging the problem of coordinating developmental and analytic process, yielded a series of papers that have appeared in the *Journal of the American Psychoanalytic Association* (Abrams & Solnit, 1998) and in *The Psychoanalytic Study of the Child* (1999). That book and those papers attempt to actualize Ms. Freud's vision of differentiating and integrating pools of data derived from different perspectives. The papers are rich in the concept of examining progressive structuralization and integrating the past object and the new object. The impact these publications have had or are likely to have on the direction of our enterprise remain unclear. If Ablon's and Mahon's papers are illustrative, however, the vast majority of child analysts appear capable of doing very rewarding work, by leveraging therapeutic action by way of mutuality and authenticity, on the one hand, or by closely attending to insight as the mode of cure, on the other.

OBSTACLES

Contemporary clinical work suggests that Ms. Freud's essentially revolutionary positions have had a relatively minor impact on child analytic practice. Why is this so? What obstacles exist to implementing her views?

Five obstacles can be delineated: (a) ambiguity; (b) the intrapsychic versus interactive; (c) the complexity of process thinking versus dynamic narratives; (d) the problem of new therapeutic tools; and (e) an identity problem.

Ambiguity. What is "developmental" anyhow? Anna Freud's developmental concept was not the only developmental point of view that surfaced in the 1960s and 1970s. All child observational researchers regard themselves as informed by a developmental approach.

Mahler's work, for example, fostered a very popular developmental school based upon the empirical feature of separation and individuation. While the inherent biological impetus that moves a child from "hatching" to the capacity for autonomy is implicit in her work, it was the facilitating or obstructing influence of the object-interaction system that most observers addressed. Furthermore, while Anna Freud noted that each new organization is characterized by a phase-specific task, this developmental school examined the *same* task—separation and individuation throughout life. In addition, the phases were not limited to those determined by biological processes introduced throughout childhood and adolescence but were extended to more socially determined phases in adult life as well. These included marriage, divorce, parenthood, grandparenthood, etc.—all of which were examined from the standpoint of the management of separation and individuation. Even death was conceptualized as a developmental phase.

Erikson's epigenetic hypothesis is a developmental theory as well. Unlike Anna Freud's, his developmental extended into adult life, was both biological and sociological, and contained implicit standards of values throughout the life cycle. Both Mahler and Erikson led people to consider how to help patients engage the tasks at each phase rather than attend to impairments in the underlying processes that make those tasks more or less difficult.

Piaget's genetic epistemology is principally a maturational system, relegating the object-interaction system to lesser significance and subordinating almost everything to cognitive progression.

The relationship between two persons also can yield a positive outcome, and this too has been designated a "developmental" outcome.

Proponents of the value of interactive relationships and intersubjectivity favor this developmental, stressing authenticity and mutual identifications as cornerstones of growth in general and of therapeutic action in analysis.[1]

In the midst of the ambiguities fostered by these multiple developmentals, it is no wonder that Anna Freud's concept became obscured. What may have obscured her contributions even further was a proposal promoted in the early 1970s in the American Psychoanalytic Association that our discipline shift its attention to a developmental orientation in the treatment of all patients, adults and children alike (Goodman, 1977, pp. 51–102). The proposal was based principally upon the work of Mahler and Erikson and was heavily influenced by object-relations and the role of societal factors. The new approaches that were created by this proposal especially invited attention to the environmental causes of developmental disorders and argued for treatment approaches that corrected mismanagement by caretakers. This had little to do with the therapeutic possibilities that Anna Freud had envisioned. Once that proposal was officially offered, it immediately became a source of controversy. The developmental was condemned as anti-analytic, and Anna Freud's work was indicted by association. As a result not only was she a victim of the developmental wars but the dichotomizing of development and analysis made attempts to coordinate the two more difficult for all future analysts. Those who won the wars were increasingly linked to interpersonal psychiatry, an orientation that began with Harry Stack Sullivan in this country and that has always been welcomed by American psychiatry. Analysts in that psychiatry look at growth and development principally from the nurture side of the equation and understand disorders as caused by defective primary objects and impaired families and societies. To be sure, the nature of the surround must never be ignored, and limitations in caregiving are or ought to be part of every child analyst's diagnostic repertoire, but that was not Ms. Freud's orienting center in her 1965 book and not the core of her "developmental."

Many theories of development provide a valuable conceptual base to examine and to help children. They have prevailed at the expense of Ms. Freud's proposal, which is more oriented in biology. Indeed, some child analysts believe that they are espousing Ms. Freud's position when they are really working in an entirely different tradition.

---

1. For a more extensive review see Neubauer (1976) and Abrams (1983, 1990).

This is a major obstacle to clinical and research activities that could bring her proposals to more concrete fruition.

The intrapsychic versus the interactive. Ms. Freud's perspective was clearly an intrapsychic one, or, to use a phrase that has become current these days, a one-person psychology. This does not mean that she was unaware of the influence of the object-interaction system or of the need to be open and available as an analyst. But while the developmental lines always incorporated the facilitating or interfering effects of the environment, the environment was viewed as a codeterminant rather than as the dominant influence on the developmental process. Internal and external mutually inform one another. Ms. Freud's dispute with M. Sperling about fetish formation, briefly summarized in her book, clearly reflects her differences with those clinicians preferentially tilted toward the external side of the equation (pp. 207 ff).

Anna Freud monitored factors that influence development by examining progressive structuralization, an intrapsychic orientation. Her theory also explains how features of the developmental process influence objects—that is, how children create parents—whereas the preferred interest in our discipline has always been how parents create children. At different times our discipline has hypothesized the existence of schizophrenogenic mothers, refrigerator mothers, the combination of a strong mother/weak father, which allegedly breeds homosexuals, and more recently the critical impact upon children of having a depressed mother during the rapproachement subphase. These have all been very popular positions. They fall within a developmental perspective that is very far from Anna Freud. Furthermore, the popularization of so-called two-person psychology, with its renewed emphasis on interaction in both causing and remedying disorders, has further shifted attention away from the intrapsychic.

The shift from the intrapsychic toward the interactive is a second factor that obscures Ms. Freud's contributions.

Process versus dynamics. Analogous to perspectives of intrapsychic versus interactive is the distinction between process thinking and constructing dynamic narratives. It is much more difficult to teach and learn process that to teach and learn about dynamics. "What makes development happen?" is a common question that produces complex answers (Mayes, 1999). Process happens, it is something that occurs without being articulated or even having to be articulated. The progression of changes in the way a child views the minds of others simply occurs over time. The child has no explanation, nor does she search for one. Regrettably, such explanatory phrases as "genetically timed elements interacting with the environment" and "underlying dimensions of development" are at high levels of abstraction, a little too removed from human beings. Fantasies and dynamic exchanges, on the other hand, are understood as residents of the unconscious, where they exist as covert informing stories and are likely to continue to have an influence unless they are accessed. And certainly there is something distinctly human about personal myths. Interpretations of stories about maternal introjects or oedipal conflicts or Jungian archetypes are concrete matters that can easily be taught and are readily embraced. But what about those semi-mystical *processes?* Anyone who suggests that one determinant of obsessive-like symptoms in early childhood is a disharmony between developmental lines is likely to be met with a glazed look. That is a far more complex concept to entertain than an aberration in the anal phase or identification with parental rigidity or even some impairment in neurophysiology. Anna Freud subsumed conflicts and relational exchanges under development, but the explanatory appeal of narratives, the understanding of personal unrecognized stories, is far greater than the appeal of explanations dependent upon complex, highly abstract processes. This tension of difference between the abstract and the concrete represents another obstacle to grasping Ms. Freud's work.

This introduces a fourth obstacle: *the problem of new therapeutic tools.* Ms. Freud claimed that there were many therapeutic possibilities made available by her revolutionary theory, yet she did not literally describe the techniques that could be used to treat the different forms of impairment. The general sense that the analyst ought to be available to provide what a child needs, sometimes referred to as a "smorgasbord" approach, seems difficult to apply in any systematic way. As analysts we know that it is sometimes important to reject an attribute assigned to us by our patients. Ms. Freud certainly knew that. She stipulated that in dealing with neurotic children such matters as external management, reassurance, and corrective emotional experiences fail to redress the intrapsychic balance (1965, p. 229). In contrast, however, she suggested that considerable benefit can result when dealing with developmentally derived disorders using mixtures of these other elements while interpretation can have little effect or might even create undesirable consequences. She explains: verbalizing and clarifying internal and external dangers help the ego deal with what it might otherwise be helpless to manage; children with "libido defects" can have a corrective emotional experience when a failure of caretaking has augmented those defects; intellectually retarded children can benefit from management that helps move them along expected developmental pathways. She adds that analysts may even redress balances in organic patients with impoverished drive activity (p. 229). These are all new therapeutic possibilities that rely on more than mere acquaintance with the developmental process. The possibilities for new modes of therapeutic action are described in her book as are some suggestions for implementing those possibilities. However, the wide array of technical interventions are only sparsely specified. Many ways of assisting a variety of possible disorders are left in a more abstract form, which simply lacks the appeal of the relatively simple interpretation of unconscious fantasies or provision of corrective emotional experiences.

This leads to a final obstacle, *an identity problem for analysts.* Is the developmental process an *analytic* matter altogether? Donald Cohen (2000) describes this as the domain issue of analysis. He asks what are its boundaries? What is and what isn't analysis? He proposes that psychoanalysis is a perspective bounded by values, principles, and theories, and he, for one, would include the propositions of developmental psychology within those boundaries. But what are the competing values, principles, and theories that make a perspective *non*-analytic?

The domain of analysis is shrouded in ambiguity these days. Sometimes it seems that anything is analysis and everyone is an analyst. On the other hand, some representatives of our discipline have a particularly restrictive view. For them analysis is therapeutic action based on insight or relational exchange where all growth rests on conflict. Is development simply too narrow for the first group and too broad for the second? If the definition of an analytic identity is so shaky, attempt to include developmental principles is bound to destabilize it further, especially since the concept of development is equally ambiguous. What a dilemma! How is it possible to bring together two concepts as ambiguous and controversial as analysis and development and promote a coherent identity? No wonder we struggle so much to define our discipline.

In brief, the problem is that analytic work is defined more in terms of content and interaction and less in terms of overall processes and principles. The metapsychological profile defines us as analysts—although different kinds of analysts, depending upon which aspects of the profile we find more congenial; the developmental profile defines us as child analysts, again depending upon which concept of development we find most congenial. Consequently, Ms. Freud's book also fails to appeal to those who are concerned that attention to a superordinate ideal like development threatens an analytic identity, an identity defined by the centrality of conflict or by a corruption in object relations.

REMEDIES

Can the obstacles to realizing the possibilities of Ms. Freud's message be overcome? Are they worth overcoming?

It certainly is possible to do effective work with children while entirely ignoring the complex developmental processes—in fact, without understanding very much about them. Many analysts find flexibility, openness, and opportunities to leverage treatment through a variety of activities described in Anna Freud's 1965 book. They honor her for these features.

Some analysts who value flexibility and openness assimilate these aspects of Ms. Freud's proposals into their pre-existing developmental concepts based on a relational system. Ms. Freud's book simply affirms what they already believe. Introducing the variations and deviations of the developmental process is seen as too complex, too abstract, too difficult to implement, too much of a strain to process— and the therapeutic opportunities may appear too vague to be taken very seriously anyway. The presentations of child analytic case reports in recent years suggest that child analysis can do very well without Ms. Freud's substantive propositions, thank you, and let's move forward into the post-modern world.

However, child analysis can do better, and perhaps it had better do better. I believe that Ms. Freud's concept of development is worth saving and promoting. The five obstacles to their incorporation into clinical work can be overcome by study and scholarship, active clinical research, and bringing together educators willing to grapple with the issues. By reaffirming the concepts of the developmental process and demonstrating the new therapeutic possibilities that arise from them, it may be possible to integrate new modes of therapeutic action usefully in our practice and thereby to extend our province.

Once that new broader terrain is widely explored, it will be time enough to decide whether to call it psychoanalysis.

BIBLIOGRAPHY

ABLON, S. (2001). The Work of Transformation. *Psychoanal. Study Child* 56.
ABRAMS, S. (1983). Development. *Psychoanal. Study Child* 38:113–139.

———— (1990). The psychoanalytic process: the development and the integrative. *Psych. Quart, LIX,* 650–677.

———— & SOLNIT, A. J. (1998). Coordinating developmental and psychoanalytic processes: Conceptualizing technique. *JAPA 46,* 85–103.

COHEN, D. J. (2000). Personal communication.

DOWNEY, T. W. (2001). Early Object Relations into New Objects. *Psychoanal. Study Child* 56.

EKINS, R., & FREEMAN, R. (1998). Introduction, *Selected Writings: Anna Freud.* London: Penguin.

FREUD, A. (1965). Normality and Pathology in Childhood: Assessments of Development, in *The Writings of Anna Freud.* New York: Int. Univ. Press.

———— (1974). A Psychoanalytic View of Developmental Psychopathology. In *Selected Writings: Anna Freud,* eds. Richard Ekins and Ruth Freeman. London: Penguin, 1998.

GOODMAN, S., ED. (1977). Psychoanalytic Education and Research. The Current Situation and Future Possibilities. New York: Int. Univ. Press.

KRIS, A. (2000). Personal Communication.

MAHON, E. (2001). Anna Freud and the Evolution of Psychoanalytic Technique. *Psychoanal. Study Child* 56.

MAYES, L. C. (1999). Clocks, engines, and quarks—love, dreams, and genes: what makes development happen? *Psych. Study Child,* 54:169–192.

NEUBAUER, P. B., ED. (1976). *The Process of Child Development.* New York: New American Library.

SOLNIT, A. J., COHEN, D. J., & NEUBAUER, P. B., EDS. (1993). *The Many Meanings of Play.* New Haven: Yale Univ. Press.

WALLERSTEIN, R. (1984). Anna Freud: Radical Innovator and Staunch Conservative. *Psychoanal. Study of the Child,* 39:65–80.

THEORY

The "Exceptions" Reviewed

The Formation and Deformation of the Privileged Character

HAROLD P. BLUM, M.D.

The "exception" is one of the three character-types Freud (1916) identi-fied in a now-classic early contribution to psychoanalytic character studies. The term has since been applied to various clinical entities with different theoretical implications. This paper explores and ampli-fies the concept of the "exception" and the "exception" as a special cate-gory of varied privileged characters. The paper re-examines Freud's and later formulations in the context of contemporary psychoanalytic thought.

THE THREE CHARACTER-TYPES FREUD IDENTIFIED IN 1916–THE "EX-ceptions," "those wrecked by success," and "criminals from a sense of guilt"—have became part of continuing psychoanalytic discourse. These are ingeniously paradoxical notions in terms of common sense. People are usually considered to be wrecked by failure rather than success; criminals were thought at the time to lack guilt and shame; and "exceptions" are likely to be thought of as spoiled and selfish rather than as individuals traumatized as children.

The dynamics and genetics of the "exception" as a privileged char-acter had never before been elucidated or connected with the very

Clinical professor of psychiatry and training analyst, New York University, College of Medicine and Department of Psychiatry, and executive director, Sigmund Freud Archives.

The author thanks Dr. Elsa J. Blum for her invaluable critique and editing of this chapter.

The Psychoanalytic Study of the Child 56, ed. Albert J. Solnit, Peter B. Neubauer, Samuel Abrams, and A. Scott Dowling (Yale University Press, copyright © 2001 by Albert J. Solnit, Peter B. Neubauer, Samuel Abrams, and A. Scott Dowling).

different character-types who arrange for their own defeat or punishment. The "exceptions" do not feel guilty but consider their demands for special treatment to be justified by their prior pain and sorrow. In contrast, those wrecked by success feel so guilty that they must "snatch defeat from the jaws of victory." Criminals from a sense of guilt are also guilt-ridden, but their guilt leads to rather than results from delinquency and crime. The "exceptions" appear to be above the usual rules and regulations, do not suffer the pangs of conscious self-reproach, and appear to be guiltless and, I might add, shameless.

Freud (1916) pointed out that everyone, to some degree, thinks of himself as an exception to the rule, with special claims and demands. But not everyone insists upon being an exception to the same degree or in characterological attitudes and behavior. In Freud's (1916) depiction, "exceptional" characters had suffered egregiously in the past and paid the price for current pleasure through prior pain. They had been through many hard knocks and harsh experiences and, according to Freud (1916), felt these torments as an injustice, especially since they had occurred in the "innocence" of early childhood. The suffering and sacrifice had therefore transpired without any provocation on their part and thus consistently supported the feeling that they were not, in any way, the victim's fault. The adult exception cannot, therefore, be understood without taking into account the importance of early childhood.

Freud's main illustration was drawn, not from his clinical experience, but from the applied psychoanalysis of Richard III, one of Shakespeare's unforgettable characters. This use of psychoanalysis to interpret a character portrayed by the great poet-dramatist was dependent upon Freud's identification with the artist in his creative work. But psychoanalytic explanation went beyond the artist's description and intuition to provide new insights into character formation and structure.

The individuals whom Freud and Shakespeare depicted are vulnerable to severe malformations of psychic structure and character. Richard's physical deformity was a metaphor for his deformed character as well as its cause. The psychological ramifications extend far beyond the immediate consequences of the physical deformity or disability. There may be compensatory fantasies of grandiosity and uniqueness alongside exceptional narcissistic vulnerability, distortions of the body image, and disturbances of body reality extended to external reality (Niederland, 1965). Related to the early psychological effects of the physical defects is later psychopathology, including the cumulative traumata experienced by the child and the parents, the unconscious fantasy elaborations, and the organizing influence of the defect in all its varied unconscious attributes and meanings.

Before further commenting about Richard III and some related clinical vignettes, let us examine some of the meanings of exception in the psychoanalytic literature. If every rule has its exception (which sharpens the definition), then the exception is the one who is above the rule, to whom the rule does not apply.

The word "exception" implies a statistical dimension, deviance from the norm, in the sense that an exception is a rarity. ("Exception" may also mean exclusion or rejection; to "take exception to" something is to object to or exclude it.) While Freud's paper deals with undesirable, devalued characteristics, "exception" also has been used to refer to those with extraordinary, highly valued qualities. Like unusual negative characteristics, giftedness is also relevant to narcissistic issues—to narcissistic rewards and injuries, narcissistic supplies and frustrations, and narcissistic entitlement and demands (Murray, 1964). (In the conclusion of his 1916 essay on "The Exceptions," Freud suggested the untenable proposition that women are exceptions, without considering the issues of frequency of occurrence and primary femininity. Feeling damaged in infancy, "undeservedly cut short" (p. 315), leads to later attitudes of entitlement and demands for special privileges.)

"Exception" in this paper refers to characterological deformity related to early physical deformity or deficiency. The related notion of entitlement due to later trauma, such as being a survivor of natural or human disaster, is also considered.

Freud had written on narcissism just two years earlier, and though he indicates the relationship of the "exception" to narcissism, his focus on the character types conveys his preoccupation with issues of guilt, particularly unconscious guilt, at that time. "Mourning and Melancholia" (1916), written in the same year as "Character Types," displays the same interest in guilt and the unconscious need for punishment. These two papers may also be regarded as forerunners of tripartite structural theory and the vicissitudes of superego function.

It is also of interest that at the beginning of the "Character Types" paper, Freud turned his attention from symptoms to character traits and character resistance in analysis. This paper thus anticipates later psychoanalytic formulations of character. Having renounced and suffered enough while feeling unfairly treated, the exceptions "will submit no longer to any disagreeable necessity, . . . and moreover, intend to remain so" (p. 312). Clinging to a privileged position becomes a formidable analytic resistance.

Freud referred to the congenital defect of Shakespeare's Richard III, who has been sent into the world deformed and unfinished, so lame and unfashionable that dogs bark at him. Richard avers, "As I cannot play the lover on account of my deformity, I will play the villain; I will intrigue, murder, and do anything else I please" (p. 314). Freud paraphrases Shakespeare's Richard III in this way: "'Nature has done me a grievous wrong in denying me the beauty of form which wins human love. Life owes me reparation for this, and I will see that I get it. I have a right to be an exception, to disregard the scruples by which others let themselves be held back. I may do wrong myself, since wrong has been done to me.' . . . Richard is an enormous magnification of something we find in ourselves as well. We all think we have reason to reproach nature and our destiny for congenital and infantile disadvantages; we all demand reparation for early wounds to our narcissism, our self-love" (p. 315).

Here Freud introduced, in the briefest manner, the notion of compensation for narcissistic wounds, quite separate from the issue of feeling guiltless and thus not subject to the restraints of internalized regulation and social prohibition. The compensation is also related, though not formulated as such, to gains from illness (Freud, 1914). The traumatized person may feel entitled to compensation as a means of redressing injury and obtaining justice and as reparation for pain and loss.

The search for compensation takes many forms, including the feeling of entitlement to extra love, comfort, and sympathy from the object world. Kris (1976) noted that demands for love, comfort, and feeding may be insatiable; persons who make such demands take without giving. In the exception, envy feeds a desire for vengeful punishment of the object world. The object, often identified with the self, is then punished by extracting payment for crimes against the self-righteous victim. What often appears as a complex combination of narcissistic demands and defenses to protect and restore narcissistic equilibrium and self-esteem coincides with inconsistent and poorly internalized standards and values in the entitled individual.

There are those who are more or less exceptional, with characteristics manifesting varying degrees of rarity or deviance from social and ethical rules and regulations. This relationship, however, is not isomorphic; the characterological concomitants of having exceptional characteristics occur on a spectrum according to the intensity or extremity of attitudes, behaviors, degree of consciousness of feeling exceptional, and degree of ego syntonicity of the exceptional status. These varying outcomes are related to familial and social responses to the deviance or deficiency.

Traits that seem to be ego- and superego-syntonic may not, in fact, imply a lack of conscious guilt. Freud's (1916) formulation to the contrary, some exceptions manifest unconscious guilt and a need for punishment (Jacobson, 1959; Moses, 1989). The unconscious need for punishment may be primary or allied with narcissistic omnipotence and entitlement. Entitlement may be associated with the projection of guilt and blame onto others or the reaction formation of humility and modesty. An individual may not be aware of regarding him-/herself as an exception, an unacknowledged privileged character. The lack of conscious shame or guilt may be associated with self-righteous and self-justified attitudes. Those who are above the rules often make their rules and try to impose them on others.

One of the most striking characteristics of exceptions noted by Freud is the apparent absence of conscious shame or guilt. Absolute conviction of privilege, tinged with infantile omnipotence, is evident in the characters of Richard III, Macbeth (Blum, 1986), and a patient described by Freud (1916), who believed "a special providence watched over him which would protect him" (p. 12). Richard III can, on the surface, intrigue and murder as he pleases. Having paid his dues in prior suffering, he can now freely inflict suffering with self-righteous pride. His self-righteousness has important narcissistic and structural considerations (Lax, 1975).

Patients who are exceptions often have a sense of righteous indignation and are determined to show the analyst the correct notions of wrong and right. They have been wronged and thus have the right to berate and belittle, criticize and condemn others for their real and fantasied faults. Justified because they feel that they have been wrongly mistreated, they attempt to extract apologies, compensations, even confessions from the analyst, parents, or others who have wronged them. Their own sense of defect may be handled by focussing on the shortcomings and defects in others; experts in faultfinding, they avoid or minimize self-criticism.

To the exceptions, parents are the repository of what is disavowed as unacceptable in their self- or love-object. The deformed child blames the parents, who themselves are full of guilt and self-blame for the child's deformity or deficiency. These attitudes are linked to the preliminary phase of superego development, to which the patient has regressed or remained fixated (A. Freud, 1965). Criticism has been internalized but is not yet self-directed in such a form that the child is able to acknowledge his/her own fault.

The exception has made a virtue out of adversity. Through projection and reversal, wrong becomes right, meriting reward rather than punishment. The privileged position defends against further narcissistic injuries and traumata. The exception may inflict castrating and belittling injury upon others to extract self-righteous punishment and revenge for any perceived injustice. Overcome by narcissistic rage when the satisfactions to which he feels entitled are thwarted (Rothstein, 1977), he may be shameless and remorseless about the infantile temper tantrums that may ensue. Some such patients fall into the category of "injustice collectors," those who remember every disappointment, which becomes a debt owed to them. These are debts that the patients ever expect to collect, although they may believe that their own debts should be readily forgiven and forgotten. Demanding and envious, the exceptions have little gratitude and little appreciation of the needs or distress of others.

A variety of counter-transferences tends to be elicited by these patients, including counter-transference to the transference of entitlement and privilege, to the patient's actual deformities or deficiencies, and to the patient's traumatic experience and narcissistic injuries.

Richard III is convinced that he is exempt from moral laws. At the same time, he is unconsciously guilty of violating oedipal prohibitions. Jacobson (1959) observed that Richard announced his goals brazenly: "For then I'll marry Warwick's youngest daughter. What though I killed her husband and her father, the readiest way to make the wench amends is to become her husband and her father" (Act I, Scene i). This is in contrast to Richard's moving monologue of self-accusation, which sealed his fate: "Oh coward conscience, how doest thou afflict me! . . ./Is there a murderer here?/No./Yes, I am:/ Then fly: what! from myself? Great reason why:/Lest I revenge. What! myself upon myself?/Alack! I love myself. . . . No: alas! I rather hate myself/For hateful deeds committed by myself. . . ./My conscience hath a thousand several tongues,/And every tongue brings in a several tale,/And every tale condemns me for a villain./. . . crying all, 'guilty! guilty!'/I shall despair. There is no creature loves me" (Act 5, Scene iii). What now needs to be clarified is that Shakespeare can be cited to support Richard III's lack of guilt as well as his guilt and need for punishment.

In Shakespeare, guilt is both latent and manifest, absent and present. Richard suffers from terrible nightmares, and he is driven to seek his own defeat and destruction. We may conclude that Richard is both guilty because of his criminal behavior and a criminal because of his unconscious guilt. It may also seem paradoxical that exceptions with congenital defects should appear to be shameless when they and their family have so often been ashamed of the defect. What is shameless in some individuals may, upon analysis, turn out to be re-action formation against the affect of shame or a pervasive attitude of feeling ashamed (Wurmser, 1981).

Freud placed the focus of Richard III's character as an exception on his apparent lack of guilt, Jacobson (1959) proposed that the cen-tral issue for Freud was Richard's refusal to accept the reality prin-ciple. She then further departed from Freud by suggesting that Richard III and the exceptions may be not guiltless but uncon-sciously guilty.

Jacobson (1959) traced Richard's inability to love women to his having been hated and despised by his own mother. But the parental reaction to the deformed or defective child and the child's reaction and reciprocal response to the parents, peers, and the social sur-round were not explored by either Jacobson or Freud. Considera-tions of structure and object relations take into account the child's actual experience with self-righteous or idealized parental authori-ties and his identification with real as well as fantasied distortions of the parents' attitudes. Both child and parent may feel that "the suf-fering I have been forced to experience" justifies his behavior with regard to the other. In fact, the poet had described the earliest distur-bance to the body ego and the primary object relationship. Richard was the product of a breech-birth after a very difficult labor. His back was deformed and so were his limbs. His teeth were already in place at birth, an oral-aggressive malformation. He also described Richard's mother's attitude: "Thou cam'st on earth to make the earth my hell./A grievous burden was thy birth to me,/techy and wayward was thy infancy" (Act iv, Scene 4). Unloved and unlovable, Richard was born to bite and to fight, ready to murder to achieve his self-serving goals. Shakespeare informs us that Richard III's oral aggression is no biting jest: "he could gnaw crust at two hours old" (Act ii, Scene 4). Richard would be able to bite his mother's nipples from birth! In-deed, the widow, Queen Margaret, forewarns, "Take heed of yonder dog!/Look when he fawns, he bites; and when he bites,/his venom tooth will rankle to the death" (Act i, Scene 3).

With escalating hate and rage across the succeeding phases of de-velopment, Richard becomes a barbaric criminal. He exemplifies the primitive narcissistic, sadistic personality in which self-love is alloyed with hate and self-hate. He is an exception, with aggression and sado-masochism dominating object relations (Friedman, 1998). Because of the failure of more mature forms of internalized parental authority and the internalization of parental rejection and rage, the benign regulatory functions of the superego are underdeveloped. Richard is shameless, without the restraining influence of conscious guilt. His conscience functions on the basis of the talion principle, with unintegrated, predominately persecutory and punitive superego precursors.

Neither the early analysts nor the poets clearly differentiated between the issues of narcissism and the issues of guilt. Moreover, some narcissistic personalities with ego-syntonic sadism, aggression, and antisocial behavior still have some empathy for others and at least vestigial capacities for guilt and remorse, while others are lacking in any significant moral considerations or judgments. There is a spectrum of narcissistic disorder from relatively benign to malignant (Kernberg, 1992). Narcissistic personalities who are ruthlessly parasitic and exploitative in some areas may have capacities for shame, guilt, and personal or group loyalties in other areas of life. Some forms of delinquent acting out with paranoid attitudes fall into this intermediate category. Megalomanic invincibility may co-exist in some exceptions with extreme vulnerability to narcissistic mortification. Such persons may be driven to attain power and position, to re-invent themselves in glorified rather than defective form. Fantasies of rebirth and restitution are common, and patients with developed capacities for sublimation may demonstrate remarkable achievement and creativity.

The narcissistic rage and revenge reactions of the exceptions such as Richard III (Kohut, 1972) are associated with intolerance for frustration and disappointment, an imperative need to remove any source of irritation or discomfort, and an omnipotent effort to eliminate any obstacle to gratification. The lack of empathy and of affect and impulse regulation in a serial killer like Richard III is a further sign of severe narcissistic disorder and the impaired primary narcissistic object relationship.

It follows that the attitude of entitlement is not isomorphic, either with considerations of narcissism or superego alone, but it is related to the complexities and vicissitudes of higher or lower levels of ego development and object relations. The more influential the role of conscious and unconscious guilt, rather than narcissism, the more likely it is that the attitudes of entitlement will be less intense and more restricted. Even where the entitlement appears to be ego-syn-tonic, it may yield when challenged. Some privileged characters may reluctantly relinquish their privileges when challenged, though they may then reassert these prerogatives or claim new ones. The interme-diate group of exceptions, who are not fixed in paranoid, addictive, and antisocial attitudes and behaviors, nevertheless often show pa-thological forms of narcissism. Patients with more neurotic forms of entitlement are capable of change, especially through psychoanaly-sis, whereas those with more primitive narcissistic forms of entitle-ment show little capacity to learn from experience or to change in analysis.

The fantasies and attitudes of the parents are critically important to the psychology of the exceptions. The parents often have fostered, fortified, or endorsed an attitude of entitlement in the child. The at-tempted denial of bodily reality and social reaction may be shared by parent and child. In one instance, the mother of a child with Down's Syndrome would eagerly display the child to other mothers while shopping, insisting that they join in her denial of any hurt, shame, or embarrassment. The other mothers were insistently expected to have pleasurable reactions and affirm the good looks of the congenitally defective child. Partially dependent upon the attitude of the parents, deformed children may want to do to others what was done to them or may have noble fantasies of being able to repair and restitute, to turn the ugly duckling into the beautiful princess or handsome prince. Damage control, strivings for revenge, and magical strivings for beauty and perfection may appear in the most varied forms, both subtle and overt.

One of the first questions asked by the typical mother after the birth of her child is whether the child is physiologically and physi-cally normal and intact. All parents react to their child's congenital defect as soon as it is recognized. Traumatic parental reactions to a severe defect or deformity long precede the child's ego develop-ment. The commonly experienced post-partum depression of such parents, however, tends to persist and to have a profound influence upon the child's psychological development. Rejecting or, con-versely, overprotective attitudes may be present from the outset. The child may be traumatized by parental impairments of empathy, affect exchange and regulation, and appropriate stimulation. Impairment of the primary object relationship may then occur, paving the way for later disturbances of development and pathogenic conflicts in the child. The physical defect is a concretizing reality to which the par-ents, child, and whole family have to adapt. The parents' fantasies also have a shaping influence upon the child's further development, as does their mourning for their child's limitations and for the normal child they did not have (Solnit & Stark, 1961). If parental depression and grief reactions persist, the child with the overt congenital anomaly remains at much greater risk for later serious psychopathology. The siblings identify with the defective child as well as with their parents' reactions.

It is well known that mothers of blind and deaf children are initially depressed and grief-stricken about their child's deficit. The mother of one child who was congenitally visually impaired regarded herself as an exception among mothers. Her nearly blind child had required special tutoring and companions and specially designed texts. There was profound concern that any worsening of the child's condition would lead to legal blindness if not actual total blindness. The mother had demanded and received special status for her child. The child was given extra care, sometimes almost to the point of protective custody. Since she could not see her foods, she was informed in advance of what food and beverage she was about to receive. One day, as a teenager, she was unknowingly served a dish at a café with a large crawling insect. After spitting and gagging on the half-chewed food, the teenager developed a psychosomatic gastrointestinal disorder. The mother then sued the food company, claiming that she, along with her child, had suffered enough and were entitled to compensation. While stating that any compensation would be used for the child's support and education, the mother also implied that she wanted punitive damages because of her daughter's condition and her apprehension about her daughter's future. They were entitled to special consideration, according to the mother, and any rules defining the grounds or limits of this type of lawsuit should not apply to her.

Actually, the mother was very guilty about her hostile ambivalence to her daughter, feeling that she had passed on defective genes. She felt that with better nurturance and medical care during her pregnancy, she might have ameliorated or prevented her daughter's congenital visual deficit. Her strong sense of entitlement was related to the displacement and projection of guilt and blame, which entitled her to the payment of reparations for her cumulative narcissistic injuries. Her daughter's sense of entitlement was related to the limitations and disappointments of her blindness but also to identification with the mother's attitudes and fantasies. The attitudes of this mother and daughter duo, who demanded justice to redress their sense of injustice, did not extend to other relationships or to global aspects of life. This mother may have transmitted messages of martyr-dom to her daughter, but there was no apparent glorification of suf-fering or sacrifice. She wanted the justice system to give her a most deserved award, as the good mother, and to punish the food com-pany, the bad mother. Despite surface similarities, while narcissistic issues are relevant to both situations, the problems of long-suffering parents of children traumatized by congenital defects are very differ-ent from those of parents with children who have exceptional gifts.

Jacobson's (1959) amalgamation of exceptionally gifted children with Freud's exceptions" overgeneralized and distorted the original concept. Jacobson gives an example of a girl of exceptional beauty who was overgratified and overindulged and felt herself in later life to be irresistible. On the other hand, an exceptionally beautiful girl may feel exploited if she feels unappreciated as a person, loved only for her superficial looks, or is treated as a sex object. A gifted child, such as a Mozart, may be exploited and used for the parents' narcis-sistic, exhibitionistic gratification. Actually, any child may be used for the parents' narcissistic gratification and compensation for narcissis-tic injuries. Freud (1914, p. 91) stated, "If we look at the attitude of affectionate parents towards their children, we have to recognize that it is a revival and reproduction of ther own narcissism. . . . They are inclined to . . . renew on his [the child's] behalf the claims to privi-leges which were long ago given up by themselves. The child shall have a better time than his parents; he shall not be subject to the ne-cessities which they have recognized as paramount in life. Illness, death, renunciation of enjoyment, restrictions on his own will, shall not touch him; the laws of nature and of society shall be abrogated in his favor; he shall once more really be the centre and core of cre-ation—'His Majesty the Baby'."

Excessive parental narcissistic investment in the child can lead to overindulgence, spoiling, and entitlement. Parental overindulgence may take such forms as waiting on the child hand and foot or shower-ing the child with material gifts instead of object love. However, such "spoiled" children are not truly exceptions, though they act and are treated as entitled and privileged characters.

The developmental disturbances of the gifted child are not compa-rable to the vulnerabilities of the child with a congenital defect. The enormous narcissistic wounds to the defective child and his/her par-ents are not comparable to the narcissistic gratification of the par-ents of the child with exceptional gifts. It is true that in highly favorable cases, creative solutions may be found, and the defective child is spurred to great adult achievement and sublimation. But the traumatization may never quite heal in the parents or the child.

While the original concept of the "exception" was tied to suffering as a result of congenital or very early defect, it has been expanded, often without regard for the differences as well as the similarities. The term "exception" is now used to encompass later severe trauma or developmental disturbance, especially with unexpected survival, surprising recovery, or irreversible damage. Thus the concept has lost its original reference to physical deformity or deficiency in infancy as the source of character deformity. When the narcissistic wounds and traumas occur in later life there is a different developmental course and outcome. For example, the survivors of disasters in which their families have died share some of the characteristics of the exceptions. Earlier fantasies and realities connected with exceptional status may be revived, and some survivors feel that they are not bound by the usual rules. Their just demands for restitution and reparation have to be differentiated from irrational or unjust feelings of entitlement.

Special aspects of life experience have contributed to the status and problems of the individuals characterized as exceptional in Freud's (1916) paper. The deformed and disabled, such as Richard III, elicit and respond to social pressures, prejudice, and stigma, as do their parents and siblings (Blum, 1999). The peers of a deformed child may not be sympathetic or compassionate; they may respond to his misfortune with embarrassment, alienation, ridicule, or rejection. Feeling defective, the deformed child may develop protective or defiant attitudes, may identify with others who are disadvantaged, etc. He may feel uncomfortable with the discomfort, demanded distance, sympathy, or pity of others. He may become self-conscious and join a support group; a blind girl, for example, might prefer socializing with blind peers to possible rejection by the sighted. The social as well as the cultural issues are overlooked or understated in the earlier psychoanalytic literature. Distress and narcissistic injury are not limited to childhood, but may appear through life and may thus influence the social adaptation of the deformed or disfigured exception.

Peripheral to the concepts of the individual exception is the parallel significance of psychosocial process. Some individuals who considered themselves a exceptions were identified with leaders and groups who were regarded as exceptions. The group narcissistic entitlement may incite antisocial reactions, especially if it is associated with splitting and the projection of aggression and denigration outside the group. Thus the Nazis were an aggrandized group, an exceptional master race, with an idealized ideology: overthrowing civilized standards, and injunctions. They were exceptions and made their own rules. They could destroy split-off, despised, and devalued groups, such as the Jews. In a split paranoid system of all-good and all-bad narcissistic objects, both aggressor and victim were regarded as exceptions to civilized rules (Blum, 1998). Dehumanized and demonized, the victims were exceptions, exempt from human consideration, subject to the new rule of genocide. Some survivors were exceptions also through identification with the unlimited entitlement and aggression of the aggressor.

The exceptions arising from later-life experience, as well as from familial and social processes represent expansion and extension of the original concept. There are now additional meanings based on models other than that of infantile bodily deformity. I particularly distinguished the dimensions of narcissism and of guilt in the formation and deformation of the character of the exception. The character of the exception is in degree rife with guilt, shame, and defenses against these affects. The exceptions also manifest humiliation, envy and rage, and compensatory demands for repair, restitution, and revenge for their narcissistic mortification. The exception is a compromise formation, often undeserving while entitled, self-punitive while omnipotently privileged. As Freud inferred, there is something of the exception in all of us, a bid for privileged position and special entitlement. Feeling like an exception, however, does not necessarily imply the intrapsychic conflicts, character structure, or experience of those described by Freud or in this paper. The exceptions have had a rather exceptional influence upon society, culture, and psychoanalysis.

BIBLIOGRAPHY

BLUM, H. (1998). The expulsion of psychoanalysis and the return of the suppressed (in press, Germany).

——— (1999). The Legacy of the dead and defective sibling. In Press, Analytic Press.

FREUD, A. (1965). *Normality and Pathology.* New York: International Universities Press.

FREUD, S. (1914). On narcissism. *S.E.,* 14.

——— (1916). Some character-types met within psychoanalytic work. *S.E.,* 14.

—— (1916). Mourning and melancholia. *S.E.*, 14.

FRIEDMAN, L. (1988). The exceptions revisited (in press).

JACOBSON, E. (1959). The "exceptions": an elaboration of Freud's character study. *Psychoanalytic Study of the Child*, 14:135–154.

KERNBERG, O. (1992). *Aggression in Personality Disorder and Perversions*. New Haven: Yale University Press.

KOHUT, H. (1972). Thoughts on narcissism and narcissistic rage. *Psychoanalytic Study of the Child*, 27:360–400.

KRIS, A. (1976). On wanting too much: the "exceptions" revisited. *International Journal of Psycho-analysis*, 57:89–95.

MOSES, R. (1989). Shame and entitlement: their relation to political process. In: *The Psychoanalytic Core, Essays in Honor of Leo Rangell*, eds. H. Blum, E. Weinshel, and F. Rodman. New York: International Universities Press, pp. 483–498.

LAX, R. (1975). Some comments on the narcissistic aspects of self-righteousness. *International Journal of Psycho-analysis*, 56:283–292.

MURRAY, J. (1964). Narcissism and the ego ideal. *Journal of the American Psychoanalytic Association*, 12:477–511.

NIEDERLAND, W. (1965). Narcississtic ego impairment in patients with early physical malformation. *Psychoanalytic Study of the Child*, 20:518–534.

ROTHSTEIN, A. (1977). The ego attitude of entitlement, *International Review of Psycho-analysis*, 4:409–417.

SHAKESPEARE, W. (1985). Richard III. *The Complete Works of William Shakespeare*. Minneapolis: Amaranth Press, pp. 575–611.

SOLNIT, A., & STARKE, M. (1961). Mourning and the birth of a defective child. *Psychoanalytic Study of the Child*, 16:523–537.

The Twin Poles of Order and Chaos

Development as a Dynamic, Self-ordering System

LINDA C. MAYES, M.D.

The diversity of theories regarding children's development is commensurate with the enormity of the task of seeking ordering designs for explaining behavioral and psychic ontogeny in infants, children, and adults. The purpose of this paper is to look at these developmental theories as epigenetic stages themselves. I shall suggest that the next stage in the epigenesis of theories of development is to see variability and disorder on a continuum with order and stability, as a constant dialectic that moves development along, whether at the level of the cell or at the level of fantasy. I shall explore four questions that are implicitly about development as an ordering process and about theories of development as methods for bringing order to what is an inherently messy, even chaotic. The first two questions—what does it mean to take a developmental perspective, and what does any theory of development need to

Arnold Gesell Associate Professor of Child Psychiatry, Pediatrics, and Psychology in the Yale Child Study Center; Faculty in the Western New England Institute for Psychoanalysis

A shorter version of this paper presented to the New York Psychoanalytic Association on November 9, 1999 on the occasion of the 1999 Heinz Hartmann Award and to the Philadelphia Psychoanalytic Society on November 17, 1999.

The author gratefully acknowledges the very productive discussions with and careful reading and suggestions for this manuscript offered by my New Haven colleagues, Drs. David Carlson, Donald Cohen, Wayne Downey, James Leckman, and Paul Schwaber, and also by Drs. Leroy Byerly and Theodore Fallon of Philadelphia.

The Psychoanalytic Study of the Child 56, ed. Albert J. Solnit, Peter B. Neubauer, Samuel Abrams, and A. Scott Dowling (Yale University Press, copyright © 2001 by Albert J. Solnit, Peter B. Neubauer, Samuel Abrams, and A. Scott Dowling).

explain—set the stage for the consideration of some different perspectives for thinking about development. These other perspectives, borrowed from general systems theory, focus on the interplay of order-stability and variability-instability in psychological development. The third question, asks what does a more detailed consideration of the variability or noise in development add to our current developmental perspectives? Exploring dynamic systems and self-ordering processes will lead to several fields not explicitly clinical, psychological, or even psychoanalytic, but I shall circle back to apply these ideas to psychoanalytic perspectives on development, change, and adaptation in the fourth and concluding question. What can these cross-disciplinary attitudes offer to the psychoanalytic developmental perspective, whether in the form of our theories or our work with patients?

IN "REFLECTIONS ON THE REVOLUTION IN FRANCE", EDMUND BURKE commented "good order is the foundation of all good things" (1973 [1790], p. 262). His reflection went beyond the social and political turbulence of the late eighteenth century to an enduring human trait. Wherever we find mystery, uncertainty, chaos, or upheaval, we search for order, stability, and meaning. Seeking order is a very human endeavor toward which we seem inevitably compelled. Our ancestors sought a stable order in the celestial constellations that guided second millennial sailors across the Atlantic and will continue to guide our descendants in the fourth millenium even on similar ocean paths. We count on the timely rhythm of the tides, try to find patterns in the weather, seek meaning in tragedy, look to historical precedent, and carefully study the ups and downs of the stock market. Implicit in our search for order is an effort to find overarching designs that go beyond the individual person or event so as to reduce uncertainty and enhance our ability to predict, thereby introducing more stability and order into our world. We have looked for our designs in deities, perfect forms, fate, destiny, evolution, genes, our parents, and even the absence of any design. The wish for order and a stable design is often so strong that we see variability or disorder as a threat and whenever possible look through the disorder to find the faintest glimpse of a predicted, stable orderliness. Even revolutions, however anarchic at the time, take on meaning and purpose in the retelling. Indeed, we may tolerate disorder only if we understand it as a reflection on our imperfect institutions, theories, predictions, methods, or measurements—in short, on our fallible nature—and not on a fallible reliance on order by design.

Perhaps nowhere is the search for order and stability clearer than in the study of human behavior. For nearly as long as recorded history, bour own behavior has caused us more confusion and more trouble than perhaps any other natural phenomenon—and we have recorded that confusion in stories, poetry, music, drawing, painting, and sculpting. The most epic human tragedy is all too often the story of caliginous confusion and order lost. The most commonplace story of love unrequited presents the same—the world gone absurdly mad even if the world is at that moment only two, three, or four persons. It is of course far too simplistic to characterize psychoanalysis as the study of everyday human disorder and instability. But in the light of our current concern, this was exactly what captured Freud's creativity: how to explain seemingly irrational behavior on the surface by conceiving of a hidden order within the mind. To be sure, the psychoanalytic version of order by design has evolved from a topographic or structural model to include a number of other design possibilities—object relations, intersubjectivity, ego psychology—but the message is the same. However disordered and unpredictable our behavior is, within the construction of our individual minds there is an explanatory order. The special creative quirk of the psychoanalytic version of an ordered mind is an inherently chaotic unconscious that seems not to follow the usual orderly rules of time and space but nonetheless brings an individual order, even driven repetitiveness, to manifest behavior and day-to-day living.[1]

What psychoanalysis also introduced to the ordered study of behavior was a schema of development—behavior explained, at least in part, by the residua of childhood memories and behavior built up in stages based on successive childhood experiences and needs. Understanding the behavior of children is a special endeavor in the search for orderly designs, and studies of child development are a special category within this search. The psychoanalytic developmental schema—indeed, any idea of something emerging from an earlier condition or form—was not possible until an evolutionary perspective challenged a creationist one. Evolutionary theory itself was one approach to introducing some explanatory order into seemingly infinite within- and across-species diversity. Taxonomic schemas only

---

1. We might stretch the metaphor a bit further to suggest that one goal of psychoanalysis is to accept disorder as inevitable—conflict shall always be with us—while at the same time understanding that every bit of chaos has its hidden order and expectability. Stretched to this point, at least metaphorically, this is a very contemporary idea—order within chaos rather than chaos as the inevitable dissolution and outer bounds of order. See, for example, Prigogine and Stengers, 1984, and Sardar and Abrams, 1998.

recorded the diversity and surely introduced a kind of bibliographic order, but they did not offer an explanation of a design plan within the diversity. Evolution changed that by introducing the related notions of ontogeny and epigenesis—one form evolving into a newer, more adapted one. Darwin's insights, so attractive and at the same time so abhorrent to some of his contemporaries, made it possible to recognize developmental processes as an ordering perspective on the study of behavior. Like biology, behavior unfolded, and Freud embraced the metaphor for his own ordered perspective on the ontogeny of the mind from childhood into adulthood.

Since the late nineteenth century, studies of children's development have flourished, and a number of theories of developmental progression have moved across the stage, some staying in the center, others lingering only briefly before passing out of view.[2] Some have focused on specific areas of development such as psychosexual stages, language, motor, or cognitive functions. Others have been more integrative, proposing grander overarching developmental mechanisms based in genes and biology, experience, family, culture, or interactive combinations of all of these. Some have been primarily taxonomic—what to expect when—and others have embedded causality within their taxonomies. Piaget's assimilation and accommodation processes are examples of causal devices embedded within the stages of cognitive development. This century's developmental theories have drawn on a number of disciplines—biology, psychology, pediatrics, education, ethology, anthropology, and psychoanalysis. Within psychoanalysis, there are several developmental theories, some more obviously epigenetic than others—that is, suggesting a progressive unfolding and ordering. The diversity of developmental theories is commensurate with the enormity of the task of finding ordering designs to explain and predict behavioral ontogeny in infants, children, and adults.

My purpose here is not to review or compare the major theories of child development (for such a review, see, e.g., Horowitz, 1987; Miller, 1989). Rather, it is to look at theories of children's develop-

---

2. This statement is a bit of a historical oversimplification. Ideas that children actually developed from simple to more complex abilities and that psychological capacities emerged over time were in the air as early as the late eighteenth century. Over two hundred years ago, Tiedemann published observations of his son from birth through his second birthday (Horowitz, 1987). Like all ideas that dramatically shift perspectives and paradigms, early ideas of ontogeny and epigenesis were taking shape by the early 1800s in biology and related fields.

ment as epigenetic stages in themselves and to ask what might be the next stages or central questions for developmental theories to address. What does our focus on development as an ordering process, as one of progressively refined, complex, well-defined, and stable capacities and functions emerging from a more undifferentiated state, leave unanswered? How do we understand individual differences and the inherent unpredictability of developmental processes—in short, the chaos and disorder embedded within ordered patterns? I shall suggest that the next stage in the epigenesis of theories of development may be to see variability and disorder not as a primitive, undifferentiated state, as threatening or unexplained noise, as regression, or as impending dissolution. Rather, I shall suggest that order and disorder[3] are essential twin poles in any developmental process, a constant dialectic that moves development along whether at the level of the cell or at the level of fantasy.

I shall explore four questions that are implicitly about development as an ordering process and about theories of development as methods for bringing order to what is inherently messy, even chaotic. The first two questions—what does it mean to take a developmental perspective, and what does any theory of development need to explain—set the stage for the consideration of some different perspectives for thinking about development. These other perspectives, borrowed from general systems theory and studies of so-called chaos, require us to shift our primary focus from emerging order to the interplay between order-stability and variability-instability in psychological development. In other words, inherent instability, or variability, shares the psychological developmental stage with progressive order and stability. The third question asks, what does a more detailed consideration of the variability or noise in development add to our current developmental perspectives? In exploring this question, I will consider three related ideas: complex dynamic, self-ordering systems, attractor states, and chaos, disorder, or variability as essential characteristics of healthy developmental systems. Our challenge will be to adapt these ideas to studies of psychological development in a

---

3. I need to make explicit what I mean by disorder when applied to development and behavior for the very word itself generates a host of associations and meanings that are surely laden by our inherent reactions to instability and disorderliness. Throughout this paper, I shall use the term "disorder" in two related ways—to indicate variability that is not expected or explained by a particular theoretical perspective and deviation from a norm or average way of behaving, thinking, or perceiving believed to be appropriate for a given age.

way that is more than attractively metaphorical. Exploring dynamic systems, attractor states, and self-ordering processes will take us into several fields that are not explicitly clinical, psychological, or even psychoanalytic but I shall apply these ideas to psychoanalytic perspectives on development, change, and adaptation in the fourth and concluding question. What can these cross-disciplinary attitudes offer to our psychoanalytic developmental perspective, in the form of our theories or in our work with patients?

One caution is in order. Throughout I will explicitly and implicitly move between the physical and the mental, between biology, the body, and psychology (and even between inanimate and animate form). This reflects an underlying conviction that the emergence of mental life is continuous with the elaboration of organic form and function, a conviction shared by many developmentalists and contemporary psychologists, neuroscientists, biologists, and psychoanalysts. At worst, it is an optimistic (and naïve) phrasing of the classical mind-brain, mind-body dualism. At best, it helps us think more universally and broadly about mechanisms of change that cut across specific domains of psychological or physical development. At least originally, psychoanalysis was rooted in this conviction. But it is a not necessarily a secure position. We must navigate between the scylla and charybdis of a false assumption of logical causality and reductionism, or overly simplifying metaphor. On the one hand, we may all too easily fall into the trap of implying that beneath every emotion, thought, fantasy, every developmental transformation in thinking and feeling, is a logically causal neural activation and transformation of an identifiable region of the brain. If only our methods were more sophisticated, we could identify that causal link in specific anatomic and functional detail—and our work as developmentalists would be neatly done. That is the fallacy on one side—an oversimplification of both brain and mind and a blinding search for simple causality. On the other hand, the language of the synapse and the language of unconscious fantasy are surely very different, and both are very complex. To equate the two in metaphor, however manifestly or phenomenologically congruent, runs the risk of requiring such oversimplification and confusion of language and models as to make the metaphor useless and uninformed by data. Thus, in proposing to present an account of complex, self-ordering developmental systems and in linking the mental and the physical, I shall try only to suggest that the general principles of change in one domain may be usefully applied in the other. I do not imply causality, nor do I imply a convergence of language between the mental and the physical.

THINKING DEVELOPMENTALLY: WHAT DEVELOPMENTAL THEORIES NEED TO EXPLAIN

What does it mean to think developmentally, whether in the consulting room, emergency room, courtroom, classroom, playroom, or delivery room? A mental health professional about to begin training to work with children remarked that she felt a need to understand development because of her work with troubled adolescents and young adults. She had a sense that the lively or deadened personalities, fixed or unstable characters, and muted or turbulent lives of her adolescent and adult patients had a discoverable and understandable etiology in their developmental past, their childhood. Hence, it seemed logical and necessary to understand children and to look at those processes that led up to a sadly entrenched adulthood. That the individual presenting this perspective was not yet aware of thinking developmentally does not mean that her portrayal of what it means to take a developmental attitude was unusual or even inaccurate. On the contrary, this young trainee's interest and understanding may represent the most commonly (and deeply) held idea of what it means to think developmentally. Her perspective implies development as historical past, written like the rings of a tree into our psychic structures and behavior, development as fate, development as blueprint (albeit shaped by experience), and development as limited to childhood and early adolescence, with little opportunity for later revision (or redemption). Such a perspective also implies that, like pictures on the walls of a cave, early developmental processes leave their indelible mark, and if we know enough or are smart enough we can figure out the clues—the developmentalist as detective. And, of course, it implies that understanding development promises to bring some order to the confusions of adult behavior and that development is, in and of itself, ultimately an ordering perspective, whether by virtue of experience, genes, or both. This is, incidentally, a point of view common not only to our trainees but also to our patients (and ourselves; Mayes, 1999).

Obscured by assumed meaning, the question what does it mean to think developmentally may at first seem trivial, especially given our baptism and conversion by evolution (and progressivism).[4] Thinking

4. It is worth noting that, like evolution and natural selection, development was (and is) quickly incorporated into social, economic, even political institutions and expectations (see Kessen, 1990). Indeed, evolution, development, and progressivism are a secular trinity for the late nineteenth and twentieth centuries. To evolve and develop is to embrace progress. To regress is to retreat. To be delayed is to be shamed,

developmentally means that something or someone grows and expands, changes, learns, matures, emerges—bigger and better. Naively stated, it means that as adults, we are not the same biologically or psychologically as when we were children. Surely, we all think we know what we mean when we use such phrases as "he will grow out of it," "she behaves just like a child," "he regressed to earlier modes of ego functioning," or "a primitively organized set of defenses." These are developmental phrases inasmuch as they imply that something less organized has emerged into something more organized or at least better—that is, a newer form emerges from an earlier one. They are also classically developmental in a value sense—earlier forms are less ordered, more primitive, more chaotic, and less adapted. But there are some important distinctions to make between development and growth, development and maturation, and development as improvement and increasing order. Making these distinctions forces us to hone in more precisely on what I will label a developmental process as opposed to often concomitant processes of growth, maturation, and increasing order and stability. Parenthetically (and paradoxically), each of these distinctions among development, growth, maturation, and increasing order and stability is best observed in situations of enhanced vulnerability or risk—children abused, neglected, orphaned, or with severe perinatal or genetic insults. In these instances, the fault lines between the concepts or processes are laid open and are thus made clearer.

Development is not synonymous with growth. To grow is to increase in size but not necessarily to change in function or form. Children gain height through gain in bone length—the essential structure and metabolic processes of the long bones do not change (though there are changes in the rate of metabolism and turnover of bone cells). Similarly, weight gain and a differential distribution of body fat occur with growth. This development need not involve new form or function—fat cells continue to act as metabolic warehouses from infancy through old age. Furthermore, gain in either height or weight is not necessarily reflective of any change in function, cognitive, motoric, or otherwise.[5] Psychologically, the simple accumula-

---

outside the mainstream. The "cultural internalization" of ideas as broad as evolution or development and their linkage with the "cultural ideal" of progress are probably inevitable—or at least understandable. But that trinity very often distorts, even disfigures, the idea of development beyond recognizable utility. At such points, it becomes important to reclaim and refigure the idea of development, to evolve another form.

5. Perhaps nowhere is the disjunction between development and growth more apparent than in instances of severe mental retardation in which children may grow physically but not psychologically (at least at the same rate).

tion of information about the world—the growth of accrued experience—also does not necessarily involve a change in function or even in the form of how information is best accumulated. Learning in its simplest form, the increase in stored information, can occur without any change in the way information is evaluated, processed, associated, or retrieved.

Of course, growth may be, and usually is, coincident with development. As children gain in height and weight and as their center of gravity changes (Thelen, 1984), they must make adaptive changes in the way they move their bodies (part of the psychological notion of "body in space"). New forms of movement emerge that in turn facilitate new modes of social interaction and new abilities to explore and learn. Thus one new form engenders new functions in other areas as well. Similarly, as children learn more information, they may develop new strategies for organizing that information (new ordering schemas) that facilitate remembering and retrieving. Again, a new form emerges coincident with an increase—in this case, in accumulated knowledge. In other words, normally, processes of growth and emerging new functions are often so closely associated that we naturally confuse the two and use the concepts interchangeably. If all goes well, children do develop as they grow, and we expect this. For example, we remind our older children they are "grown up," meaning that they should behave differently and have a totally different set of psychological needs. Or we often refer to growth in the course of a therapeutic relationship to imply a reordering of the patient's familiar object-related templates or defensive structures and responses. Surely also, we may see psychological change and growth literally associated in children. For example, children in considerable psychological distress often stop growing. If and when their distress is lifted, whether by their adaptations, their family's interventions, or psychological assistance from another adult, their linear growth often resumes. New psychological organizations and adaptations bring growth back on-line. Nonetheless, in its most concrete sense, growth does not necessarily indicate emerging new form or function in our children or our patients.

Similarly, development is also not necessarily coincident with maturation although again the two processes often occur simultaneously and developmental events are usually dependent upon successful maturational processes. Most basically, maturation implies increasing refinement of an existing function. Things simply get better and more efficient. For example, commonly in newborns, some hepatic enzyme systems, while functional at birth, do not function at full efficiency but are induced by exposure to certain metabolic products.

The enzymatic system matures through the effects of feedback, supply and demand, but it does not change its essential mode of functioning—it is just more widely available and thus able to handle the increased metabolic needs of the maturing infant.[6] A classic example of the codependence of maturation and development is the appearance of a social smile. In this case, the neuromotor mechanisms for smiling mature at a given rate, and non-social smiling appears in infants on a relatively fixed timetable. But if the smile is not met socially in repeated interactions with caring adults, it disappears as a social behavior. Maturation occurs but the adaptation of a matured motor behavior to a new use and function—the developmental event—does not occur. Psychologically, we might also see internalization as a maturational process and the reworking and integration of those internalized interactions and relationships into parts of the self as the essence of a developmental process. In a sense, maturational processes prepare the way for developmental reorganizations and integration across different functional domains—and one cannot think developmentally without understanding maturation. If the proper biological or psychological substrate is not adequately matured or available, then concomitant developmental events may not be possible or may be compromised. Of course again, if all goes well, maturational and developmental processes are seamlessly interwoven—where one begins and the other ends is not so evident or even so useful to distinguish.

This differentiation between growth or maturation and development prepares the way for an examination of development as increasing order and stability. I define a developmental process as one that involves new functions or forms emerging through change in an old function or through the reorganization of different functions into a new integrated unit or ability. Single sounds come together as words, words come together as sentences; physical feelings of discomfort—hunger, cold, fatigue—gain word and experiential representations as emotional states. This implies that growth is a change in size and maturation is a process of improving efficiency in a function that does not itself necessarily acquire other new characteristics or cause change in any other domain. The function gets better with age, but of course this begs the question of how that efficiency, that matura-

6. Of course, this difference in efficiency is not a trivial fact, and many an error or miscalculation in drug dosage or attribution of understanding is made by not recognizing that young, immature systems do not function at the same level as mature or adult systems. Again, in a popular sense, just understanding these kinds of differences in functional efficiency is "thinking developmentally."

tion (or growth), is really achieved. For example, when one becomes a faster typist over time, is this simply the learned effect of practice? Or has there been reorganization at a neural level that permits a more automatic, newer form of connection between the motor action of striking the keyboard and the association between thoughts or words written in script?[7] Viewed from afar, some processes such as the neuromaturation of facial muscles into the pattern of a smile seem ordered and on a fixed, relatively non-perturbable timetable, like a program running its course. However, viewed up close, there may be much reorganization of muscle groups into different patterns of coordinated movement that make up smiling. Similarly, viewed from afar, independent locomotion seems one of those maturational events that occur relatively consistently and within a fairly narrow chronological time band. But, again, there is much neural and muscular reorganization that must happen before walking independently is possible and even then, in the first months, the ability to step in walking motions or even walk with support is easily altered by different social and caring contexts. When viewed up close, what we take to be a simple maturational event is a complex layering of emerging new form and function. And the more closely we look, the more blur these distinctions among maturation, growth, and developmental processes blur.

This blurring depending on where we place our observational lens is the essence of seeing developmental processes as increasing order and stability versus as chaotic, messy, and more probabilistic. It is surely true that for most developmental processes whether at the biological or psychological level, there is a remarkable global regularity. Surely, when looked at from afar, development is progressive or directional, linear inasmuch as one gain usually follows another, and quantifiable inasmuch as it is incremental. Progressive order is the name of the game. Walking, language, even abilities for symbolization and imagination emerge on more or less uniform timetables and in more or less uniform patterns for children even across differ-

---

7. Self-organization or new forms of typing abilities on a global scale may also be seen in the design of the typewriter. In 1873, an engineer named Christopher Scholes designed a typewriter keyboard with the familiar QWERTY layout which was intentionally inefficient. If a typist on a standard typewriter moved too fast, the keys jammed. The QWERTY layout slowed the typist down sufficiently to diminish this possibility. However, when this particular layout was mass-produced and typists across the world began to use it, their efficiency improved, other companies imitated the same keyboard layout, and soon this intentionally inefficient typewriter became the standard that typists used with great efficiency (example from Waldrop, 1992).

ent cultures. There are on average diminishing degrees of freedom with development. That is, as simple functions become more complex, there is less room for change and/or recovery. So compelling are the collective observations of development as regular, coherent, and expectable across individuals that many theories of development present progressions as nearly clean, or at least predictable, phase shifts from one stage to another as if one set of skills or abilities regularly replaces another over a window of time.[8]

But surely development is also the opposite of all of these characteristics when looked at closely in our laboratories and in our patients. Progressions are preceded or followed by regressions,[9] one area of ability may far outstrip another, increments are blurred, and order is lost in considerable variation within and between individuals. When studied at close range, what looks from a distance like an orchestrated, cohesive, even predictable process from a distance takes on a more exploratory, opportunistic, and function-driven character. In short, development is both minimally messy and maximally chaotic.

An example from studies of children's understanding of numerical concepts illustrates these different, though complementary perspectives—development as ordered and moving toward parsimonious complexity versus development as increasingly flexible and moving toward more options, greater variability. Considering children's understanding of concepts of addition, several cognitive psychologists have proposed an ordered progression beginning with counting from one, moving to counting up from the largest of the numbers, and so on until the child reaches the more or less adult strategy of relying on retrieval from memory (e.g., Ashcraft, 1987). These different strategies are typical of specific age ranges from preschool to pre-adolescent children. (This stair-step representation of developmental progression is applicable to any number of areas, including social and psychosexual development [Case, 1992].) When studied at close range, however, children rely on all of these addition strategies depending on the type of task as well as on their age (Siegler, 1996). While their reliance on one strategy over another

8. Psychoanalysis offered one of the earliest and most elaborate stage-based theories of development, but there are of course many others, dealing with cognition, language, motor skills, and social development.

9. Indeed, it is not uncommon for children learning a new skill to lose temporarily gains in other domains. Thus, recently gained motor skills may seem to be lost as new language skills came on-line. At least, gains in one area may be paralleled by the temporary slowing of gains in other domains.

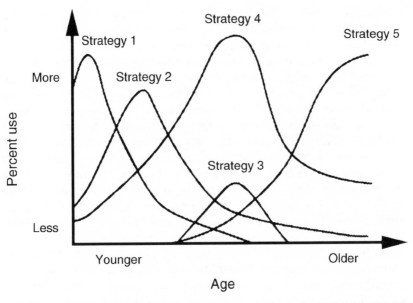

Figure 1. From *Emerging Minds: The Process of Change in Children's Thinking* (p. 89) by Robert S. Siegler. Copyright 1996 by Oxford University Press, Inc. Used by permission of Oxford University Press, Inc.

does change with age, they may readily fall back on so-called early strategies given a change in the task setting or demand. Indeed, when we look at the choice of strategy by age, an increasing flexibility or variability in choices as more strategies become available seems more apparent than the replacement of one "more advanced strategy" by another (graphically illustrated in figure 1).

Similar cases can be made for other aspects of children's cognitive development and for their understanding of social meaning. While it is generally true that there is an ordered progression in children's ability to understand certain concepts and in the ways they approach learning, it seems equally true that one strategy or level of understanding does not supplant an earlier one but that all remain in the repertoire. In a sense, greater flexibility and choice—or more variable strategies—are just as much features of development as are increasing stability and order and diminishing degrees of freedom. While one strategy or level of understanding may be relied upon more often during a particular phase of development, other strategies remain in place and available.

How to reconcile these different perspectives—increasing order versus increasing flexibility and options? These are complementary perspectives—twin poles of developmental processes. Traditionally, most perspectives on child and adult development have asked when certain developmental stages or capacities are most evident (Omaya, 1985). When do children on average walk independently, when does a child understand the difference between pretense and reality, when do children understand consequences and experience conflict and guilt? Hand in hand with "when" questions are those asking about orderly sequences—what comes before and after. What are the apparent preconditions for language and communication, what are the sequences of independent walking or a fully mature grasp, what are the phases of individuation and separation, what precedes a capacity for symbolization or, later, for abstract thinking? Asking about developmental sequencing and patterning focuses on average performance and on prediction and thus highlights stability and consistency in performance. It orients us clinically, behaviorally, educationally, and predictively. But these perspectives on developmental sequencing do not address the question of how new forms and functions appear—what moves children from one average stage to another. Is development a process of moving from one essentially stable phase to another with only brief, unstable, transition phases, or is the process of change more fluid and more variable? One perspective permits us to see the landscape on average while the other permits us to get closer to some essential questions about how novel forms and functions emerge.

Focusing on the appearance of new functions not as an average but as an individual process draws our attention to the process of change as well as the product of change—to the variability and flexibility as well as order in developmental change. By emphasizing the variability in developmental progressions, we begin to ask questions about what conditions and contexts favor the use of one strategy (or one defense, fantasy, ego capacity, internalized object) over another. We also can begin to look at interactions among domains of development. How does change in one domain reshape or reorder strategies or choices in another? For instance, how does the ability to walk independently reorder an infant's repertoire of social cues? What social experiences increase in attractiveness, salience, or importance with the reorganization of independent locomotion? Also, by focusing on how rather than when, we shift our emphasis from explanation and prediction to likelihood, probability, and multiple possible outcomes and pathways.

Thus, thinking developmentally implies not just mapping the emergence and maturation of function, nor does it imply only understanding average stages either pre- or postdictively. I mean it to indicate especially the dynamic evolution of new forms, functions, and adaptations that are the hybrids and reorganizations of old forms and functions put to new use.[10] It means understanding that change in one domain influences change across many other domains and that our theoretical separation into individual domains, while conveniently orienting, often obscures complexity and novel combinations. Thinking developmentally also means focusing on questions of how change occurs, on variability as much as stability, and on a dynamic, dialectic process as much as a progressively emerging, ordered one.

What a theory of development needs to take into account is, first, the origins of novelty in any developmental progression (see also Thelen and Smith, 1994). Novelty occurs in any individual's adaptation to a given set of life circumstances, and novelty occurs from the level of cellular metabolism and gene expression to individually unique mental representations of a bodily experience. Traditionally, theories of development do not easily account for novel psychological or biological adaptations.[11] The second requisite of a developmental theory is to reconcile global or average regularities and patterns with local variability and sensitivity to environmental context. In other words, a robust developmental theory needs to allow for stability and instability side by side. Thirdly, the theory should allow us to integrate developmental data at many levels of explanation. We should be able to integrate psychological perspectives on the impact of early trauma with those examining the emergence of arousal systems in the brain or the emergence of a cognitive capacity for symbolic representation with the elaboration of a fantasy life that influences perception, thought, and social relationships. Fourthly, we should be able to account for how local processes or adaptations can

10. The creation of new form and function is not limited to childhood. It may occur throughout life, as with the learning of a new language or a musical instrument in adulthood. Each of us struggling to learn a new skill as an adult has had the experience of painfully plodding progress initially, followed gradually by increasing proficiency and then by a sense of automaticity. Actions or thoughts initially taken in slow, conscious steps are smoothly integrated into a seamless whole that occurs nearly without conscious vigilance—a new skill has developed.

11. Wolff (1987, p. 240) has suggested that "the induction of novel behavioral forms may be the single most important unresolved problem for all the developmental and cognitive sciences."

lead to more global outcomes. For example, how does a child's local, moment to moment response to a parent's unremitting depression contribute to an enduring and pervasive character and defensive structure in adulthood? Once again, understanding 'how' is far different from simply recognizing an association between an early condition and, for example, a later character structure. "How" brings us closer to appreciating the complexity and dynamic nature of developmental systems. It turns our attention away from prediction and toward explanation, albeit not a mechanistic explanation but one that takes into account the behavior of complex systems. We intentionally choose the term "systems" in contrast to "developmental domains" or "tasks" in order to begin to bridge between ideas of development and ideas of general systems.

A New Developmental Triptych

Dynamic systems, self-ordering processes, and attractor states—these ideas form a possible novel developmental triptych and are the language of a different field—really several fields—physics, mathematics, chaos and general systems theory, among others. By invoking the image of triptych, I imply that these three ideas tell a story and are of a piece. The story is rooted in some very classical assumptions about how we understand complex processes, whether at an atomic or economic level, whether the flow of rivers, the ups and downs of the stock market, the emergence of language in a child, or even the ebb and flow of associations in an analytic hour. It is also rooted in some classical assumptions contrasting order and disorder, with order being the desired or perfect state and disorder signaling dissolution and breakdown. Recognizing complexity is of course not new, but how we think about such complexity within developmental systems requires changing some of our classically inherited attitudes.

For one, much of modern Western science is analytical. And we have inherited or adopted a similar stance when we think about complex clinical or developmental processes. We study the whole by studying its component parts and assume that the more clearly we define and describe those component parts, the better we will understand the process as a whole. We deduce the properties of the whole system from the properties of its parts—the concept of reducibility or its more negative guise, reductionism. In other words, we assume if we take apart the individual harmonies played by each member of the developmental orchestra and add them sequentially we will hear the symphony once again as a whole. Each part will retain its unique individual character and function even when acting within the whole system. Vice versa, when outside the system, the part will function just as it does when it is a part of the integrated whole. So, for example, by understanding the component steps of phoneme recognition and production, we will have a clearer understanding of the acquisition of language in a social context. Or by studying when infants recognize distinct emotion-cueing facial expressions, we will understand more about the communication of emotions between parents and their three-month-olds. To be sure, there is a very important element of truth (and practicality) in these assumptions. God is often in the details, whether these are about a particular fantasy configuration in an analysis or coordinated visual gaze as an early communicative strategy. The more we understand about the details of any developmental domain, the more we can appreciate the degree of complexity within that domain.[12] By understanding the details, we also understand better what needs to be the product of any process of change, and by better understanding the product, we can at least hypothesize what must be the process.

But another complementary approach is to study the symphony as an orchestrated whole as well as the behavior of its individual parts, for when the individual parts are brought together, their behavior as a whole may also be different. We might think of complex systems as entities in and of themselves rather than (or in addition to) the sum of individual, more easily understood parts. What are complex systems? Naively stated, these are systems composed of many parts, which may be of the same or different kinds, and may be connected physically or functionally in more or less complicated fashions. Like complexity, the idea of systems is not new. Proposed in the 1950s and 1960s (Bertalanffy, 1968), it ushered in a whole field of systems theory that impacted biology, neuroscience, psychology, psychiatry, economics, management, and ecology to name only a few. Indeed, early on, a few psychoanalysts recognized the applicability of general systems concepts to the field (e.g., Charny & Carroll, 1966; Loeb & Carroll, 1966). Similarly, a number of developmental psychologists appreciated the applicability of general systems notions to developmental theory (e.g., Sameroff, 1989).

---

12. This too is an oversimplification, for we often make inferences about parts from our observations of the whole, whether these are animate or inanimate, physical or psychological forms. For example, we infer from the turbulence in a stream that there may have been an obstruction upstream. We infer the central location of a cerebral hemorrhage from a paretic gait and slurred speech. We infer a specific fantasy configuration from the stream of associations in an analytic hour.

Examples of complex systems come from every branch of the natural and social sciences (e.g., Haken, 1977, 1988). Flowing rivers, clouds, crystals, lasers, steam engines, automobile engines, chemical reactions in which many molecules participate and form new molecules, weather patterns, population growth and decline, factories, disease epidemics, individual societies, cultural beliefs, peer review committees, professional organizations, hospitals, academic departments, analytic institutes—all of these are complex systems. Biology abounds in complex systems. A single cell is a complex system composed of a cell membrane, a nucleus, a cytoplasm, and each of these in turn contains many other components. Thousands of metabolic processes, many understood in quite clear isolated detail, go on simultaneously in any one cell. Organs are complex systems composed of millions of cells working in integrated fashion. Groups of neurons are complex systems as is every region of the brain and of course, the whole brain itself. Systems are not only complex because they are composed of many parts but also because of complex behavior, such as attentional systems, memory, imagination, independent locomotion, or symbol manipulation. In psychoanalysis, we may think of the ego as a complex system made up of many individual functions. We might also argue that patient and analyst are a complex system, for their individual psychic worlds function interactively during the course of any analysis.[13]

Thinking in a complex systems perspective may at first seem only another way of saying that it is impossible to know all the component parts or variables or meanings in any one behavior, event, or structure—holistic and non-specified thinking in the guise of a new technical language. An analytic hour cannot be distilled into its component parts, interactions between parents and their children are more than a sum of conversational verbal and nonverbal bids. But what is key is the idea that the integrated whole produces behaviors and patterns different from the details—that is, the idea of a dynamic, self-organizing integration, not just an additive one. In other words, complex systems manifest patterns of behavior that may be very different from the content and function of their individual parts. When we

13. Seeing an analytic hour as a complex system may be one solution to the very troubling issue of how we can ever know that what the analyst reports about what happened clinically in any one hour or series of hours represents a "verifiable" account. If we take the analyst's report as one perspective on the complex system of analyst-analysand, so-called inter-observer reliability refers not to agreement about the analysand's observed behavior but rather to how other analysts might think about the material as presented by the treating analyst.

proceed from a more detailed or elemental, microscopic analysis to a more holistic, macroscopic[14] one, new properties, patterns, and qualities emerge in the system that are not evident in any of the individual components. Networks of individual neurons firing produce a series of complex movements not evident in mapping the individual action potentials of each neuron. Associations emerge between patient and analyst that are not available to either in his or her own mental world or reflective time. Or consider a flock of geese taking off in confused mass. Within minutes the geese have organized their group or system to a form that flies in synchrony and spells the leader at prescribed intervals. The behavior of the geese in a flock is novel, not apparent in the flying abilities of a single bird or even a pair of birds. Thus, complex systems are dynamic—they organize as a whole, produce patterns of behavior, and come together or fall apart in novel ways not predictable from their individual elements. The self-organizing quality of a complex system is not necessarily intuitive and is worth pausing over, for this is the most salient property of a complex system for developmentalists interested in the process of change and emerging novel form (see, for example, Kelso, 1995; Thelen and Smith, 1994).

In part, this idea of self-organizing complex systems is seeing very common phenomena in a new light. It requires us to think of the system as a whole and of the behavior as a property of that system rather than of its components summed together. It also asks us to remodel another classical scientific tenet that pervades even our studies of mental phenomena. Classical views of systems such as flying geese, excitatory neurons, air flow, the crawling infant's move to upright walking, the organization of babbling into language hold that these

---

14. Of course, even the terms "macroscopic" and "microscopic" are relative. Studying the chromosomal patterning in a genetic disorder is surely a more microscopic approach to studying the behavior of a child with a particular mutation. On the other hand, studying the length of the telomere or the process of cleaving DNA into relevant segments is a more microscopic perspective than the chromosome patterning. In other words, while there is often a implicit higher value placed on more detailed (e.g., more microscopic) data as being more likely to reveal the true nature of the system in question, the degree of resolution is more accurately judged by the question needing to be addressed. Counting the number of looks away may or may not be a relevant measure of the conversational synchrony between two individuals, though it may be one that is easily verified and agreed upon. The data required to study the behavior of any complex system will necessarily be more macroscopic than those data relevant to the function of individual components of the system. Data regarding the behavior of a complex system must take into account the interactions among a number of components.

systems are organized by forces outside the system or outside the behavior, so to speak. For physical phenomena, we cite temperature,
gravity, electromagnetic fields; for biological and psychological phenomena, we cite genetic code, environment and experiences, biological substrate, interactions among all of these. We think of structure
as emerging from these external, prescriptive, "designing" elements—form from matter—and we assume that the prescription or
design for the form is contained within the matter. Children learn to
walk independently on the basis of genetic prescriptions or codes
that regulate cortical myelination and increasing interconnectivity.
The brain develops on the basis genetic codes that are turned on or
modulated by expectable experiences.

Influenced by nearly three centuries of ideas borrowed and translated from Newtonian principles, we understand these prescriptive
elements as the stabilizing, organizing forces for complex systems.
They constrain the system toward an equilibrium or steady state, and
when the system is not stable, it is near dissolution or breakdown.[15]
We assume that we can model complex processes with linear forms,
X leads to *Y*, steady states, equilibrium, and harmony. Walking is a
hallmark of a structural steady state—the coming together of behavioral and neural functions into a stable behavior. Achieving the capacity for abstract thinking or for delay of gratification is another
structural steady state. When we speak of regression, we are implying
a retreat from a steady state of psychological functioning to an earlier
mode of behavior. If one or more of the prescriptive elements are
dysfunctional, these steady states are disrupted, or structures do not
emerge or do so in unstable fashion. Magnets do not function if they
are overheated, if the temperature conditions are not the properly
prescribed ones. Genes may be mutated, not turned on or off at the
proper time, or not correctly transcribed, and thus, they may produce a dysfunctional protein. Environments may be abusive and ne-
glectful or overwhelming. The breakdown in these prescriptive or
necessary blueprints or preconditions breaks the system and leads
to increasing disorder—neoplasm, delayed development, disruptive
behavior, increasing psychological distress, regression, depression.

Conversely, if all goes well, change and a steady state come about
because the prescription works well. For development, it is writ in
our constitution—our genes as they are turned on or off by critical

15. Indeed, many theories of development from the late nineteenth and early
twentieth century drew extensively on the laws of thermodynamics, particularly the
second law, which allowed for the inevitable increase in disorder in the world—or the
constant increase in entropy.

experiences. The rate of change may vary but the engine for change is given to us prescriptively in our endowment. Most developmental theories are based on this idea of steady state or at least developing toward this prescribed steady state and stable developmental capacities. Implicit in these theories is that with maturation there is diminishing fluctuation or room for change in any capacity—in other words, that we achieve a predictable steady state. When that steady state begins to break down, the individual is in trouble, entering senescence, or near death. Built into our biology and psychology are some corrective mechanisms that allow, within a range, adaptation to disruptions, but the goal of adaptation is to return our biology and our psychology to a stable, equilibrated relationship and state. For psychoanalytic theories of development, these ideas of equilibrium or harmony versus disharmony are most resonant in Anna Freud's developmental lines (and surely, conflict and defense). Development proceeds well when there is "harmony" among the various lines. Although it is common, even expected, that there will be disequilibrium along the way, synchrony and ultimately stability are an ideal outcome.

Unquestionably, there are value and truth in these points of view. Of course, individual developmental paths are shaped by interactions among genes and experiences; and from one perspective, as we have already discussed, on average there is a remarkable stability and steady state to systems as complex as our brains and our psychology. However, perspectives from dynamic systems hold that even well functioning systems are often never stable, never at equilibrium or even at steady state. The hallmark of all complex systems is not that they operate consistently at equilibrium or a steady state but rather that they operate constantly on the edge of dissolution, always poised between stability and turbulence (or what has been called "the edge of chaos" [Sardar and Abrams, 1998]).[16] Instead of signaling impending dysfunction, being far from equilibrium is a precondition for emerging order and structure. Order emerges from variability and from systems nowhere close to a steady state. And the emerging order itself is also never quite stable—disorder is always possible and even necessary for continued self-organization. The more choices, the more flexibility, the greater the degrees of freedom, the more chance for disorder but also for self-organization. These observations were originally made in chemistry in work on so-called dissipa-

16. The science of "complexity" emerged in the early 1980s with its roots in chaos theory. See Gleick, 1987; Prigogine and Stengers, 1984.

tive systems (Prigogine and Stengers, 1984)—that is, systems that require energy to keep them running[17]; the brain and body are salient
biological examples. These systems are open to influences and exchanges with the surrounding environment. But observations of dissipative systems were quickly applied to biological and social systems
to study patterns of population growth, the organization of neuronal
groups, and, more recently, developmental questions such as the
organization of independent locomotion and aspects of cognition
(Thelen and Smith, 1994).

Looking beyond the hydraulic, thermodynamic, even mechanical
syntax of energy and flow,[18] this systems point of view presents a different take on the orderliness of development among other presumed ordered processes. Classical ideas of the orderliness and
predictability of nature are complemented by a recognition that beneath what seems like order in our most cherished, accepted forms
there is a remarkable disorder—and this is especially true for behavioral and psychological development. Actually, disorder or apparent
randomness has always been visible to us. But so steeped have we
been in the belief that the goal of rational natural and social science
is to describe and discover trends (or "essences" [Omaya, 1985]), we
are often tempted to relegate findings that do not fit a set of beliefs
or expectations to experimental noise or imprecise observation. Or

17. The simplest example of a dissipative system may be a rolling ball. Classical
views of the energy needed to start a ball rolling expressed a simple relation between
the mass of the ball and its speed. But these simple, linear perspectives do not take
into account such dampening forces as friction, which makes a simple linear problem
non-linear inasmuch as the impact of friction will change the relation between mass
and speed as the ball continues to move. Thus, more energy will be needed to keep
the system moving. Otherwise, the ball will stop. This is the difference between a so-
called closed system and an open one. The former is a system that is stable, at a state
of entropic equilibrium. No new behavior can emerge without the addition of energy.
Open systems, while often behaviorally stable, are always far from thermodynamic
equilibrium because of the continuous flow of energy to keep the system functional.

18. There is, of course a familiar, perhaps even historically regressive tone to this
kind of language—energy, equilibrium, steady states. It is reminiscent of the hydraulic, mechanical language of the earliest psychoanalytic models of mental functioning—drives seeking discharge, excess quanta of energy, mass, and force. It is also
reminiscent of the applications to human behavior of principles of thermodynamics,
particularly the second law regarding the inevitability of increases in disorder or entropy, to human behavior if the restraints of defense and ego are adequately in place.
Even contemporary models of cognitive functioning use mechanical or computa-
tional metaphors, though this is beginning to change in some quarters (see review in
Siegler, 1996). One difference in these views of complex dynamic systems is in the focus on variability, not as a signal of regression or dissolution, but rather as a desirable,
necessary property of the system.

we have looked through the disorder to strain for that near perfect approximation of order. A view of self-ordering systems places the emphasis on periods of disorder and great variability as the nidus for change. The possibility of new form and structure is contained within the disorder. The more variability is built into the complexity of the system, the more opportunity there is for self-organization and self-preservation. The new point of view is that self-organizing processes have an absolute requirement for random fluctuation, for disorder, at points in their developmental history.

And here is the apparent paradox. Within an inanimate or animate system's disorder and potentially chaotic behavior, which we have traditionally regarded as flawed, inaccurate, or dissolving, there is another level of order. We come back to order again, but this time, the order hidden within disorder and order as a self-generating property of the system, not necessarily as a predefined prescribed process and outcome. Detailing how complex systems came to be seen as self-ordering is a story that others have told as chapters in the unfolding narrative about chaos theory.[19] In all of its details it is an interesting but distracting side road for our purposes. Nonetheless, there are two landmarks in this narrative that provide an important conceptual foundation for the third idea in our triptych—how self-ordering emerges from variability, or the idea of attractor states.

A central property of the self-ordering processes of complex systems is their sensitivity to small changes in initial conditions, popularly called the "butterfly effect" to indicate major changes resulting from something even as manifestly insignificant as the flapping of a butterfly's wings.[20] Here we mean adaptive in the sense of respond-

19. In a way, chaos is a paradoxical term, for in its technical usage it indicates not so much instability and disarray as another level of orderliness, which is hidden in apparently random behavior, a kind of "organized disorder." The term also indicates a phenomenon that defies prediction, not because it is random and disorderly, but because it is not linear. Chaotic structures, functions, and behaviors follow non-linear dynamics and non-linear models. Development is inherently non-linear even though our long accepted ideas of stages, phases, and apparently dramatic transitions in developmental abilities lead us to think of a relatively stable, relatively programmed process.

20. The "butterfly effect" was first noticed in studies of weather patterns and weather forecasting. Very small changes may be quickly magnified through various feedback loops so that a tropical rain cloud generates a hurricane hundreds of miles away. In other words, theoretically, even large-scale changes can come from small perturbations such a gale force winds can eventuate from a change in air currents produced by the flapping of a butterfly's wings. The elegance of the so-called butterfly effect is that it involves randomness—that is, because of such sensitivity to external conditions, weather patterns (and other behaviors) are never quite predictable—but

ing to changes in the environment or contexts surrounding the system. Population growth responds to changes in prosperity, political climate, cultural shifts. The brain organizes and reorganizes neuronal connections to learn from experience as Edelman (1987) has elaborated in his views of neuronal selection. The interconnectedness or feedback among the many components of a complex system means the system can respond to even tiny shifts in external conditions. In other words, most complex systems are very adaptive and sensitive to small changes in initial conditions inasmuch as the impact on one component in the system may be magnified through the feedback loops among the many components to have a major effect throughout the whole system. Psychologically, we might think of the very common observation that events very early in an analysis, such as how analyst and analysand first greet one another or how they set up the conditions of their therapeutic relationship, often reverberate and resurface for years hence. Or in infancy, apparently small changes in parental behavior or usual routine may temporarily upset the infant's sleep and feeding patterns and even growth.

A second property of complex systems is infinite complexity or possibilities within finite constraints. Based originally on observations from topography,[21] the idea of fractal-like complexity within a prescribed form is evident throughout biology—for example, in the structure of the pulmonary tree, the near infinite capillary branching of the circulatory system, and the intricate synaptic networks linking neuronal networks. This idea of complexity within constraints returns in another guise to the earlier idea of different perspectives when development is viewed up close and from afar. For all systems, what we observe depends on where we place ourselves as observers and how we make our observations. The more closely we look, the more detail we see; and the more detailed our measurements, the more complex the system appears. This perspective of greater complexity nonethe-

---

at the same time, accounts for richly complex, ordered (though non-linearly) behavior. For an accessible description, see Gleick, 1987.

21. The idea of infinite complexity within finite constraints emerged from a remarkably simple, yet intuitive, question and classic paper, "How long is the coast of Britain?" (Mandelbrot, 1977). The answer depends on one's perspective. If we measure in miles, the answer will be different from a measurement made in inches or centimeters. The closer we look, the more detail and variety we see. What we observe depends on where we are positioned as observers and how we make our measurements. What looks flat from afar is three dimensional up close. Thinking in fractions of dimensions or fractals (e.g., 2.2 dimensions, not just two then three dimensions) captures the idea of moving continuously closer or farther away as an observer and thus seeing more or less of the targeted observational field.

less is bounded by the finite constraints of the system we are observing. For example, the more closely we look at the conversational synchrony between a mother and infant the more we will see in the way of turn-taking, missed turns, even overlapping turns. This complexity is still bounded by the constraints of the infant's motor, cognitive, and social development and the mother's interest in and dedication to her parenting role. Similarly, the more closely we examine any dream or fantasy, the more details will emerge that connect to other fantasies, earlier dreams, and waking events. But the capacities of the analyst, the openness of the analysand, and the time limits of the hour put finite constraints around the complexity that can be observed.

Both properties, sensitivity to initial conditions and the possibility of infinite variation within finite constraints, mean that all complex systems fluctuate within a set of conditions, paths, or states. The system fluctuates because of the sensitivity to context, and it stays within a set of states or paths, albeit a potentially very large set of paths, because of the finite constraints. These states or paths are so-called attractor states—that is, patterns of change or fluctuation along which the system may move and states at which the system eventually settles, at least at one point in time.[22] Socially, we might think of chiefs of state, institutions, families, religious leaders, or coaches as attractors—states or persons around which others tend to congregate. Repetitive patterns of behavior, persistent fantasies, enduring configurations of conflict and defense also represent attractor states. Most systems, animate or inanimate, have many different attractor states or possible paths within their finite constraints. For example, the human body is constrained to a general form, but within that constraint there is a seemingly infinite variety for the expression of individual form. Similarly, the brain is constrained to a particular shape and organization but again within that shape, no two brains are alike in their patterns of connectivity and types of networks. Or developmentally, most children learn at least one language, but how they learn that language, how they pronounce individual words, how they use the language to convey meaning are infinitely variable. The choice of one or more preferred attractor states or paths at any point in time reflects the systemic sensitivity to external conditions.

22. Perhaps the clearest example of an attractor state comes from watching a ball rolling in a bowl. Unless disturbed, the ball eventually settles to the bottom of the bowl. This is the attractor point or state. Consider too that pendulums tend to swing regularly, it does not usually snow in July in temperate climates, and infants tend usually to babble before they speak in words. Each of these "on average" behaviors defines a set of attractors or preferred states.

In a sense, this is really no more than another way of talking about individual differences shaped by experience (as well as endowment) that we all recognize as inherent to biology and psychology. In other words, our endowment or experiences provide finite constraints for developmental outcomes that may vary remarkably from individual to individual. But there is another twist that makes the idea of attractor states different from the usual emphasis on differences between individuals. When we speak of different paths or states along which individuals vary, we are especially speaking of *within-individual variation* across developmental time. Any one system has a set of states or paths that it follows on average and will move between these paths on the basis of initial conditions or changes in the external environment. The greater the variety of possible paths, the greater the complexity and within-individual variability in the system's behavior across time. The idea of attractor states or pathways applied to psychological development maps, not the variations across individuals, but the variations for any one of us at any point in our development. the more possibilities for functional paths, or the greater the number of attractor states we are able to function along, the more adaptive or resilient we are to changes in environment or context, the greater our degrees of freedom.[23]

Can these ideas of dynamic, self-ordering systems adapting around various states of attraction or salience be usefully applied to developmental processes? The very complexity poses some empirical chal-

23. The dynamic, changing behavior of complex systems along their attractor states may also be represented graphically in so-called phase space. We are accustomed to looking at representations of three-dimensional objects, such as a building, in two-dimensional drawings. But behavior can also be represented in two dimensions such as the swinging of a pendulum, where one axis shows the horizontal location and the other the vertical location. At any point in time, with these two points, we can locate the pendulum in space. Phase space takes this representation of motion one step further and represents change or motion. One axis represents, for example, the velocity of the pendulum, another the location on the vertical axis, another the point in time. Phase space diagrams take information from moving, changing parts and represents the behavior of the whole system over time. If the behavior is steady and unchanging, the phase space diagram is a single point. If the behavior is repetitive or periodic, the phase space diagram shows a loop. If the behavior is a mixture of repetitive and changing patterns (e.g., order and disorder), the phase space diagram assumes the shape characteristic of many complex systems and represented prototypically by the Lorenz attractor (see figure 2; Lorenz, 1995). The Lorenz attractor, initially described in studies of weather patterns, was dubbed "strange" (Ruelle, 1993) because of the intricate phase space diagram that depicts non-linear, complex, non-predictable processes. The more degrees of freedom in the system, the more complex the phase space diagram and the "stranger" or more complex the set of attractor states.

lenges, not the least of which is finding the most appropriate measures that are available to us methodologically but do not at the same time look at individual components of the system as reflective of the system as a whole. This is a crucial challenge and one that is only beginning to be met, even in discussions of methodological designs or in the creation of appropriate investigative techniques (Thelen, 1989; Sameroff, 1989). It is why, despite the theoretical and metaphorical attractiveness of a complex-systems application to children's development, few empirical or clinical studies have as yet been modeled on these types of perspectives (Kelso, 1995; Quinodoz, 1997; Thelen and Smith, 1994).

But hard as it is to model empirically or clinically, it is perhaps useful to conclude this section by rephrasing one example of development familiar to analysts into the language of complex systems (for clinical examples phrased in general systems language, see Loeb & Carroll, 1966; Quinodoz, 1997). Consider the phenomenon of separation-individuation late in the first and early in the second year of life, a period preceded usually by apparent wariness toward strangers and increased concern and distress when parents leave, even if briefly. Various theoretical perspectives describe this phenomenon and developmental period in different terms. But all focus on the increasing psychic differentiation between the infant and parent—that is, on the infant's growing awareness of himself as a separate, individual agent able to act on his own and be acted upon from the outside. Several of these perspectives also point to the ability to hold inanimate objects in mind even if out of sight as the necessary precursor for remembering significant others when they are away. Other perspectives, such as attachment theory, suggest that the degree of separation distress provides a window on the stability and soundness of the infant's earliest relationships. Interactive approaches to the separation-individuation phenomenon underscore the comingled contributions of parental care, biologic readiness, maturational level, and cultural expectations.

A complex systems point of view assumes that these factors are not just individual contributors to the phenomenon but rather define the system—a child with his own biology in the care of his parents, who are parenting under a given set of cultural norms and their own internalized parenting experiences. The parents' own expectations, beliefs, and fantasies affect their responses to the child's behavior. In turn, their child's behavior effects changes in parents' responses. How the child responds to novel or stressful events, a capacity in part reflective of experience and in part of genetic endowment, also renders his behavior and responses to the ordinary and not so ordinary actions of parenting. The system develops along a set of salient paths reflecting the merged and interactive product of these components. This complex system is also "held" in a particular societal or external space that places a number of demands and constraints on it, and these constraints shape the preferred paths or adaptive trajectories the system will follow. These include economic and job-related demands on the parents, societal expectations for how parents and children should behave, the experience of other caring adults who share the responsibility of child rearing, the extended family's support, and even the availability of mental health interventions for the parent or child during more stressful or extraordinary times. In this point of view, the child's internal and external response to separations and his moves toward individuated independence are not an insulated developmental event impacted and shaped uniquely or interactively by genes, environment, and experience. Rather, we understand the child's internalized response to separation and the adult's degree of flexibility or stolid repetitiveness in metabolizing losses throughout life as reflective of this continually active, dynamic, self-ordering "object relations" system. We begin to think about the range of adaptive choices for both child and adult as the hallmark of their adjustments to separation and loss. Such a perspective also potentially expands our clinical field by shifting our focus from thinking about childhood antecedents or lines of development to thinking about emerging form, function, and adaptation in a larger system context.

CIRCLING BACK TO PSYCHOANALYSIS: THE IMPLICATION OF SEEING, DEVELOPMENT AS COMPLEX SELF-ORDERING SYSTEMS

As we circle back explicitly to psychoanalysis and development in this concluding section, it may be useful to look back over the salient points we want to bring under the psychoanalytic lens and into the consulting room. So far, we have suggested a number of possibilities for how very common analytic observations and theoretical constructs can be placed in a self-ordering systems point of view—for instance, the ego or the analyst-analysand relationship as a self-ordering system. Indeed, as others have also suggested (Quinodoz, 1997), thinking of a whole system as well as of individual components may be more comfortable for psychoanalysts than for developmentalists from other traditions. As analysts, we more often think in terms of larger systems—"ego functioning," "unconscious fantasy," "defensive structure." Through our clinical work, we understand intuitively if not empirically through our clinical work the applied idea of a complex system—the interactions and feedback loops among the many components of, for example, internalized objects and fantasies. Nonetheless, however intuitively compatible these ideas are or aren't, what is perhaps more relevant to our concluding task is to suggest some of the explicit implications for psychoanalysis involved in a rephrasing of development in terms of complex, self-ordering systems.

The main points we have made thus far are that development involves the process of creating new forms and functions through remodeling old ones, combining several old functions into a new one, or even taking apart an old form or function to make a new one from the component parts—a point of view echoed by other analysts rethinking psychoanalytic theories of development (e.g., Neubauer, 1996). Development is about the creation of novelty. So, for example, we might think about how internalized objects are reworked and revised over the course of development and how new persons are matched to old objects or new ones are created. We often see patients when they are trapped in repetitive patterns, endlessly using the same behaviors and fantasies over and over again even as the world changes around them. Novel forms and functions seem lost, even threatening. If such begin to appear, we think about therapeutic action and change. Sometimes we even put it in terms of development regained or development back on track.

We have also suggested that classically, we think of developmental processes as moving toward greater order, more constraints, less flexibility, more refined and complex abilities. While there is merit (and truth) in this point of view, developmental processes viewed up close are not as increasingly constrained as some theories suggest, or perhaps as feels comfortable to believe. In many areas, the hallmark of development is to add strategies, to increase the number of adaptive options, to add to the range of attractor states or pathways. The hallmark of healthy development is more options, more flexibility, psychically and behaviorally, instead of less, at least in some areas. Having access to a range of strategies, some very old, at least chronologically, others only newly acquired, increases one's ability to adapt to any number of changing and novel demands and conditions. This is surely reminiscent of Loewald's point of view that every individual has access to earlier modes of thought and fantasy and that these modes remain active in our mental lives across development.

The third point we have suggested is that developmental processes may be fruitfully viewed as self-ordering. Built into the complexity of the system as a whole is a sensitivity to change in context and an inherent ordering ability—finding a new path, state, or attractor that is more adaptive to the conditions at hand. While the language may be different, this point of view is of course reminiscent of the ego psychologists' emphasis on processes of adaption in ego development. What is different in our application of the metaphor of self-ordering systems is not just that the individual adapts (or does not) to a changing environment or life's experiences but that the capacity for adaptation is an inevitable byproduct of the developmental process itself. If all goes well, the capacity for adaptation is an inevitable byproduct of the developmental process itself. If all goes well, the capacity for adaptation is part and parcel of the developmental engine (Mayes, 1999).

How do these three points impact upon our view of analysis with our patients? For one, even as theoretically and abstractly phrased as these notions of self-ordering systems, development as novelty, order and disorder may be, they are nonetheless closer to the day to day, moment to moment developmental snapshots we see in our clinical work. More often than not, clinically, whether with adults or children, development does not proceed in ordered, staged, or phase manner. It is a far more dialectic process and the microscopic detail afforded by the analytic lens usually highlights the messiness and chaos of developmental events, processes, or phrases. This is not to say that there is no merit in the more traditional and classic theories of developmental progression proposed by analysts and non-analysts. These are surely useful orienting guides and they do capture important features of the developmental landscape on average. But they are not dynamic in the sense of something constantly in motion and changing. Classical views of development emphasize short- and long-term prediction while these more contemporary views of systems, self-ordering, and novel forms emphasize probability. Given one set of conditions for an individual at one point in time, there are a number of possible paths, adaptations, or states, some more probable than others. The idea of attractor states and sensitivity to initial conditions also puts the emphasis on a range of options and on maintaining flexibility, not on how development may stay "on track" despite varying contexts, cultures, and experiences. This point of view in essence turns our wonder at the complexity of development upside down. Instead of being amazed by the variety of individual choice, we find it more amazing that there is regularity amid the variety of individual possibilities, conditions, experiences, and cultures.

Shifting away from prediction and from looking for average or usual patterns also brings into focus what it means to say, for example, that a behavior is regressed or even primitive or that development is off track. These ways of phrasing developmental observations put the emphasis on progressive, ordered unfolding and on the desirability, even better psychic health, of relying on later acquired, more expectable or average behaviors, defenses, fantasies, adaptations, or ego functions. Once again, these points of view have merit and cannot be discarded, but they do not allow for a view of development as self-ordering, opportunistic, and disordered as well as ordered. Seeing development as a dialectic, dynamic, self-ordering process makes it perhaps more accessible, if not permissible, to ask why using an old strategy, an old behavior, or an old fantasy seems necessary given a set of conditions or experiences.

We return at this point to a paraphrase of the question implicit in

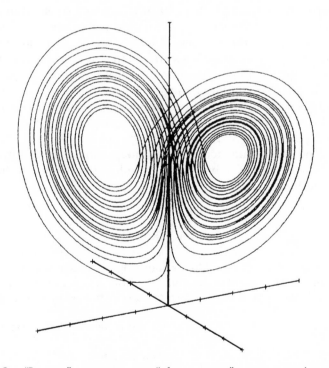

Figure 2. "Lorenz" attractor—a "phase space" representation of the change in a complex system over time (adapted from Sardar & Abrams, 1998). Copyright James Gleick. Reprinted from CHAOS (p. 28) with permission of Carlisle & Company L.L.C.

our young trainee's interest in development. How does an understanding of developmental processes as self-organizing systems contribute to our clinical work with children and adults? We can surely accept that thinking about development is close to root of every bit of therapeutic work with children. But with adults we may sometimes fall into the same belief as our trainee—development is for children, it is past history already writ upon the lived present, and our job is to elaborate the story. What happens in our adult patients is not "developmental". We, and our patients, often subscribe to a view of development as genes, fate, prescribed stages, order by design, happening (or not) in spite of us (Mayes, 1999). But when we shift our focus to developmental processes as self-ordering, we begin to appreciate that what is in our developmental design is the capacity to learn and shape according to context and need—self-ordering. Development does not happen in spite of us but rather is within us—and accepting this means accepting a responsibility for our development as an ongoing process, not as a psychic text by which we live or within which we chafe or hide. With this more dynamic, self-ordering system perspective, we modify our emphasis to a focus on individual self-righting and on how we all move back and forth between different modes or paths of functioning depending on our internal needs and external conditions. Development going well preserves and enhances this flexibility. The ability to stay ordered, on a fantasied even keel, is ironically preserved by never quite settling into a fixed pattern or set of options but by keeping open a mixture of old and new strategies molded together as needed into new adaptations. Order within disorder, stability and instability side by side—herein is the developmental riddle.

BIBLIOGRAPHY

ASHCRAFT, M. H. (1987). Children's knowledge of simple arithmetic: A developmental model and simulation. In J. Bisanz, C. J. Brainerd, & R. Kail (Eds.), *Formal Methods in Developmental Psychology*. New York: Springer-Verlag.

BERTALANFFY, VON L. (1968). *General system theory*. New York: George Braziller.

BURKE, E. (1790). *Reflections on the Revolution in France* (1993). New York.

CASE, R. (1992). *The mind's staircase: Exploring the conceptual underpinnings of children's thought and knowledge*. Hillsdale, NJ: Erlbaum.

CHARNY, E. J., & CARROLI, E. J. (1966). General systems theory and psychoanalysis: Theoretical considerations. *Psychoanalytic Quarterly*, 35:377–387.

EDELMAN, G. M. (1987). *Neural darwinism*. New York: Basic Books.

GLEICK, J. (1987). *Chaos: Making a new science*. New York: Basic Books.

HAKEN, H. (1977). *Synergetics: An introduction*. Heidelberg: Springer-Verlag.

———— (1988). *Information and self-organization: A macroscopic approach to complex systems*. Heidelberg: Springer-Verlag.

HOROWITZ, F. D. (1987). *Exploring developmental theories: Toward a Structural Behavioral Model of Development*. Hillsdale, NJ: Erlbaum.

KELSO, J. A. S. (1995). *Dynamic patterns: The self-organization of brain and behavior.* Cambridge, MA: MIT Press.

KESSEN, W. (1990). *The Rise and Fall of Development*. Worcester, Mass: Clark University Press.

LOEB, F. F., & CARROLL, E. J. (1966). General systems theory and psychoanalysis: Application to psychoanalytic case material. *Psychoanalytic Quarterly,* 35:388–398.

LORENZ, E. (1995). *The essence of chaos*. London: University College London Press.

MANDELBROT, B. B. (1977). Physical objects with fractional dimensions: seacoasts, galaxy clusters, turbulence, and soap. In R. Balian and J.-L. Peube (Eds.) *Fluid dynamics*. Pp. 555–78. London: Gordon and Breach.

MAYES, L. C. (1999). Clocks, quarks, and engines—love, dreams, and genes: What makes development happen. *Psychoanalytic Study of the Child,* 54:169–192.

MILLER, P. H. (1989). *Theories of developmental psychology*. New York: W. H. Freeman and Company.

NEUBAUER, P. Current issues in psychoanalytic child development. *Psychoanalytic Study of the Child,* 51:35–45.

OMAYA, S. (1985). *The ontogeny of information: Developmental systems and evolution*. Cambridge: Cambridge University Press.

PRIGOGINE, I., AND STENGERS, I. (1984). *Order out of chaos: Man's new dialogue with nature*. New York: Bantam.

QUINODOZ, J. M. (1997). Transitions in psychic structures in the light of deterministic chaos theory. *International Journal of Psychoanalysis,* 78:699–718.

RUELLE, D. (1993). *Chance and chaos*. London: Penguin.

SAMEROFF, A. (1989). Commentary: General systems and the regulation of development. In Gunnar, M. and Thelen, E. (Eds.). *Systems and development: The Minnesota Symposia on Child Psychology*. Pp. 219–235. Hillsdale, NJ: Erlbaum.

SARDAR, Z., & ABRAMS, I. (1998). *Introducing chaos*. New York: Totem Books.

SIEGLER, R. S. (1996). *Emerging Minds: The process of change in children's thinking*. New York: Oxford University Press.

THELEN, E. (1984). Learning to walk: Ecological demands and phylogenetic constraints. In L. P. Lipsitt (Ed.), *Advances in Infancy Research* (vol. 3, pp. 213–250). Norwood, NJ: Ablex.

———— (1989). Self-organization in developmental processes: Can systems approaches work. In Gunnar, M. and Thelen, E. (Eds.). *Systems and Devel-*

opment: The Minnesota Symposia on Child Psychology. Pp. 77–117. Hillsdale, NJ: Erlbaum.

——— & SMITH, L. B. (1994). *A Dynamic Systems Approach to the Development of Cognition and Action.* Cambridge, Mass: MIT Press.

WALDROP, M. (1992). *Complexity.* New York: Touchstone.

WOLFF, P. (1987). *The development of behavioral states and the expression of emotions in early infancy: New proposals for investigation.* Chicago: University of Chicago Press.

In Search of
Winnicott's Aggression

BEATRICE MELMED POSNER, M.S.S.S., ROSLYN WOLFE GLICKMAN, M.S.W., EITHNE COYLE TAYLOR, M.S.W., JOYCE CANFIELD, M.D., and FRANCINE CYR, Ph.D.

Going beyond Winnicott's widely known ideas about creativity, in this paper the authors ask why some people are able to live creatively while others suffer recurrent feelings of anger, futility, and depression. Examining Winnicott's reframing of aggression as a life force, it attempts to answer this question by tracing the evolution of his thinking on the nature and origin of aggression. It argues that because he saw aggression as inherent and as central to emotional development, interference in its expression compromises psychic maturation. The paper explores how Winnicott arrived at the conception of a combined love-strife drive and demonstrates that for him, there is no love without aggression, no subject, no object, no reality, and no creativity. That is, for Winnicott, aggression is an achievement that leads to the capacity to live creatively and to experience authenticity. Clinical vignettes illustrate the

---

The authors are the members of the Montreal Winnicott Study Group. Beatrice Melmed Posner is a member of the Canadian Psychoanalytic Society, psychoanalyst in private practice, teacher and supervisor at the Argyle Institute for Human Relations; Roslyn Wolfe Glickman is a psychoanalytic psychotherapist in private practice, psychiatric social worker, Montreal Children's Hospital; Eithne Coyle Taylor is a psychoanalytic psychotherapist in private practice and at the Infant/Parent Program, Douglas Hospital, Montreal; Joyce Canfield is an adult and child psychoanalyst, child psychiatrist, Montreal Children's Hospital, past president of the Quebec English branch of the Canadian Psychoanalytic Society; Francine Cyr is a child psychoanalytic psychotherapist, professor of clinical psychology, Université de Montréal.

The Psychoanalytic Study of the Child 56, ed. Albert J. Solnit, Peter B. Neubauer, Samuel Abrams, and A. Scott Dowling (Yale University Press, copyright © 2001 by Albert J. Solnit, Peter B. Neubauer, Samuel Abrams, and A. Scott Dowling).

therapeutic use of these conclusions and their value for psychoanalytic theory.

WINNICOTT'S IDEAS ABOUT THE TRANSITIONAL PROCESS AND ITS CON-sequences for living creatively are well known. This paper explores his less well known ideas about aggression and its link to creativity and discusses their source in what he finally called the "love-strife drive" (1969b, p. 245).

For Winnicott, the word *creativity* describes ordinary living; the do-ing that arises out of being. It is the coloring of the whole attitude to-ward reality, in which the individual experiences himself as being both alive and real.

According to Winnicott, the transitional process is made possible through the opportunity for illusion afforded the infant by the mother's adaptation to him at the beginning of his life. He argued that "creativity . . . is the retention throughout life of something that properly belongs to the infant's experience" (Winnicott, 1970a, p. 40). Creativity is at the heart of the mother-infant relationship; therefore, failure of maternal adaptation has significant implications for the psychic development of the infant.

In this paper, we attempt to go beyond the broadly accepted un-derstanding of Winnicott, according to which the child bathes in the light of mother's love, is nurtured through the illusion of omnipo-tence in imaginative play, and grows into a creative, playful adult. Where is the dark side in all this? How can one account for the per-son who is unhappy, depressed, or destructive? We believe that Win-nicott provides answers to these questions in his exploration of ag-gression and its link to creativity.

Winnicott did not construct a coherent theory and disclaimed hav-ing one. In his obituary for Winnicott in 1971, Martin James said, "Winnicott . . . practiced and taught 'piecemeal tinkering', and was an enemy of grand schemes that overlook the individual." As Dra-peau (1995) reminds us, Winnicott cautioned Klein about the dan-gers of constructing a theory that was not open to being questioned, played with, rediscovered, and reformulated by creative people (p. 56). We believe that Winnicott was developing such an open model.

One cannot talk about Winnicott without talking about his style. In a commemorative speech, Marion Milner (1987b, p. 250) quotes Winnicott as saying to his students, "What you get out of me, you will have to pick out of chaos." Jeremy Walker (1996) elaborates: "We might take this as a joke, or an expression of humility and regret. It's a boast. His words actually meant, 'I am going to think and talk creatively, and if you hope to take anything in, you must listen creatively.'"

In attempting to track the important ideas in his rich body of writing, we are faced with the daunting deceptiveness of his language, which readily disguises the complexity of his thinking. Winnicott used everyday words in very particular, idiosyncratic ways, at times in the commonly understood sense and at other times not. What appears to be simple is not so simple after all. He forces us to deconstruct his language to arrive at his meaning. This makes him difficult to study and can lead to a reductionist understanding of his ideas. His linguistic inconsistency may even have interfered with his reception and acceptance by the psychoanalytic community.

It is clear that from the outset Winnicott was strongly influenced by Darwin's idea that the survival of a species is dependent on its successful adaptation to its environment. Winnicott inverted Darwin's theory, insisting that babies need a facilitating environment and that failure of the human environment has serious consequences for the developing personality. Philips (1988) comments, "By introducing a language of reciprocity into the story of early human development, Winnicott revises part of Darwin's account. He reverses the Darwinian equation by suggesting that human development is an often ruthless struggle against compliance with the environment" (p. 5). In his revision of psychoanalysis, Winnicott derived everything from this model of the mother-infant relationship.

Winnicott was both a part of and apart from the psychoanalytic world in which he lived and wrote. In the 1930s and 1940s in Britain, this world, dominated first by Sigmund Freud and then by Melanie Klein, faced serious splits between the followers of Klein and Anna Freud. Winnicott was reluctant to align himself with one party in the controversy over the other and pursued an independent direction. This enabled him to continue to draw upon the theories of both Sigmund Freud and Melanie Klein while formulating his own unique vision. While he did not explicitly take a position that contradicted either Freud or Klein, he proceeded to elaborate a path of human development that included a radically revised theory of aggression.

Winnicott acknowledged his indebtedness to Klein and valued her seminal work, including her theories of the world of internal objects and of infantile anxieties and their vicissitudes. However, he took significant exception to other aspects of her work, particularly her emphasis on internal experience to the exclusion of the "actual" environment. His very different view of the world of the infant stressed the importance of the environment and its role in facilitating inherent maturational processes.

From Winnicott's perspective, Klein's conceptualization enclosed the developing infant in an inner fantasy world in which inherent destructiveness played out its inevitable course. Winnicott also saw destruction or aggression as innate and as central to the emotional development of the individual. However, he reframed aggression as a life force (Winnicott, 1954c, p. 216), not as the death force of Freud or the overwhelmingly destructive force of Klein. That is, he saw aggression as a *potential,* the constitutional element with which a child is born, as distinct from *actual* aggression. How this potential is expressed is a function of the environmental provision. A dependable facilitating environment makes it possible for the child to negotiate the path of development toward a healthy expression of actual aggression. Both compliance and antisocial destructive aggression are responses to inadequate environmental provision.

The implications of this restructuring of theory are significant. In refuting the idea of inevitable destructiveness, Winnicott not only posited an alternate explanation for actual aggression, but also elaborated a highly original and subtle developmental path. We will trace this path, describing both the evolution of his thinking about aggression and his ideas about the transformations in aggression at various stages of human development.

APPETITE AND GREED

Before he wrote about aggression, Winnicott wrote about appetite and greed. His written explorations of this subject began with a 1936 paper, "Appetite and Emotional Disorder." He was not yet explicit about the connection between appetite and aggression. Rather, he explored the revelations of appetite and attitudes toward instinctual life, suggesting that a discussion of this relationship was long overdue. He also called attention to the important link between appetite and emotional development, connecting disturbances of appetite with various psychiatric illnesses and psychosomatic disorders. Disturbances in appetite are a main indicator of development gone awry. An infant's attitude toward food is a precursor of his or her relationship with other people and with his own desire. "The revelations of appetite, the study of greed was at the same time the study of the first relationship that would enable Winnicott to formulate his developmental theory" (Phillips, 1988, p. 72).

Winnicott's ideas about greed are original and provocative. He saw greed as love in a primitive form. "It is the primitive love impulse, the thing we are always frightened to own up to, but which is basic in our natures" (Winnicott, 1945, p. 170). He referred to it as having a "very definite meaning, joining together the psychical and the physical, love and hate, what is acceptable and what is not acceptable to the ego. . . . Greed is synonymous with life, appetite, excitement" (Winnicott, 1936, p. 33). Winnicott differentiated greed from greediness. He believed that when greediness appears in human behavior it is always in a disguised form—that is, hidden behind a symptom, reflecting the anxiety attached to it. "The word *greed* is used in the theoretical statement of the tremendous instinctual claims that an infant makes on the mother at the beginning" (Winnicott, 1956, p. 312). It is the "pre-ruth" primitive love impulse, unintended ruthlessness, so designated because the infant is unaware of mother's separateness.

In "The Observation of Infants in a Set Situation" (1941) Winnicott's ideas on the subject of greed are further clarified and refined. He observed the behavior of babies between the ages of 5 and 13 months when confronted with a spatula. Variations in hesitation in picking up the spatula indicate the degree to which greed and appetite have been allowed to develop. A child whose greed is inhibited may avoid picking up the spatula on his own or may cling to or check with the mother. In contrast, a child who can play with or use the spatula creatively has been given the freedom to express his greed (appetite).

At the same time, Winnicott recognized the significance of normal anxiety. "Normal" hesitation may sometimes result from the existence in the baby's mind of the *fantasy* of a strict mother. In allowing for this possibility, he drew on Klein's ideas about fantasies in infancy, but he used Klein in his own way, seeing these fantasies as the imaginative elaboration of the body functions of eating: "the growth of the personality through imaginative eating" (Winnicott, 1957, p. 110). The infant who cannot enjoy the spatula must have had *actual* experiences of frustration and unhappiness or some degree of disallowing of the aggressive impulses. "In the normal hesitation of the baby, Winnicott could see the beginnings of a sense of concern for the impulses of destruction" (Davis, 1993, p. 60). Nevertheless, infants who have a good relationship with their mothers will feel free to express their greed (appetite). Therefore the "set situation" gives important clues to the state of the infant's development.

Winnicott's earliest statement on aggression as such is found in a paper simply entitled "Aggression" (1939). In this paper he wrote, "Instinctual aggressiveness . . . is originally a part of appetite or of some other form of instinctual love" (pp. 87–88). Typically, Winnicott used different words to describe the same phenomenon. For primary aggression, he sometimes substituted "theoretical greed," "instinctual aggressiveness," "primary appetite-love," or "mouth love." But despite the variability of his terminology, his argument is consistent and clear—all those aspects of aggression in the newborn that may be experienced by the mother as cruel, hurtful, or dangerous are so *by chance.* This point is crucial to Winnicott's thinking (Abram, 1996, p. 10). It was obvious to him that a baby kicking in the womb cannot be assumed to be trying to kick his way out, any more than an infant a few weeks old thrashing away with his arms or sucking hard on the nipple can be assumed to be attacking. This initial activity or motility Winnicott called *primary aggression.*

Of course, Winnicott stressed that aggression changes in quality as the infant grows and matures within the context of environmental handling. In his rich and complex paper "Aggression in Relation to Emotional Development" (1950–55), he developed these ideas more fully. He asked a very provocative question: "Does aggression come ultimately from anger aroused by frustration, or has it a root of its own?" While he recognized that it is possible to detect some reactive response very early in the life of a child, he believed it to be important to try to answer this question in order to prevent confusion about what really goes on.

Winnicott did not wish to set up a rigid developmental theory and insisted that developmental processes are not consolidated once and for all: "These things develop gradually, and repeatedly come and go, and are achieved and lost." Nevertheless, in "Aggression in Relation to Emotional Development," he wrote about "aggressiveness as it appears in the various stages of ego development" (1950–55, p. 205). His premise is that initially there is unintentional aggression. In the very early phase, one of pre-integration, there is purpose (wanting to eat, to move, to chew the nipple) but without intent (to hurt). In the second stage there is integration of the personality, with concern or guilt. (This can be seen as comparable to Melanie Klein's depressive position.) Finally there is the stage of interpersonal relationships and conflicts, both conscious and unconscious. Aggression that belongs to this stage is familiar through the work of Freud.

Winnicott held that primitive love also exists before there is a capacity for taking responsibility and that it has a destructive quality even when there is no intent to harm, as with the biting aspect of primitive greed (love) described above. Destruction becomes an ego responsibility only after there is integration and organization of the ego sufficient for the existence of anger. For the same reasons, Winnicott insisted that hate is relatively sophisticated and does not exist in these early stages. In this way he made the case for the examination of primary aggression, as distinct from reactive aggression.

By 1955, he drew a distinction between motility and aggression, describing motility as a "part-function." "Part-functions" are organized gradually as the child becomes an integrated person. As we have seen, it is only with integration that a person can have purposive behavior and that aggression can be intentional.

It is important to understand that "for Winnicott there is no room for ideas about evil, wickedness, cruelty or being destructive, or concepts of being murderous or violent in this notion of innate aggression" (Walker, 1998, p. 2). Winnicott said, "We can get nowhere with our study of aggression if in our minds we have it irrevocably linked with jealousy, envy, anger or the operation of the instincts that we name sadistic. More nearly basic is the concept of aggression as part of the exercise *that can lead to the discovery of objects that are external*" (Winnicott, 1970b, p. 287).

Motility begins in the womb, in the impulses of the fetus coming up against opposition. It is part of the inherited potential, purely physical at first. It is seen in spontaneous gestures—reaching out, encountering the environment. It is this motility that is expressed in the pre-ruth era. There are many variations in the infant's capacity to use his motility.

In one pattern, the environment is constantly discovered and rediscovered, and contact with the environment is an experience of the individual. Winnicott called this healthy: the child has been held by the good-enough mother and has been allowed to come up against opposition. His own experience permits him to discover the environment, and the development of his sense of what is real (himself, external reality, and the difference between the two: the Me and the Not-Me). In health, the individual needs to look for appropriate opposition and can enjoy doing so.

In the second pattern, the environment impinges on the infant,

and instead of a series of individual experiences there is a series of reactions to impingements. Withdrawal to rest becomes the individual
experience, and motility is then experienced only as a reaction to impingement (Winnicott, 1950–5, pp. 211–212). Ill health results at
this very early stage because the life force is taken up in reaction to
impingement. Boundaries between the Me and the Not-me are not
clear.

In the third pattern, the life force is totally thwarted by the need to
react to impingements, so that the individual develops as an extension of the impinging environment. There is a failure to evolve an individual. There is no authentic core. Winnicott calls this the extreme
false self: the individual exists by not being found. These patterns are
manifest in the antisocial individual who is unable to contain his "destructive aggression" in fantasy, and in the overly compliant individual who is inhibited in his ability to live creatively.

Aggression in Relation to an Object

Winnicott developed his ingenious concept of *the use of an object* in a
series of papers, of which "The Use of an Object and Relating
through Identifications" is the most vexing and contentious. When
he presented it in 1968 to the New York Psychoanalytic Society, the
response was intensely negative. Winnicott's last significant paper, it
continues to challenge understanding. He did not revise it because
of his final illness. Nevertheless, "The Use of an Object" represents
the culmination of his thinking. Its central postulate is that development of the capacity to use the object, resulting from the natural
growth processes and their interaction with the good-enough environment, permits the child to escape the limited confines of his internal world of projective-introjective mechanisms and the illusion of
omnipotence.

At the beginning, the infant experiences only the subjective object
and moves gradually, enabled by transitional experience, through
object relating to object usage. Transitional experience takes place
in the space where illusion holds sway: where the baby creates the
world. It is neither inside nor outside, just as the baby at this moment
is neither a part of nor separate from mother. It is on the border between the beginning inner life and the beginning ability to recognize
external reality.

Object relating involves projective mechanisms; the object is
meaningful, but not yet experienced as wholly other. The subject is

still an isolate and does not recognize the object as "an entity in its own right" (Winnicott, 1968, p. 222).

Object usage involves the "acceptance of the object's independent existence, its property of having been there all the time" (Winnicott, 1968a, p. 221). The object must be objectively perceived and must belong to shared reality. Winnicott described this process in the following way: "After 'subject relates to object' comes 'subject destroys object' (as it becomes external); and then may come 'object survives destruction by the subject'" (Winnicott, 1968a, p. 222). If the object survives—that is, if it does not change in quality or attitude, if it does not retaliate—the child can now use the object. It has value because it has survived; it has its own life. Object usage is the destruction of the object in fantasy and its survival in reality.

This idea is an inversion of our usual understanding of reactive destruction, in which aggression is seen as a response to confrontation with reality. Winnicott held that the destruction in fantasy plays a part in making the reality. The child experiences the limits of his omnipotent control and arrives at the realization that the object is wholly other, outside his (the subject's) boundaries.

Importantly, Winnicott (1968a) stated, "Although destruction is the word I am using, this actual destruction belongs to the object's failure to survive. Without this failure, destruction remains potential. The word destruction is needed, not because of the subject's impulse to destroy, but because of the object's liability not to survive" (p. 225).

We can see that although Winnicott accepted the idea of inherent aggression, his ideas about the nature and meaning of this aggression differed significantly from Klein's. For him, the paradoxical destruction and survival of the object leads to the recognition of reality (the external object which has survived) and to the distinction between the internal object and the external object. He linked this to a joyful awareness of both the external world and the survival of the object: "*There is no anger* in the destruction of the object to which I am referring, though there could be said to be joy at the object's survival. From this moment, or arising out of this phase, the object is *in fantasy* always being destroyed. This quality of 'always being destroyed' makes the reality of the surviving object felt as such, strengthens the feeling tone, and contributes to object-constancy. The object can now be used" (Winnicott, 1968a, p. 226).

This is different from Klein, who linked destruction of the object with the depressive position, and the inevitability of guilt, and the need for reparation. For both Winnicott and Klein, the impulse to destroy is in fantasy. For Klein there is resolution but it is guilt-ridden; there is no emphasis on an external object which survives. But for Winnicott, destruction is an achievement because the child has risked the aggressiveness, has experienced the survival of the object, with its implication of constant love, and is able to contain the destruction in fantasy. The child experiences the limits of his omnipotence. The destruction is an achievement because it signifies tolerance of ambivalence and the acceptance of personal aggressiveness. Without this achievement (the risk of destruction and the experience of survival of the object), the child cannot develop the capacity for concern, which Winnicott understood to be beyond guilt.

As Winnicott conceived the process, object usage is not exploitation of the object but, rather, the development of creative potential. The relationship with the object (which at once can be destroyed in fantasy, but in fact survives in reality) allows for the individual to feel free to be creative and to experience both his own authenticity and that of the object. According to Winnicott, then, we can live creatively and with zest only if we can risk destroying the other. The capacity to use the object signals the capacity for living creatively as a separate being.

Winnicott's last statement on the subject may be found in "The Use of an Object in the Context of Moses and Monotheism" (1969b). In this paper he arrived at a formulation of aggression that is crucial in pulling together all of his previous ideas on this subject. "The crux of my argument is that the first drive is itself one thing, something that I call 'destruction,' but I could have called it the combined love-strife drive. This unity is primary. This is what turns up in the baby by natural maturational process. The fate of this unity of drive cannot be stated without reference to the environment. The drive is potentially 'destructive' but whether it *is* destructive or not depends on what the object is like" (p. 245). Here he beings together love and aggression not as opposing forces but as aspects of the same basic drive toward integration and toward the self that can live creatively and feel real.

CLINICAL MATERIAL AND COMMENTARY

His introduction to *The Maturational Processes and the Facilitating Environment* (1965) makes clear Winnicott's intention to explore those failures of development in infancy that lead to serious disturbance.

He believed that patients with such problems cannot be treated by Freudian analysis alone. He stressed the importance of waiting until the patient has the ability to *use* the analyst—that is, to use his interpretations. Winnicott maintained that with these patients, change depends first on the analyst's survival. They need the analyst to provide an ego-adaptive setting. Initially, an insightful interpretation is less important than sufficient support of ego development. Once the patient achieves integrity of the self and is able to feel real, he will become able to use the analyst in a way that he could not risk with his parents.

The following case material illustrates the initial recognition, acceptance, and working through of aggression in the individual, from actuality to fantasy.

JUAN: CLINICAL ILLUSTRATION 1

Juan was five-and-a-half when he began three-times-weekly psychoanalysis. He exhibited a number of symptoms, including distractibility, impulsivity, and difficulty sitting still. Juan was afraid to go to the family playroom alone and frequently went to his parents' bed in the middle of the night. He also had a history of speech delay and temper tantrums. But the incidents that brought him into therapy were far more serious: At three, Juan had entered the family car alone, put it in gear, and crashed it through the garage door. This brought him to treatment in a group setting. Then at five, he set a fire that destroyed his bedroom. This prompted Juan's parents to seek further help in individual psychotherapy.

Juan's birth was greeted with ambivalence. His parents had recently moved from another country. His mother was frequently unavailable, emotionally or physically, since she was busy attending to her husband's needs as well as to the demands of her own profession. Juan's care was left to a series of baby nurses during his first two years, after which he had a single caregiver. Moreover, he appears to have been a challenging infant: for example, it was reported that he cried constantly and could not be soothed easily.

Juan's inner world is illustrated by what happened in the first session. In the playroom, Juan selected a small car from a toy-box and asked, "Will it go by itself?" He then tried the car on the floor, crashed it into the wall, and exclaimed, "It didn't break!" Then he took out a pig with nursing piglets attached and said, "I wonder what kind of animal this is." He placed a number of toys inside a fence, which his analyst assembled for him at his request, and said, "Now they can't get out. The baby pigs are trying to get back inside the mother."

Breaking some modeling clay into pieces, Juan said, "This will be food for the animals." Then he removed the animals from inside the enclosure and placed them by the "food" so "they can't get it and eat it all up." He added, "I wonder if these animals bite?" The analyst commented that he wanted to keep the food safe from the biting animals.

Juan rolled a piece of clay and said, "This is a cobra. It is a snake that could kill. It can kill an alligator, a rhinoceros and a fire-eating dragon." The analyst responded, "It sounds as if a cobra is more dangerous than any of these other dangerous biting animals." Juan answered, "Yes, if a cobra touches the sink, it would fall apart. If a cobra touches a house, the house would fall down. If a cobra touches water, it would cause a fire and make the fire alarm go off." The analyst commented that there had been a very dangerous fire in Juan's house.

Juan went to the window and reported seeing an ambulance. "Maybe it is going to a fire," he said. The analyst said, "Firemen also go to fires." Juan replied, "The fire is already over." He then said, "Butterflies can't fly, only airplanes can."

Juan picked up various toys from the toy drawer and began to mark each one with a crayon. He put marks on a boy doll and a baby doll. He then picked up the mother doll and threw her in the corner of the toy drawer. He took out a white crayon and declared, "I'm going to draw. The white crayon is the whole color of all the crayon world!"

Going back to the animals and covering them with modeling clay, he said, "I'll keep them all in a pile and fix it so they can't get out." The analyst said, "I wonder if the animals are being punished?" Juan smiled and said, "No," but kept putting modeling clay on top of them.

As the session ended, Juan took some masking tape, marked on it, and stuck it on his toy drawer. He asked the analyst to write his name on another piece of tape, which he then attached to the radiator. The analyst commented that, as with the toys, Juan now was marking both his drawer and the radiator so that this place would be "just for him."

COMMENTARY

To consider this vignette according to Winnicott's way of thinking, Juan's behavior makes insistent demands on the environment for care and management; he continues to search for an object to whom he may relate. He declares his anxiety about his continuity of being when he asks of the small car, "Will it go by itself?" By smashing it repetitively against the wall and declaring, "It didn't break" Juan reassures himself that both he and the house are not damaged. He also illustrates his continued demand that the environment meet his self-expression. His only way of "being" seems to be that of finding opposition, of coming up against something.

By questioning the animal's identity, Juan is letting his analyst know about his own precarious sense of self. He is asking: Who am I? Am I only a bundle of projections (as in the stage of object-relating), or can I use you to find myself and experience realness (as in object usage)? The piglets trying to get back inside their mother may indicate that returning to the safety of the womb offers a solution in fantasy to fears of his own destructiveness.

Juan goes on to play out a scenario in which he has to keep food safe from biting animals. This could be understood as a portrayal of his early oral greed, which was not understood or accepted as normal ruthless loving (primary aggression) but rather was regarded as purposive anger (secondary aggression). He may be expressing anxiety about his mother's role as nurturer and as survivor of his greed. The dangerous cobra-boy vividly portrays the sense of destructiveness felt by Juan. His sense of vulnerability is revealed by the comparison of butterflies to airplanes. A defensive use of omnipotence may underlie his reference to "the white crayon . . . the whole color of all the crayon world." When he subsequently marks the toys and radiator with his name, he is personalizing and valuing the analytic situation. This is the constructive gesture that will enable him to get to his experience of destructiveness. As Winnicott (1960b) wrote: "People have to understand that their primitive destructive urges belong to their early love. Perhaps it is true to say that human beings cannot tolerate the destructive aim in their very early loving. The idea of it can be tolerated, however, if the individual who is getting towards it has evidence of a constructive aim already at hand of which he or she can be reminded" (p. 139).

CATHY: CLINICAL ILLUSTRATION 2

Cathy, 45 years old, came to a second analyst after her first analysis was terminated prematurely. She was dissatisfied with her marriage, depressed and suicidal. She had been a compliant and well-mannered child who never felt that she could win her mother's approval. Regardless of what she did, her mother criticized her.

It seemed that her first analyst had provided primarily a holding environment. Cathy had idealized him and now demanded perfect adaptation from her new analyst, constantly comparing his failures to the perfection of her first analyst and equating them with her parents' failures. However, during the first year of treatment she worked through this idealization and came to understand that what she may have taken from her previous analyst was the hope that there would be a cure.

During the next two to three years, treatment was characterized by intermittent use of the analyst's small failures. For example, one day when the analyst was slow to greet her at the door, she said, "I thought you had not waited for me, that you had left, that you don't like me, that you hate me and want to get rid of me. You are just like my mother, who was never there for me."

In the fourth year of treatment, instead of the usual description of herself as "panicky, fearful, needy and psychosomatic," Cathy was beginning to acknowledge that she was constantly angry and always critical. In one session she said, "I am thinking a terrible thought! I hope that my mother doesn't die soon because I am starting a new job next week." The analyst commented, "You feel you ought to be ashamed of the bit of you that longs for the stimulation of an interesting job, and seem inappropriately ashamed of this wish to not have any impingement on your concentration as you begin it." Cathy next said that she had found her father's violin when she was cleaning closets. She wondered bitterly why he had never played for the family, only for his quartet. The analyst said, "You are linking his 'selfishness' with what you believe to be your own." Cathy continued, "I still haven't sent the check for my mother's burial plot. Mother wants me to buy her a plot beside father. But it is like I will have buried her already if I do that! She will be angry, even though she told me to buy it." The analyst said, "This is the projection of your anger onto mother. It is you who, behind all your compliance, have been angry at mother who constantly denigrated you. Would you consider that buying the plot may be too close to your unconscious murderous rage at her?"

In subsequent analytic work the focus was on the secondary aggression that had built up over a lifetime of compliance. This work led Cathy to a measure of empathy for herself and a beginning capacity for taking responsibility for her own angry feelings. Although this capacity waxed and waned, eventually Cathy was able to say, "It is nice to be at the point where what I do I feel comfortable with, and that I can do things without 'should' or 'should not' coming into it. But still I get agitated and irritable, and I don't like the disappointments." The analyst said, "This is the precariousness of *doing*." Cathy said, "I don't like being down." The analyst continued, "When you dream up your world, you have to be prepared that the outside world may not greet you in return. Using your imagination or creativity means risking the interplay between what is inside you and the control of the outside."

COMMENTARY

In this vignette, the patient's experience of the analyst's survival of her attacks eventually enables her to explore both primary and secondary aggression. The implications of the concept of the survival and use of the analyst are that the patient comes to take the risk of not protecting the analyst from "destruction." The destructive activity is an attempt to put the analyst outside the sphere of influence— outside the patient's omnipotent control—so that she can use the analyst. Winnicott says that when this happens, the positive changes that come about are profound; they depend not on interpretive work but on the analyst's survival of attacks without retaliation. *Reliability* in these moments of attack is all that matters.

Interpretation at these moments can seem to the patient like the analyst's self-defense (Winnicott, 1968a, p. 224). "Usually the analyst lives through these phases of movement in the transference, and after each phase there comes reward in terms of love, reinforced by the fact of the backcloth of unconscious destruction" (p. 225). Sufficient use of the analyst leads to working through the moments between primary and secondary aggression. In the session about the burial plot, the analyst first interprets the patient's inappropriate shame for wanting to go forward in her life. Only later in the session, after the patient experiences anxiety about her selfishness, can the analyst interpret unconscious rage and evidence of a death wish toward mother.

Once some self-reflective mechanism is at work, the analyst can interpret the risk of playing, imagining, and creating. The psychoanalyst Harry Guntrip provides us with a vivid illustration of how Winnicott himself used such interpretation. Recounting his own analysis with Winnicott, Guntrip (1975) writes, "Right at the end of my analysis I had a sudden return of hard talking in session. This time he [Winnicott] made a different and extraordinary statement. He said: 'It's like you giving birth to a baby with my help. You gave me half an hour of concentrated talk, rich in content. I felt strained in listening and holding the situation for you. You had to know that I could stand your talking hard at me and my not being destroyed. I had to stand it while you were in labour being creative, not destructive, producing something rich in content. You are talking about "object relating," "using the object" and finding you don't destroy it'" (p. 153).

In this excerpt, Winnicott demonstrated eloquently the implications of his formulations about aggression creativity and the use of the object.

CONCLUSION

Tracing Winnicott's theory as it evolved throughout his life, we have come full circle: searching for the relationship between aggression and creativity in Winnicott, we found them together. In his final formulation, Winnicott (1969b) came to see love and aggression as different expressions of the same drive. This one drive, the love-strife drive, is the life force. Love and aggression are inherent and are expressed in the activity, motility, spontaneous reaching out, aggressive, greedy loving of the infant. Primary creativity, primary aggression, primitive love, greed, appetite, destructiveness, and unintentional aggression are all expressions of this drive. After all, can we say that the spontaneous gesture expresses only love and not strife or creativity, or that the creation of the transitional object is creative alone and not also loving? Isn't biting mother's breast also an expression of love? Love and strife, creativity and aggression, all involve moving out to the world, taking hold of one's world and making it one's own. They are the basic elements of the life force made manifest in the infant. So how can we distinguish one from the other?

To return to our original question, why do some people go on to live creatively while others suffer recurrent feelings of futility, anger, and depression? Consider the infant who bites the breast. When the mother does not recognize this biting as an expression of the infant's inherent love and feels it only as an aggressive act, this is experienced by the infant as an impingement. Repeated impingements of this kind interfere with the infant's developing capacity to live with zest and spontaneity. Such experiences underlie the ennui, anger, recurrent bouts of depression, and sense of futility that are felt in adulthood. Alternately, when the mother is able to accept the baby's biting as an expression of his life force (his love and his aggression), the infant is able to continue spontaneously reaching out to the world. This formulation brings us back once again to Winnicott's central idea of the dynamic interplay between the infant's natural developmental path and the facilitating environment. It gives vivid meaning to his constructs and is especially powerful in elucidating the link between creativity and aggression.

The linking of creativity and aggression and the idea of the unity of the love-strife drive are Winnicott's original contributions to the psychoanalytic theory of the development of the psyche. They represent a definitive departure from the theories that preceded them and from most other current psychoanalytic thinking. To our knowledge, this understanding of Winnicott has not been clearly demonstrated or appreciated before.

For Winnicott, without aggression there is no love, and there can be no subject, no object, no reality, and no creativity. In the beginning, creativity and aggression exist as potentials; in the healthy individual they have become achievements. The recognition of one's personal aggression and potential for destruction, the acceptance of this destructiveness, its containment in fantasy, as well as the recognition of its origins in and links with primitive love lead to the possibility of living creatively and with zest. Together, creativity and aggression play profound and essential roles. In the child, they propel development and growth. In the adult, they make possible meaningful and authentic living.

BIBLIOGRAPHY

ABRAM, J. (1996). *The Language of Winnicott: A Dictionary of Winnicott's Use of Words.* London: Karnac Books.

DAVIS, M. (1993a). "Destruction as an achievement in the work of Winnicott." *J. Squiggle Foundation,* 7:85–92.

——— (1993b). Winnicott and the spatula game. *J. Squiggle Foundation,* 8:57–67.

——— & WALLBRIDGE, D. (1981). *Boundary and Space: An Introduction to the Work of D. W. Winnicott.* New York: Brunner/Mazel.

DRAPEAU, P. (1995). Situer Winnicott (1) La science et le point de vue du jardinier. *Revue de psychanalyse,* 6:53–89.

EIGEN, M. (1981). The area of faith in Winnicott, Lacan and Bion. *Int. J. Psychoanal.,* 62:413–433.

——— (1970b). Individuation. In *Psychoanalytic Explorations,* ed. C. Winnicott, R. Shepherd, & M. Davis. Cambridge, Mass.; Harvard University Press, 1989, pp. 284–288.

GOLDMAN, D. (1993). *In Search of the Real: The Origins and Originality of D. W. Winnicott.* Northvale, N.J.: Jason Aronson.

GUNTRIP, H. (1975). My experience of analysis with Fairbairn and Winnicott. *Int. Rev. Psych-Anal.,* 2:145.

JACOBS, M. (1995). *D. W. Winnicott.* London: Sage Publications.

MILNER, M. (1987b). *The Suppressed Madness of Sane Men: Forty-Four Years of Exploring Psychoanalysis.* London: Tavistock Publications.

NEWMAN, A. (1995). *Winnicott's Words: A Companion to the Work of D. W. Winnicott.* New York: New York University Press.

PHILLIPS, A. (1988). *Winnicott.* London: Fontana Press.

SAMUELS, L. (1996). A historical analysis of Winnicott's "Use of an object." *J. Squiggle Foundation,* 11:41–50.

SOLNIT, A. J. (1972). Aggression: A View of Theory Building in Psychoanalysis. *JAPA,* 20:435–50.

WALKER, J. (1996). *Winnicott: Making sense out of chaos.* Unpublished manuscript.

——— (1998). *D. W. Winnicott: On aggression.* Unpublished manuscript.

WINNICOTT, CLARE (1978). D. W. W.: A reflection. In *D. W. Winnicott: Psychoanalytic Explorations,* ed. C. Winnicott, R. Shepherd, & M. Davis. Cambridge, Mass.: Harvard University Press, 1989, pp. 1–18.

WINNICOTT, D. W. (1936). Appetite and emotional disorder. In *Collected Papers: Through Pediatrics to Psycho-Analysis.* London: Tavistock Publications, 1958, pp. 33–51.

——— (1939). Aggression and its roots. In *Deprivation and Delinquency,* ed. C. Winnicott, R. Shepherd, & M. Davis. London: Tavistock Publications, 1984, pp. 84–92.

——— (1941). Observation of infants in a set situation. In *Collected Papers: Through Paediatrics to Psycho-Analysis.* London: Tavistock Publications, 1958, pp. 52–69.

——— (1945). Primitive emotional development. In *Collected Papers: Through Paediatrics to Psycho-Analysis.* London: Tavistock Publications, 1958, pp. 145–156.

——— (1945). Thinking and the unconscious. In *Home Is Where We Start From.* New York: W. W. Norton, 1996, pp. 169–170.

——— (1950–5). Aggression in relation to emotional development. In *Collected Papers: Through Paediatrics to Psycho-Analysis.* London: Tavistock Publications, 1958, pp. 204–218.

——— (1952). Anxiety associated with insecurity. In *Collected Papers: Through Paediatrics to Psycho-Analysis.* London: Tavistock Publications, 1958, pp. 97–100.

——— (1953). Transitional objects and transitional phenomena. In *Playing and Reality.* London: Tavistock Publications, 1971, pp. 1–25.

——— (1954a). The depressive position in normal emotional development. In *Collected Papers: Through Paediatrics to Psycho-Analysis.* London: Tavistock Publications, 1958, pp. 262–277.

——— (1954b). Metapsychological and clinical aspects of regression within the psycho-analytical set-up. In *Collected Papers: Through Paediatrics to Psycho-Analysis.* London: Tavistock Publications, 1958, pp. 278–294.

——— (1956). The antisocial tendency. In *Collected Papers: Through Paedi-*

atrics to Psycho-Analysis. London: Tavistock Publications, 1958, pp. 306–315.

———— (1957). On the contribution of direct observation to psycho-analysis. In *The Maturational Processes and the Facilitating Environment*. New York: International Universities Press, Inc., 1965, pp. 105–114.

———— (1958). The first year of life: modern views on emotional development. In *The Family and Individual Development*. London: Routledge, 1969, pp. 3–14.

———— (1960a). The theory of the parent-infant relationship. In *The Maturational Processes and the Facilitating Environment*. New York: International Universities Press, Inc., 1965, pp. 37–55.

———— (1960b). Aggression, guilt and reparation. In *Deprivation and Delinquency*, ed. C. Winnicott, R. Shepherd, and M. Davis. London: Tavistock Publications, 1958, pp. 136–144.

———— (1962). A personal view of the Kleinian contribution. In *The Maturational Processes and the Facilitating Environment*. New York: International Universities Press, Inc., 1965, pp. 171–178.

———— (1963a). The value of depression. In *Home is Where we Start From*. New York: W. W. Norton & Company, 1986, pp. 71–79.

———— (1963b). The development of the capacity for concern. In *The Maturational Processes and the Facilitating Environment*. New York: International Universities Press, Inc., 1965, pp. 73–82.

———— (1963c). Morals and education. In *The Maturational Processes and the Facilitating Environment*. New York: International Universities Press, Inc., 1965, pp. 93–105.

———— (1964). The roots of aggression. In *Deprivation and Delinquency*, ed. C. Winnicott, R. Shepherd, and M. Davis. London: Tavistock Publications, 1984, pp. 92–99.

———— (1965). Notes made on the train. In *Psychoanalytic Explorations*, ed. C. Winnicott, R. Shepherd, & M. Davis. Cambridge, Mass.: Harvard University Press, 1989, pp. 231–233.

———— (1966). The child in the family group. In *Home is Where We Start From*. New York: W. W. Norton & Company, 1986, pp. 128–141.

———— (1968a). The use of an object and relating through identifications. In *Psychoanalytic Explorations*, ed. C. Winnicott, R. Shepherd, & M. Davis. Cambridge, Mass.: Harvard University Press, 1989, pp. 218–227.

———— (1968b). The use of the word use. In *Psychoanalytic Explorations*, ed. C. Winnicott, R. Shepherd, & M. Davis. Cambridge, Mass.: Harvard University Press, 1989, pp. 233–235.

———— (1968c). Comments on my paper "The use of the object." In *Psychoanalytic Explorations*, ed. C. Winnicott, R. Shepherd, & M. Davis. Cambridge, Mass.: Harvard University Press, 1989, pp. 238–240.

———— (1968d). Roots of aggression. In *Psycho-analytic Explorations*, ed. C. Winnicott, R. Shepherd, & M. Davis. Cambridge, Mass.: Harvard University Press, 1989, pp. 458–461.

—————— (1968e). Communication between infant and mother, and mother and infant, compared and contrasted. In *Babies and their Mothers,* ed. C. Winnicott, R. Shepherd, & M. Davis. New York: Addison-Wesley Publishing Company, Inc., 1989, pp. 89–103.

—————— (1969a). Contribution to a symposium on envy and jealousy. In *Psycho-analytic Explorations,* ed. C. Winnicott, R. Shepherd, & M. Davis. Cambridge, Mass.: Harvard University Press, 1989, pp. 462–464.

—————— (1969b). The use of an object in the context of Moses and Monotheism. In *Psycho-analytic Explorations,* ed. C. Winnicott, R. Shepherd, & M. Davis. Cambridge, Mass.: Harvard University Press, 1989, pp. 240–246.

—————— (1970a). Living creatively. In *Home is Where We Start From.* New York: W. W. Norton and Company, 1996, pp. 35–54.

—————— (1970b). Individuation. In *Psychoanalytic Explorations,* ed. C. Winnicott, R. Shepherd, & M. Davis. Cambridge, Mass.: Harvard University Press, 1989, pp. 284–288.

—————— (1971a). Playing: a theoretical statement. In *Playing and Reality.* London: Tavistock Publications, 1971, pp. 38–53.

—————— (1971b). Creativity and its origins. In *Playing and Reality.* London: Tavistock Publications, 1971, pp. 65–85.

DEVELOPMENT

On the Ethical and Evaluative Nature of Developmental Models in Psychoanalysis

RACHEL BLASS, Ph.D.

This paper points to the ethical/evaluative positions that underlie two psychoanalytic models of development and their ideals of maturity, Freud's concept of genital maturity and Winnicott's concept of the True Self. The author also explores the nature of the justifications, if any, of these ethical/evaluative positions and addresses the implications of her findings for the assessment of the validity of other psychoanalytic developmental theories and for the application of developmental theories in psychoanalytic practice.

THIS PAPER ADDRESSES ONE SPECIFIC DIMENSION OF THE ETHICS OF psychoanalysis, namely, the ethical/evaluative nature of psychoanalytic theories of development. In its concern with the fact that ethical and value statements are embedded in psychoanalytic developmental theories and with the available justifications of these statements the present study complements three other areas of psychoanalytic investigation.

One such area is the investigation of the ethics of psychoanalytic treatment (e.g., Bornstein, et al., 1983). Here we find primarily a concern with the impact on the analysand of the analyst's person and

---

Senior lecturer in the Department of Psychology, The Hebrew University of Jerusalem, and candidate at the Israel Psychoanalytic Institute.

I am grateful to Dr. William Meissner for his comments on a previous draft of this paper. An earlier version of parts of the paper was presented at a conference on "Freud at the Threshold of the Twentieth Century" in Jerusalem, December 1999.

The Psychoanalytic Study of the Child 56, ed. Albert J. Solnit, Peter B. Neubauer, Samuel Abrams, and A. Scott Dowling (Yale University Press, copyright © 2001 by Albert J. Solnit, Peter B. Neubauer, Samuel Abrams, and A. Scott Dowling).

personal morals and of the analytic setting, and to a lesser extent with what may be considered ethical conduct between analyst and analysand (e.g., Klimovsky, et al., 1995). The issue of technical values—i.e., values that are built into the structure of the analytic praxis (such as self-understanding, authenticity, truth)—has also been recently addressed (Meissner, 1996). In general, the conclusion of such studies is that self-awareness will mitigate any harmful effects of the analyst's personal morals on the analysis, allowing the analysand the optimal development of independent morals and values. While this conclusion is often presented with a greater awareness than Freud might have had of the intricacies of the psychoanalytic situation and the inevitable involvement of the person of the analyst, nevertheless, it resembles Freud's early position that optimal analytic progress requires that the analyst overcome the desire to force his ideals on his patients (1918, pp. 164–165).

By pointing to ethical dimensions inherent in the developmental theories that inform analytic practice, the present study stresses that factors additional to those related to the analyst's person must be taken into account in any attempt to prevent the imposition of ideals on the analysand. That is, if (as I will contend) the developmental theories that guide the analyst's work include ethical positions, then the analyst's awareness of his personal value system and of the values inherent in analytic practice will not suffice to mitigate a directive influence of those values on the analysand. Additional steps will be needed in this regard.

Another area of research to which the current study is relevant attempts to delineate the goals, aims, and ideals of psychoanalysis. This kind of research has emerged out of purely theoretical concerns (e.g., Rieff, 1961; Wallwork, 1991), as well as out of clinical interest (e.g., Grinberg, 1990; Hartmann, 1939; Sandler and Dreher, 1996). The research as a rule notes the influence of a kind of ethic, moral world-view, or ideal of health and well-being on psychoanalytic theory and practice. Ideals of truth and autonomy are considered central to this ethic, and various kinds of adaptive relationships to the environment are noted as well. But what characterizes much of this work is that it provides descriptions that are essentially observational rather than critical. That is, it describes the kind of ethics that prevail in psychoanalysis but, in the main, does not attempt to justify or refute them.

Hartmann's early and famous paper on "Psychoanalysis and the Concept of Health" (1939) is interesting in this regard because it reveals a major difficulty in maintaining such an observational stance.[1] Noting that ethical and other evaluative systems play a part in psycho-analytic conceptions of health, Hartmann makes it clear that the question that faces the analyst is "not whether these norms are justi-fied" but rather what is "the genesis and structure of behavior which has, in fact, for whatever reason, been assigned a place in a scale of positive and negative values. . . . [W]e may ask ourselves what con-ceptions of health have been advanced and not whether certain con-ceptions 'ought' to be advanced" (p. 8). But as he proceeds to answer this question it becomes quite clear that Hartmann is not merely de-scribing existing conceptions. He is, rather, advancing a conception that he thinks *ought* to be advanced—namely, a conception of mental health that gives greater weight to adaptation to reality. While it may be argued that this emphasis on adaptation merely allows for a more accurate definition of what is conventionally meant by the term "mental health," it would seem that Hartmann is, in effect, suggest-ing that conventions regarding the meaning of mental health must change in order to take into account the value of adaptation. For ex-ample, he thinks that many people have conceptions of mental health that downplay this component in favor of conceptions that give "undue prominence" to the capacity for instinctual expression or for rationality (p. 9). Thus the focus on adaptation reflects Hart-mann's own view of the ideal, not an attempt to better capture some objective given state.

It is at this point that the inherent difficulty with an observational position in relation to psychoanalytic values becomes apparent. What constitutes mental health and pathology is not a given fact to be sim-ply observed but something that psychoanalysis, through its theoreti-cal formulations, plays a part in determining. And, indeed, psycho-analysis does not usually seem to regard itself as a mere agent of society, charged with propagating those values that happen to be broadly accepted. Rather, it seems to regard its goals, aims, ideals, and, more broadly, its ethic as its very own. Moreover, even when so-ciety offers some general notion of what is healthy, often there are dissident views, and the analyst must make a choice among them. This choice is also not merely observational—it is not founded on given facts regarding health and pathology—but rather reflects a value judgment. The purely descriptive stance that Hartmann sees as

1. This difficulty persists in Hartmann's later book *Psychoanalysis and Moral Values* (1960).

appropriate for psychoanalysis, and which is continued in present-day studies of this kind (Sandler and Dreher, 1996), is inherently problematic.

The present paper may be seen to be a contribution to this area of study in that it both explores central values embedded specifically in psychoanalytic developmental theories and raises the neglected critical question of whether sufficient justification is provided for them.

A third area of research to which the present work is relevant is that of psychoanalytic developmental theories. If, as I contend, these theories are guided in part by ethical/evaluative considerations, then acknowledgment of these considerations contributes to our understanding of the theories. Further, these ethical/evaluative factors may serve to explain some of the differences and disputes between developmental theories which are not accounted for by terminological idiosyncrasies, empirical findings, and clinical interests and focuses.[2]

In this paper I use the term "ethical/evaluative" to cover a wide range of phenomena, all united by the fact that they refer to that which is inherently good. That is, any statement that some act or way of being is desirable because it is what is inherently good to do or be is here considered an ethical/evaluative statement. Included would be statements regarding what is moral, ethical, and virtuous and statements regarding what is of value existentially (i.e., what is the right kind of way for a person to live).

In this context, it is very important to distinguish between this kind of inherent good ("the good") and "goods"—things that are beneficial or of worth to someone in some way. Satisfaction of a desire or pleasure of any kind is always beneficial in some sense, but not all beneficial things are good in the ethical/evaluative sense that I intend here. In order to attain what is inherently good it is sometimes necessary to forfeit various benefits—for example, giving up some of one's own goods in order to be just or to act charitably. This is also the case when one manifests a certain virtue that runs counter to one's inclinations. In these instances the individual relinquishes

---

2. Psychoanalysis has discussed the issue of ethics in some additional ways as well (Erikson, 1976, Sosnik, et al., 1992, Strenger, 1997, Wallerstein, 1976)—for example, in its theories on the development of the superego. But these discussions almost never address the inherently ethical nature of the development concepts, and when this dimension is acknowledged it is not regarded critically. That is, the question of the value and foundation of the ethical dimension is not raised, nor is its incorporation into the broader psychoanalytic framework considered problematic (Blass, 1999).

some goods, not in order to obtain greater goods (i.e., benefits), but rather in order to attain, or to do, what is inherently good.

This leads me to one more point of clarification. Thus far my explanation of my use of the term "ethical/evaluative" has focused primarily on ethical/evaluative *statements*. But these need to be distinguished from ethical/evaluative *theories*. While the former (statements) propose what is good, the latter (theories) provide some framework or justification to explain how or why this is so. To say that one ought to be charitable or productive is to make an ethical/evaluative statement. To explain why charity is a virtue or why productivity is an important existential value is to put forth an ethical/evaluative theory. Most people hold views comprised of many ethical evaluative statements, but few have developed or adopted well-formed ethical/evaluative theories.

I turn now to examine the evaluative/ethical nature of the developmental theories of Freud and Winnicott. In each case my focus will be on one aspect or model of each theory. In reference to Freud I will relate to the goal of genitality, in reference to Winnicott to the development of a True Self. I will not attempt to provide comprehensive formulations of these aspects of the theories but will rely on my readers' general familiarity with the theories and will describe the *ways* in which they are put forth by their authors. In each case I will first point to the factual nature of the description—that is, how the model is presented as something discerned through acquaintance with factual matters relating to the individual. I will then show how alongside the factual description ethical/evaluative statements are to be found. In other words, the description refers not only to what exists and what state of affairs brings about another state of affairs but also to the value or goodness of what exists and the state of affairs one should seek to attain. Finally, I will indicate the nature of the justification provided for the ethical/evaluative statements.

FREUD'S MODEL OF THE DEVELOPMENT OF MATURE SEXUALITY

THE FACTUAL NATURE OF THE DESCRIPTION OF THE CONCEPT

The most detailed description of Freud's concept of sexual development is to be found in his *Three Essays on the Theory of Sexuality* (1905). There he explicitly refers to his conclusions regarding sexual life as statements of "fact" (p. 197) and as "findings" derived from a combination of psychoanalytic investigation reaching back into childhood and the direct observation of children (p. 201). As is well known, Freud presented these "findings" in a model that describes various pregenital and genital organizations of the libidinal drives and that focuses on their essential qualities, primarily their sources, aims, and objects. This model elucidates the biological and environmental factors that influence the course of development as the individual moves from organization to organization, ultimately arriving at the mature state in which the drives of the earlier stages become subservient to the genital drive. While Freud later changed his views on the timing of this shift, in *Three Essays* he ascribes the transition from autoerotism to a relationship to an extraneous sexual object to this final stage. Both the sensual genital desires and the affectionate currents that evolved through repression that took place in latency are directed toward this extraneous object. The aim of these desires (for men) is satisfaction through discharge.

The following passages illustrate the factual way in which Freud presents some of these processes. For example, regarding the nature of the early object choice he writes:

> It may be regarded as typical of the choice of an object that the process is diphasic, that is, that it occurs in two waves. The first of these begins between the ages of two and five, and is brought to a halt or to a retreat by the latency period; it is characterized by the infantile nature of the sexual aims. The second wave sets in with puberty and determines the final outcome of sexual life (p. 200).

Regarding the transformation to the mature state of puberty he writes:

> The sexual instinct has hitherto been predominantly auto-erotic; it now finds a sexual object. Its activity has hitherto been derived from a number of separate instincts and erotogenic zones, which, independently of one another, have pursued a certain sort of pleasure as their sole sexual aim. Now, however, a new sexual aim appears, and all the component instincts combine to attain it, while the erotogenic zones become subordinated to the primacy of the genital zone. . . . The new sexual aim in men consists in the discharge of the sexual products. . . . The sexual instinct is now subordinated to the reproductive function (p. 207).

Freud here seems to be simply presenting his findings on observed changes in psychological and biological functioning at different points in the life-cycle. There are no immediately apparent ethical/ evaluative statements involved. This is particularly so when the focus is on the biological dimensions of development—for example, when

Freud refers to the genital stage as founded on "the manifest growth of the external genitalia" and a concomitant development of the internal genitalia such that they are now able to discharge the sexual products (p. 208). But there is no striking shift in tone when he describes psychological developments such as the changes that take place in the nature of the object choice, or the effects of mental life on sexual excitation (p. 203).

A similarly factual approach is apparent when Freud points to the obstacles in the path of development. For example, he notes that there may be difficulties in satisfying the aim of the genital drive if a "component instinct shall already during childhood have contributed an unusual amount of pleasure" (p. 211). Such overly pleasurable experiences and the fixations and repressions they bring about are also described as the source of later difficulties in finding an appropriate sexual object (p. 200).

THE ETHICAL/EVALUATIVE STATEMENTS EMBEDDED IN THE FACTUAL DESCRIPTION

The ethical/evaluative nature of Freud's developmental model emerges primarily from an examination of the ways in which he defines and determines what he considers the mature state of sexual development. Were he to define maturity as an inevitable outcome of the developmental process or in terms of what tends to be the end of this process or what people tend to *regard* as its desired end, then a factual approach to maturity would be maintained. Accordingly, an observational method would be applied to determine the course leading to maturity; there would be no question of the involvement of ethical/evaluative determinants. On the other hand, if Freud were to consider the end-state of development not as inevitable but as open to variation, or if he were concerned not with the end people *do* arrive at but rather with the end they *should* arrive at, and were he to define this possible end-state not as what he *believed* people desired but rather in terms of what *is* indeed desirable, then what maturity is would no longer be a simple matter of fact or an event to be simply observed but rather would reflect some kind of choice or preference by Freud. In this case two possibilities would arise. One is that the preference would be determined by the goods that this specific notion of maturity allows for (e.g., the experienced pleasure). In this case Freud would be putting forth his conception of maturity merely as one possible path of development open to those who wish to reap the benefits it offers. The other possibility is that the preference would be determined by an ethical/evaluative position. In this case it is Freud's position on the inherent good toward which a person should develop that would determine what maturity is. I contend that in Freud's writings the mature state of development is indeed determined by such an ethical/evaluative position.

The ethical/evaluative statement that underlies Freud's factual description of his conception of mature genitality is not always easy to discern. At times it seems as though he is speaking of inevitable processes or general tendencies and beliefs. Yet careful analysis shows that what determines Freud's position is a value. Let us look at the covert evaluative statement that emerges in the following key passage from Freud's very factual *Three Essays:*

> The final outcome of sexual development lies in what is known as the normal sexual life of the adult, in which the pursuit of pleasure comes under the sway of the reproductive function and in which the component instincts, under the primacy of a single erotogenic zone, form a firm organization directed towards a sexual aim attached to some extraneous sexual object (p. 197).

At first sight there seem to be several possible factual interpretations of this passage. It may be suggested that the outcome of which Freud speaks here is inevitably final; it is a fact of nature that the possibility of reproductive functioning emerges last. And it is another fact of nature that the aim of the genital drives is "discharge of sexual products" (p. 208). In speaking of the pubertal development of the genital zone, Freud, indeed, affirms that "the starting-point and the final aim of the process . . . are clearly visible." Alternatively, it may be suggested that Freud is speaking here of what is commonly found to be the final outcome. He would thus be stating that most people tend to arrive at the developmental state he is describing. This would be in line with Freud's later references to "characteristic" and "typical" processes of the pubertal phase (p. 199). Yet another possible interpretation arises if one takes Freud's reference to "what is known as the normal sexual life of the adult" as a statement regarding common belief regarding the normal, and hence desired, state of development. Such an interpretation would be in accordance with Hartmann's view that psychoanalysis treats social values as facts regarding mental health.

But these interpretations are ultimately untenable. Indeed, it may be a biological or psychological fact that the genital drives, zones, and reproductive functioning develop last and that the aim of adult sexual drives is discharge. But Freud's model of mature genitality does not simply posit such facts. Rather, it refers to one specific way in which the facts are to be dealt with. According to Freud, there is a normal, appropriate, and desired way of expressing genital sexuality. It should allow for some partial inhibited expression of the pregenital drives. It should involve the convergence of the affectionate and sensual currents. There should be a single extraneous object, different from the objects of childhood, toward whom these currents are directed, etc. Alternative ways of dealing with the newly emerging genital drives, such as their complete inhibition or an expression of them in relation to numerous objects without any concomitant affection, also take into account the very fact of the presence of the genital drives, but do not constitute what Freud would consider mature developmental states but rather pathological ones. In short, while the emergence of genital drives may be regarded as an inevitable factual event, how the mature individual deals with it is not.

Regarding the possibility that Freud's model of genital maturity depicts common practice or belief, it may be seen that such an interpretation would be highly inconsistent with his more general critical view of many social conventions. Freud would not adopt conventions without careful scrutiny of their sources, meanings, and implications. His analyses of the misguided nature of humankind's belief systems and the faults of present-day civilization are central to his thinking (e.g., Freud, 1927, 1930). Indeed, in the present instance there may be some overlap between what is characteristic of pubertal sexuality, what is believed regarding sexual maturity, and what Freud himself considered to be the ultimate state of development, but Freud did not and would not determine his views by statistics or opinion polls. For example, he did not consider hysteria normal simply because many girls manifested its symptoms (e.g., Freud, 1896). Nor did he think that the sexual behavior of most men reflected the attainment of mature genitality; many, for example, fail to bring about the convergence of the sexual and the affectionate currents or to reach satisfaction (e.g., Freud, 1912). Furthermore, no positive findings are presented suggesting that what he is putting forth as mature indeed corresponds to such practices and beliefs.

Further support for this argument that Freud did not define maturity in terms of some factual event is found in the manner in which he presented his remarks. They appear at the very beginning of the section entitled "Phases of the Sexual Organization" and are followed by Freud's most explicit description of the developmental stages. That is, *prior* to the presentation of any evidence, Freud affirms that genital sexuality is clearly the final outcome of sexual development, and no subsequent evidence is added. Factual considerations simply do not come into play.

But if the nature of maturity is not defined or determined by facts, there is still the possibility that a personal preference is coming into play. That is, one could perhaps argue that Freud was describing only one possible course of development among many others from which the individual may choose depending on his preferences. Such a description would not involve an ethical/evaluative stance on Freud's part. This view, however, must also be rejected. Freud makes no reference to such an open perspective on development. He does not suggest that alternate routes of equal value exist. Rather, the opposite is suggested. Alternate routes that certain individuals may take are viewed in the light of his own preferred route and are deemed pathological. Those who do not arrive at mature genital sexuality *fail* to attain it (p. 200).

Ultimately, there is, according to Freud, only one fully desirable developmental path. People should attain mature sexuality, and not because of the facts or because of the possible benefits. People should attain this state of maturity because it is inherently good. In other words, the final outcome of development is defined and determined by an ethical/evaluative stance, by what Freud held as the "ideals" of mature sexuality and of human development in general (p. 200).

From this recognition of the ethical/evaluative nature of Freud's model of maturity there follows an ethical/evaluative reading of the specific developmental aims maturity entails. Rather than being viewed as observational data, these aims must now be regarded as statements regarding how a person should be. In effect, Freud is affirming that one *should* move beyond autoerotic pregenital pleasures to a complex relationship to an external other, that this other sexuality *should* be felt along with affectionate feelings that one *should* not be inhibited from serving the reproductive function, etc. Values of concern and affection for the other and for society in general, as well as the importance of active fulfillment of one's biological potential, are here expressed.

It is important in this context to be aware of the centrality of these ethical/evaluative statements to the broader developmental model. They are not merely one dimension of the model but shape its essential nature. For it is in light of the conception of the mature state that Freud proceeded to formulate the developmental process as that which leads to maturity. Freud explicitly acknowledged this. In *Three Essays on the Theory of Sexuality* (1905), after describing the desired final outcome of the developmental process, he explained that his understanding of the stages leading up to this outcome was derived from the study of "inhibitions and disturbances" in its attainment (p. 197). That is, once we know the final outcome, the ultimate goal, we can understand positive development in terms of progress toward it and pathological development in terms of the factors that impede it. It is not that the facts of development reveal the genital goal; rather, the ethical/evaluative view that this is the goal to be attained shapes the understanding of the developmental process.

One further dimension of this view should be noted. In positing that the final genital goal is good Freud did not make explicit the *exact* sense in which it is good. It seems, however, that he was referring to good not in a moral sense but in an existential one. That is, Freud described the failure to attain genital sexuality not as morally or ethically wrong but as exemplifying a kind of lack in the individual's existence. If a person does not attain genital maturity something in his/her being remains incomplete, "inhibited" (p. 208). There is one point, however, where an ethical dimension does come into play: when Freud explicitly states that the failure to attain an aspect of the developmental goal is *not* a matter of ethics. He reiterates this view at various points. For example, in *Civilization and its Discontents* (1930) Freud claims that society's prohibitions on extragenital satisfaction and same-sex object choice are the source of serious injustice because they "disregard . . . the dissimilarities, whether innate or acquired, in the sexual constitution of human beings" and thus "cuts off a fair number of them from sexual enjoyment" (p. 104). Freud maintains here that no ethical dimensions worthy of consideration underlie the prohibitions that stand in the way of the individual's sexual enjoyment. This point is further developed in his famous response to a letter of a concerned mother of a homosexual:

> Homosexuality is assuredly no advantage, but it is nothing to be ashamed of, no vice, no degradation. . . . [W]e consider it to be a variation of the sexual function, produced by a certain arrest of sexual development (Jones, 1957, pp. 195–196).

Were Freud merely to assert that as a psychoanalyst he could describe different sexual constitutions and developmental arrests as well as their behavioral consequences but could make any statement on their ethical value, his position would not be an ethical one. But once he affirms that certain forms of sexual behavior should be considered morally acceptable on the ground that they are the best ways to attain sexual satisfaction, given a person's constitution and development, once he suggests that a certain instance of developmental arrest has no ethical consequences, then a metaethical position is being taken. It should be noted here that Freud did not consistently maintain that all activity is ethical if it is a form of gratification determined by one's constitutional and developmental capacities. Such a view would logically require that cruelty, if pleasing to its perpetrator, be regarded as ethical, and Freud clearly did not maintain this (Freud, 1933, p. 214). For Freud additional factors come into play in determining the overall morality of an act, such as the harm the act causes to others and the degree to which its performance precludes participation in other forms of higher cultural activities. Nevertheless, in determining whether a certain act is ethical, one of Freud's considerations is its developmental determinants. He felt that an ethical judgment was possible, at least in part, on the basis of his psychoanalytic understanding of these determinants.

The combination of Freud's position on the value of genital sexuality and his position on its non-ethical status results in the view that genital sexuality is a developmental state that people should seek to attain, but that failure to attain it is not necessarily immoral. To arrive at sexual maturity is most desirable and valuable, and yet an action that is based on developmental limitations should not be considered unethical but should be understood as a pathological variation in human functioning and consequently of no inherent ethical implications.

THE JUSTIFICATION OF THE ETHICAL/EVALUATIVE STATEMENTS

Did Freud provide an ethical/evaluative *theory* that would explain or provide a framework for understanding his ethical/evaluative *statements?* In a general sense the answer is no. This might be expected inasmuch as Freud apparently considered his model to be wholly factual and not ethical/evaluative. Nevertheless, there is the possibility that beyond the specific context of his developmental conception, from an analysis of the entirety of his works, some implicit justifying theory is available. Such a thesis is put forth by Wallwork in *Psychoanalysis and Ethics* (1991). There he argues not only that Freud's conceptions have implications for ethical theory but that these conceptions in their entirety contain a significant and yet latent ethical perspective, and that in an implicit way Freud also provides grounding for this perspective.

Wallwork's very detailed understanding of Freud's implicit ethical theory may be briefly summarized as follows: Happiness is what is good or of value, but not just any happiness, only those forms of happiness that are based on strong feelings of pleasure, and only when the pleasure attains certain personal and social aims. Those specific pleasures are of value because they are those that are experienced by a person in a state of developmental maturity. The pleasures experienced in this state *should* be sought because that is the state the person *should* be in. And finally, that is the state that the person *should* be in because in that state the person fulfills his true function. Here Wallwork relies on ancient Greek theoretical conceptualizations that link the notion of "function" with the notion of "good." According to Wallwork, this link allows Freud to "*logically* pass from . . . purported *fact* about human development [the nature of human function] to a normative ideal [what is the good or valued way to be]" (p. 256).

It may be seen that two kinds of values are involved in this exposition. There are valued acts and interactions which, when carried out by the mature individual, are also experienced as pleasurable. And there is a valued state of being, the mature state of development, which, while not pleasurable in itself, provides the ground for valued pleasures. That is, Wallwork posits that in Freud's formulation it is only because of the value of the state of the experiencer that what he experiences as pleasurable is indeed of value. Wallwork's study focuses primarily on the former kind of values, but the latter kind is more fundamental. It is also of greater concern to the present study inasmuch as it is more directly concerned with Freud's conception of the mature state and its grounding as an ethical value.

Careful analysis of Freud's justification of his ethics and, more specifically, his justification of the value of the mature state of development reveals severe limitations. Formulations of the kinds of happiness and pleasure that are to be valued do not constitute a justification of Freud's ethics or even an explanatory theory; they simply further elaborate Freud's beliefs regarding what kinds of things are worthy. They are informative, but dogmatic. That is, they provide a more lucid picture of the things Freud approved of (e.g., the kinds of pleasures and consequences he considered important), but in and of themselves they offer no explanation of why these things are worthy of approval. The final step, in which there is a turn to the essential function of the person, differs from all the previous steps in this regard. Here Freud attempts to answer the question of why what is being put forth as a value is indeed a value. Here, however, I contend that the argument presented is fundamentally flawed.

In this final step Freud, according to Wallwork, implicitly makes the move from desired pleasures to the desired state of being—i.e., the state of developmental maturity. The problem with this argument lies in its claim that maturity as depicted by Freud is the state in which the person fulfills his function. Firstly, without further evidence that it is specifically this state (depicted by Freud) that fulfills the person's function, the statement is merely another dogmatic assertion. Secondly, the notion that that which is inherently good is derived from the person's function rests on a teleological framework in which all natural things have a desired end (see, e.g., Aristotle's *Nichomachean Ethics,* Bk. I: Ch. 1). Only if a natural thing is considered to have an inherent end could its very function be good. But rather than speak of function in terms of inherent ends, Wallwork focuses on function in terms of what is "characteristic" or "normally expected" of things:

> From such factual premises as "This knife cuts well" and "This fisherman catches lots of fish every day," the evaluative conclusions validly follow that "This is a good knife" and "He is a good fisherman." These arguments are valid because the concepts of a knife and a fisherman are functional concepts; that is, *knife* and *fisherman* are defined in terms of the purpose or function that knife and fisherman are normally expected to serve (1991, p. 256).

Wallwork concludes that since the human being is similarly a functional concept "[it follows] from the factual statement . . . that [a certain] woman is flourishing in the sense of being a loving, self-reliant, creative contributor to society . . . that she is a good person."

But Wallwork's examples are misleading and his conclusion is faulty. A knife and a fisherman do not have inherent ends and thus are not inherently good. When we say that a knife is good what we mean is that an object designated to serve a certain end (to cut bread), is serving that end well, or that something intrinsic to the form of a certain object makes it well-adapted to serving that designated end. When we say that a fisherman is good, what we mean is that he is fulfilling an end that he had been assigned or taken upon himself, or that he is well-suited to fulfill that end. In contrast, when we say that the person per se or other natural things (e.g., animals or trees) are good (beyond whatever ends are momentarily assigned or designated to them[3]), we are speaking of the ends of this person and these things in themselves. To speak meaningfully of such inherent ends and to ground them adequately a metaphysics is required. Wall-

---

3. Momentary ends are often assigned to human beings and other natural things, such as when a person is needed to fill a certain task or a tree is needed that would block sunlight.

work does not suggest that Freud presented or adopted one, and in fact there is no evidence that he did.

As a consequence of the failure of this final and crucial step of justification, the notion that the state of maturity as defined by Freud is a good one lacks adequate grounds. In terms of Wallwork's project, the significant implication of this conclusion is that Freud's broader ethics, so carefully described, is without firm foundation. But in terms of the present study, the significant finding is more specifically that the value Freud ascribes to the mature developmental state has no apparent justification. Wallwork's efforts did not succeed in providing a theory that would adequately explain or ground Freud's statements on the value of genital maturity.[4]

WINNICOTT'S MODEL OF THE DEVELOPMENT OF TRUE AND FALSE SELVES

THE FACTUAL NATURE OF THE DESCRIPTION OF THE MODEL

This model is described in terms of two kinds of facts: the fact of the existence of True and False Selves, and the facts that pertain to the ways in which they evolve.

The True Self is usually described in a somewhat ephemeral fashion. For example, Winnicott writes that in the earliest state it is "the theoretical position from which come the spontaneous gesture and the personal idea" (1960a, p. 148). It is also described as having an originally biological character: "The True Self comes from the aliveness of the body tissues and the working of body functions, including the heart's action and breathing." And finally, it is considered to have a strong experiential component. In the earliest stages, Winnicott explains, "it does no more than collect together the details of the experience of aliveness." Later, it is regarded as the core of the person and functionally as the sole source of creativity and the feeling of being real.

The False Self, in contrast, is viewed as a kind of reactive organization of the personality, but one that lacks wholeness or integrity since it is founded on compliance to external demands (p. 142). Winnicott

---

4. At this point it should be recalled that Freud's ethical/evaluative statements regarding genital maturity were of two kinds. One emphasized the value of that developmental state, the other pointed to its non-ethical status. Wallwork's attempts to justify Freud's ethics do not directly address the latter kind of statement. Although his discussion of Freud's value of autonomy is relevant, it does not constitute an attempt at grounding or justification.

describes this False organization primarily in terms of its functions relative to the True Self. "The False Self has one positive and very important function: to hide the True Self, which it does by compliance with environmental demands" (pp. 146–147). Winnicott describes the various ways in which this hiding function comes into play on a continuum from the least healthy forms of organization to the healthiest. At one extreme, "the False Self sets up as real and it is this that observers tend to think is the real person;" at the other extreme the False Self is behind the individual's "polite and mannered social attitude" (pp. 142–143). Between these extremes there are varying degrees of domination of the True Self by the False Self.

Like the existence of the True and False Selves, the developmental process through which they evolve is presented as a matter of fact.

> Periodically the infant's gesture gives expression to a spontaneous impulse; the source of the gesture is the True Self, and the gesture indicates the existence of a potential True Self. . . . There are now two possible lines of development in the scheme of events. . . . *In the first case* the mother's adaptation is *good enough* and in consequence . . . [t]he True Self has a spontaneity. . . . *In the second case,* . . . the mother's adaptation to the infant's hallucinations and spontaneous impulses is deficient, *not good enough,* . . . The infant gets seduced into a compliance, and a compliant False Self reacts to environmental demands (pp. 145–146).

In other words, Winnicott proposes that a condition exists in the infant (e.g., ego needs) which, when responded to in one way (that of the good-enough mother), results in the formation of a certain state of affairs (a True Self), and when responded to in another way (that of the mother who is not good-enough) results in the formation of another state of affairs (a False Self). In this context the good-enough mother is operationally defined as one who is capable of meeting the infant's omnipotence or, in more practical terms, of recognizing and complying with what is expressed in the infant's spontaneous gesture rather than imposing her own demands on him. Winnicott refers to these capacities as the mother's essential function.

It is interesting to note that Winnicott not only presents a factual picture of development but at times explicitly emphasizes the importance of doing so. In an earlier paper, for example, he points to the specific nature of psychoanalytic theory and practice and specifically stresses its limited moral import (Winnicott, 1945). He writes that psychoanalysis is "an instrument of scientific research or a therapy, but it never makes a direct philosophical or a religious contribution.

Freud took pains to point this out, and those who come to psycho-analysis for the first time will do well to be quite clear about the limitations of its aims and aspirations" (1945, pp. 11–12).

There are three main ethical/evaluative statements embedded in Winnicott's model of the development of the True and False Selves. All three are latent in his writings regarding this conception, and the first two are intimately connected. (1) What is of value in a person qua person is the True Self; (2) it is good to develop this True Self; and (3) one should at certain points limit this True Self in order to maintain one's connection with society.

The first statement may be seen from the way in which Winnicott defines the True Self. The term indeed is used to refer to a certain kind of organization in the psyche, but it also comes to designate that part of the psyche that is regarded as most significantly human, or as the source of our value as unique human beings. Only a person with a healthy True Self "exists" (p. 150), has "true experience," and begins to live (p. 148). That organization not only makes us feel real (once again, a factual matter) but is what is most real. It is not only the source of our creativity (another fact); our humanity lies in that creativity. It is not merely a dimension of our self but rather, our *True* Self. As Winnicott (1971) explains elsewhere, only the person who has developed a True Self can say, "I AM, I am alive, I am myself." He concludes that "from this position everything is creative" (p. 66). As such, the very definition of the True Self contains implicit value judgments regarding our existence. Winnicott, in effect, asserts the evaluative position that what is most authentic in our existence is that psychological organization that allows us to feel real and creative. The evaluative nature of this position is highlighted when it is compared with alternate conceptions regarding what is true to our selves. For example, some conceptions, such as that of Kant, see humanity precisely in the transcendence of all biological or psychological tendencies and offer not different empirical pronouncements but different value judgments. Religious conceptions, which view the value of the person in terms of his *relationship with God* rather than in spontaneous gestures arising from biological needs or personal creativity, also differ from Winnicott on the basis of value judgments. And even within the psychoanalytic realm, a Kohutian conception, which views the essence of the self in terms of an idealized parental imago and a grandiose self evolving in part through the parents' expectations and hopes for their child, would offer a different pronouncement regarding what is of value in the human being.

The second ethical/evaluative statement is that the True Self should be developed; it should become the central structure of the personality, leaving the False Self to play a minor role. To some extent this statement is derived from the previous one. If what is of value in a person qua person is the True Self, it follows that the True Self should be developed. It is the essence of what is of inherent value that it should be sought after. Here, however, what is added is the comparison with the False Self and the developmental dimension. A True Self is better than a False Self, and the path leading to the formation of the True Self should be preferred over that leading to the False Self. In other words, I am suggesting that Winnicott's delineation of two developmental routes, one that emerges when the mother provides good-enough responses to her infant and the other when she does not, cannot be taken as a mere description of causal relationships. Rather, it includes statements regarding the desired state of affairs, the desirability of the development of the True Self, and the undesirability of the development of a full-blown False Self. The developmental route leading to the one is referred to as good, healthy, normal; the route leading to the other as not good enough and pathological (Winnicott, 1960a, p. 147).

It may be seen that the desirability of the state of affairs is not presented as derived from the benefits it offers. Winnicott's statement is not simply that those who follow the route he recommends will probably be happier or more successful. If this were the case the choice would be left to the discretion of each individual. Winnicott is saying something else. He is speaking of the full development of the True Self as a state of normalcy, of health. The more developed the True Self, the healthier the person is. This healthy state is presented as inherently good. No matter what personal benefits the individual may be gaining from his or her defensive False Self structures, they are nevertheless defensive, hiding the True Self, and thus hiding the expression of what is truly, and inherently of value (ibid., pp. 142–143).

It should also be clear that Winnicott's ethical/evaluative statements regarding the True Self are not merely a developmental formulation of social norms regarding what is ethical and of value. This would run contrary to the very heart of Winnicott's thinking. Were this the case, his model would be directing the individual toward social conformity rather than toward the experience of his or her unique creative potential.

This leads to the third ethical/evaluative statement; namely, that the individual should at certain points limit this True Self in order to maintain his connection with society. Although the True Self is what is of value in one's person and its development should be sought, Winnicott nevertheless argues that the False Self has an important, albeit restricted, role even in health. It is responsible for the individual's "polite and mannered social attitude" (p. 143). Were people always to be true to their True Self, their social functioning would suffer. One's "place in society . . . can never be attained or maintained by the True Self alone." A psychic organization that is, in a limited way, compliant to external demands is helpful in this regard.

Here Winnicott's evaluation of the importance of being polite comes into play. His developmental model does not offer a choice in this regard but rather contends that one must develop the capacity to be polite (i.e., a healthy False Self), even at the expense of living most truly (i.e., in accordance with one's True Self). This particular assertion is clearly based on Winnicott's view of the role of a certain kind of social relationship to the good life.

THE JUSTIFICATION OF THE ETHICAL/EVALUATIVE STATEMENTS

Did Winnicott offer any ethical/evaluative theory that could justify these statements? As in the case of Freud's developmental conception, the fact that the ethical/evaluative statements are latent does not allow for the possibility that Winnicott would present overt and explicit justifying arguments. However, it may be possible to seek justifying arguments of a more latent kind.

I have found one such predominant implicit argument, based on the affinity Winnicott posits between the failure to develop a True Self and physical suffering, even death. Throughout Winnicott's writings, he often connects a psychological failure to thrive with the suffering and death of the True Self, with physical suffering and death. For example, he writes that "When the mother's adaptation is not good enough at the start the infant might be expected to die physically, because cathexis of external objects is not initiated. The infant remains isolated. But in practice the infant lives, but lives falsely. . . . The clinical picture is one of general irritability, and of feeding and other function disturbances" (p. 146). Winnicott also speaks of death as a way to avoid the annihilation of the True Self (p. 143).

If this connection between failure to develop a True Self and physical suffering and death is intended as analogy, then it only serves to help clarify or reaffirm the values associated with the True Self and its development. In effect, it would be just another way of saying that the True Self is what exists authentically in the person and that it is very important to develop the True Self rather than the False Self. However, if what Winnicott means is that the infants who do not receive good-enough mothering indeed suffer in a physical and obvious way, and in extreme cases narrowly escape death, then an implicit justifying argument emerges. The gist of the argument is that if the failure to develop a True Self has such terrible and even fatal consequences, then the development of a True Self must be a value. That is, since physical suffering and death run counter to the good of the person if this is the consequence of the developmental process, it must be wrong, and its alternative must be good. This argument would refer most directly to the second ethical/evaluative statement; namely, that one should develop a True Self rather than a False Self.

I will not take issue here with the factual premises of this argument. Rather, I contend that even if failure to develop a True Self indeed results in severe suffering or death, this does not mean that the development of a True Self is in and of itself a valued end. That discomfort, physical or psychological, follows from the absence of some event or entity is not sufficient grounds for the claim that that event or entity is a value. This may be seen in two ways: Firstly, it would not be strange to say that one is willing to suffer discomfort in order to maintain a certain value, for the fact that a certain value results in discomfort does not in itself disqualify it from being a value. Secondly, were discomfort the sole criterion of value, then any developmental process that causes discomfort, such as the development of the superego, would be deemed to be without value. This contradicts not only conventional views of what is ethical and of value but also Winnicott's own developmental theory. Elsewhere, for example, he emphasizes the importance of being able to tolerate unpleasant experiences, such as frustration and anger, in the aim of achieving a higher level of development (1960b). Clearly, we would be willing to have a child suffer the pains of an operation in order to save her life or improve her motor or mental abilities. The question of when physical discomfort is acceptable and when it is not returns us to the question of the values for which we are willing to suffer. Thus these values stand beyond the suffering per se.

It does seem more obvious that if death is the result, the developmental process must be wrong. In the case of an adult, it may not be too difficult to think of situations in which someone may choose to forfeit his life for the sake of a value. However, the infant is never in a position to make such a choice, and situations in which the infant's parents may make such a choice for the sake of their developmental values are hard to imagine. But this does not mean that the end of the developmental process is to be valued. Were failure to develop a True Self to result in death, this would mean not that a True Self is good but that the True Self is necessary for life, and life is good. The claim that a True Self is necessary for life makes the True Self not a value per se but a *means* to a value, just as sleep may be necessary for life, or aggression may, at times, be necessary for survival. The value of these means independent of their contribution to life may be questioned. We tolerate suffering and even death for the sake of our values, but the means to attain these values and to avoid negatively valued outcomes are not necessarily valued in themselves. Thus, the possible fact that the development of a True Self is required in order to live and to avoid unnecessary physical suffering or even death does not justify the notion that the True Self is a value.[5]

In sum, the ethical/evaluative statements embedded in Winnicott's factually described developmental conception of the True Self remain without apparent justification. Attempts to justify them by pointing to the physical suffering that follows from the failure to develop a True Self ultimately fail. The transition from the fact of suffering to the evaluative judgment regarding the good or its absence is not tenable.

DISCUSSION

This study has pointed to the presence of ethical/evaluative statements in two apparently factually based developmental models. It was shown that these statements were not borrowed from social norms regarding what is ethical or of value, nor mere statements regarding what is beneficial. Rather, they emerged as statements of what Freud and Winnicott, respectively, believe to be inherently good. While both men clearly intended to describe facts of development, they were inadvertently and in a very latent way describing the ideals of development, including how the person should experience and relate to him/herself and his/her society, and the morality of failing to do so. It is important to recognize that these ideals are not trivial aspects of these developmental models but lie at their very heart. They constitute the goals and endpoints of the development

5. It should be noted here that the value Winnicott ascribes to the True Self is not merely as a means to the value of life. He specifically maintains that the True Self is a good form of life and that it is possible but not desirable to live with a less developed True Self.

processes and determine the proper course and direction of these processes. In fact, it is only in light of these ideals that the earlier steps of development can be posited. Thus, were the evaluative dimension of these models to be discarded, numerous potential paths of development would need to be elaborated, and references to progression, regression, or defense would lose all meaning.[6]

After pointing to the existence of the ethics underlying the two developmental models, we turned to the kinds of justification offered for them. It was shown that attempts at justification were hard to find. Since the fact that ethical/evaluative statements were present in the factual descriptions was not acknowledged, no ethical/evaluative theory was put forth in their support, and no explicit attempts to justify them were offered. Nevertheless, it was possible to propose some implicit ones. These were found to suffer from severe limitations: On the one hand, they seemed to rely on other conceptions that were laden with their own ethical/evaluative statements. The ethical/evaluative statements of the developmental models were shown to be grounded on the ethical/evaluative statements of these additional conceptions, but no grounds were offered for the latter statements.

On the other hand, the attempts at justification seemed to aim at grounding transitions from some facts regarding human nature to the ethical/evaluative statements in question (e.g., from the fact of how the person functions to the value of genitality, or from the consequences suffered when a person fails to develop a True Self to the value of the True Self). Here we found that the grounds put forth rested on faulty argumentation. Ultimately, the bare facts regarding what empirically exists in the person's nature, his or her potential for flourishing or for suffering, did not support the contentions put forth regarding how the person ought to be.

It may be seen that the failure of these attempts was determined by their basic approach. Clearly, there is no way that one value could be grounded by another unless ultimately reference was made to some kind of non-evaluative foundation. And there is no way that a purely empirical fact, without the support of some broader evaluative or metaphysical framework, could indicate how a person should be.

6. For example, if there is no inherent value in the development of a True Self, it is just as much a defense against the development of a False Self as the False Self is a defense against the True Self, and the necessary steps to avoid the development of a True Self (given a good-enough mother) need to be elaborated. Obviously, such a change in perspective would have far-reaching implications for the clinical setting as well.

The fact of suffering could contribute to our understanding of how a person should be if we hold the ethical view that all suffering should be avoided. And the fact that the person has certain unique functions may contribute to such an understanding if we hold some metaphysical position on the significance of the presence of unique potentials. Facts may be relevant to one's ethical/evaluative positions, but they cannot in themselves determine it. As Hume (1739) made clear over two hundred years ago, the goodness or badness of an event cannot emerge from close scrutiny of facts alone. That we are here dealing with psychological facts does not change the matter. Thus, once justification was sought either through other values or through pure empirical facts, failure was the necessary outcome.

The implications of this study extend beyond the two developmental models we have analyzed. We suggest that any psychoanalytic model that describes how a person ought to be, not how it is possible, normative, inevitable, or beneficial to be, will contain ethical/evaluative statements. Moreover, these statements will never find justification by reference only to other ungrounded values or psychological facts. Thus, in examining the validity of a developmental theory, it is important to explore the ideals proposed and the nature of their foundations. If they describe what is possible, normative, inevitable, or beneficial, their validity should be determined by the factual evidence brought in their support. If, however, they refer to how a person ought to be in the ethical/evaluative sense of the term, then to validate the theory a non-factual form of justification must be sought. This may require recourse to forms of philosophical argumentation that are commonly employed in attempts to justify ethical and evaluative positions. Alternately, there is the possibility of leaving the theory with inadequate validation and offering it to others who share the same values.

Further investigation is necessary in order to determine the nature of the ideals set forth in other developmental theories and the kinds of arguments brought in their support. I believe such investigation will reveal that beneath their very factual descriptions many of the ideals of familiar developmental formulations are actually ideals in an ethical/evaluative sense. In speaking of the importance of individuation (Mahler), autonomy (Erikson), the fusion of love and aggression (M. Klein), the cohesiveness of the self (Kohut), etc., norms and benefits may play a part, but ultimately it is the ethics and values inherent in the specific developmental model that are finding expression. If this is not apparent, it may be because the factual tone of the descriptions are deceptive, or because we so deeply share in these values or have so grown so accustomed to them that we tend to see them as facts. I also believe that investigation of additional developmental theories will reveal that where such values are present they are not acknowledged as such, and if any evidence is brought in their support it is of a factual kind (clinical and developmental) and hence insufficient. Only detailed analyses, of the kind carried out in the present study, can support or reject these initial impressions.

In conclusion, I would like to highlight the importance of recognizing the ethical/evaluative nature of seemingly factual statements. If such statements are not recognized for what they are,

(1) *Developmental theories will contain many unfounded propositions.* It is only when the nature of a proposition is determined to be ethical/ evaluative or factual that the appropriate form of justification can be sought.

(2) *Dialogue between competing theories will be limited.* If indeed there are ethical/evaluative differences between competing developmental theories, the discussion of differences in terms of clinical and empirical findings alone will not further understanding.

(3) *Psychoanalytic theory will unwittingly be serving certain value systems.* Most developmental psychoanalysts believe that psychoanalytic developmental theories are dealing with facts regarding development. The public, which shares this belief, would be unwittingly influenced by the implicit ethical/evaluative statements contained within them.

(4) *Psychoanalytic practice will unwittingly be serving certain value systems.* The analyst, rather than being directed by developmental facts, will be directed by developmental ideals of which he or she is unaware. For example, when a Winnicottian analyst responds in a way that facilitates the development of a True Self, she is not merely facilitating development, as she may believe, but is facilitating a certain *kind* of development, based on certain values of how a person should be. Other kinds of development, based on other ideals, are possible. If the analyst and the patient are not aware of this, the analyst is unwittingly guiding the patient toward one ideal of development and away from possible others. This may not be directly problematic when the values are generally agreed upon (e.g., the value of having contact with reality, or the value of having some degree of autonomy). However, as we have seen, the values found within developmental models are much more specific and less obviously accepted (e.g., the value of the True Self, or more specifically of maintaining a

polite relationship with others at the expense of being true to one-self).[7]

As noted at the beginning of this paper, there is a growing awareness of the impact the analyst's personal values can have on the course of a treatment. A parallel awareness of the infiltration of values in the form of developmental theories has yet to emerge. The present study suggests that the time is ripe for this. To be aware of the values found in the developmental theories is not merely to acknowledge their existence but to be willing to find ways of critically examining them.

BIBLIOGRAPHY

BLASS, R. B. (1999). The impact of psychoanalysis on the ethical dimension of personality theories. Paper presented at "Freud at the Threshold of the Twentieth Century" conference, Jerusalem, December 1999.

BORNSTEIN, M., ISAY, R., MEERS, R., & SLAP, J. (EDS.) (1983). Values and neutrality in psychoanalysis, *Psychoanalytic Inquiry,* 3:4.

ERIKSON, E. H. (1976). Psychoanalysis and ethics—avowed and unavowed. *Int. Rev. Psychoanal.,* 3:409–415.

JONES, E. (1957). *The Life and Work of Sigmund Freud,* Vol. 3. New York: Basic Books.

FREUD, S. (1896). The aetiology of hysteria. *SE* 3:90–115.

——— (1905). *Three Essays on the Theory of Sexuality. SE* 7:130–243.

——— (1908). Civilized sexual morality and modern nervous illness. *SE* 9:181–204.

——— (1912). On the universal tendency to debasement in the sphere of love. *SE* 11:179–190.

——— (1918). Lines of advance in psychoanalytic therapy. *SE* 17:159–168.

——— (1927). *The Future of an Illusion. SE* 21:5–56.

——— (1930). *Civilization and its Discontents. SE* 21:64–145.

——— (1933). Why War? *SE* 22:199–215.

GRINBERG, L. (1990). *The Goals of Psychoanalysis.* London: Karnac Books.

HARTMANN, H. (1939). Psychoanalysis and the concept of health. In *Essays on Ego Psychology.* New York: Int. Univ. Press, 1964, pp. 3–18.

——— (1960). *Psychoanalysis and Moral Values.* New York: Int. Univ. Press.

7. One may argue that as long as the analyst carefully upholds the value of the patient's autonomy and freedom such dangers will be averted. A response to this argument is beyond the scope of the present paper, but it should be noted that it is not without problems. There are different ideals of autonomy and freedom, and there are different ideals regarding the nature of the self whose autonomy and freedom is to be facilitated.

HUME, D. (1739). *A Treatise of Human Nature,* ed. L. A. Selby-Bigge. Oxford: Oxford Univ. Press, 1888.

KLIMOVSKY, G., DUPETIT, S., & ZYSMAN, S. (1995). Ethical and unethical conduct in psychoanalysis: correlations between logic, ethics and science. *Int. J. Psychoanal.,* 76:977–989.

MEISSNER, W. W. (1996). *The Therapeutic Alliance.* New Haven: Yale University Press.

RIEFF, P. (1961). *Freud: The Mind of the Moralist.* New York: Doubleday.

SANDLER, J., & DREHER, A. (1996). *What do Psychoanalysts Want? The Problems of Aims in Psychoanalytic Theory.* London: Routledge.

SOSNIK, R. A., CHIARANDINI, C., & HILKERT, F. G. (EDS.) (1992). The ethical texture of psychoanalysis. *Psychoanalytic Inquiry,* 12:4.

STRENGER, C. (1997). Further remarks on the classic and romantic visions in psychoanalysis: Klein, Winnicott, and ethics. *Psychoanal. & Contemp. Thought,* 20:207–244.

WALLERSTEIN, R. S. (1976). Introduction to symposium on "Ethics, Moral Values and Psychological Interventions." *Int. Rev. Psychoanal.* 3:369–372.

WALLWORK, E. (1991). *Psychoanalysis and Ethics.* New Haven: Yale Univ. Press.

WINNICOTT, D. W. (1945). Towards an objective study of human nature. In, *Thinking about Children.* London: Karnac Books, pp. 3–12.

——— (1960a). Ego distortion in terms of true and false self. *The Maturational Processes and the Facilitating Environment.* London: Hogarth, 1979, pp. 140–152.

——— (1960b). The theory of the parent-infant relationship. *The Maturational Process and the Facilitating Environment.* pp. 37–55.

——— (1971). *Playing and Reality.* London: Tavistock.

The Mother-Daughter Love Affair Across the Generations

LEENA KLOCKARS, Lic. Psych.,
and RIITTA SIROLA, M.D.

The relationship between mother and daughter is the basis for all love relationships throughout life. Through the eyes and hands of the mother, the intimate and caring nature of love is transmitted from generation to generation. Mother-daughter love is also the beginning of heterosexual love and of sensual pleasure. However, sexuality separates and alienates mother and daughter. As a consequence, the daughter's identification with the mother becomes the most important transmitter of love.

We review psychoanalytic studies of the development and fate of the mother-daughter love relationship, with particular attention to the change of the daughter's early love for the mother to identification with the mother and falling in love with a man, and to the significance of sexuality in this developmental process.

FROM BIRTH ON, THE IDEAL OF MOTHERLY LOVE IS LINKED TO EVERYthing that is good. The mother's lap is the paradise of our fantasies. Our love affair with the mother forms the basis for all later love relationships. Because the mother is usually the first object of our love, the more developed emotions have a certain maternal and feminine quality (Tähkä 1993).

For a girl, the mother is the object of both love and identification, and the girl never abandons either of these relationships, although

Leena Klockars is an adult and child psychoanalyst, a member of the Finnish Psycho-analytical Society. Riitta Sirola is a psychoanalyst and an associate member of the Finnish Psycho-analytical Society.

The Psychoanalytic Study of the Child 56, ed. Albert J. Solnit, Peter B. Neubauer, Samuel Abrams, and A. Scott Dowling (Yale University Press, copyright © 2001 by Albert J. Solnit, Peter B. Neubauer, Samuel Abrams, and A. Scott Dowling).

their quality and manifestations vary from one developmental phase to another. Sexual desire is a feeling that separates mother and daughter and changes the quality of their love relationship, although the mother's impressions of sexuality exert an essential influence upon the daughter's sexuality. Maternal love and the loving relationship between mother and daughter are at the same time real and subject to fantasy, as is their point of origin, the mother's inner space, her physical and mental motherly functioning. Many important matters in our lives, such as mother tongue, family stability, and various family traditions, are conveyed through the maternal inner space and the love affair between mother and daughter.

The mother-daughter love affair exists in the mother's fantasies long before the daughter's birth. Every little girl imagines that she will one day give birth to a daughter. She has memories and fantasies of her love affair with her own mother, and perhaps of her grandmother's love as well. The present-day relationship is the product of a long chain of love affairs of mothers and daughters. Many authors have described such a lineage, among them Blum (1980), Chodorow (1978), Hägglund (1988), and Welldon (1988).

An essential part of the mother-daughter love affair is a man, the mother's beloved, the daughter's father. For the mother, a daughter is a desire of a manifestation of a love affair, a gift from a man. For the daughter, the mother is a woman who loves a man in the first place. The mother's ability to love a man and her way of loving are transmitted to her daughter and influence the daughter's way of loving a man and her choice of a life companion. Fathers' fantasies about the love affair of mothers and daughters also have a crucial influence on these relationships.

ANTICIPATING MOTHERHOOD AND THE BIRTH OF A DAUGHTER

Vilja Hägglund (1988) describes how we carry throughout our lives the internalized world shared by a mother and a child and transmit it to later generations. In the expectant mother's fantasies, the baby in her uterus is linked to a good internal object: the good enough mother of the mother's own early childhood. She converses with her embryonic baby even during pregnancy and creates fantasies about the child to come. These images have a great influence on the mother's future attitude toward her offspring.

The woman's fantasies have a special effect on the interaction between mother and child when the waited-for baby is a girl, since every mother has, in addition to her fantasies, memories of her relationship with her own mother, and these experiences and fantasies color her expectations of the future. The mother's attitude toward a baby girl differs from that toward a baby boy, just as her mother responded to her in a different way as her father. This difference persists throughout life. Gender is our fate—it influences how the mother will react to us.

A mother's wish to have a child is often so taken for granted that her underlying motives are hardly considered. Brazelton and Cramer (1991) list some of these motivations for motherhood:

- Identification with the mother and with women in general. Every woman has experienced some kind of maternal care and has fantasies and emotional memories of it. As early as 12–18 months of age a little girl starts to nurse her dolls and soft toys in a motherly way. Her gestures, facial expressions, tone of voice, touch, and movements reflect caring and empathy that cannot be explained entirely by learning.
- The wish to be complete and omnipotent. There is a narcissistic tendency to gratify these wishes by pregnancy and by a child.
- The desire for fusion and oneness with another. Pregnancy and nursing of the baby bring fantasies about fusing with another human being, about a totally shared existence.
- The wish to mirror oneself in the child, a hope that she can duplicate herself, to have a sense of immortality.
- An infant, especially a girl, gives the mother an opportunity to see herself in another person and—at least in her dreams—to reach for ideals and possibilities previously lost to her. A child presents a new future.
- A child enables the mother to renew or repair her relationship with her own mother.
- The opportunity both to replace and to separate from one's own mother by matching now her own all-powerful mother.
- The mother's attempt to bind a man to herself through a child—or, conversely, the wish to prove the man's secondary position compared to a child's.

Motherhood and pregnancy are normal developmental crises for a woman. These crises commence with an intense sexual relationship leading to conception (Grete Bibring 1961). Pregnancy begins a new phase in a young woman's life. The object of love, the embryo, becomes a part of the woman's self until the fetal movements interrupt this initially narcissistic process. A new task in her psychic development is to create a picture of the child as a separate individual inside her body. With birth, she becomes irrevocably and forever a mother. Pregnancy and delivery do not usually lead to individuation of the embryo in the mother's mind. The baby is often seen as a totally separate individual when there will be another child.

Difficulties and shortcomings in the mother's relationship with her own mother complicate her pregnancy and subsequent relationship with her child. Disappointments in the maternal relationship may turn a woman's desire to have children into a compulsive demand (Marita Torsti 1996). The woman may tend to idealize her own motherhood, making herself too important to discern what the baby needs and dispossessing the baby of his or her central role. The child is not allowed to have his or her own space but has to prop up maternal grandiosity. The mother becomes the great giver, without whom the child does not have permission to survive. A mother who has not been permitted to fulfill her own early needs may thus try to use her child to repair her own deficit. An idealizing mother cannot endure imperfection, in the child or herself.

Although the idealization of motherhood often has painful consequences for the child, sometimes it is the only way for the woman to cope with motherhood. By idealizing her flawed relationship with her own mother, she makes possible a love affair with her baby that surpasses that earlier relationship. At least in her fantasies, she creates a new kind of relationship to her mother and to the mother-daughter relationships of the previous generations.

Pregnancy brings many questions to the fore in the mother's consciousness (Elina Mäenpää-Reenkola 1997): Will motherhood make her similar to her mother, and does she wish to be similar? Is giving birth to a child usurping her mother's place or executing a smashing victory over her? Will her mother exact revenge?

THE GENESIS OF THE MOTHER-DAUGHTER LOVE AFFAIR

The birth of a baby is an expected and longed-for event, but at the same time it is an ambivalent and frightening situation for a woman. The expectant woman is at the same time the mother of the child to be delivered and the daughter of the mother who has given birth to her. Thus pregnancy poses a significant test for the mother-daughter relationship of the previous generation (Pines 1993). Early mother identifications will be evoked and compared with the current mother-daughter relationship.

Elina Mäenpää-Reenkola (1977) describes how the baby becomes a part of the mother's self while still nested within her. Pregnancy and childbirth transform the mother's body and body image: The boundaries of the mother's body will never be definitely closed; for the mother, the child will remain unconsciously part of her even when the child is grown.

A child is narcissistically important and cathected for the parents (Furman, 1997; Freud, 1914). In the very beginning, the child is a narcissistic object for the parents rather than a separate individual. The narcissistic cathection never totally ends although the child's significance as a personality in her own right will increase with age. McDougall (1980) adds that the relationship between mother and child is also a sensual one. For the mother the child is not only a source of narcissistic gratification but also, from the outset, a source of libidinal satisfaction.

The narcissistic cathexis is naturally different for girls and for boys. It is easier for the mother to experience her daughter than her son as a variant and continuation of her own body and psyche. Shared experience and empathic understanding develop more easily between mother and daughter. The narcissistic cathexis of the daughter contains the fulfillment of all maternal expectations, new prospects, and fantasies of womanhood and femininity, motherhood and motherliness. During a successful development this narcissistic union with the mother converts into a good enough love affair, first with the mother, then with the father, and finally into a daughter-mother-father triad (Mäenää-Reenkola 1997). Thus a love affair with the mother forms an essential basis and opportunity for love experiences in later life.

The firm physical union between mother and child continues even after the birth of the baby. Bibring (1961) notes that a woman's gaze, her grasp, her gestures, and the rhythms of her cradling derive from her body. The child's first image is formed by her sensations of the mother's body and by what she gradually comes to see in her mother's eyes (Hägglund 1988). A girl builds her self by mirroring herself in her mother's eyes and in interaction with the mother's body. Her earliest self experiences, her initial impressions of the female body and femininity, are totally dependent on the quality of the mother-daughter relationship. In psychoanalytic terms, the girl's first reality is her mother's unconscious mind. Torsti (1996) says that the early interaction between a child and her mother is determined by the mother's unconscious and that the nature of the female inner space is nonverbal. When the mother speaks to her baby the emphasis, from the baby's point of view, is not on the words she says but on the tone, rhythm, and volume of her voice.

When the child is a girl, the mother's unconscious fantasies are transferred to the next generation through physical sensations and corporal memory. The mother knows, more or less consciously, that she is guiding and teaching a potential mother-to-be, and this has an influence on the early care of a baby girl. The first identifications start to take shape in actions of care. As the daughter grows, shared experiences increase and mutual identifications multiply. The mother gradually promotes her daughter to the role of a woman, her colleague, and, with growing age, to her own nurse-mother. This calls for the mother to deal well enough with the pain and sorrow caused by envy, competition, aging, and abandonment.

The child's grandmother has been a granddaughter in her time, she transmits the experiences of previous generations to the next ones. In her newborn granddaughter she sees, colored by her own experiences, the beginning of her own life and her daughter's life as well as a new possibility to repair or change the mother-daughter relationship. Suggesting a name for the newborn, helping in her care, and sharing experiences reveal the character of the maternal traditions of the family.

The baby and mother also share physical sensations in connection with breastfeeding. In nursing, both mother and baby have a fantasy of totally owning and controlling the other's body. Both experience synchronous bodily sensations, as during pregnancy. The nursing mother learns to judge by the amount of milk in her breasts when the baby starts to become hungry. She conveys to her baby how to relate emotionally to receiving the breast and becoming gratified. While breastfeeding, she allows her baby to enjoy even intense sucking and at the same time calms the baby down and controls excessive agitation.

Like all the other fantasies about the child, the mother's fantasies related to nursing are different in the case of a boy and a girl. Lactation influences the relationship between daughter and mother. By prolonging lactation the mother is able to maintain simultaneously the reality and a fantasy of mutual dependency and mastery of her daughter's body and mind. Similarly, the daughter cherishes a fantasy of owning and ruling her mother.

THE PREOEDIPAL LOVE IDYLL

In the preoedipal phase the child believes that everything is received from the mother, who is experienced as omnipotent. The child feels that the mother has no needs of her own but is always in the service of the child (Alice Balint 1939). Love for the mother is totally self-centered; the child feels that the mother should always give her preference over others and that her needs should be her mother's.

The gratifying experiences and richly sensual sensations that mother and daughter share in nursing, feeding, cleaning, bathing, and other caring form unforgettable images of perfect love. The mother creates meaning for her daughter's body and sexuality by her gaze, touch, and voice. As Winnicott says, the mother tempts her child to life, she evokes the sensuality of her daughter's body. Stoller (1968) illustrates how the mother's acknowledgment of her baby's sex has a crucial influence upon the formation and strengthening of the child's core sexual identity.

According to Freud (1914), an individual is unable to give up gratification, once experienced; one is not willing to be without the narcissistic perfection of childhood. Later on, the awakening of critical judgment makes one realize that it is not possible to maintain the illusion of perfection. The individual attempts to recover this in a new form, as an ego ideal that he or she is trying to reach. The ego ideal is the bearer of the lost narcissism of childhood, a substitute for the forfeited experience of perfection.

For a child, motherhood is the ideal of love. Only later, when the mother has differentiated in the child's mind into an individual, does she become an object of love and desire. Furman (1997) maintains that the genetic core of womanhood lies in the potentiality of motherhood. A girl recognizes her mother first as a mother, a gratifier of needs, and only later as a woman. Judith Kestenberg (1982) notes the very early origin of the capacity for motherliness. When a little girl plays with her doll one can see the child's love for and identification with her mother and motherly activities (Torsti 1996; Mäenpää-Reenkola 1997). The more gratifying is the girl's relationship to her mother, the more devotedly she takes care of her doll. This idealizing love also appears in the girl's other plays. She acts out endless domestic scenes, draws pictures to give to her mother, and sings to her. The mother is the center of her entire early love. In therapy with a preoedipal girl this phase often takes the form of languor and pining when the mother is absent from the session.

Sexuality changes the early preoedipal mother-daughter love relationship. As early as the third year the girl finds through masturbation the excitement produced by her genitals, and the sexual pressure grows. The central doll phase of the early maternal relationship is then left behind.

The girl's relationship to her mother goes through a crucial metamorphosis at this time (Bollas 1997). The mother has given meaning to her daughter's body by nursing her. She has characteristic ways of touching the sensual and sexual parts of her daughter's body. Because of her own sensations, the mother may have oversexualized her daughter's body in her fantasies. On the other hand, she may have to deny the sexual gratification of the body. The daughter soon develops the ability to recognize maternal desires and needs and the wish to fulfill them. Bollas claims that autoerotic sensations of pleasure increase significantly by the age of three and are transferred to the mother-daughter relationship. In the child's mind the mother becomes a sexual being.

The girl drifts into a crisis in her relationship to the mother as she senses that the object of her mother's desires is someone other than she. The preoedipal dream is broken, and a man has entered the previously self-contained mother-daughter paradise. Until now, the mother has been an object of love. When the daughter comes to identify herself with the mother, the object of her love is displaced. If there are problems in identification with the mother, there will also be problems in changing the object of love. If identification does not allow for a good enough feeling of autonomic identity, the girl remains stuck with her early love to the mother. If, on the other hand, sexualization of the girl's body has taken place too early, the objects of identification and love cannot become differentiated.

In this phase of development the mother-daughter relationship is very vulnerable. As development proceeds, the mother has to give up her daughter's love, which earlier created narcissistic pleasure, and trust in the pleasure and love identification can bring. Furman (1982) beautifully describes this phase in her paper "Mothers are there to be left." Many other analysts have written about the influence of preoedipal problems in the mother-daughter relationship on the daughter's later potential to turn toward a man and on her sexual development. Chasseguet-Smirgel (1970) writes that the girl's too early desire to free herself from the power of the mother, whom she experiences as omnipotent and castrating, may lead to overidealization of the father and denial of her own femininity.

From Dyadic to Triadic — the Girl's Oedipality

Freud (1925, 1931, 1933) considered castration anxiety, the sense that one's own body is defective, caused by the lack of a penis and penis envy, the major motives for the girl's replacement of the mother by the father as an object of her love. The girl becomes disappointed with the mother because of her lack of a penis and turns to the father in the hope that he will compensate her for this intolerable defect and repair her imperfect body.

The girl becomes frustrated in her desire to love because she does not have anything the mother needs from her and with which she could bind herself to the mother. Mother and father complement each other sexually in a powerful way, which enforces their bond and commitment. When the little girl can no longer experience herself as wanted and loved by her mother, her desire to have mother/woman exclusively to herself turns into a desire to *be* a woman (McDougall 1995). This evokes in the girl a wish to be loved by the other sex and to become a mother in the future.

Tähkä (1993) divides the girl's triadic development into three phases. In the first phase, she recognizes that the father plays the role of an object of love in the mother's mind. She tries to be similar to the mother and more lovable than the rival father. At this stage, the mother is an object of both love and identification. In the second phase, it dawns on the girl that the mother loves the father because of his dissimilarity, not his similarity. Now the girl attempts to gratify her mother as her father does, trying to be better than he is in all respects. In the third phase of the oedipal triad the girl transfers her love to the father. She has earlier idealized the mother, but now the object of the mother's desire becomes the idealized object of the girl's desire—i.e., a phallus. This is, according to Manninen (1991), an unconsciously created and maintained illusion of the incomparable power of the father-man bodily equipment and its derivatives in reaching the desired gratification. In this developmental phase, the father becomes idealized as an object of love, but the mother remains an idealized object of identification.

Ogden (1987) describes the reorganization of desires of the oedipal age as a transitional phenomenon. The mother has been increasingly recognized as a separate person, with wishes and desires that the daughter can no longer gratify. To the girl this feels like a deception. The man, the father, becomes the main representative of otherness, of an external object. The event is gradual and transitional. The mother's heterosexual love is based on her love for her own father and on the good enough fantasy of a daughter-father love affair, and this fantasy exerts an unconscious influence upon the daughter's fantasies. A little girl falls in love first with the man in her mother's daughter-father fantasy, the man in the mother's mind, the father in the mother. If the mother's image of her relationship with her own father is good enough, she will allow her daughter to fall in love with her father. By identifying with the father of her own good father-daughter relationship, she is able to observe her daughter through her husband's eyes and thus can allow for the narcissistic gratification the daughter can receive from her father's gaze. In this way the mother becomes a unifier of motherly and fatherly love and an agent in her daughter's oedipal development. If the mother's father fantasy contains disappointment, conflict, devaluation, and envy, these emotions will be transferred to the daughter's world and will negatively influence her love relationships.

Pentti Ikonen (1987) writes that oedipal love is often the greatest emotion in human life. From the point of view of a developing individual, oedipal experience means a thoroughly new orientation toward others, oneself, and existence as a whole. Great love always contains an oedipal part, although it may have other components as well. Oedipal love always leaves its mark. Both the desire to rediscover it and the fear of doing so unconsciously guide later choices of love objects and the formation of love itself. The oedipal experience also means loss of the initial object of love, followed by shock, denial, hatred, and finally, sorrow. If the loss is not worked through, the girl can protect herself from oedipal disappointments only by excessive defense actions such as the devaluation of differences between generations, sexes, and bodies, which cause feelings of oedipal inferiority, the creation of non-sexual ego ideals, and other attempts to deny oedipal reality.

Ikonen (1987) states that the girl gives up her oedipal wishes because of her own vulnerable self-esteem. She seeks to transfer the wish for erotic-sexual fulfillment from a concrete desire to a world of fantasy and hopes for the future. In addition, she has to be able to abandon both the early symbiotic-narcissistic love for the mother and the erotic love for father and mother and to find objects of love outside the family. The girl's feelings change and motivate a displacement from a dyadic to a triadic relationship. Jealousy, feelings of being an outsider and of inferiority, and insight into the impossibility of attaining her own wishes evoke shame and hatred and the wish to repress oedipal tendencies.

The oedipal relationship between mother and daughter is highly susceptible to problems. In the negative oedipal solution the girl does not find in the mother a good and desirable father fantasy; the mother herself remains the object of love and the father a rival for the mother's love. Ideally the mother should be able to lead her daughter to the heterosexual, complementary world. The mother and father as the objects of the daughter's love become differentiated in the course of oedipal development, and the love the daughter cherishes toward them receives differentiated tones. The diversification of feelings of love forms the basis for later development, in which different people will act as different objects of love.

NEUTRALIZATION OF THE MOTHER-DAUGHTER RELATIONSHIP — LATENCY

Although Freud originally regarded latency as a time of stagnation in sexual development, many later writers (e.g., Maenchen 1970, Etchegoyen 1993) claim that it is a part of the psychosexual moratorium phase, in which the girl works through her grief at the loss of childhood and the impossibility of returning to the mother's inner space and owning her. The obligatory separation from the parents leads to reorganization of defenses, development of the ego and superego, and working through of oedipal problems.

In her preoedipal solution, the girl feels deceived by her mother and, in her oedipal solution, by her father. She realizes that the primary object of her mother's love was the father, and that the primary object of her father's love and physical desire is the mother. The girl has to survive outside the dyad and to give up even the triad; she has to find her objects outside the family. If the girl has experienced her parents as good and loving, it is easier for her to accept their love affair and to feel relieved and delighted by their mutual love. Thus her desires lose their omnipotent and frightening character. Although the girl has been disappointed in her love affair with her parents, her ability and will to identify persist, growing stronger with development. Latency is thus a period of psychic reparation and rebuilding, apart from grief work. The girl has learned to tolerate loss and has acquired more developed psychic defense mechanisms. Her relationship to her parents, particularly the mother, improves and becomes more intimate.

In this developmental phase the girl has realized, by means of the oedipal situation, the multiplicity of the parental relationship and of her feelings of being an outsider. Bion calls this learning by understanding connections. Cognitive faculties increase and bring the complexity of the external world within the girl's reach. Friends, interest, and school wean the girl from her family to a circle of peers. After having become disappointed with her parents, the girl has to find a separate identity and the importance of friends increases. Nevertheless, the presence of the parents is crucial for the development of identity. The earlier development of identification turns into the development of identity.

Although the latency girl has seemingly abandoned her sexual desire for her parents, sexuality has not vanished from her mind. Sexually toned play, curiosity about her own body and others', and masturbation are common but are considered forbidden and shameful. The resolution of the oedipal situation and sexual prohibitions significantly influence the development of the superego. The enforcement of its code via the development of morality and feelings of shame and guilt is a central function of the latency period.

If the earlier mother-daughter relationship has been good, mother and daughter can easily enjoy each other during the girl's latency. They do all sorts of things together, and the girl really enjoys participating in mother's and women's activities. The grandmother is an important object of female identification for the girl and may be a necessary support person in everyday life.

Life in the community of three female generations is often supportive and free of conflicts at this stage. For the girl latency is a period of internal clarifications, of consolidating her strength and finding her own capacities. The whole personality has been budding, ready to burst into a powerful change with the advent of puberty and its sexual development.

Conflict in the Mother-Daughter Love Affair

When the daughter reaches adolescence and the mother middle age, great changes start to take place in their relationship. Some authors stress the crisis character of adolescence and the conflict it causes in the mother-daughter relationship; others emphasize attachment and the process of continuous identification.

In adolescence, the girl's normal identity crisis is at its strongest, and the battle for independence at its most intense. After the peaceful latency phase, the daughter changes externally and internally. These changes force her to face all the difficulties of the mother-daughter interaction deriving from an earlier phase and earlier unsolved problems, though in a different form. The girl has to abandon her close companionship with the mother—often very quickly—and her desire to be regressively intimate with the mother. The girl withdraws from the mother—in fact, opposes her; she argues, accuses, attacks, quarrels, and is otherwise at odds with the mother. They argue about everything and anything—clothes, chores, friends, interests, and even about the mother's life style, which the girl formerly accepted and admired. Now she criticizes, demands, and rises up in open rebellion. She tries to enlist the father to her side, against the mother, or looks for support from friends, stepparents, mother's friends, and even her grandmother.

According to Dahl (1989, 1993, 1995), one can make a distinction in psychoanalytic theory between current problems of the mother-daughter relationship and the girl's dealings with her internal relationship with the mother. The developmental task of the adolescent girl is to integrate fantasies of the mother of the moment and the internal mother of childhood. The fantasy of the mother of childhood as omnipotent, controlling, and domineering turns into a picture of an independent woman in charge of her femininity, motherhood, and her own identity, with whom the daughter can identify, whom she can love, and whom she can depend on when needed. The fight against the contemporary mother is in the service of the internal separation process. Pining for a mother who relieves the girl from loneliness, an outsider's position, and psychic pain from time to time evokes powerful homosexual wishes and fears.

In adolescence, the oedipal situation is reactivated. The girl has to be able to abandon the object of her preoedipal love, the internal mother, and turn toward the internal father-man. The change of object is again a burning issue. If the girl has not been able to identify with her mother, she returns to an earlier stage in their relationship, and the mother-woman again becomes the object of love.

The central motivational force of adolescence is sexual need, which increases in puberty and requires an object. According to Tähkä (1993), this activates oedipal objects, which have been idealized and repressed both as objects of love and as ego ideals. This leads to their gradual, unconscious re-externalization and comparison with the real parents of the present.

The changes in the girl's body contribute to conflicts in the mother-daughter relationship. The girl cannot hide from her sexuality and maturation. She wants to catch up with or surpass her mother and at the same time fears to do so. The change in the shape of her body is on the one hand a source of joy and pride, on the other hand a cause of shame and confusion. After the menarche the girl's life has changed in a fundamental way; she has become a woman, heir to her mother's life style in many respects. The bodies of daughter and mother have differentiated only by becoming similar.

The mother's ability and wish to contribute to her daughter's change and growth at this phase are crucial in the development of the mother-daughter love affair. The ability to be supportive but not invasive, close but not too intimate, warm but not too involved promotes the daughter's growth. The mother's flexibility is under a heavy strain. Sometimes the daughter curls up beside the mother to chat about this and that. Sometimes she slams out of the room, full of anger, shouting that only her friends understand her. Sometimes she pretends to know everything about everything and turns down all her mother's suggestions; sometimes she asks for advice and pours out all her troubles to the mother. Gradually, the girl comes to realize that her mother's personality and life style are different from hers. She may fear her mother's envy of her youthful exuberance, feel empathy and tenderness because of the disappointments of her mother's everyday life, and feel sorrow because of the psychic and physical separation that looms ahead. The latter part of the adolescence is once again a period of reparation and rebuilding in the mother-daughter relationship.

The mother faces simultaneous new challenges in her relationship with her own mother, who is aging and may be lonely, infirm, helpless, and hoping for aid from her daughter. A woman in her middle age experiences pressure from both directions. Sometimes she herself longs for mothering. In her relationship with her own mother she may meet situations that she has never faced before. She may be forced to take care of her helpless, sick mother, to become a mother for her own mother. Touching and psychic and physical intimacy enter the mother-daughter relationship in a new way. Once again the unsolved problems of the shared history will reappear. Preoedipal fears and homosexual impulses cross both the mother's and the grandmother's mind. The same grandmother who found it easy (or difficult) to touch or feed her newborn daughter now wishes or fears to be touched and fed by her daughter. The mother who once was experienced as omnipotent and domineering is in need of her daughter's love and help.

SEXUALITY — THE DIFFERENTIATION OF THE MOTHER-DAUGHTER LOVE RELATIONSHIP

Almost everything in the mother's and daughter's lives has been shared: the bodily connection during pregnancy and lactation, reciprocity in the relationship as the mother nursed the daughter, mutual love and identification. The girl's early sensual pleasures have been mainly linked to the mother. In terms of sexual feelings of pleasure, however, the girl becomes disappointed and hurt by the mother; normally the mother does not overtly offer sexual pleasure and may even forbid it by signals from her behavior. Sexuality forces the girl to differentiate from the mother. It may well be the only thing mother and daughter do not share.

As oedipal development progresses, the girl realizes that she is not the most important object of her mother's love. The father-man has something that the mother prefers to have, that is the object of her love, and that gratifies her. As the girl identifies herself with the mother, the object of mother's love becomes the central object and organizer of the daughter's desire. According to Grünberger (1985), it is of fundamental importance for the girl to realize that the mother who has given birth to her cannot be the object of her real love, and that she cannot be an object of her mother's love in the way a man can.

As we have noted, a problematic preoedipal relationship complicates the girl's sexual development. Benjamin (1990) describes difficulties resulting from the fact that the girl, in normal development, has to identify with the mother, who is regarded as the object of desire, and not with the father, who is considered the subject of desire. Kulish (1998) also stresses the girl's need to resolve the conflict between being an object (identifying with the mother) and a subject of desire. How can she be faithful to her mother and at the same time sexual? Sexual desire separates the daughter from the mother. Identifying with the mother binds the daughter to her.

The bodily changes and sensations of adolescence draw the daughter's attention to her own body. Memories of sensual pleasure brought about by the mother's care in early childhood cause homosexual fears and wishes (Dahl 1985, 1993, 1995). Identification with the mother's body and intense relationships with girlfriends create similar pressures. Sharp and even obsessive separation from the mother may cause conflicts between mother and daughter; external separation is often used in the service of internal separation.

How the mother responds to her daughter's sexuality is of crucial importance for the girl's future relationships. The mother's fantasies and experiences in relationships with men, her own sexuality, and her parents' sexual life are revived in her as she observes her daughter with boyfriends and male relatives. The mother's attitudes toward sexuality were conveyed by the way she nursed her daughter as a baby and reacted to the girl's wish to examine and nurse her own body. The girl's sexuality develops partially by identifying with the mother's mental world. Later on, the mother should have the ability and will to allow the daughter to live her own sexual life. As stated earlier, sexuality may be the only domain the mother cannot share with her daughter.

CONTINUATION OF THE LOVE RELATIONSHIP TO LATER GENERATION

During her adolescence the girl rediscovers her mother, now on a more realistic basis. The mother is at least partially differentiated from the internalized mother image of the daughter's childhood. The girl has also met other women. Her fantasies of women, womanhood, femininity, and motherhood become more varied and allow for new objects of admiration and identification. She is not so dependent on her mother as she builds her own feminine identity. In a similar manner she abandons her father and her father-man-image. Mother and daughter no longer share the same man, even in their fantasies. In this respect, both mother and daughter become differentiated, although identification with womanhood gives them an opportunity to continue their reciprocal commitment and mutual love. Mother and daughter never become fully differentiated from each other.

The girl's original love for the mother has turned into love for a man from outside the family. This man is not a part of those fantasies the mother and daughter once shared. The daughter's life is now dominated by a man whom she herself has chosen and who is unknown to the mother. In this situation, the mother may feel like an outsider, forced to give up the daughter who was a part of her in the womb and whose growth into an independent adult she has supported as an important collaborator and empathizer. The mother may feel abandoned and rejected. On the other hand, she is proud of the fact that her life continues in her daughter and that she may one day have a granddaughter as well.

A granddaughter represents a repeat of a woman's own childhood and that of her daughter, which she now is able to enjoy. Her life continues in her daughter and granddaughter. Joy and sorrow, receiving and yielding, go hand in hand.

The mother is able to live her life in a more relaxed way without taking care of her daughter's everyday needs. Menopause may be confusing, but then again sexual life becomes liberated once the fear of pregnancy has vanished and children have left home. The mother has space for herself and her feelings. Pines (1993) describes the sex life of an aging female patient. In the act of making love to her, her husband is not only her lover, who satisfies her adult body and helps her to forget growing older and facing death, but in foreplay, when touching her wife's body in a way that both of them enjoy, he unconsciously conjures up the mother of his wife's early childhood and her love for her little daughter. These sensual, bodily memories and the illusion of the mutual love of childhood extend to the end of life.

At the same time that the mother learns to give up the earlier form of her relationship with her daughter, she has to part with her own mother and her daughter-mother relationship. The death of the old mother indicates finally and concretely that it is not possible to regain the lost paradise of childhood, the absolutely reciprocal relationship of mother and daughter. The woman feels ultimately abandoned and lonely. As she confronts the death of her mother, she has to go through the bodily attachment and dependence of the mother-daughter relationship once more. She nurses and feels, touches and caresses her mother as her mother once cherished her. Conflict may arise if the aged and dying mother wants to possess her daughter again. It may be difficult for her to detach herself from her daughter, whose intimacy and care enable her to experience the same protection her mother gave to her long ago. In connection with separation anxiety, the mother goes through experiences of psychic attachment and dependency by reminiscing, accepting, forgiving, and sensing gratitude. The mother has lost two previous important generations of women, but at the same time she views two future generations with whom she is able to share giving and receiving, identification and love.

BIBLIOGRAPHY

BALINT, A. (1949). Love for the mother and mother love. *Int. J. Psycho-Anal.* *30*:109–127.

BENJAMIN, J. (1990). The Alienation of Desire: Woman's Masochism and Ideal Love. In Zanardi, G. (ed.) *Essential Papers on the Psychology of Woman.* New York: New York University Press.

BIBRING, G., DWYER, T., HUNTINGTON, D., & VALENSTEIN, A. (1961). A study of the psychological process in pregnancy and of the earliest mother-child relationship. *Psychoanal. Study Child.* 16:9–44.

BLUM, H. P. (1980). The maternal ego ideal and the regulation of maternal qualities. In S. L. Greenspan and G. H. Pollock (eds.): *The Course of Life: Psychoanalytic Contributions Toward Understanding Personality Development,* vol. 3, Adulthood and the Aging Process. Washington, NIMH.

BOLLAS, C. (1997). Hysteria on our time. A paper given at the Finnish Psychoanalytical Association 27.9.1997.

BRAZELTON, T. B. & CRAMER, B. G. (1991). *The earliest relationship.* Karnac Books, London.

CHASSEGUET-SMIRGEL, J. (1970). Feminine guilt and the Oedipus complex. In *Female Sexuality* (ed.) Chasseguet-Smirgel. Karnac. London 1985.

CHODOROW, N. (1978). *The Reproduction of Mothering.* Berkeley: University of California Press.

DAHL, E. K. (1989). Daughters and mothers: Oedipal aspects of the witch mother. *Psychoanal. Study Child,* 44:267–280.

DAHL, E. K. (1993). The impact of divorce on a preadolescent girl. *Psychoanal. Study Child,* 48:193–209.

DAHL, E. K. (1995). Daughters and Mothers. Aspects of the Representational World During Adolescence. *Psychoanal. Study Child,* 50:187–204.

ETCHEGOYEN, A. (1993). Latency—a reappraisal. *Int. J. Psycho-Anal.* 74, 347–358.

FREUD, S. (1914). On narcissism. *S.E.* 14.

FREUD, S. (1925). Some psychological consequences of the anatomical distinction between the sexes. *S.E.* 19.

FREUD, S. (1926). The question of lay analysis. *S.E.* 20.

FREUD, S. (1931). Female sexuality. *S.E.* 21.

FREUD, S. (1933). Femininity. *S.E.* 22.

FURMAN, E. (1982). Mothers have to be there to be left. *Psychoanal. Study Child.* 37:15–28.

FURMAN, E. (1996). On Motherhood. In Richard, D. & Tyson, P. (eds.) *The psychology of woman: psychoanalytic perspectives.*

GRUNBERGER, B. (1985). Outline for a study of narcissism in female sexuality. In Chasseguet-Smirgel, J. (Ed.): *Female Sexuality.* London: Karnac Books.

HÄGGLUND, V. (1988). Äidin ja lapsen varhainen maailma. In Psykoanalyysin monta tasoa. Psykoanalyytikko, professori Tor-Björn Hägglundin juhlakirja 10.3.1988. Nuorisopsykoterapiasäätiö.

IKONEN, P. (1987). Oidipuskompleksin ilmenemismuotoja myöhemmäsä elämässä. Duodecim 1987.

KESTENBERG, J. (1982). The inner-genital phase—prefallic and preoedipal. In Mendell, D. (Ed.): *Early Female Development.* New York: SP Medical & Scientific Books.

KULISH, N. M. (1986). Gender and transference: the screen of the phallic mother. *Intern. Rev. Psychoanal.* 13:393–404.

MAENCHEN, A. (1970). On the technique of child analysis in relation to stages of development. *Psychoanal. Study Child.* 25:175–208.

LEHTONEN, J., KÖNÖNEN, M., PURHONEN, M., PARTANEN, J., SAARIKOSKI, S., & LAUNIALA, K. (1998). The effect of nursing on the brain activity of the newborn. *J. Pediatrics.* April 1998.

MANNINEN, V. (1991). Pojan polku, isän tie. Psykoanalyyttisia tutkielmia pojan kasvusta, isän merkityksestä ja miehen tavoitteista. Helsinki. Kirjayhtymä.

MANNINEN, V. (1993). Tyydytys ja tyytymys. Helsinki. Kirjayhtymä.

McDOUGALL, J. (1980). *Plea for a Measure of Abnormality.* New York: Int. Univ. Press.

McDougall, J. (1995). *The Many Faces of Eros*. London: Free Association Books.

Mäenpää-Reenkola, E. (1997). Naisen verhottu sisin. Helsinki: Yliopistopaino.

Ogden, T. H. (1987). The transitional oedipal relationship in female development. *Intern. J. Psycho-Anal.* 68:485–498.

Pines, D. (1993). *A Woman's Unconscious Use of Her Body. A psychoanalytical perspective*. London: Virago Press.

Stoller, R. (1968). *Sex and Gender*, vol. 1. Maresfield Library. London, 1984.

Torsti, M. (1996). *Äitiys*. In Roos, E., Manninen, V., Välimäki, J. (Eds.) Helsinki: Kohti piilotajuntaa. Yliopistopaino.

Tähkä, V. (1993). Mielen rakentuminen ja psykoanalyyttinen hoitaminen. WSOY. Porvoo-Helsinki-Juva.

Welldon, E. V. (1988). *Mother, Madonna, Whore. The Idealization and Denigration of Motherhood*. London: Free Association Books.

Wrye, H. K. & Welles, J. (1989). The maternal erotic transference. *Intern. J. Psycho-Anal.* 70.

Body Self

Development, Psychopathologies, and Psychoanalytic Significance

DAVID W. KRUEGER, M.D.

Ego development or, more broadly, the sense of self has at its core a cohesive, distinct, and accurate body self. Compromise of body self development as a result of early overstimulation, empathic unavailability or nonresponse of the caretaker, and inconsistency or selectivity of response can lead to specific developmental arrests, including body-image distortions, nonintegration of body self and psychological self, and difficulties in the regulation of tension states and affect. The individual may then attempt to repair those disrupted developmental needs by such symptomatic expressions as eating disorders, compulsive exercise, substance abuse, and the creation of physical danger, as a step toward integration of mind and body as well as a defensive antidote to painful affect.

In the psychoanalytic treatment of these patients, the need for the analyst's attunement to the patient's development of body self as well as psychological self development is illustrated by clinical vignettes of the enactments and attempted restitution of specific developmental trauma.

FREUD (1923) RECOGNIZED THE BODY EGO AS THE FOUNDATION FOR subsequent ego development; however, except for the work of Schilder (1956) and Hoffer (1950), the body and its evolving mental

Clinical professor of psychiatry, Baylor College of Medicine; training and supervising analyst, Houston—Galveston Psychoanalytic Institute; faculty, The Institute of Contemporary Psychoanalysis and Psychotherapy, Washington D.C.

The Psychoanalytic Study of the Child 56, ed. Albert J. Solnit, Peter B. Neubauer, Samuel Abrams, and A. Scott Dowling (Yale University Press, copyright © 2001 by Albert J. Solnit, Peter B. Neubauer, Samuel Abrams, and A. Scott Dowling).

representation have been largely absent from developmental and psychoanalytic theory. Clinicians in psychotherapy and psychoanalysis have therefore focused almost exclusively on the psychological self. Yet the need for attention to the body self as a developmental foundation and ongoing container of the psychological self has been vividly expressed by some of our patients in their emotional, behavioral, or psychosomatic symptomatology. The body is often the narrator of feelings they cannot bear to hold in conscious thought, much less express in words.

The body self is the core foundation, the container, of the psychological self; in normal development body self and psychological self together form the sense of self. In certain early developmental disruptions, body self awareness and evolving integration do not occur, giving rise to various types of psychopathology. Effective psychoanalytic work with these individuals requires first that the developmental arrest of the body self and its subsequent impact on psychological self-awareness and integration be specified. For individuals with a prior developmental arrest involving the body self, affect regulation and tension reduction at times require a regressive retreat, at least in part, to a bodily experience.

Somatic experiences, the first form of affect, often occur in an analysis as particular affect states are accessed. Just as a crucial aspect of early development is the verbalization of somatic states, so developmental arrest can prevent differentiation, verbalization, and desomatization of emotions (Krystal, 1997).

Developmentally, the subjective experience and processing of body state and somatic affect through mirroring and reciprocal interactions with caretakers are prerequisite to the differentiation of affect and its correct coupling with language (symbolization). The patient must have differentiated and distinguished specific feelings in order to repress them defensively later; similarly, he must have integrated mind and body to split them defensively. The concept of defensive splitting is applicable only after the attainment of a certain developmental awareness and integration. A fundamental thrust of early development is the child's increasing "ability to extend the range of his interests beyond his body" and "sublimination in which the body is only forgotten in order to be better remembered" (Phillips, 1998, pp. 29, 34).

Attempts to effectively regulate basic affect states of emptiness, depression, and alexithymia through such activities as vigorous exercise, rage outbursts, participation in or creation of physically or emotionally dangerous situations, and the abuse of drugs, alcohol, or food stimulate mental alertness as well as regulating endorphins, enkephalins, and catecholamines (Grotstein, 1997).

BODY SELF AND PSYCHOLOGICAL SELF AS AN INTEGRATED LINE OF DEVELOPMENT

The infant's body is determined through the intersubjective definition, attachment, and mirroring of both interior and surface by significant others; that is, it is organized and given meaning in a relational matrix. Attachment needs are, first and foremost, body-based needs. Bowlby (1980) has described a network of emotional and behavioral response patterns in caretaker and infant that he termed the attachment system, defined by Siegel (1999, p. 69) as "an inborn system within the brain that evolves in ways that influences and organizes motivational, emotional and memory processes with respect to significant caretaking figures." The initial attachments are formed by the age of seven months, involve only a very few other persons, and lead to specific changes in the infant's brain function and behavior (Main, 1995). The attachment interactions with primary caretakers may be the central foundation from which body self and psychological self develop and integrate.

Developmentally, the body self is a hierarchy of experience and intellectual mechanisms progressing from images, to words, organizing patterns, and superordinate abstractions and inferences that regulate the entire self experience (Krueger, 1988a). Close and careful attunement to all sensory and motor contacts form the initial unity of mind and body, predicated on the establishment of the body self as container for the evolving psychological self. Winnicottt (1965) and Stolorow and Atwood (1992) have emphasized how the caregiver's affect attunement, conveyed through consistent and accurate sensory motor interaction with the infant's body, allows the evolution of the infant's psychological self.

The earliest imprint of the mother on the child is through bodily sensations and feelings—attunement to his body fluids and sensations, sensory matching, and secure holding—from a time before the child has words. In an elegant and innovative work, Wrye and Welles (1994) reconstruct this development from the powerful preverbal body experiences and memories that emerge in the transference experiences of adult analytic patients. [The earliest somatic awareness via caretaker physical contact and sensory experience relies on the mother's attunement to body processes of the child.

These experiences form later maternal erotic transferences and countertransferences.] Wrye and Welles (1994) contend that for some patients the identification, toleration, and eventual understanding and integration of the preverbal origins of erotic transference can create the first true intimacy they have ever experienced. Dramatic findings of research on early development and expanding awareness of neurobiological and intersubjective experience inform this appreciation.

Most developmentalists agree that the body self consists of the full range of kinesthetic experiences on the body's surface and in its interior. Lichtenberg (1978; 1985) has described the body self as a combination of the psychic experience of body sensation, body functioning, and body image. He hypothesized that reality testing occurs in a definite developmental sequence of increasing awareness and integration of body self.

THE EARLY PSYCHIC EXPERIENCE OF THE BODY

The infant's first awareness of self has been widely investigated (Emde, 1983; Mahler, 1968; Papousek and Papousek, 1975; Stern, 1985; Winnicott, 1965). Mahler (Mahler and Furer, 1968) has indicated that the earliest sense of "self" derives from sensations within the body, especially proprioception. These stimuli enable the infant to discriminate the body's self-schema from its surroundings. Tactile sensations, the primary body experience during the first weeks and months of life, may be the first developmental experience of the body self (Kestenberg, 1975).

Spitz (1965) noted the baby's inclination to concentrate on the mother's face, particularly on the eyes, during periods of feeding. The mother's hands outline and define the original boundary, the body surface delineation. Kestenberg (1985) emphasized the rhythmic movement between mother and child and the match of their movement styles as a foundation of the bond between them and a catalyst for the infant's development.

The mother's empathic resonance with the infant's internal experience provides a mirroring and a reciprocity that not only reinforce and affirm but form body self awareness (Winnicott, 1971). Her empathic alignment with the baby is the child's first experience of effectiveness: his affect produces a reciprocal response in the mother. Emde (1983) has suggested that this is the infant's chance to control parental behavior, to be *effective* in determining something—to be a cause.[1] The accuracy of the empathic attunement is crucial because it is the initial linking of mind and body experiences. If the mother is not accurately and consistently attuned to the infant, the basis for a mind-body division is established, inhibiting the child's development of the ability to "see the world feelingly" (*King Lear* IV.6.151).

A number of early developmental experiments have demonstrated the existence of a motivation for mastery—the wish to actively determine an outcome and experience effectiveness (Papousek and Papousek, 1975; Kestenberg, 1975; Demos, 1985). The desire for competence becomes a factor in psychic development as early as four months of age (Demos, 1985). The motivation for effectiveness continues throughout development but changes in expression, form, and content. White (1959) called the subjective experience of competence "effectance pleasure."

Lichtenberg (1989) has suggested that the earliest developmental need/motivational system is based on the psychic regulation of physiological requirements occurring within the infant-caregiver unit (Sander, 1980). Optimally, this becomes internalized as a pattern for self-regulation. When empathic failures occur at this early developmental level and attempts at self-regulation and symbolic representation are ineffective, symptoms later emerge as unconscious attempts to regulate affect and tension states physiologically. Plassman (1998) has demonstrated that reciprocity of prenatal and postnatal "body psychology" is a "dialogue with the body" that has its origin in the "dialogue with the primary objects."

DEFINITION OF BODY SURFACE BOUNDARIES AND DISTINCTION OF THE BODY'S INTERNAL STATE

Beginning at a few months of age and extending into the second year of life, the child develops a sense of reality based on the emergence of an integrated body self from newly discovered body boundaries and body internal states. Outer boundaries of the body become more specific and delimited.

Anzieu (1985) and Kuchenhoff (1998) have described the body images or ego-boundary representation and stated specifically that the skin serves the psychological function of defining and differentiating self and object. Body self-awareness functions to contain

---

1. I am assuming that the neurophysiological components necessary to the formation of the body self exist. First, of course, is an intact sensory system, with the innate ability to distinguish one's own body from the body of another and to develop imaging capacity.

and organize the intrapsychic space of the evolving psychological self. The "skin-ego" (Anzieu's term) serves as a stimulus barrier to preserve this evolving development.

Empathic parental mirroring and reciprocal interactions mold both internal and surface sensations into distinct and coherent functions of the child's self. Inner and outer, what is "me" and what is "not me," are distinguished. The child's experience becomes that of a unit rather than a collection of parts (Winnicott, 1971). He develops criteria for identifying where his body ends and the rest of the world begins, corresponding with the development and differentiation of psychic representation and functioning (psychological self) within the container of body self-development. He can now tolerate brief absences from the need-satisfying object and temporary suspensions of empathic contact. This sense of body self-unity is essential for subsequent ego integration, the development of physical coordination and grace, and the ability to experience pleasure in bodily activity.

But prolonged physical or empathic absence of the caregiver, characterized by inconsistencies of response or failure in the mirroring function, may lead to disavowal, splitting, or defensive fusion in the infant, with resultant distortions of body self and subsequent ego development. Body boundaries may not be distinguished, resulting in a failure to develop cohesive recognition and distinction of internal states.

Active attempts to define the body surface may include wearing heavy, loose clothing to stimulate the skin, developing a preoccupation with textures, yearning for yet fearing the touch of another, compulsive weight-lifting to outline the body muscle mass distinctly, or body mutilation. The receipt of pain establishes (or regressively re-establishes) a boundary—an experience of existing as a bounded, contained entity. The following vignette illustrates pathology at this stage of development. (This and the other vignettes presented are intended to illustrate not psychoanalytic process but a specific aspect of development, its pathology, and attempted reinstitution.)

Vignette 1: Cindy

Cindy, age 15, presented with a severe depression and compulsive self-mutilation. She had no evocative body image and little awareness of any feeling other than emptiness, alternating at times with severe tension.

With Cindy's birth, her mother had become extremely depressed and withdrew from the child emotionally, turning over her care to a succession of babysitters. Cindy's father, an international airline pilot, was available only episodically, and when he was home he reportedly attended primarily to his depressed wife.

When Cindy could not evoke or provoke responses from her parents, she felt as if she didn't exist. She would then repeatedly rub the skin on her arms with a pencil eraser until she bled. Seeing blood from her self-mutilation made her feel more real. This sensation, established through pain (and, unconsciously, the boundaries of her skin), was confirmed by bleeding and later by scarring (an hypertrophied boundary). She was reassured temporarily when she found that she could not erase herself; she was indelible, permanent. The pain, as well as her primitive sense of permanence, relieved her tension for a brief time. The reality of her most basic self—her body—buttressed her feelings of existence. Thus she created a temporary organization of her chaotic state by establishing the boundary via her skin, outlined by pain and accentuated by scars.

THE DEFINITION AND COHESION OF THE BODY SELF AS A FOUNDATION FOR SELF-AWARENESS

A new level of organized self-awareness begins at about 15 months. This is confirmed by observational studies of the infant discovering himself in the mirror at 15–18 months (Spitz, 1957) and by his acquisition of the semantic "no." Spitz defined the capacity for and function of "no" as evidence of the emerging distinctness of the "I" and "not-I," moving toward autonomy and self-awareness. "No" developmentally states, "I am not an extension of you and your body or your desire; this is where you end and I begin—my body is mine and mine alone."[2]

In normal development the experiences and images of the inner body and the body surface become organized and integrated into an experiential and conceptual whole. Consolidating a stable, integrated, cohesive mental representation of one's body, with an evolving sense of distinctness and effectiveness, is a key developmental task during this period, prerequisite to an internalized sense of psychological self, providing a unity and continuity over time, space, and state (Demos, 1985). Analytic literature does not provide a clear or consistent conceptualization of the evolution of body self and image (Rizzuto et al., 1981; Button et al., 1977). Body image is assumed to be something one has or does not have, as if it were fixed and

2. Beginning at 16–18 months, the infant discovers that he is what creates the image in the mirror. He reaches for the label on his own forehead (Modaressi and Kinney, 1977) and touches a smudge placed on his own nose rather than the image in the mirror (Lewis and Brooks-Gunn, 1979). Mahler (1968) and Piaget (1945) agree (from different theoretical vantage points) that in normal development a cognitive sense of separate existence and of body self can exist by 18 months. Exploration and familiarity with body parts have already begun by this age.

either accurate or distorted (Bauman, 1981; Van der Velde, 1985). With the beginning of concrete operations, at approximately age six, a true separation of self and object and a more distinctly complete body image become possible.

PATHOLOGICAL SEQUENCES IN BODY SELF DISORDERS

Research on deficiency states in infancy has demonstrated that failure to develop a normal psychic representation of the body may result from insufficiently intense stimulation as well as from cognitive and emotional overstimulation (Dowling, 1977; Shevrin and Toussieng, 1965; Wolff, 1960). Failure to adequately achieve the psychological regulation of physiological needs or the overgratification of these fundamental needs may produce such clinical syndromes as eating disorders, substance abuse, compulsive shopping or sexuality, or addictions to exercise, self-mutilation, or online computing (Farber, 1997).

I should like to propose a more specific link between certain developmental disruptions in body self-formation and evolution (what Battegay [1991] has called "hunger diseases") and the restorative efforts manifested as psychopathology. The nature of the developmental trauma itself seems to determine the form of the resulting psychopathology. All the deficits described begin in infancy and continue through the first few years of life. Each motivational system identified by Lichtenberg (1989) and Fosshage (1995) develops from and is shaped by the lived experiences within a relational matrix. Early developmental arrests in the process of establishing a stable, integrated, cohesive body image seem to result from one or several maladaptive interactions (Krueger, 1989a, 1997). These early developmental pathological sequences fall into three groups, which may not be mutually exclusive: overintrusiveness or overstimulation; empathic unavailability; or inconsistency or selectivity of response.

OVERINTRUSIVENESS; OVERSTIMULATION

Overly intrusive parents attempt to remain merged with the child from his infancy onward, impeding his effective pleasure in mastery and disrupting individuation. The parents' behavior toward the child is characteristically controlling, protective, and enmeshing, with predominant demands for conformity (Bsormenji-Nagy and Spark, 1973). When this pattern is so extreme as to produce developmental arrest, the child may experience the body self and image as indistinct and blurred or, alternatively, as small, prepubescent, asexual, and undifferentiated (Krueger, 1989b). Such a child experiences his body as separate from himself and easily invaded; he may attempt to establish body and self distinctness in such rudimentary ways as exercising to feel physical sensation, refusing to eat, compulsive weight lifting to establish a firm body outline, or various sexual perversions that force recognition and response, such as exhibitionism.

An individual who experiences physical and emotional intrusiveness and overstimulation may mobilize primitive protective measures that result in the development of a higher threshold to stimuli or a tuning-out or withdrawal (Demos, 1985); the latter may subsequently interfere with psychic representation at a higher level, affecting integration of physical and psychic representation. In later life he may require more intense, more extreme experiences in order to produce psychic representation or recognition of feeling. Sequelae include such distortions of tactile stimulation as limpness when held, an intense fear or wish to be touched, a desire for or avoidance of physical intimacy, sensations of numbness or somatic inattentiveness, or misperceived body image.

One type of transsexual male is an extreme clinical example of overstimulation/enmeshment; body and psyche remain so intermingled with the mother that somatic and psychic differentiation does not occur (Krueger, 1983). Thus a transsexual male at age four and a half reportedly looked at his arms and asked, "Are these my arms or Mother's?" The mother had intermingled with him physically to the extent that he had no independent psychic representation of his body or self.

Intrusiveness upon the child's personal integrity may include actual invasion of his body space—for example, by sexual assault or forced feedings (Dowling, 1977), evacuations, operations, or unrelenting body contact. Penetration of the child's emotional world may include manipulation of his feelings or thoughts, devaluation of his attempts at mastery, and demands that the child's perceptions be negated or denied. Overstimulation can occur in either a physical or an emotional way, resulting in an experience of being overwhelmed, unable to integrate or control bodily sensations. These overwhelming states create regression to a preoccupation with the body self and archaic bodily imagery (Peto, 1959) or, if they occur early enough, failure to develop beyond such a preoccupation. A later compensatory effort to develop a complete and distinct body self may employ intense sensory stimulation to provide perceptions of the body. At times of emotional stress, such an individual regresses to body self stimulation as an attempt to regulate affect and reduce tension. Stimulation and reintegration of the basic body self are the most primitive adaptive attempts at psychic reorganization.

Vignette 2: Joan

Joan, a 16-year-old girl, tried desperately to control her overwhelming compulsion to exercise. She reported, "I tried and tried not to give in and exercise, but the anxiety was overwhelming. I felt that if I didn't exercise I would lose it—that I would just fade into everyone else—like my body would just become a blob mixed in with everyone else around me. Then I'd be like everyone else—not special." She regressively attempted to vividly reestablish her body self experience and boundaries—to feel real and distinct.

She later showed me a letter written to her by her mother: "We need to give you our love and receive yours in return. We are all hurting so much. You are and always will be a part of our bodies." In a family therapy session, the mother told the therapist that "When she left home it was like losing a part of me—like my arm or part of my body."

EMPATHIC UNAVAILABILITY AND NONRESPONSE

The parent may be unable to resonate accurately and consistently with the child's internal experiences or to respond to the subtleties of his emotional and physical experiences, movements, and affects. The infant's experience does not become a point of reference for the parent. Body boundaries may not be consistently or accurately defined by caress, touch, or secure holding, preventing the infant from developing a reliable body boundary and sensory awareness. Later, the child's body self development and awareness are incomplete, and body image is distorted. His projective drawings of body image are distorted, shapeless, and excessively large, with blurred boundaries (Krueger, 1989b). These findings are most notable in those diagnosed as bulimic, borderline, or chronic narcissistically depressive characters. Their body images often fluctuate with their mood and self-image, oscillating several times a day. When the individual is experiencing a depleted self-image, his body image may become several times larger than actual body size.

Niederland (1976) has described several artist-patients in psychoanalysis who showed marked changes in body experience and perception during periods of intense creativity. Each had fantasies of being deficient, incomplete, misshapen, or ugly. During creative periods, their bodily experience changed to a perception of completeness, wholeness, and freedom from deficiency or inadequacy. When difficulties arose in their creative work, their perceptions of insufficiency and defect returned. These artists' fantasies of incompleteness and deficiency were based on the failure to form a distinct body image due to early trauma and failure in bonding with their mothers.

Many behaviors regarded as impulsive, addictive, or unrelenting are designed to evoke or establish boundaries. Spending sprees, often attempts to counter the experience of helplessness at a time of the rupture of an empathic bond, create the illusion of power and limitlessness, with the purchase of articles, usually clothing, to make the individual attractive to others (Krueger, 1988b). Stimulation of skin, the psychic envelope, affirms and delineates a body boundary, as do wearing large, loose clothing so as to feel a rubbing sensation, wrist cutting, and compulsive sexuality. Internal body awareness may be stimulated by such behaviors as binging, vomiting, the abuse of laxatives or diuretics, and the heart palpitations that follow extreme exercise.

Later in development, temporary losses of body control, such as soiling, crying, or even tripping and falling, can create overwhelming feelings of shame and embarrassment. These feelings involving insults to the body self may strain the sense of self cohesion and body reality beyond tolerance and are often described as a desire to escape from one's body or shed one's skin (Lichtenberg, 1978). At times of intense affect, the individual's focus of attention shifts from mastery to basic aspects of body self intactness and preoccupations with body sensations, body schema, and body language.

INCONSISTENCY OR SELECTIVITY OF RESPONSE

Parental response to selective stimuli from the infant creates a selective reality. For example, the mother may ignore affective and kinesthetic stimuli and respond only to physical needs or physical pain. This response pattern teaches the infant to perceive and organize experiences around pain and illness in order to obtain attention and affection. Effectiveness is via the body self; affect regulation never gets desomatized. The affirmation of body self and psychological self through pain and discomfort becomes entrenched in personality and characteristic modes of interaction, with a resultant predisposition toward psychosomatic expressions.

Vignette 3: Ashley

Ashley, now 19 and a very attractive television model and college student, described a ritual of several years' duration. Whenever she felt overwhelmingly anxious and fragmented, she would get into very hot bathwater and scrub herself so hard with a brush that her skin would be raw and bleeding. She said that this did not cause pain but was relieving, reassuring. Her "scrubbings" began at pubescence, when she felt "dirty" and needed to "scrub away the dirtiness." She recognized, in reconstructions, that illnesses and accidents were the only way to effectively engage the concern and attention of her highly self-absorbed and largely absent mother. Earlier physical and sexual abuse had skewed the experience of her body and of pain, raising a pain threshold already elevated because of her mother's empathic neglect of her child's sensorimotor development.

A Model Developmental Arrest of Body Self: Eating Disorders

What follows is a clinical illustration of the process of developmental arrest involving both body self and psychological self, a composite gleaned from almost two decades of both psychoanalytic and intensive inpatient work with individuals presenting with eating disorders. Most persons with anorexia nervosa and bulimia suffer from an incompletely developed body self and psychological self; the previously described stages of body self development have become derailed in one or more psychopathogenic interactions, and the eating disorder is an attempt at affect regulation as well as developmental restitution. These patients have limited ability to describe themselves and their feelings meaningfully. Like many other psychosomatic patients, they tend to have constricted emotional expression and describe extraordinary details of symptoms as substitutes for feelings and internal experiences. They inhibit fantasy, limiting their capacity to symbolize and to play. Unaccustomed to accepting themselves as a point of reference or describing their own internal experience, they perform for others, are perfectionistic, and yearn for recognition (Bruch, 1973a; 1973b). They engage in obsessive vigilance about their bodies, food, calories, and how they appear to others.

Patients who suffer from anorexia nervosa and bulimia have an inadequate internal regulation system, to the extent that they may be unable to recognize such basic body sensations as hunger. They oscillate rapidly between grandiosity and self-depreciation, relying vulnerably on external cues. At times of major increments of separation-individuation, such as pubescence, early adulthood, marriage, and pregnancy, each involving some form of bodily change, these individuals become aware of their pervasive reliance on external cues to direct them and of the absence of an internal center of initiative and regulation. Their developmental arrests affect body self and schema, psychological self, and some cognitive capacities, particularly those influencing the sense of one's self as a whole and the permanence and completeness of body image. Sensorimotor development is often delayed with the persistence of some pathological neurological reflexes and other soft neurological signs of arrest of body self-development. With treatment, these pathological signs and reflexes normalize (Donatti et al., 1990).

These disorders manifest as deficiencies of self-regulation, and the patient often has little or no recognition of an internal center of initiative or reference (Krueger, 1988a). Feeling particularly ineffective in affect regulation (Bruch, 1973), she used food to compensate for a deficient integration of mind and body. Relying on others for affirmation, enhancement, function, and esteem, the patient searches for a way to internalize the source of these emotional goods, often with the result that she feels that her body—indeed, her self-organization—is easily invaded, influenced, exploited, and overwhelmed by others. The frenetic exercise that is often characteristic of anorexics may appear to be undertaken for the purpose of losing weight, but at another level it is a desperate attempt to experience the reality of the body, for which they do not have an accurate or distinct mental representation. It is also an effort (like extreme dieting or vomiting) to counter the anguish of internal emptiness, boredom, and deadness. As a young anorexic woman explained, "I feel completely helpless and ineffective, and I don't know what's wrong or how to feel better. At least when I focus on food and feel fat, I have *something* I can control and do something about."

The anorexic individual establishes an artificial boundary by saying "no" to food proffered by parents. In a quest for her own identity, she creates a distinctness by her opposition to her parents and to her own hungry body. She reviews her body as an unintegrated part of her environment, something that must be resisted. One anorexic woman stated this vividly: "My body grew up without me. I never got any affirmation; it was like I was invisible as a child." Her food refusal is a demonstration of independence from her parents, an effort to bring into concrete focus that which is otherwise incomprehensible. The result is a visible need for nurturance and care as her body becomes weaker and more childlike.

The bulimic individual attempts to supply for herself what is missing via the symbolic equation of food and nurturance. This dynamic, incorporating symbolism and magical thinking, was summarized by a patient: "When I am in the middle of a binge it's like I have anything and everything I've always wanted. By getting rid of it all immediately, I don't even have to pay the price of getting fat." Food not only is used to regulate affect and tension states but often has been used historically by the family of origin to reward, punish, or nurture (Krueger, 1997). In addition, bulimia is often an attempt to define internal aspects of body self experience; thus binging produces the sensation of fullness and distention, and purging or using laxatives to cause diarrhea produces a specific, defining pain. The individual can then eliminate what she perceives as "bad": acidic vomitus or feces.

Vignette 4: Jennifer

Jennifer, a college senior with a four-year history of bulimia, represents a typical symptom/dynamic composite. Her bulimia worsened at the beginning of her senior year, two months prior to her presentation for treatment.

As we examined a bulimic episode in detail, she described first being aware of feeling both empty and uncomfortable, sometimes depressed. She turned immediately to food to fill the void. During the binge itself, she felt pleasure, sometimes euphoria. She experienced a magical omnipotence in which she could have, for a moment, whatever she wanted. During the binge she often was frantic, rushed, or anxious. Afterwards she experienced a distended and painful stomach. This gave her "bad" feeling both reality and localization; it was also something she created—both by the sequenced action of binging and by the "bad" food she chose—sweets or "junk" food. Her dysphoria was now an entity that had form, shape, and remedy. She could actively and immediately rid herself of the problem by purging. "Feeling fat" was deemed the cause of feeling bad. Various active maneuvers—dieting, taking diuretics or laxatives, and especially incessant exercise—could then be directed at this malady, enabling her to achieve the illusion of control by literally getting rid of what she had eaten (the bad feeling/object). Then followed a period of feeling guilty for these actions, interspersed with feeling tired and relieved at having managed these events.

For Jennifer feeling "bad" was the result of feeling ineffective, particularly in maintaining an empathic connectedness with an important other or with her ideal self. Her goals of perfection (which of course were unattainable) centered on grades, weight, and other highly valued social referents. Jennifer yearned to be able to control something external, concrete, and specific, in order to feel effective when her internal state was unfocused. "When I felt empty and lonely as a girl, I would wish something really bad would happen to me, like an accident and bleeding, so that I would have a real reason for feeling really terrible and so that others could see my hurting and believe it. Then I could believe it too and know what it was. I didn't understand what was the matter. After something bad would happen to me in my fantasy, I'd feel better. Then I would have someone to comfort me. I would imagine, for example, being hit on the head and getting a bruise so that someone could see I was hurt. When I binge and feel fat and see my distended stomach—it is something for me to feel bad about. I created it. I wished to get skinny so that people could see how skinny I was and see me as sick. Sometimes I wish they'd find something wrong with me physically so they could see it and get rid of it."

Jennifer recognized more detail. "I feel helpless, worthless because I can't control how someone responds to me. That's what brings me back to my body. Binging is a substitute for the things I can't get and want. I'm out of control. I take in something to feel better, then I feel more in control." When I commented that this must seem the only way that she can feel effective, she responded, "Yes. If it's not the way I want it to be, I can eat my way into feeling better—at least for a little while. Then I'm back to where I was before: miserable."

The search for a focus for dysphoric affect is an attempt at mastery by converting passivity into activity and eliciting specific response/validation from an important self-object. This narcissistically vulnerable young woman described having used food as an affect regulator since early childhood, when both parents were away and she was cared for by a series of nannies. These issues became more manifest in the transference as she saw me as the embodiment/withholder of what she needed; any perceived empathic failure on my part led to an episode of symptomatic binging and purging.

DISCUSSION

These three types of pathological interaction seem to result in specific developmental arrests. They all impact the sense of self at a basic body self level, with the absence of a coherent, accurate, organized body image. The individuals described have a poor sense of their body boundaries, if any (Garner and Garfinkle, 1981; Krueger, 1989a; Rizzuto et al., 1981). Lacking internal evocative images of a body self or a psychological self, they rely on external feedback and referents, such as the reactions of others to their appearance and actions or their reflection in mirrors. There is a distinct lack of object and internal image constancy. As illustrated by the model of eating disorders, this arrest in body self development parallels the arrest in the development of psychological self.

The failure to achieve autonomy and separation stems from an early nucleus of arrested development, encountered when the sense of self emerges from mirroring experiences with the mother in the first weeks and months of life. This process extends, in changing forms, throughout development. The preverbal experiences in the first year of life have failed to acknowledge and confirm a distinct and accurate body self (Krueger, 1988b; Peto, 1959; Rizzuto et al., 1981). A more severely narcissistic individual may not have a consolidated body image and ideal to either deny or achieve.

Disturbances in differentiating self and other affect the ability to create symbols and to distinguish the symbol from the object symbolized; this in turn promotes a particular kind of developmental arrest: concrete self-referential thinking without the capacity for abstraction or representation of the body and its contents, including affect differentiation. Though these individuals may be quite articulate and accomplished, they feel lost when focusing internally and do not have a language in which to express feelings (Krystal, 1988). Thus they elicit self-representation and regulate affect via the felt experiences of their own bodies. Their representation of self must emerge from the body self experience, not from a symbolic representation of the self, because they have never developed a viable representational image of the self. The psychological distance required for developmental progress beyond a transitional object is unavailable at this concrete non-symbolic operational level. Symbolic equations are experienced as the actual object rather than as emblem, as in Jennifer's use of food (Segal, 1978). There is no "as if" quality as in true symbols, only an all-or-nothing concrete experience. At times of insult or perceived empathic disruption, these individuals engage in action sequences or symptoms that in some way stimulate the body (e.g., pain, gorging, starvation, overexertion, body mutilation) so as to create a sensorimotor experience of the body self. These patients are not primarily denying body awareness and feelings, for they have not developmentally attained desomatized and differentiated affect and bodily sensation and have not as yet integrated mind and body enough to split them defensively. At the time of a current emotional insult, their organizing function is to direct focus to the first and most basic organizer of ego experience and structure: the body self.

Higher-order, more structured pathology involves regressive retreats to more intact body self-representations and regulation at times of threatened self-representation. In certain patients "concreteness" may be a defense against ongoing differentiating processes (Bass, 1997); by contrast, developmentally arrested patients who have not yet fully differentiated with intact body self/psychological cohesion may be concrete as a result, especially in reference to themselves and their internal states (though being quite intelligent and abstract in other areas).

Patients with more developmentally advanced psychopathology, such as that organized around oedipal issues, may have an integrated body schema, with more highly organized and dynamically/symbolically significant loss fantasies, such as castration anxiety or immobilization. Unconscious fantasies of losing vital body parts or functions occur in conjunction with emotionally charged relational interactions and oedipal issues. In individuals with more structurally intact psychopathology (e.g., psychoneurosis), fantasies of loss occur without severe threat to the sense of self-cohesion. Body self-cohesion and representation are basically intact and play an important role in these instances, but these symptoms occur at the level of fantasy rather than in action symptoms.

TREATMENT IMPLICATIONS

The restitutive attempts described here are a central issue in treatment. They can be understood initially as attempts to meet arrested developmental needs as well as to defend against painful affects. The entire psychodynamic scenario within which the action symptom is embedded must be empathetically understood and interpretatively addressed, as it is much more than simply defense through action.

Lichtenberg, Lachmann, and Fosshage (1992) have described five motivational systems, each built around a basic need: the need for psychic regulation of physiological requirements, the need for attachment and later affiliation, the need for exploration and assertion, the need to react aversively through antagonism and/or withdrawal, and the need for sensual enjoyment and sexual excitement. Deficiencies in the development of any of these tracks can result in specific action symptoms as attempted restitutive enactments.

As we have noted, these patients typically describe themselves and their feelings in a paradoxically concrete way. They convey a vague sense of incompleteness, emptiness, unhappiness, and a feeling that something is missing. Their emotional expression and capacity to fantasize, symbolize, and play are constricted (Krystal, 1997). Often they present a specific external focus of symptomatology ranging from a separation crisis to a specific action symptom or scenario, such as addiction to food, money, or sex. Lacking a consistent, internally regulated image of a body self and its desomatization to a psychological self, they addictively rely on external feedback and referents, such as other people, possessions, or objects. Psychoanalytic treatment for such patients must address the psychodynamic scenario of the present moment in which the attempted restitutive symptoms occur as well as the underlying developmental deficits.

The initial phase of analysis does not focus on interpreting unconscious fantasies, decoding symbolism, or even interpreting defenses against anxiety enacted in the symptom scenario. The empathic failures experienced throughout early development may have resulted in an unconscious core organizing assumption of badness or defectiveness (Stolorow and Atwood, 1992), later projected onto the body (Plassman, 1998). First, the analyst must emphatically resonate with and convey understanding of the patient's investment in the symptom, its immediacy and power in reducing tension, and the difficulty and anxiety of relinquishing the symptom. Consistent therapeutic attention and empathic listening must focus on the motivation in using the symptom (developmental restitution as well as tension reduction and defensive purpose), enactment, and the patient's experience before, during, and after the symptomatic act. Then, the use of the action as a defense and the avoidance of an internal focus on experience to counter painful affect can be collaboratively explored.

Because the patient may not have differentiated specific feelings, the analyst requires a somatic and affective focus intended to expand the accuracy of the patient's reading and labeling of internal signals. The patient can then internalize the experience of effectiveness and the process of empathic attunement as self-empathy and can resume developmental growth. The fusion of feeling and action creates a potential space for fantasy, contemplation, and symbolism. The analytic process can then evolve to transference phenomena, including the understanding and interpretation of those structured by the patient's internal object world (Ogden, 1997).

SUMMARY

[First, the body self is the *function* of another, the intermingling with the caretaker who regulates physiological and psychological requirements.] Next, it is immediate, felt *experience:* the emerging extension experience of unsatisfied need. Next, the body self is *form,* an internalized representation including body image with objectively distinct patterns of behavior, as well as the subjective and systematic experience of reality. Finally, it is *concept,* a relatively enduring internal frame of reference, comprised of bodily and emotional images and the perception and processing of these experiences. The body and its evolving mental representation form the foundation of integrated ego functioning.

Pathological sequences in body self-disorders include parental overintrusiveness with overstimulation, empathic unavailability and nonresponse, and inconsistency or selectivity of response. Each gives rise to a specific failure in body self and body image development and integration, related to symptomatic expression in some form of action sequence. With such arrests in development, the ego's capacity to regulate tension and affect states is compromised. At times of stress, psychological management requires a regression to the body self.

Transference phenomena and process will reveal critical qualitative aspects of the level of pathology and the nature of defect in internal structure, preferred mode of affect regulation, functional dynamics, and the role of action/enactment in the reestablishment of intrapsychic equilibrium. The integration (or lack thereof) of the body self and psychological self must include an understanding of developmental phenomena within the individual's subjective frame of reference and intersubjective/relational perspectives over time.

BIBLIOGRAPHY

ANZIEU, D. (1985). *Le Moi-Peau*. Paris: Bordas.

BASS, A. (1997). The problem of concreteness. *Psa. Quart.*, 46:642–682.

BATTEGAY, R. (1991). *Hunger Diseases*. Lewiston, N.Y.: Hogrefe and Huber.

BAUMAN, S. (1981). Physical aspects of the self. *Psychiat. Clin. North America*, 4:455–469.

BOWLBY, J. (1980). *Attachment and Loss*. New York: Basic Books.

BRUCH, H. (1973a). *Eating Disorders*. New York: Basic Books.

——— (1973b). *The Golden Cage*. Cambridge, Mass.: Harvard University Press.

BSORMENJY-NAGY, I., & SPARK, G. (1973). *Invisible Loyalties*. New York: Harper & Row.

BUTTON, E., FRANSELLA, F., & SLADE, P. (1977). A reappraisal of body perception disturbances in anorexia nervosa. *Psycholog. Med.*, 7:235–243.

DEMOS, V. (1985). Affect and the development of the self: a new frontier. Self Psychology Conference, New York.

DONATTI, D., THIBODEAUX, C., KRUEGER, D., & STRUPP, K. (1990). Sensory integrative processes in eating disorder patients. American Occupational Therapy Association National Meeting, New York.

DOWLING, S. (1977). Seven infants with esophageal atresia: a developmental study. *Psychoanal. Study Child.*, 32:215–256.

EMDE, R. (1983). The prerepresentational self. *Psa. Study Child.*, 38:165–192.

FABER, M. (1985). *Objectivity and Human Perception*. Alberta, Canada: University of Alberta Press.

FARBER, S. (1997). Self-medication, traumatic enactment, and somatic expression in bulimic and self-mutilating behavior. *Clin. Soc. Work J.*, 25:87–106.

FOSSHAGE, J. (1995). An expansion of motivational theory: Lichtenberg's maturational systems model. *Psychoanal. Inq.*, 15:421–436.

GARNER, D., & GARFINKLE, P. (1981). Body image in anorexia nervosa: measurement, theory and clinical implications. *Int. J. Psychiat. Med.*, 11:263–284.

GROTSTEIN, J. (1997). Mens sane in corpore sano?: The mind and body as an "odd couple" and as an oddly coupled unity. *Psychoanal. Inq.*, 17:204–222.

HOFFER, W. (1950). Development of the body ego. *Psa. Study Child* 5:18–24.

KESTENBERG, J. (1975). *Children and Parents: Studies in Development*. New York: Jason Aronson.

——— (1985). The use of creative arts as prevention of emotional disorders in infants and children. National Coalition of Arts Therapy Associations meeting, New York.

KRUEGER, D. (1983). Diagnosis and management of gender dysphoria. In: Fann, W., Karacan, I., Pokorny, A. and Williams, R. (eds.), *Phenomenology and Treatment of Psychosexual Disorders*. New York: SP Medical and Scientific.

——— (1988a). Body self, psychological self, and bulimia: developmental and clinical considerations. In: Schwartz, H. (ed.). *Bulimia: Psychoanalytic Treatment and Theory*. New York: International Universities Press.

——— (1988b). On compulsive spending and shopping: a psychodynamic inquiry. *Amer. J. Psychother.*, 42:574–584.

——— (1989a). *Body Self and Psychological Self: Developmental and Clinical Integration in Disorders of the Self*. New York: Brunner/Mazel.

——— (1989b). The "Parent loss" of empathic failures and the model symbolic restitution of eating disorders. In: Dietrich, D. and Shabab, P., *The Problems of Loss and Mourning: New Psychoanalytic Perspectives*. New York: International Universities Press.

——— (1997). Food as selfobject in eating disorder patients. *Psychoanal. Rev.*, 84:617–630.

——— (2000). The use of money as an action symptom: A Psychoanalytic view. In Benson, A. (ed.). *I Shop, Therefore I Am*. New York: J. Aronson and Sons.

KRYSTAL, H. (1988). *Integration and Self-Healing: Affect—Trauma—Alexithymia*. Hillsdale, N.J.: The Analytic Press.

——— (1997). Desomatization and the consequences of infantile psychic trauma. *Psychoanal. Inq.*, 17:126–150.

KUCHENHOFF, J. The body and ego boundaries: A case study on psychoanalytic therapy with psychosomatic patients. *Psychoanal. Inq.* 18:368–382.

LEWIS, M. & BROOKS-GUNN, J. (1979). *Social Cognition and the Acquisition of Self*. New York: Plenum Press.

LICHTENBERG, J. (1978). The testing of reality from the standpoint of the body self. *J. Amer. Psychoan. Assoc.*, 26:357–385.

——— (1985). *Psychoanalysis and Infant Research*. Hillsdale, N.J.: The Analytic Press.

——— (1989). *Psychoanalysis and Motivation*. Hillsdale, N.J.: The Analytic Press.

————, LACHMANN, F., & FOSSHAGE, J. (1992). *Self and Motivational Systems.* Hillsdale, N.J.: The Analytic Press.

MAHLER, M., & FURER, M. (1968). *On Human Symbiosis and the Vicissitudes of Individuation.* New York: International Universities Press.

MAIN, M. (1995). Attachment: Overview, with implications for clinical work. In: Goldberg, S., Muir, R., and Kerr, J. (eds.). *Attachment Theory: Social, Developmental, and Clinical Perspectives.* Hillsdale, N.J.: The Analytic Press.

McDOUGALL, J. (1989). *Theatres of the Body.* New York: W. W. Norton.

MONDARESSI, T., & KINNEY, T. (1977). Children's response to their true and distorted mirror images. *Child Psychiat. Human Develop.,* 8(2):94–101.

NIEDERLAND, W. (1976). Psychoanalytic approaches to creativity. *Psychoanal. Quart.,* 45:185–212.

OGDEN, T. (1997). *Reverie and Interpretation: Sensing Something Human.* Northvale, NJ: Jason Aronson, Inc.

PAPOUSEK, H., & PAPOUSEK, M. (1975). Cognitive aspects of preverbal social interaction between human infants and adults. In: *Parent-Infant Interaction.* Chicago Foundation Symposium. New York: Associated Scientific Publishers.

PETO, A. (1959). Body image and archaic thinking. *Int. J. Psychoanal.,* 40:223–231.

PHILLIPS, A. (1998). *The Best in the Nursery.* New York: Pantheon.

PIAGET, J. (1945). *Play, Dreams and Imitation in Childhood.* New York: W. W. Norton.

PLASSMAN, R. (1998). Organ worlds: outline of an analytical psychology of the body. *Psychoanl. Inq.* 18:344–367.

RIZZUTO, A., PETERSON, M. & REED, M. (1981). THE PATHOLOGICAL SENSE OF SELF IN ANOREXIA NERVOSA. *Psychia. Clin. North America,* 4:471–487.

SANDER, L. (1980). Investigation of the infant and its caregiving environment as a biological system. In: Greenspan, S. I. and Pollack, G. (eds.), *The Course of Life,* Vol. 1. Rockville, Md.: National Institute of Mental Health, pp. 117–202.

SCHILDER, P. (1956). *The Image and Appearance of the Human Body.* New York: International Universities Press.

SEGAL, H. (1978). On symbolism. *Int. J. Psychoanal.,* 59:315–319.

SHEVRIN, H., & TOUSSIENG, P. (1965). Vicissitudes of the need for tactile stimulation in instinctual development. *Psychoanal. Study Child.,* 20:310–339.

SIEGEL, D. (1999). *The Developing Mind: Toward a Neurobiology of Interpersonal Experience.* New York: Guilford Press.

SPITZ, R. (1965). *The First Year of Life.* New York: International Universities Press.

———— (1957). *No and Yes.* New York: International Universities Press.

STERN, D. (1985). *The Interpersonal World of the Infant.* New York: Basic Books.

STOLOROW, R., & ATWOOD, G. (1992). *Contexts of Being: The Intersubjective Foundations of Psychological Life.* Hillsdale, N.J.: The Analytic Press.

Van der Velde, C. (1985). Body images of one's self and of others: Developmental and clinical significance. *J. Amer. Psychiat. Assoc.*, 142:527–537.

White, R. (1959). Motivation reconsidered: The concept of competence. *Psychol. Rev.*, 66:297–333.

Winnicott, D. (1971). *Playing and Reality*. New York: Basic Books.

———— (1965). *Maturational Processes and the Facilitating Environment*. New York: International Universities Press.

Wolff, P. (1960). *The Developmental Psychologies of Jean Piaget and Psychoanalysis (Psychological Issues. Monograph 5)*. New York: International Universities Press.

Wrye, H., & Welles, J. (1994). *The Narration of Desire: Erotic Transferences and Countertransferences*. Hillsdale, N.J.: The Analytic Press.

CLINICAL CONTRIBUTIONS

The Effects of Medication on the Psychoanalytic Process

The Case of Selective Serotonin Reuptake Inhibitors

GEORGE A. AWAD, M.D.

This paper deals with two analysands who developed serious symptoms of anxiety and depression during the middle phase of their analysis. The symptoms were severe enough to disrupt the previously established analytic process. After a consultation, both patients were put on a selective serotonin reuptake inhibitor (SSRI). Both responded well to the medication, not only in terms of symptom reduction but also in re-establishing the analytic process. Both patients made very little reference to medication after an initially negative reaction to the suggestion of a psychopharmacology consultation. The process of seeking a consultation, the prescription and monitoring of the medication, the concept of medications as parameters, and the possible reasons for the virtual absence of references to medication are discussed.

> The future may teach us to exercise a direct influence, by means of particular chemical substances, on the amount of energy and their distribution in the mental apparatus. It may be that there are other still undreamt-of possibilities of therapy.
> —Sigmund Freud 1940, p. 182

Training and supervising analyst, Toronto Institute of Psychoanalysis, and associate professor of psychiatry, University of Toronto, Ontario, Canada.

The Psychoanalytic Study of the Child 56, ed. Albert J. Solnit, Peter B. Neubauer, Samuel Abrams, and A. Scott Dowling (Yale University Press, copyright © 2001 by Albert J. Solnit, Peter B. Neubauer, Samuel Abrams, and A. Scott Dowling).

THE DEVELOPMENT OF NEW MEDICATIONS HAS INFLUENCED THE PRAC-
tice of psychiatry and subsequently that of psychotherapy and psychoanalysis. A preliminary study by Roose and Stern (1995) indicates
that in some psychoanalytic practices up to one third of patients may
be medicated. One group of medications, the selective serotonin-re-
uptake inhibitors (SSRIs), is used to treat depression, anxiety, and
obsessive-compulsive disorders. Since these conditions form a large
part of most psychoanalytic practices, it is important to understand
how advances in neurobiology may influence psychoanalysis (Reiser,
1984; Cooper, 1985) and how psychoanalysis may help in treating
specific problems such as obsessive-compulsive disorder (Esman,
1989) and anxiety and panic disorders (Busch et al., 1991; Busch,
1995).

The focus of this paper is clinical rather than theoretical. It does
not deal with the important topic of psychopharmacology and
metapsychology but instead presents two cases, focusing on the decision to use medications, their impact on the analytic process, and the
process of discontinuing their use.

THE LITERATURE ON MEDICATION AND PSYCHOANALYSIS

I have arbitrarily divided my comments on the literature into three
areas: the dynamics of prescribing medications, the meaning of medication use, and the effects of medications on psychoanalysis. Discussions of the integration of psychotherapy into a general psychiatric
practice (e.g., Goldhamer, 1983; Gutheil, 1982; Kahn, 1991; Karasu,
1982; Nevins, 1990) are not relevant to this paper and are not dealt
with here.

A small but growing body of literature examines the dynamics of
prescribing medications in psychoanalysis (Anonymous, 1992; Cohen, 1992; New York Psychoanalytic Society, 1992; Kantor, 1989,
1990, 1993; Sharf, 1992; Rodriguez-Boulan, 1992; Roose, 1990; Wylie
and Wylie, 1987). Most of this work consists of case presentations and
discussions of why and when medications should be introduced and
by whom, the psychoanalyst or a consultant. In these cases medications were first prescribed when certain symptoms, such as clinical
depression or anxiety, became disruptive. The authors suggest that
medications treat one aspect of the patient—mood—while analysis
deals with character style, compromise formations, and unconscious
fantasies. In all case studies, the introduction of medication is treated
as a parameter that could have been handled analytically.

Finally, some papers discuss the relative merits of combined treatment, in which the analyst prescribes and monitors the medication, and split treatment, in which another physician prescribes and monitors. In all the cases presented the analysts were medical doctors who prescribed and monitored the medications. Yet only Ostow (1962, 1979, 1990), probably the most experienced in using medications in psychoanalysis, recommends combined treatment. In the practices of lay analysts, medications have to be prescribed and monitored by someone else. Thus, any comments on split treatment made by medical analysts will be speculative.[1]

A second area discussed in the literature is the meaning of medication use for both analyst and analysand. Most authors suggest that the conscious and unconscious beliefs of the analyst are a major factor in how their patients experience the medications. And most focus on the realistic and countertransferential issues, including the therapist's ability or inability to accept the slow pace of treatment or to tolerate his own affective states in response to the patient's pain—the wish for omnipotence and idealization, anger at the patient, giving up on the patient, etc. Even though some authors allude to countertransferential issues in the *non*prescribing of medication, all the clinical examples given presented are about countertransferential prescribing. In cases of severe anxiety or depression, to refrain from suggesting medication may indicate a lack of current knowledge about their use or more serious countertransference issues. As for what medications mean to the patient, some authors have developed the theoretical formulation that the medications are experienced as transitional phenomena (Hauser, 1986) or transitional objects (Adelman, 1985). In addition, patients express specific meanings, such as fears of biological deficiency, dependence, and abandonment.

A third area dealt with in the literature is the effect of medications on the analytic process. As might be expected, most of the cases described are more tumultuous than the average. Some of the patients were suicidal, with psychotic symptoms and frequent hospitalizations, and required major tranquilizers. These patients cannot be compared with the usual analysands. A valid study would require comparison of two similar patients (i.e., outpatients, with character pathology and mood disorder), one patient medicated and the other not (Karush, 1992). Nonetheless, all the authors of these case presentations, including a few who described "the average" analytic pa-

---

1. The dynamics of split treatment will differ depending on whether it is practiced by a medical or a lay analyst. The fact that the medical clinician has a choice while the lay analyst does not will also affect both transference and countertransference.

tient (e.g., Wylie & Wylie, 1987), believe that an analytic process is possible when the introduction of medication is handled analytically. In some situations, the introduction of medications facilitated rather than inhibited the analysis of transference.

CLINICAL CONSIDERATIONS

The dynamics and meaning of the use of medications during analysis are influenced by such factors as the different dynamics and diagnoses of analysands, their attitude toward medication, the analyst's attitude toward it, the timing of the prescription (before, at the start of, or during analysis), the reasons for prescribing it, the types and number of medications used, the presence or absence of side effects and the ease or difficulty of monitoring them, the length of time the medications are used, and the person who decides or does all of the preceding.

In general, there are three ways of prescribing medications. No one method is likely to be best for all patients. The first method is for the medical analyst to diagnose a condition that requires medication and to prescribe and monitor both dosage and side effects. The second is to refer the patient to another psychiatrist, who will prescribe and monitor. The third is for the analyst to refer the patient for a consultation about pharmacological interventions but to take responsibility for prescribing and monitoring them.

For the two patients discussed in this article, I chose the third course. Both patients were university graduates with professional careers, and both had moderately severe character pathology with serious problems in relating and in self-esteem regulation. They were in analysis for a year or more before manifesting pronounced anxiety or depressive symptoms. I proposed a consultation, and after some initial resistance they decided to take the medication prescribed (an SSRI), and took it regularly and responsibly. They responded favorably to the SSRI, experiencing some mild initial side effects that subsided over the long term. Medical management of the SSRIs faded into the background, consisting only of prescription renewal on request.

In my view, depressive or anxiety symptoms form part of the analytic process. However, when the symptoms intensify to the point where the clinical picture becomes a clear Axis I diagnosis, I start considering medication. In doing so, I do not consciously take into account the difficulty of the analysis. For example, in a journal issue devoted to this topic, Karuch (1992) presents a case in which medications were not used but (it is suggested) could have been. In my reading of the case, I saw no reason to consider medication, despite the length and complexity of the analysis, since the material did not suggest anxiety or affective disorders according to standard psychiatric diagnosis.

In suggesting a consultation, the therapist shifts from a psychoanalytic listening mode (introspective, dynamic, and interpretive) to a psychiatric, medical mode (extrospective, phenomenological, and suggestive). Hoffman (1998), in discussing the analytic process, describes the dialectic between ritual and authority, on one side, and spontaneity, on the other. I extend the concept of dialectic beyond Hoffman and suggest that with some patients a dialectic between a psychoanalytic and a psychiatric attitude is unavoidable. Usually I listen for unconscious motivation and meaning. However, when a diagnosed disorder persists and continues to disrupt the analytic process or the patient's life, I introduce the idea of a consultation about the possibility of medication. It may take several months to reach this stage because many Axis I diagnoses can be resolved analytically— and we can wait for that, if the symptoms are not too disruptive. In the two case vignettes presented here, I introduced the idea of a consultation; a similar procedure would apply if the patient asked for medication.

The main goal of the consultation is to obtain a psychiatric diagnosis based on a diagnostic interview and to educate the patient about the disorder and the use of medications. I indicate that my bringing up this issue obviously implies that I think medications might be helpful; however, I do not make a unilateral recommendation to try them. If the patient agrees to a consultation, I give her the name of a consultant who I know understands the complexity of the psychoanalytic process. I use a consultant because my knowledge of medications is limited and because I am reluctant to shift my analytic stance and assume a diagnostic and didactic role. The patient makes the appointment.

The consultant's report, by prior agreement between us, details the possible medications, the range of doses, and the timing and amount of increases. After receiving the report, I give the analysand a copy and discuss her reactions. I ask the patient to decide whether or not she wants to take the medication. If she decides to do so, and I make it clear that I am willing to assume the medical responsibility for prescribing and monitoring it.

The advantage of this method is the implication that everything that happens to the patient, including the taking of medications, interests the analyst, forms part of the analysis, and is an analyzable interaction. Monitoring keeps the analyst aware of changes in the patient's mood and symptoms and their possible influence on the analytic material. Otherwise, the analyst has to depend on communications from the psychopharmacologist or the patient, which may be inaccurate or untimely.

I believe this method is consistent with a psychoanalytic stance. The medical information acquired by the analysand is equivalent to but not the same as an insight gained through an interpretation during a unique relationship (the transference-countertransference). It differs from general factual knowledge deduced by a specialist and told to the patient. However, the analysand does learn something about herself and a course of action that may alleviate her symptoms. She can then make an informed choice, which, in my opinion, is the ultimate goal of psychoanalysis. However, what is also different from the usual psychoanalytic stance is that as medical psychoanalysts we have a legal and clinical responsibility in prescribing the medication. We are also legally and clinically responsible for the patient's violent behavior toward herself or others.

Taking medical responsibility may or may not influence the analytic process. As yet we have no empirical evidence on whether such a shift in the analyst's role is beneficial, harmful, or neutral. This method may have disadvantages: the analysand may view the suggestion of a consultation negatively, and the shared responsibility may become an arena of conflict and struggle for control.

Certain types of patients—e.g., patients who are taking a number of medications that require continuous evaluation, and patients who constantly demand new medications or resist taking them—may require split treatment. In one psychotherapy case that I supervised, arguments between the patient and the psychiatrist over medications filled most of the sessions, to the point that no other work could be done. Splitting medication prescription and therapy allowed for removal of a constant irritant between patient and therapist and permitted the resumption of therapy.

I present my method to the patient in an intentionally rational manner to indicate my belief that the use of medication has a strong realistic element. However, every step of the process also has unconscious meanings and transference-countertransference implications for both parties. The case vignettes that follow illustrate some of these.

CASE VIGNETTE 1: MEDICATION AS A HOLDING ENVIRONMENT

Ms. A, a 27-year-old single white female professional, came to analysis because of anxiety and low self-esteem. She was seen four times a week and used the couch. She had been in a 6-year previous analysis in another city. That analysis was terminated when she lost her job and could not find another job in that city.

Analysis revealed symbiotic fantasies that she constructed to deal with her fear of abandonment by an angry, preoccupied, and threatening mother. Aggression arising from the frustration of her wishes for attachment changed those wishes to fantasies of revenge and omnipotent control of the mother. However, the mother did not tolerate her expression of aggression or allow it to be modulated and resolved. Thus, primitive defenses against aggression characterized Ms. A's clinical picture: turning aggression on herself through verbal and physical attacks on herself, futile rages and anxiety, and fantasized expression of aggression through the symbiotic fantasy (e.g., poisoning the mother). In addition, guilt about her aggression and a need for punishment resulted in a sadomasochistic style of object relationships.

She could work therapeutically on genetic reconstructions but became enraged by my attempts to analyze transference-countertransference interactions. The only transference interpretations she could hear were that she was angry and hateful toward me because she saw me as a threat to her equilibrium, which focused on the centrality of her mother in her life and vice versa.

Approximately 18 months into the analysis, partly as a result of uncovering these fantasies, her chronic anxiety increased and she began to have panic attacks several times a day. Her anxiety grew so severe that analytic sessions became chaotic and unproductive and interfered with her ability to perform at work. At first I was reluctant to suggest a consultation, hoping that she could resolve her anxiety psychotherapeutically. I rationalized that I had successfully treated two patients with anxiety and panic attacks psychotherapeutically (an adult in analysis and an adolescent in psychotherapy), although in these situations the decision not to take medications had been theirs, not mine. Then I realized that my wish to maintain the ideal of a "pure" analysis and my withholding the possibility of relief by medication may have been an expression of my anger at Ms. A for not being the ideal—i.e., unmedicated—analytic patient.

In the following session, I suggested a psychopharmacological consultation. The anxiety the patient expressed during this session was typical of the preceding few weeks:

Ms. A: Nothing happened, but I hardly slept last night. I freaked out after Bob [her boyfriend] left. . . . Having Bob around helps. I am trying to systematically destroy the life I have. I have not called my friends; I feel at the end of my rope. . . . Part of why I am suffering this anxiety is that part of me needs to be born. I am so much at the end of my rope that I'll either go crazy or figure it out.

Analyst: The anxiety feelings increase when you are alone and decrease when you are with someone?

Ms. A: Yes. Sundays are the worst. . . . It has been two years since I have been able to sleep most of the night. . . . It's excessive worrying; the wheels are spinning. I feel I cannot survive another day like this. But I say, A, you have to. I don't know what kind of help I need. I need to be tucked in bed. I want my mother.

Analyst: Is the anxiety there all the time? In the evening you need something to calm you down, like a mother tucking in her baby?

Ms. A: It is there more or less. Very rarely is it not there. There is a driving force behind it. When I talk about being tucked into bed, I am asking for a way to calm me down.

Analyst: You have been very anxious for several months. At times, medications can help a person to calm down. Would you like to see a colleague of mine who is a specialist in medications and anxiety, to find out whether he thinks that medications can help you?

Ms. A: My mother was on antidepressants. I thought I was getting better and now I am not. When I heard medications, I thought of my mother. I will be like her and need medications forever. I am afraid of it; I don't know why.

The next day she said that she wanted a consultation but was going to fight me about it.

Ms. A: I guess I don't trust you as much as I thought I did. I can't depend on you to watch out for me. I'd better watch out for myself. . . . The attack on my anxiety is an attack on me. I am the problem. If you solve the problem, what happens to me? I will vanish. Dismantling my anxiety means dismantling me. Maybe there will be a new version, but it won't be me. It will be someone else. There will be no sense of I. Anxiety is what holds me together. If I were not anxious, who would I be, what would I do?

Analyst: At one level, you seem to experience my suggestion of consultation as an attack on you.

Ms. A: On my integrity. On what holds me together. There is nothing to replace it if it is dissolved. I doubt that medications will work like magic. What happens if they dissolve the anxiety—will I hold together? I'm afraid of falling on the floor in pieces.

A couple of weeks later, she started wondering, "Maybe I am angry because you are stopping me from ruining my life." Then she screamed, "Fuck off, I hate your guts. There is nothing I can do to make you react like I want you to react; to throw me out. You say you don't have an agenda. I don't believe you!"

Analyst: You are angry at me for suggesting the consultation.

Ms. A: I am afraid that you are pulling a fast one on me like my mother's shrink. He put her on chemicals and nudged her out of therapy. I am not willing to deconstruct my anger.

Analyst: And you wonder whether I am trying to use chemicals to get rid of your anger, and of you.

Ms. A: Yes. There is a part of me that is accepting and part that is not. Well, that is the real part of me and I am not going to get rid of it. I don't accept myself. But I am damned if I am going to follow anyone's agenda.

Throughout this session and others, I listened to her calmly. I was accustomed to her attacks and had learned that if I listened empathetically, expressed my understanding of her feelings, and waited, she would eventually calm down and analyze. My interpretations centered on her fear of biological vulnerability and the possible loss of her sense of continuity if she changed. Then she attacked me for being a "fucking optimist" because "You have the nerve to think that I could end up being happy." She was angry because I wanted her to get better; that meant forgiving her mother. However, as she awaited the consultation, she indicated that part of her was looking forward to taking medication because she could no longer tolerate her anxiety. Yet she was aware of her conflict between wanting to get better and wanting to stay enmeshed.

The consulting psychiatrist diagnosed her as having generalized anxiety disorder and panic disorder and suggested that both might respond to the same drug, Zoloft. Ms. A was afraid that medication would calm her down to the point where she would stop working on her problems; then she would "wake up" twenty years from now to find herself, like her mother, a "bitter, fat, menopausal woman in a dead-end situation."

Ms. A: My strategy is to avoid the problem, and if the medication reduces the anxiety then I may stop working. . . . I am afraid of taking drugs.

Analyst: As you and I discussed, the ultimate resolution is internal. How do you find a middle ground or alternatives to the black-hole experiences you have described? The medication may help you calm down to work on it.

Ms. A: I am an avoidaholic. I feel I should avoid talking about medications and deal with the real issues. Dr. Y [the consulting psychiatrist] said not to consider taking this medication as a weakness, but I do. I fundamentally believe there is something wrong with taking medications. I wonder if this comes under "suffering is good for the soul" or because I don't want to change. I will lose my grip because I consider medications psychological muscle relaxants. If I relax I will die. I also don't want to be like my mother. This may be strange but the only way to separate from my mother is to realize that I am like her in some respects. . . . Part of me feels like you are trying to change me. You don't accept me as I am. However, I don't think you have an agenda but you hope the best for me.

A few weeks later she started a session by saying, "I wrote in my diary about my relationship with my mother. I cannot go backward or forward. It is like salmon jumping upstream. In Dr. Doolittle, there is a character with two heads, called a Pushmi-Pullyu. It is not a case of wanting to go in one direction and being afraid—it is going in two directions. It is the irresistible force meeting an immovable object." Later, she told me that she had written two poems but had "accidentally" forgotten to bring them to the session. She did not want me to see what she was writing about or to understand what the poems were.

> *Analyst:* The struggle seems to be between two states: amorphous-like, diffuse, versus focused attention and clarity.
> *Ms. A:* For me, focusing is the ultimate enemy. If I do, everything will come tumbling down; it is a house of cards but it is my house. So will my fantasies, that I am number one. That my brother will be put in his place. Something about penises. I am going to lose my mother, lose number one. What will I gain? [sarcastically] "You will get a loving relationship." I hate arithmetic, two plus two equals four. I don't want to be mother's little girl. I want to have been mother's little girl.
> *Analyst:* You want to change the past and not achieve something new.

It took Ms. A three or four months to decide to take medications. Ultimately, it was her intolerable anxiety that made her decide to start. For two years she took 150 mg of sertraline (Zoloft) daily, which controlled her anxiety and panic symptoms. During that time she worked hard in her analysis and achieved a sense of separateness from her mother: her preoccupation with her mother lessened, and she became more involved with other objects, interests, and issues. She reconstructed the development of her symbiotic fantasy and understood the anxieties and seductions of symbiosis. She understood her fears about achieving a sense of separateness, particularly the role of genital anxieties in keeping the fantasy alive. She also expressed guilt about moving ahead with her life and leaving her mother behind.

What was remarkable during that period was the absence of any reference to the medication other than periodic requests for renewal of the prescription. She had no side effects. She had little sex with her boyfriend, but her sex life was like that before medications. Although she was aware that decreased libido was a possible side effect of the medication, she could not tell whether her sex drive was lower than it had been. Her previous anxiety had interfered with her sexuality, and she felt no differently now. Nor could I find any symbolic or unconscious reference to the medication; it seemed to have faded into the background. Ms. A indicated that she could now distinguish between her "physical anxiety," which responded to medication, and the "psychological anxiety" that she still experienced and could resolve through analysis. Toward the end of the third year, and for the first time during her analysis, she was able to reflect on our relationship, to allow the analysis of transference, and to see, in the here and now, her attempt to create a sadomasochistic relationship with me, her need for omnipotent control, and her efforts to destroy her analysis.

After two years, Ms. A decided to stop the medication. She felt that the insight she had achieved over that period might help her better manage her anxiety. She reduced the dose gradually over three months, consulting with me at each step. However, within a week after she had discontinued the use of the medication she became preoccupied with her mother in a different way: instead of wishing for symbiotic union, she was angry and vengeful. Ms. A wanted to hurt her mother, was frustrated by her inability to do so, and was enraged that "the bitch" was going to get away with having been a bad mother. This change in the nature of her preoccupation reflected intrapsychic changes that had occurred in the previous two years. In addition to becoming aware of her wish to be taken care of by her mother, she became more aware of the anger and hatred she felt toward her. However, the expression of intense anger and hatred reflected a lack of resolution of her feelings.

It is not clear whether the recurring preoccupation with her mother was related to discontinuation of her medication. One possibility we entertained was that she felt comfortable and "tucked in" while on medication. She felt she had a "holding environment" consisting of the medication, her relationship with her boyfriend, and her relationship with me. Stopping the medication upset the equilibrium of this environment and caused a regression to preoccupation with her mother, albeit with a new twist. A coincidental external event may have also precipitated Ms. A's reaction. Her mother was able to get an exciting new job in Europe, where she was going to work with her husband. This was not the "bitter, fat, menopausal woman" who was being left behind by her daughter. Overnight, the guilt Ms. A had felt about leaving her mother behind turned into rage about being left behind herself.

Whatever the reasons, Ms. A continued in analysis after she discontinued her medication (which occurred five years ago) without a recurrence of her debilitating anxieties. Instead of dealing with her symbiotic fantasies, she is addressing other conflictual issues, such as an absence of clear ego-ideals, a harsh and punitive superego, and the vengeful nature of her narrative.

CASE VIGNETTE 2: EMPATHETIC FAILURE OR DEPRESSION?

Ms. B was a single, professional woman who came to see me at age 32 because of her grief over a failed love affair. She was seen four times a week, on the couch. Three years of analysis revealed that she was driven to succeed to fill an inner emptiness, had a need to be led, and made massive use of denial. She reconstructed a family situation in which she felt no emotional connection with her mother: "I did not grow up wanting to be like my mummy and there was emotional flatness between us. She was always busy, there was no dialogue. I always had the feeling that my mother did not like me as much as she liked the boys. . . . What a bitch! I feel angry because I was not the favored one." She was able to establish a tenuous connection with her father, but at a price: her acceptance of his Old World views, particularly that women are scheming and that "good" women wait to be discovered by men. Her lifelong wish was to join two groups which would not have her: the male world of her older brothers, and the wealthy milieu of her ethnic group.

During this period we were able to work together to analyze her transference (which was primarily idealizing) and to identify empathetic failures that could be mended. Because of conflicts over personal and work-related issues, however, her relationship with her boss, John, deteriorated, as did her job performance and her confidence level. She became depressed, anxious, and lost because she had lost John's guidance. These changes were reflected in the analytic relationship.

> *Ms. B:* I have questions about where I am in analysis and where I am go-
> ing. There is the issue of falling back. I wonder whether you are aware
> of the struggles I will be encountering. I feel that you know more, but
> you are not telling me, because it is better to get there myself.
> *Analyst:* You seem to attribute hidden knowledge to me and an attitude
> of wanting you to work harder to get that knowledge.
> *Ms. B:* There is a fear that you do not understand the anxiety I have be-
> cause I have not expressed myself fully. My fear is that if I expressed
> my despair you would say "you are right, you are hopeless." Either you
> will stop or the object of the analysis will change.

Despite her belief in my knowledge, any explanation I suggested
met with a strong negative reaction. For example, it had become evident that she was a follower of John and was not self-directed. She
said:

> *Ms. B:* I feel a bubble has been burst during analysis. I gained an appre-
> ciation of things I do not do, that I was not as self-directed or indepen-
> dent as I thought, and I fear more revelations will be equally upset-
> ting.
> *Analyst:* It seems that realistic appreciation of your abilities is seen as a
> failure.
> *Ms. B:* That is true. It is one thing to talk about omnipotence and talk
> about how I was deceiving myself about the realities of myself, the
> sense of omnipotence was developed by John, and I was glad to go for
> the ride [very upset tone].
> *Analyst:* You have a catastrophic reaction to any insight you make.
> *Ms. B:* The things I found out that I lacked—the ability to integrate, an-
> alyze, to be self-directed—were fundamental. They terrified me. I
> could not function because of these issues.

For almost a year, it seemed that I could do nothing right. My efforts to be with her, listen to her, make empathetic comments, and
not interpret were all experienced as abandonment. On the other
hand, she experienced any interpretation as pointing out her inade-
quacies, displaying insensitivity, and attacking her; she responded as
though she had discovered a new catastrophe about herself. Several
attempts to attune myself to her, to understand her experience of me
and what I was doing or not doing to contribute to the impasse, led
to global responses about either fear of abandonment or the feeling
of being attacked. We both found this year difficult: she was suffering
and I could not find a way to help her. I could not use her responses
to modify my stance and resolve the impasse. Within three months of
this year, as she developed a picture suggestive of depression, I was

unsure whether she needed medication to treat it. She must have sensed what I was thinking.

> *Ms. B:* I feel depressed. It feels cyclical and not related to psychic events. I question my ability to deal with things. I feel limited either psychologically or it is related to neurotransmitters. . . . I wonder whether this will work or will I have to submit to Prozac.
>
> *Analyst:* Why is it either Prozac or analysis? Why not both?
>
> *Ms. B:* One is your comment that this is not organic. [Two years earlier she had wondered whether she had organic brain syndrome; after investigating what this meant to her, I reassured her that she did not have it.] The other is that I will not be dealing with my feelings. Having to go on medication is an admission of illness. It would be a tantamount to having something that cannot respond to psychotherapy.
>
> *Analyst:* Organic can mean two different things. In the past, when you explained your understanding of organic, you talked about your brain structures being affected, and that is what I assured you about. However, organic as in depression can be due to neurotransmitters.
>
> *Ms. B:* I understood that what was happening to me was psychological and not due to neurotransmitters. My feeling is that I can work things out. I brought up the issue of medications; you did not challenge me. . . . Do you think that I am a candidate for medications, or can I work things through?
>
> *Analyst:* I am not sure that you need medications now, but I don't rule anything out in the future.
>
> *Ms. B:* Bringing up medications makes me angry and makes me feel worried about my prospects and potential. I appreciate your honesty, but I feel angry that this is not what I thought. All of a sudden I feel different from my family or friends, and I feel more separate and alien than before. It does make me angry at you for even considering medication in the future. It is a sign of giving up at a certain level. When I despair I feel I cannot work it through.
>
> *Analyst:* I feel you trapped me. You asked me a question and you somehow expected me to say no to medication but the fact that I kept the door open is making you angry.
>
> *Ms. B:* I am angry at putting so much faith in the process. I thought that you did not think that this was organic and thus I needed no medication. If we had a misunderstanding about the term organic, why not other subjects?

Further attempts to bridge the gulf in empathy failed. Her suffering continued, and because she sensed that she was about to be fired from her job, the medication issue was discussed again. I comfort I had developed about the use of medications during my work with Ms. A helped me to raise the issue. The consultant diagnosed Ms. B as having a depressive disorder and prescribed 20 mg of paroxetine

(Paxil) a day. After some initial reluctance she agreed to take the medication. A week after she began the medication, she was fired. However, she was given a good severance package that allowed her to defer seeking re-employment immediately.

The period that followed was remarkable, both analytically and extra-analytically. Ms. B felt that the medication "immuned" her against feeling devastated by her firing. In fact, by the time the medication was expected to be fully effective (one month), she was feeling well and had no side effects. This did not stop the analytic process but restored it. I was able to listen without her feeling abandoned and to interpret without injuring her. She was able to reflect on what had gone wrong at work and in her life in general. Extra-analytically, she decided not to look for a job right away and spent a year doing adventurous and productive things that she could not do while working. The medication did not recede into the background, as with Ms. A; however, Ms. B mentioned it only with a sense of gratitude for how it made her feel and what she was able to do, and regret that she had not started earlier and saved herself a lot of suffering. In addition, in keeping with her professional background, she reflected on the medication in a scientific way. She felt that she had a depressive illness and could see evidence of a family history. She experienced the symptom relief as an opportunity to work analytically to resolve her conflicts and build a sense of self that would enable her to resolve traumas and anxieties without depression and without medication.

After taking the medication for about a year, she decided to discontinue it slowly. As she did so, she became concerned that although she had had an excellent year of living, it perhaps had not been equally productive analytically; in other words, she might not have gained enough insight to be able to manage without the medication. This concern was followed by one of her most insightful series of sessions. She painfully realized that she was so driven to succeed that she participated in making immoral decisions (such as cheating on expense accounts and claiming unauthorized expenses) that were a source of unconscious guilt and anxiety. She also realized that she, like her hated boss, had superego lacunas. These insights made her choose a different type of job, in the public service with lower pay.

After reducing her dose to 15 mg and then to 10 mg, she was reluctant to stop the medication completely and decided to stay on the lower dose for a few more months. She was having job interviews after a year's absence and found that the process made her anxious. She felt that she could distinguish between two types of anxieties: "focused anxiety" related to conflicts, which could be worked through in analysis, and "unfocused anxiety," which was general and did not seem related to conflicts. Medication relieved her "useless, unfocused" anxiety and helped her analysis by allowing her to "see the fallacies that I constructed about myself that are based on how people look at me." We talked about the period before medication, and I shared my experience of not knowing what to do. She agreed that her depression was a factor in the impasse, but added that exploring reasons was foreign to her family style. After she had finally discontinued the Paxil (four years ago), neither the symptoms nor the analytic impasse recurred.

DISCUSSION

These cases demonstrate that in situations with clear indications, where there is a well-considered procedure for prescribing medications, and when they are effective and cause few long-term side effects, their use does not disrupt the analytic process. Neither patient indicated a wish to leave analysis because she felt better. Thus symptom removal does not necessarily cause patients to give up on analysis.

However, the influence of medications on the psychoanalytic process is a more complex matter. An analysand sees an analyst to be helped with problems. They meet several times a week; while the analysand free-associates, the analyst listens and intervenes with clarifications, confrontations, and interpretations. Even though a therapeutic alliance develops, resistance is an inevitable part of the process. Interpretations, particularly transference interpretations, can lead to insight, followed by a working-through process that results in structural changes. I will focus here only on the aspects of the process that I believe were affected by medication, assuming that its influence on the other aspects was neutral.

During her previous analysis Ms. A had learned to free-associate and had formed a partial therapeutic alliance with me; we could work together on certain issues (such as her relationship with her mother), where I could make genetic interpretations. However, she would not accept transference interpretations because they impinged on the importance of her relationship with her mother. After uncovering some fantasies, Ms. A became extremely anxious and chaotic; she lost her limited therapeutic alliance and her ability to reflect and to use my interpretations to gain insight. Medications decreased her anxiety and restored the alliance; she regained her ability to use extratransference interpretations and to free-associate. Subsequently, she was able to use transference interpretations.

Ms. B was able to free-associate, formed a therapeutic alliance with me, and could consider transference and extra-transference interpretations. Her depression resulted in a loss of these functions. She complained instead of free-associating, lost her therapeutic alliance with me, and started to experience my interpretations as attacks. Medications relieved her depression so that she was able to re-establish her therapeutic alliance and her ability to free-associate and to gain insight from interpretation.

I think of the analytic process as occurring in a transitional space created by the analyst and analysand, where they can communicate, co-create, and co-discover. Whatever interferes with this process is resistance. Resistance is often created by defensive maneuvers or an affective state that prevents reflection and dialogue in the transitional space. An agitated affective state created by the resisting analysand can be managed by interpretations. But a biologically based mood, such as anxiety or depression, can interfere with the analytic process by weakening the analysand's ability to reflect; it can disrupt the therapeutic alliance by interrupting the dialogue. Medications may help by reducing the anxiety or depression and allowing the analysis to proceed.

It is interesting that both patients talked about two types of anxieties. Ms. A differentiated between "physical" and "psychological" anxieties and Ms. B between "focused" and "useless, unfocused" anxieties when they were anxious, they experienced anxiety globally and could not differentiate different types of anxieties. Medications may help by treating a mood that interferes with the ability to reflect and differentiate affects.

I believe that there were three factors that account for the positive outcome of these two patients: analyzing the transference-countertransference interactions around the medications, the procedure used for prescribing the medications, and the effectiveness of the drugs.

The analysis of the analyst's conscious and unconscious beliefs and countertransference are probably most important in how both parties experienced the medication. I think that the conscious and unconscious beliefs of the analyst influence how medications are presented to and experienced by patients. My conscious beliefs were affected by my psychiatric training and my long association with an academic department of child psychiatry. Recently, however, I became influenced by the progress in biological psychiatry and the centrality of medications to many psychiatric conditions. I had used medications with some of my child patients and with adult patients who were interested in symptom relief rather than psychotherapy. Despite this experience, I came to realize that unconsciously I drew the line with analytic patients, excluding them from medication even if they suffered from a psychiatric disorder known to be responsive to it. Furthermore, I realized that I believed that analysis without medication is superior to analysis with medication. It was important for me to realize that not suggesting a consultation was a negative countertransferential reaction to a disappointing patient.

Both patients initially experienced the suggestion of a consultation as a narcissistic injury—a symptom of weakness, biological vulnerability, having a sickness, or being a devalued family member. Inevitably, their anger turned on me, the bearer of bad news. They interpreted the suggestion as an indication that I believed they were sicker than they thought, I was disappointed in them, I was abandoning them, or I didn't accept them as they were. They may have been right. I accepted their anger as a legitimate response to my suggestion and did not try to rationalize it. Instead, I handled their responses as I would any other analytic material: I tried to understand and interpret it.

An interesting finding is the belief that psychotherapy is a higher form of treatment than pharmacotherapy. To some extent I do believe that. I still think that if a condition can be resolved by psychotherapy within a reasonable period, it is preferable not to use medication. Thus, if a patient develops anxiety or depression as a result of material brought up in analysis or external situations of loss or conflict, an attempt should be made to resolve the situation therapeutically. Very often such psychotherapeutic resolution is successful. This helps the patient develop a sense of competence in her ability to work through and resolve difficulties. Such a resolution may also reflect positively on the analyst. We analysts may be wary of medications because improvement will be attributed to the medications and not to our therapeutic skills. Furthermore, no medication is completely safe; wherever possible, avoiding taking them is a good general rule. However, this attitude should not become a general belief in the superiority of psychotherapy over medications. Clearly there are situations on which medications are indicated and are more effective than psychotherapy. The literature often suggests that the therapist imposes his belief in the superiority of psychotherapy on the patient. While there is truth in this, I believe that patients also hold this belief, independently of therapists, and that analyzing the belief and the narcissistic injury implied in patients' acceptance of their biological vulnerability is as important as the psychoanalyst's self-analysis.

One issue highlighted in the literature is the countertransferential prescription of medications. Equally important is the countertransferential nonprescribing of medication when there are clear and almost universally accepted indications for prescription, such as depression (American Psychiatric Association, 1993). In addition to the medical-legal implications of nonprescribing (Klerman, 1990; Stone, 1990), there is its import to the analyst. What does it mean for an analyst to cling to a belief system that runs counter to all evidence, a belief that is scientifically unsound and unproved? Is it the cathexis of our method over the welfare of our analysands? Is it an angry attack from a disappointed analyst or punishment of the patient for not giving us the glory of a "pure" analytic cure? In addition, there is its meaning to the patient: Most analytic patients are aware of the analyst's status as a physician and understand something of the biology of psychiatric disorders and the role of medication. Do they experience our nonprescribing as withholding? As a punishment for depriving us of a therapeutic victory? Or as a conspiracy of silence about their "psychiatric" diagnosis. Thus, countertransferential nonprescribing needs to be analyzed as much as countertransferential prescribing.

Another factor in a successful outcome is the procedure followed in introducing, prescribing, and following medications. Even though this constitutes a shift from the psychoanalytic interpretive stance, it is not a total shift to the extrospective psychiatric stance. We do not become the authority on medication and tell the patient what to take. Instead, a pharmacotherapeutic alliance (Gutheil 1982), similar to the psychotherapeutic alliance, develops. The therapist and patient discuss and analyze the issue together; then it is up to the patient to decide. Medications are another form of analytic material, something that has meaning, involves both analysand and analyst, and becomes the focus of analysis. As something that affects the analysand, it must be acknowledged and dealt with by the analyst.

The suggestion of a consultation can be considered a parameter, defined as a noninterpretive intervention (Eissler, 1953; Moore and Fine, 1990). It fulfills the four conditions Eissler lists as essential to the introduction of a parameter: (1) the psychoanalytic process would otherwise come to a standstill; (2) a return to standard technique is possible; (3) the parameter is dispensable after fulfilling its usefulness; and (4) the patient can gain insight into its function. However, I would like to abandon the concept of parameters, which reflects the belief that interpretations are the most, if not the only, effective interventions we can make. There is no evidence for the claim that interpretations are more effective than other forms of intervention, such as support (Wallerstein, 1986). A conception of the analytic process as a dialectic (Hoffman, 1998) would allow us to regard the suggestion of a consultation as part of the process and not necessarily a parameter.

A third factor in the success of these outcomes was that SSRIs proved effective in alleviating symptoms and required little or no monitoring of dosage or side effects. They were thus practical for me to prescribe. A continuous medical role for the analyst, such as asking about the dosage or side effects and requesting blood tests or electrocardiograms, might interfere with the analytic process. I therefore cannot make a blanket recommendation that the medical analyst should always prescribe medications. The presence of uncomfortable side effects may complicate the analytic situation. No matter how rationally the medications are prescribed and how they are consciously experienced, at some level the patient may blame the analyst for her dry mouth, dizziness, or blurred vision. This could create serious transference-countertransference complications. On the other hand, a feeling of well-being, uncomplicated by side effects, could also be attributed to the analyst and could enhance the therapeutic alliance. However, neither of my patients experienced me as an omnipotent figure who could magically take the pain away.[2] Instead, the reduction of the symptoms was attributed to the medications. Yet they were grateful for my having suggested a consultation, since it had resulted in an improvement in their life.

One interesting finding was the relative infrequency of references to the medication during analysis by both patients. This finding is open to challenge: some may suggest that I was not looking properly. However, the finding of references to the medications in vague mate-

---

2. While prescribing medications did not result in idealizing me, a different outcome occurred in a different situation. In the past few years I have been experimenting with the use of medications with a small number of preschoolers suffering from a pervasive inability to regulate themselves: sleep-wake cycle, feeding, attention, activity level, behavioral inhibition, and affect. Life, for the children and their families, was very difficult. They have been through several assessments and failed treatments. Most of the children responded to my plan of interventions that included low doses of SSRIs. The improvement in the child and the quality of life of the family has resulted in idealizing me to a degree that I have not experienced with any of my successful analysands. The fact that lay analysts do not have a choice will also have an impact on the transference and countertransference.

rial may be imposed by analysts who think that the analysand should have fantasies about the medication.

Some of the early literature concerns schizophrenic and borderline patients whose repression of primary process material is not very successful. My patients, who were neurotic with character disorders, may have been able to repress primary process material about medications, if it was there. Furthermore, earlier medications had serious and often unpleasant side effects that became part of the patient's life. Thus, it is possible that SRRIs may be a special group of medications because they fade into the background, relieving symptoms with no side effects to remind patients of their presence. One side effect reportedly mentioned by many patients, decreased libido, was not mentioned by either of my analysands, probably because they were not very active sexually before medication.

A second reason for the paucity of references to medication may be that analysands are less likely to talk about feeling good than about other issues that concern them. In addition, both of my patients had been in analysis for two years more or less before they started medication. Both were insightful and had worked through many issues. They therefore took a rational view of medication and saw it as treatment for a psychiatric disorder with a biological basis. They welcomed the relief their medication offered and saw it as an opportunity to work on issues they knew were not amenable to medication.

Finally, these were highly educated patients who were aware of advances in biological psychiatry and the biological roots of some psychiatric disorders. This knowledge helped them deal with the narcissistic injury of taking medication.

Psychoanalysis and psychopharmacology address two different but not separate realms in the same person, the brain and the mind. Neurobiology deals with the brain—its anatomical relationships, structures, neurochemistry, and neurotransmitters. Human beings can be motivated by or become symptomatic from dysfunction of these biological systems. Medications are taken to alleviate symptoms that result from such dysfunctioning. Psychoanalysis deals with the mind, with how the mind organizes an individual's narrative, and with motivation and meaning. It deals with those symptoms that result from conflict and compromise formation. Thus, Kantor (1990) is correct in stating that some patients may suffer from two distinct disorders, a biological one that is not defensive and has no roots in conflict, and a psychological one that arises from conflict. However, he is incorrect in stating that the biological disorders are devoid of dynamic significance. A biological disorder will always create a mental state, and there is no mental state that does not have dynamic significance.

Advances in biological psychiatry need to be incorporated into psychoanalytic practice. However, at this stage we need more clinical reports about various medications before we can establish any general guidelines about their use in psychoanalysis.

BIBLIOGRAPHY

ADELMAN, S. A. (1985). Pills as transitional objects: A dynamic understanding of the use of medication in psychotherapy. *Psychiatry* 48:246–253.

AMERICAN PSYCHIATRIC ASSOCIATION (1993). Practice guideline for major depressive disorder in adults. *Amer. J. Psychiat.* 150(Suppl 4):1–26.

ANONYMOUS (1992). The case of Ms. A. *J. Clin. Psychoanal.* 1:70–92.

BUSCH, F. N. (1995). Panel: agoraphobia and panic states. J. Amer. Psychoanal. Assoc. 43:207-221.

BUSCH, F. N., COOPER, A. M., KLERMAN, G. L., PENZER, R. J., SHAPIRO, T., & SHEAR, M. K. (1991). Neurophysiological, cognitive, behavioral, and psychoanalytic approaches to panic disorder: towards an integration. *Psychoanal. Inq.* 11:316–332.

COHEN, S. K. (1992). The use of medication with patients in analysis: Panel of the New York Psychoanalytic Society, March 26, 1991. *J. Clin. Psychoanal.* 1:26–35.

COOPER, A. M. (1985). Will neurobiology influence psychoanalysis? *Amer. J. Psychiat.* 142:1395–1407.

EISSLER, K. (1953). The effect of the structure of the ego on psychoanalytic technique. *J. Amer. Psychoanal. Assoc.* 1:104–143.

ESMAN, A. (1989). Psychoanalysis and general psychiatry: Obsessive-compulsive disorder as paradigm. *J. Amer. Psychoanal. Assoc.* 37:319–336.

FREUD, S. E. (1940). An outline of psychoanalysis. *S.E.,* 23:144–208.

GOLDHAMER, P. M. (1983). Psychotherapy and pharmacotherapy: The challenge of integration. *Can. J. Psychiat.* 28:173–177.

GUTHEIL, T. (1982). The psychology of psychopharmacology. *Bull. Menninger Clin.* 46:321–330.

HAUSER, R. (1986). Medication and transitional phenomena. *Int. J. Psychoanal. Psychother.* 11:375–398.

HOFFMAN, I. (1998). *Ritual and Spontaneity in the Psychoanalytic Process.* Hillsdale, N.J.: The Analytic Press.

KAHN, D. A. (1991). Medication consultation and split treatment during psychotherapy. *J. Amer. Acad. Psychoanal.* 19:84–98.

KANTOR, S. J. (1989). Transference and the beta adrenergic receptor: A case presentation. *Psychiatry* 52:107–115.

——— (1990). Depression: When is psychotherapy not enough? *Psychiat. Clinics. N. Amer.* 13:241–254.

———— (1993). Analysing a rapid cycler: Can transference keep up? In *Psychotherapy and Medication: A Dynamic Integration,* ed. M. Schacter. Northvale, N.J.: Jason Aronson, pp. 291–311.

KARASU, T. B. (1982). Psychotherapy and pharmacotherapy: Towards an integrative model. *Amer. J. Psychiat.* 139:1102–1113.

KARUSH, N. P. (1992). The case of Ms. B, part II: Summary of psychoanalytic treatment. *J. Clin. Psychoanal.* 1:111–128.

KLERMAN, G. L. (1990). The psychiatric patient's right to effective treatment: Implications of Osheroff v Chestnut Lodge. *Amer. J. Psychiat.* 147:409–418.

MOORE, B. & FINE, B. (1990). Parameters. In *Psychoanalytic Terms and Concepts.* New Haven: The American Psychoanalytic Association and Yale University Press.

NEVINS, D. B. (1990). Psychoanalytic perspectives on the use of medication for mental illness. *Bull. Menninger Clin.* 54:323–339.

NEW YORK PSYCHOANALYTIC SOCIETY (1992). The use of medication with patients in analysis: Panel of the New York Psychoanalytic Society, March 26, 1991. *J. Clin. Psychoanal.* 1:1–133.

OSTOW, M. (1962). *Drugs in Psychoanalysis and Psychotherapy.* New York: Basic Books.

———— (1979). *The Psychodynamic Approach to Drug Therapy.* New York: Psychoanalytic Research and Development Fund.

———— (1990). On beginning with patients who require medication. In *On Beginning an Analysis,* ed. T. Jacobs & A. Rothstein. Madison, Conn.: International University Press, pp. 201–227.

REISER, M. F. (1984). *Mind, Brain, Body: Toward a Convergence of Psychoanalysis and Neurobiology.* New York: Basic books.

RODRIGUEZ-BOULAN, M. (1992). Ms. C: A clinical vignette. *J. Clin. Psychoanal.* 1:129–133.

ROOSE, S. P. (1990). The use of medication in combination with psychoanalytic psychotherapy or psychoanalysis. In *Psychiatry,* Vol. 1, ed. R. Michels. Philadelphia: Lippincott, pp. 1–8.

———— & STERN, R. (1995). Medication use in training cases: A survey. *J. Amer. Psychoanal. Assoc.* 43:163–170.

SCHARF, R. J. (1992). The use of medication with patients in analysis: Panel of the New York Psychoanalytic Society, March 26, 1991. *J. Clin. Psychoanal.* 1:14–25.

STONE, A. A. (1990). Law, science and psychiatric malpractice: A response to Klerman's indictment of psychoanalytic psychiatry. *Amer. J. Psychiat.* 147:419–427.

WALLERSTEIN, R. (1986). *Forty-Two Lives in Treatment.* New York: Guilford Press.

WYLIE, H. W., & WYLIE, M. (1987). An effect of pharmacotherapy on the psychoanalytic process: Case report of a modified analysis. *Amer. J. Psychiat.* 144:489–492.

"I want to know, too"

Psychotherapy with a Visually Impaired Boy

HENRIK ENCKELL, M.D.

This paper discusses the psychotherapy of a latency boy who suffered from a progressive visual impairment. It first describes some of the problems blind and visually impaired children meet in their development: (1) difficulty in constituting objects, (2) as this is accomplished, difficulty in separation, (3) the need to establish concrete contact with the object world, and (4) aspects of their identification. The psychotherapeutic treatment of Peter is presented with emphasis on the following themes: (1) Peter's demands to be allowed to enter the "secret room" (which seemed to reflect concretized but ungraspable aspects of the therapist), (2) functions of Peter's profuse questioning, (3) Peter's attempts to handle excitement, and (4) concreteness in Peter's experiences and also in his identifications. The themes are discussed from the point of view of the progressivity of his visual impairment.

IN A STUDY OF THE EXPERIENTIAL WORLD OF THE BLIND, GUNNAR Karlsson (1999) makes a distinction among the different sense modalities in their ability to establish a direct contact with material objects. Same sense experiences provide immediate contact with things, and others do not. Sight and tactility fall into the former cate-

---

Department of Psychiatry, University Hospital of Kuopio, Finland.

The author wants to thank Vilma Korkee and Erna Furman, for their very helpful comments on this case and Johannes Lehtonen, Simo Salonen, and Gunnar Karlsson for their valuable comments on an earlier draft of this paper.

gory, providing a direct perception of the existence of an object. They are therefore primary sense functions.

The other sense modalities are, of course, also meaningful, but *in themselves* they do not provide a world of material objects. The other senses may get the necessary support from tactility and sight, and with them create a more or less rich experience of the world and the people around us.[1] The following pages describe what may happen when one of the primary sense modalities is not intact, and how this is reflected in a psychotherapeutic process.

During the 1960s and 1970s the psychoanalytical community was actively interested in the experiences of blind children. This interest was concentrated around two centers: Hampstead's Research Group on the Study of Blind Children, with Dorothy Burlingham as a central figure, and another in Ann Arbor, Michigan, initiated by Selma Fraiberg. The work done in these centers is well documented, based in the former case on close observations of blind children in a day-care-center environment (e.g., Nagera and Colonna, 1965; Wills, 1965; Curson, 1979) and in the latter on observations of young blind children in a home environment (e.g., Fraiberg, Siegel, et al., 1966; Fraiberg, 1968. See also Wills, 1970). Extensive work with mothers of visually impaired children is also described in the literature (e.g., Wills, 1979). But I have found only two actual case histories of psychotherapeutic work with visually impaired children (Omwake and Solnit, 1961; Segal and Stone, 1961), and the second of these cases is complicated by many factors not related to visual impairment.

PROBLEMS OF CONSTITUTING THE OBJECT WORLD

The blind infant finds himself in an extremely unpredictable situation vis-à-vis the object world. Objects are there when they are felt, especially when they are the subjects of active investigation through fingering and mouthing, but they disappear when the tactile contact comes to an end. For the young blind child this means that the object turns up out of nowhere only to disappear into nothingness (Burlingham, 1965).

One might suppose that hearing, for example, would provide con-

---

1. Piha (1998) has come to an analogous result through another route. He has noted that sound impressions are transferred to the visual sphere; because of its transient and amorphous character, the exclusively heard cannot find a foothold but is bound in more stable visual representations. The heard searches a base in the visual world of experience.

siderable compensation for the lack of vision, but at the outset this is not the case. A study by Fraiberg, Siegel, and Gibson (1966) of the blind child's reactions to objects only heard reveals that hearing becomes significant for the congenitally blind fairly late in development. Sound cues alone do not lead to reactions in the blind infant, whereas they lead to searching behavior in the sighted. This can be understood if the division into primary and secondary sense modalities is taken as a point of departure. The blind individual has only one primary sense, tactility, and when this cannot be used, objects disappear. The sighted can build up a representational matrix via two senses, and this can function as a base for the other senses as well. Poor eyesight causes the primary representational matrix to grow more slowly or to be weaker. Thus the blind child reaches for an object on sound cues alone at about eleven months, while the sighted does this five or six months earlier.

There are comprehensive descriptions in the literature of how the behavior of blind children is often characterized by autism and passivity (see, e.g., Sandler, 1963). When objects are extremely unreliable, experientially speaking—when they come out of nothingness and disappear into it again—this is understandable. At the same time it is clear that the blind child is handicapped in all his efforts to grasp an object. It is convenient for such a child to remain in a behavior pattern characterized by the ambition to observe and control his own body directly instead of using an object to take possession of it. His own, often repetitive methods of confronting somatic experiences easily come to the forefront, while the possibility of getting support from an object is often a less utilized path to development.

Many blind children never take the step out into the object world, but when they do, the problem of separating becomes apparent (Nagera and Colonna, 1965). This may be interpreted in two ways. Because of his handicap, the blind child has a limited capacity to introject. His mother and the world around him are internalized through the senses that are accessible, but these are limited; as a result, the blind child has a relatively weak comforting introject, which makes him dependent on the tangible accessibility of a caring adult. This can also be seen from the perspective that the blind child *de facto* is extremely helpless without a helping hand. Thus he often turns to—and relies on—whatever adult is available at the moment (Wills, 1970). The child is forced by his own helplessness to utilize all the assistance he can get for the moment, and he does this without much discrimination.

Fraiberg (1968) relates a vignette that illustrates this separation problem. Kathy was born blind, but was privileged in that her mother was very experienced, sensitive, and at the same time active and supportive in her relationship to her daughter. The child made very good progress: her speech and motoric development were good. At 20 months, however, problems arose. Kathy suddenly refused to let go of her mother, and her father would no longer do as a comforter; she insisted on being carried and tried to wind herself around her mother so that the contact surface between them would be as large as possible. The situation became so difficult that Kathy began to withdraw, trying to sleep as much as possible. Her mother said she had a feeling that the whole thing was somehow connected with the initial stages of walking. Hitherto Kathy had not walked on her own, but she seemed to hesitate when faced with the possibility of taking an active step. Fraiberg says that the mother proved to be absolutely right. Shortly after this difficult clinging stage Kathy began to walk, and the difficulties disappeared as if by magic.

This case demonstrates the blind child's special difficulties in connection with the acquisition of skills that make him not only more mobile but also more independent. Kathy was trying to reach as large a concrete contact surface as possible because she was in a quandary about leaving the bearing arms of her mother. The blind child who has begun to make use of, and get support from, another is subject to great internal and external dangers when he leaves this protecting object.

The Form of Contact, Concreteness, and Fantasy

In relation to his parents, then, the blind child is in a position quite different from that of a sighted one. This difference may also be reflected in the type of contact the child establishes with parents or other caring adults.

A sighted child has a chance not only to "see" whether his mother is concretely present in the same room as himself but also to observe how she is behaving and relating. Is she psychically accessible, and what is her attitude toward me? The blind child is not only uncertain about how and when the object will turn up, but also about whether and to what extent the caring adult shares his experiences (Klein, 1962). In order to reassure himself of his mother's psychic presence, he is therefore forced to make use of special means. Thus Kathy, on her way toward taking her first steps into an unknown space, demands the greatest possible concrete contact surface with her mother.

One of my aims in this study is to show how the blind child's contact with the caring adult is characterized by concreteness. Since he cannot reassure himself visually of his mother's psychic presence, it is often necessary for him to do so concretely. Only this will provide enough certainty.

Concreteness in relationships can also be understood from a more general perspective. The sighted child has a good chance to approach and investigate things, space, and people actively; the blind child is exposed to reality in a different way. The sighted can prepare himself for approaching dangers; the blind one is forever in the risk zone—unable to prepare himself. The result is, understandably, an unremitting preparation for disaster. In this regard the blind child's situation is similar to that of a severely traumatized child. Grubrich-Simitis (1984) has described how such a child experiences the world in concrete terms since he has learned that reality may ruthlessly intrude at any time. Leaving this experiential pattern, in which reality is raw and merciless, is much too risky. In other words, the blind child tends to maintain a concrete contact in order to reassure himself that a contact exists. At the same time he concretely keeps to reality in general, since this is all there is to keep him prepared for the concreteness of the reality he is exposed to. The logical consequence is that blind and sighted children probably have greatly different fantasies. While the sighted can indulge in fantasy scenes, the blind child has learned to keep to reality in an intimate, concrete way.

IDENTIFICATION IN THE BLIND

Psychic development is based to a great extent on identifying with gratifying and admired objects (Tähkä, 1993). When I do things in the same way as the person I admire, I am just as good as he is and manage just as well; at the same time, through this acceptance, I take him with me.

The blind child runs up against two difficulties on this developmental path.

For the most part the world we live in is the world of the sighted. This is a matter not only of practical arrangements but also of language and culture. The blind person is under pressure to adapt, for example, to concepts that do not correspond to his experiential world (Burlingham, 1965). The models he has are usually sighted and for that reason differ from him. Even if parents are sensitive to their blind child's special needs, it is still difficult for them, from their outsider position, to offer models that suit his needs, possibilities, and experiences; the inevitable differences in experiential worlds make it more difficult for the adults to suggest productive ways of being that are appropriate for the child. It must also be pointed out that the visually impaired child's therapist faces some special difficulties. It is not always easy to feel one's way into an experiential world quite different from one's own; this is a problem that affects not only the blind child's sighted parents but also his therapist.

Further, the blind have relatively limited opportunities to perceive the identification object; therefore the method of "taking in" a model for action and behavior is also limited. Like the contact mode, identification may well be characterized by concreteness—"being like" is expressed in concrete action patterns, which the blind child must learn by other than visual means.

Thus for the visually impaired child the constituting of the object world rests on a relatively unsteady base, since only one primary sense is available to him. If objects become meaningful, separation from them will be troublesome, and the visually impaired child will make use of concrete means to maintain the contact. This concreteness can also be seen in general in the experiential world. It can be interpreted as a consequence of the fact that it is safest for the visually impaired child to maintain a behavior pattern that constantly takes concrete reality into consideration. Finally, the visually impaired child's identification process is complicated when the identification object is sighted and must be "taken in" by other than visual means.

PETER

Peter was born blind, but his blindness was not immediately diagnosed. When he was six months old a congenital cataract was diagnosed, for which Peter was operated on successfully. After this initial gain the quality of Peter's vision had fluctuated. It inexorably worsened but through surgery the situation could be improved at intervals. By age 8, when he first came for treatment, Peter had gone through ten operations, and it was somewhat unclear how well he could see. He could move fairly freely in familiar environments but sometimes bumped into furniture in strange places. It was clear that he would eventually be totally blind, something Peter himself did not acknowledge. His mother also told me that Peter did not want to believe that other children could see better than he could.

Peter's mother sought psychotherapy for her son primarily because of his problems in school. Peter attended a boarding school for the visually impaired. The classes were very small, but Peter was sometimes so restless that he had to be given individual instruction. Occasionally his disquiet was expressed in quarreling, but mostly it was a matter of his trying in various ways to make himself heard, noisily, and to "poke his nose" into what both adults and other children were doing. He wanted to take part in every discussion and often began to ask adults questions when they were talking among themselves—all this so vehemently that the others often became exhausted.

Peter had two older siblings and one younger. His parents divorced when Peter was four years old, and both parents had new families. His mother had custody of the children from this first marriage. Peter saw his father regularly. During the week he lived at school in the capital city; he went home for weekends and holidays. Naturally enough, Peter was homesick during the week, but his parents had made the decision that the boy should go to a special school for the visually impaired—especially considering his severe restlessness.

THE FIRST HALF YEAR

For a fairly long period at the beginning of the therapy my meetings with Peter were rather bewildering. During the first interview Peter made immediate contact by at once exploring the therapy room with his fingers and by bringing things very close to his eyes. At the same time he asked openly and frankly about various things, including what kind of doctor I was. When I told him I was a doctor who tried to understand the things children worry about, Peter said he didn't have any worries. The bewildering aspect of this period of the therapy was partly connected with this immediate, extremely forthright contact and partly with Peter's facial expressions, which were very meager and difficult to interpret. It soon became quite clear that it would be difficult to read Peter's emotional state accurately.

Thus, compared to most visually impaired children, Peter was from the beginning remarkably active both in seeking contact and in investigating the material we had available. Even during the first session I had an inkling that something other than problem-free curiosity underlay this activity. Peter began to talk about Pippi Longstocking—the strongest girl in the world. She behaved exactly as she wanted to, but this was no problem since she was so strong, he said.

The police came to take her to an orphanage, but Pippi just tossed them up into a tree. She was so strong that she could even lift her own horse. I commented that if she was so strong she surely didn't need to be afraid because she could cope with all kinds of dangers. And maybe it was worrisome for Peter to talk with me since we didn't know each other yet? Peter interrupts: "Is there hot water here? Does hot water come to the bathroom here? How does it get here?"

This is how Peter introduced a procedure that would recur constantly: he interrupted with a question concerning concrete reality. It was probably no coincidence that Peter asked this question just when I was talking about his insecure feelings in the presence of an unfamiliar person—and one he might perceive as someone who would take him to a strange place, an "orphanage." By this means he changed the subject at the same time that he got me to speak about the nature of reality in a way he tried to control. One might suspect that Peter's activity in general had a defensive side: by actively exploring his environment and by one means or another giving shape to it, he is able to control and avoid internal dangers.

Even during the first weeks, despite a curiosity about technical equipment and technical details that immediately became evident, Peter focused his attention on my person. "Do you have a family? How did you get here today? What language does your wife speak?" During one session Peter discovered a locked door in my office, and he immediately asked where it led. "What's there behind it?" I tried to tell him that I was interested in what he himself thinks, even though, of course, I understood that he was interested in these things—but that it was considerably more difficult for me to understand what he thinks and feels if I tell him everything about myself. At the same time I tried to say a little about how you can use your imagination and sort of play inside your head, in your thoughts, when you don't know something for certain. Peter's reply was that he didn't do that. It gradually became clear to me, too, that this was true.

A few sessions after his discovery of the locked door, when we had finished playing a game of Memory (in a version for the visually impaired), Peter said, "Now we are going to think!" *Aha—good—what shall we think about?* "About what is behind that door!" *Well—what's your idea?* "My idea is: What is there?! What's there?! I want to know!" For Peter, thinking about something was the same as trying to find out how reality was constituted. As can be seen, this ambition was extremely strong.

Peter soon evinced great confidence in my ability to know what he had done and what he thinks. At the beginning of a session he might say, "Now we'll play Memory. Did you know that?" He might believe that I knew what lessons he had in school that day and wonder whether I was on the school board; not only do I seem to know what Peter experiences, but being on the school board I also decide about many things pertaining to the circumstances of his daily life. Peter starts a game: we are to take turns writing down the name of an animal and the other will try to guess the animal. The one who guesses right most often has won. I interpreted this game as an effort not only to find out but even to control what the other was thinking. That it was animals we were to write was perhaps not a coincidence.

Peter told me that the previous night he had fallen out of his bed, the upper berth of a bunk bed. He said he had begun to sort of walk in his sleep, and then he fell. He woke up during the fall itself. I wondered aloud how it felt to wake up in midair. Peter answered by repeating in concrete detail how the whole thing happened—how Anna, his nurse, came in, how he went to bed again, etc. I said it must have been frightening to wake up in the air, in the middle of the fall. *It sounds terrifying.* Peter interrupted: "Can eagles eat people? How big is an eagle? How high up on me would an eagle reach? Can vultures steal a small child?"

It turned out that Peter was soon to go through another eye operation. We established when it was to be done, and then Peter began again to ask about dangerous animals. "Can a fox kill a person? If 3,000 roosters attack a person, can they kill him? If a fox claws someone's throat like this [Peter scratches his throat], can he die?" I said that often when we speak about the operation Peter begins to ask about these dangerous animals, wondering how dangerous they really are. Perhaps he is frightened of this operation. Peter denies this categorically. Just before the operation his questioning about dangerous animals escalates, but Peter does not admit that he is afraid. Later it turned out that Peter invariably came down with a fever just before an operation and that the anesthesiologist finally interpreted this fever as psychogenic.

When I speak about the operation and especially about the fears he might have in connection with it, Peter interrupts in order to get an immediate description of a danger that may threaten from outside. In this way he seems to be trying to give an image to a danger so that it can somehow be handled. Internal dangers are thus quickly transformed to external ones. That the dangers take on the shape of various animals can be linked to the question game, in which we are also to think of animals. What the other is thinking—to himself—constitutes a threat that must be met by concrete configuration.

THE SECOND HALF-YEAR

After the summer, when the second half-year of the therapy began, Peter's interest was more oriented toward my person—what I do when he is not present—and toward the person or persons who might occupy my time. "Who has been here before me? Why is the chair placed like this? Was it a man or a woman who was here before me? Tell me now! I'll give you five seconds to answer." When we play the guessing game Peter develops a "thought sound." I must begin to think about what animal Peter has written down when he begins to tap his pencil. When he stops tapping I must tell him what I have thought. In other words, there is not much time for me to make my own choices as to when and what to think.

Peter begins to ask about royalty. Have I seen the king or queen? "How do they live? How big a castle do they have?" When I tell him what I know about this, Peter exclaims, "What? That's not possible! Why aren't two rooms enough?!" He expresses his aversion to the queen—queens should not be allowed to rule. "Is the queen really as old as forty-five? An ugly old hag!" Peter very much wants me to try to get hold of pictures of the royal family. Clearly there is some connection to me, since Peter often asks about the royal family and mine by turns, and even gives my children royal names.

During a session in the middle of the autumn, Peter begins by saying: "Remind me later of my jacket so that I don't forget it." *Sure*, I say. We play a game of Memory and Peter goes to the bathroom—as he often does. At intervals he calls out, "What time is it?" I tell him. "What are you doing now?" calls Peter after a while. *Waiting for you.* Peter comes out and asks resolutely but pleadingly, "What's behind the door? Can't you tell me?" I say that, yes, I can probably tell him, but first we have to think about what he imagines. Peter says that maybe it's a broom closet or perhaps a room with a table and two chairs. "Tell me now. What else shall I say to make you tell?" I say that I understand it's troublesome when I don't always answer these questions. Peter said he doesn't want to be thinking about this all the time. He wants to get rid of the thinking!

I tell him that I live on the other side. "Is that so? Do you come from an important errand and go in through the door there?" Is it like this? [Peter stands up to dramatize] *I might do it that way.* "I want to go in there. Why can't we?" I say but I think we had better sit here and think instead. I understand quite well that Peter would love to go in and see what it's like there in reality. Peter says that if he found a key he would certainly go in. "How many square yards is it?" *Well, what do you think?* "Maybe a hundred." *Approximately,* I reply.

Peter says he would like to live here, in my office. It would be nice to be here all the time. He thinks he will buy this space from me when I retire so he can settle down here. Then he wants us to change seats, and I say that now—using my chair—he's like me. When the doorbell rings, signaling that he is to be picked up, Peter says, "Remind me of my jacket." *Certainly. Remember to take your jacket with you.* "Good that you reminded me," says Peter. "Have a nice weekend!"

Evident here is Peter's intense desire to establish a concrete, tangible contact with me. His own ideas or thoughts are not sufficient. Pete wants hard facts, not only about my person but also about what might occupy my time. This also applies to what I think of Peter himself. When I open the door in response to the doorbell, he says, "What did it sound like? What were you doing when it rang?" And he may then ask, "Do you know why I rang so many times?" *Tell me.* "Because you didn't open right away!"

In my work with Peter I came by degrees to tell him something about myself and my circumstances. The immediate reason was that when he didn't get an answer Peter began to retire into a shell where I could no longer reach him. It was also clear to me that what I was able to tell him corresponded to what a sighted child could see for himself without asking. You might say that in one way or another the visually impaired child needs to acquire elements for representation in order to have something to work with. At the same time it was a question of giving him something to hold on to in order to facilitate an identification. Our way—Peter's and mind—was for me to tell him more than I would have told a normally sighted child.

In the session described above it also became evident how Peter concretely tries to adopt what is me and mine. It is perhaps no coincidence that Peter expresses this identification in connection with what I tell him about myself—of what is on the other side of the door. Because I tell, Peter is probably grateful. At the same time, he can also have the experience of having something tangible to identify with.

At this point we abandoned the guessing game. Peter begins to write doctors' certificates, and just before Christmas he asks, "What do you do if someone is ill?" And he tells me about Emil from Lönneberga, a character in a book, who in a blizzard took a dying farmhand to the doctor all by himself. I say that I think Peter is musing about what to do when you have big problems—how you should handle them—and wondering what I would do in such a situation. Then perhaps he could do likewise himself? And perhaps he is thinking especially much about this as we will soon have the Christmas break? Peter wonders about my address, saying, "What would you say if I wrote you a letter? Would you be happy then?" I reply that I would always be happy to hear from him.

THE THIRD HALF-YEAR

In time Peter began to make up games with some imaginative content. To be sure it was strictly constructed play with repetitive dramaturgy. As time passed, I began to see that Peter's questions pertained somewhat less to the trivia of the outside world and touched more on matters of feelings and bodily sensations. So Peter might ask, "What does it mean when you win—when you play or wrestle and win—and you say 'Yes sir!' *It means that you are happy to have won.*

At the next session Peter goes to the bathroom and calls out from there, "Henrik?" *Yes?* "What are you doing?" *I'm waiting for you.* "Here I come! Now we must sing! Let's sing *Frère Jacques* as a round. Henrik?" *Yes.* "Henrik, I have a question—can you listen?" *Sure.* "When you clear your throat, what makes the phlegm come up?" *Air.* "Henrik. Henrik, I have a question for you. Shall I say?" *Say.* "When you clear your throat, what gets the phlegm up?" *It's air.* "How strongly does the air come up?" I take Peter by the hand and draw my own along the back of his hand to show how hawking brings up the phlegm, explaining at the same time how the air sort of presses upward. I say that Peter is thinking about what happens in his body when he clears his throat, and this is the way it goes.

The questions begin more to concern psychic reality. Asking is no longer only a way to first externalize internal dangers and then conquer them through my interpretation of this material reality. In other words, the questions also touch on his own experiences and thus come to serve more immediately as configurations of them.

During this period Peter develops what he calls our "sketch." In this he plays a boy and I am to act the father. The dialogue is in English. Peter, who decides on the lines, quickly develops the drama. The boy wants to stay up to watch TV, but his father says ("Here you have to be sharp, tough, strong, and strict," Peter commands) that the boy must turn off the TV and go to bed. The boy is "boiling mad."

Then the father must be still stricter, at which point the boy gives in. Then it's morning, and the father rouses the boy from bed and takes him to his day care center.

Over several months we often play this sketch. In one session I tell him that I will be changing consulting rooms, explaining where the new office will be. Peter wants to go there at once, and when that is not possible, he says that then he wants to know what kind of room is behind the closed door. And, in English, "I give you five seconds time!"—partly playful, partly threatening. I say that this situation is like the sketch, "I want to look, I want to know, and I am boiling mad if I am not allowed to watch." Peter replies by asking me to play the sketch with him. At the next session, in connection with his wish to know what is going on at my place, he says, "I want to know. . . !", but then he makes a slip and says, "I want to watch. . . !", which is the reply the boy in the sketch makes when he is told to go to bed.

I tell him that I think that with me Peter is like the boy in the sketch. He wants to "watch," wants to know about me, and gets angry when he is "not allowed." My impression is that this dramatization— which is repeated many times—signifies an effort to control his wish to get a distinguishable "visualization" of me. The drama has in part the character of play, but the sketch in its repetitive and strict form is also a way of establishing a "sharp, tough, strong, strict" rule around his effort to be allowed to "watch." Before we played the sketch Peter always enjoined me to be sharp, and in this way he received external help in keeping his own wish to "know" and "see" in check.

During the first session in the new consulting room Peter notices that there is an automatic telephone answering machine. He gets very excited, fingers it, and happens to turn it on. He hears a fragment, which he interprets as me speaking to someone else. Peter asks whom I was talking to. I say that I understand that this is very interesting to Peter: whom can Henrik have been talking to? And what can he have said? Peter replies by asking where I bought the answering machine, what it cost, etc. For a long time Peter's curiosity about the contents in the answering machine was extremely intense.

The new office consisted of two rooms—the therapy room and a kitchen—separated by a curtain. Shortly before the summer break Peter asks once again what I had said to that other person on the answering machine. "If you don't tell me I'll go to the kitchen!" Rather cautiously Peter then did this and walked straight to the refrigerator, which he eagerly investigated. "Where does all this food come from?" I tell him that he wants to know this just as he wants to know about the answering machine. He wants to know what these things contain and where they come from. Peter asks what kind of message I have dictated into the machine and I tell him. "Now let's play that I'm calling you!" And so we play this—I rattle off my message, Peter leaves a message, and we do it in reverse. Peter is jumping with enthusiasm, crying, "I want an answering machine, too!"

In Peter's interest in the "other room" a pattern can be discerned. The room behind the locked door, the messages on the answering machine, the room on the other side of the curtain, the contents of the refrigerator—these are all initially closed and therefore outside Peter's store of knowledge, and they all have a connection to me. It might be said that they are like the part of me that Peter senses lies outside his immediate sphere of knowledge: my mind. For him, the issue was not that going into the other room was a symbol for entering my mind, but rather an effort to take concrete possession of this other room. In all probability Peter did not experience the other rooms as metaphors but more as concrete, desirable reality.

THE FOURTH HALF-YEAR

Peter began habitually to sit in my chair. He wanted to know about various dangerous situations I had been involved in, "where you had to call for an ambulance or the police, for example. If there had been a burglary, for example." I say that perhaps Peter is wondering about what I did when I encountered these dangers in order to know what he himself would do later on if he faced danger. "Yes," Peter says. "Tell me now!" He is very impatient, saying that he'll go to the kitchen if I don't tell him.

In the kitchen Peter's attention is first drawn to the refrigerator, then to the stove. He checks to see how cold the refrigerator is and how quickly water freezes in the freezing compartment. "What keeps the refrigerator cold? What is the sound you hear when you close the door?" I take Peter's hand and, guiding it to the rubber packing on the door, I tell him how he can feel how this insulates the refrigerator, keeping it cold, and how it also gives off a sound when you close the door.

The stove is perhaps even more exciting, particularly the oven. Peter investigates how you put on the fan, how quickly the oven gets hot. "What can you do in different temperatures?" I tell him, at the close of one session, *Well, in 50° C you can, for example, dry fruit.*

Peter begins the next session by asking, "Henrik, I have a question. Do you have patience?" *Oh, yes.* "What can you do in the oven at 50°C?" I say that you can dry fruit at that temperature, noting that this was clearly very fascinating for Peter: what can you do in different temperatures? Peter answers with a question: "What kind of oven do you have at home?" Peter is very excited during this session, testing how quickly the oven gets hot. Twice during the session he goes to the bathroom. I speak of how fascinating and exciting it is to know what kind of oven Henrik has, what you can do in it, and with it. Peter replies that he wants to have a similar oven and starts to wonder about whether there might be room for his family to live in my office.

Here we might see how Peter is trying concretely to identify with me—for example, by sitting in my chair—but also how in order to conquer internal dangers he is trying to get help from the methods I use to deal with them. When I relate some incidents in which I have called for an ambulance, Peter memorizes them. It is as though he were writing these events in his memory, then repeating them to himself.

His preoccupation with the refrigerator and the oven may also be seen in this context. Penetrating them, exploring them, and seeing how he can regulate them are fascinating and exciting since this is a way to become acquainted with my control of excitement very concretely, in the same way that the identification is concrete. What do you do to get it cold, and what do you do to get it to heat up?

THE THIRD YEAR

Peter begins to write his own short stories and also to write down lyrics to familiar songs. He says he is doing this so that he can leave something behind; these texts will be here after his therapy is over. Psalms dominate the lyrics: "Blossom Time," "Safe with Jesus," "Silent Night," "Fairest Lord Jesus,"—i.e., songs about how good God is, how He makes nature bloom, and how we are uplifted by all this. We sing together. When I try to talk about what we are doing, Peter interrupts, "Where is Saltsjöbaden [a place outside the town where Peter's school was situated]?" The questioning, however, subsides somewhat. A kind of rhythm sets in. Toward the end of the session the questions again begin to crop up.

At one session we talk about public swimming pools and Peter asks if I have been to a certain outdoor pool. *Yes, I've been there.* "When was the last time?" *Last summer.* "How old were your children then?" I answer that I think that now Peter is trying to draw a picture in his head of what it was like when I was there. I take his hand and draw in his palm with my finger. *This is what I think you are doing: this is the way you draw a picture of my family and me swimming.* "Where do your children go to school?" Peter thinks they go to a school for sighted children he has visited. I say, "Yes, you've been in that school, so you have a picture of it and now you can put my children into it. Then I say that I am not telling him everything about myself; if I did that, I couldn't know what kind of picture Peter himself draws. Peter says, "If you tell me, I'll erase the picture I've made." I answer by telling him that I think it is hard for him to draw a picture by himself and then be doubtful about whether that picture corresponds to reality.

THE FOURTH YEAR

Peter's behavior during the sessions gradually became calmer. Previously he had a habit of calling through the mail slot when I did not immediately open the door, but he stopped doing this. The questioning also lost some of its compulsive character, and it was also more possible to think together about it. On the whole I have the feeling that Peter is now less controlling. I'm happy that he can now occasionally say, "I'm thinking about something," and that he likes to share those thoughts with me. Sometimes he says that he doesn't want to think about anything disagreeable—which is a step forward considering that previously he denied that anything unpleasant or frightening existed for him.

Peter also begins to tell me about various memories, things that happened a long time ago. These events are related in concrete detail, but I have the impression that Peter now perceives his experiences to a greater extent precisely as experiences; he doesn't act so much on the spur of the moment but is able to capture an experience in words and can even share it with others by telling about it. This probably reflects an increased ability to think of our minds as separate entities; an increased ability to perceive these as functioning separately.

This may be analogous to a discovery reported by Omwake and Solnit (1961) from the treatment of a blind girl. At the beginning of her treatment this girl immediately enacted her reminicenses. There was no infantile amnesia, but during the course of the treatment this amnesia was established. Analogously, it is conceivable that Peter gradually begins to have a feeling of having experiences instead of just acting instantly.

It was especially gratifying to discover how Peter found himself both thinking and enjoying sharing these thoughts with me. For example, he might say, "Do you know what I was thinking today?" *Tell me.* And then Peter tells me how angry he was when everybody else wanted to decide what he should do in school while he wants to decide for himself.

Yet it was still clear that much of his need for concrete reassurance persisted. During one session Peter tells me he thinks it is unnecessary for a classmate to come along on a sports event. I say that maybe Peter really doesn't want this classmate to come? "What did you eat for breakfast today?" *Of course I can tell you, but first we have to talk about this.* Peter says, "Maybe you had a sandwich and coffee." I comment that perhaps Peter is trying to get a picture of me as I sit having breakfast, and now he wants to know if this picture corresponds to reality. Peter replies, "If you don't tell me, I'll erase the picture when I leave." *Aha, so that's your way?* I say that perhaps it is especially important for Peter to find out whether his picture is correct since he doesn't see so well? Perhaps it's particularly important since everything is so uncertain when you have poor sight and that's why Peter wants reassurance? Peter says that anyway he does see something. But then, "What did you have for breakfast?" I tell him, and Peter is surprised that I put honey on my sandwich. Then we talk about how this tastes.

DECISION TO TERMINATE THE THERAPY

Since the situation with Peter has gradually become less hectic, and both his parents and his school are satisfied with how he is now managing, we make plans to terminate the therapy. The termination date is set for a day more than a half year later, in mid-autumn.

This alters the situation again—in the therapy, but not outside it. Peter begins to question me more intensively. Happily, though, it is still possible to talk about this—and even to curb the questioning so that Peter listens to what I have to say. Outside the therapy Peter's newfound stability continues.

Shortly before the summer preceding the termination date we have a problem with dates for a couple of sessions. We try to find alternative times for the canceled sessions, and Peter is very anxious for this to succeed. I say that perhaps he feels it is important to get these sessions in, now that the summer break will soon begin, and perhaps also because we are going to terminate the therapy in the autumn. Peter asks, "How do children in orphanages dress? In their own clothes, in clothes they have gotten from their parents, or in clothes provided by the orphanage?" I reply that Peter is now beginning to think about what abandoned children look like, and perhaps he feels as though I am abandoning him. Peter says, "There's no connection here, is there?" *Well, I'm not so sure about that. You began to picture abandoned children when I talked about your terminating therapy this autumn.* "It's hard to picture them when you don't know how the children are dressed," says Peter. *Yes, that's true.*

At the last session before the summer break I talk once again about the termination. Peter asks, "How does your daughter usually read the paper? What's the address of your place in the country? What color is the house?" And I comment that now that the summer break is about to begin Peter is trying to picture me in the summer so that he can somehow see what I am like then. "Have I been trying to picture you for four years?" *I think so.* "Have I always asked a lot of questions before the summer break?" *Quite often.* "Why am I asking more questions now?" *What do you think?* "Maybe because I'm going to leave in the autumn."

THE FINAL MONTHS

During the final stages of the therapy Peter's questioning escalates, but—to a fair degree—it is possible to discuss this. We discuss how this questioning is connected to his constantly worsening sight, and to the approaching end of the therapy.

At one session Peter asks about various cities in Denmark—where they are located, how large they are. He does this in a way that is exhausting, seemingly endless. I say that Peter wants to get so much information from me because the therapy is soon to end. Perhaps he wants somehow to retain his "sight"—his "eyes"—and Peter replies that it is hard for him to listen to what I am saying because he is waiting so eagerly for an answer.

At the next session Peter asks me about Denmark's royal family and I speak again about his wish to get me to tell him things. Peter replies that he asks when he doesn't know something, and that he gets so impatient because he doesn't know whether he will get an answer before he leaves. I say that Peter wants security before he leaves—he wants to know what things are like, and he wants to have the feeling of security this provides. And he wants to have it before he leaves me. *In other words, you get this feeling of security when you know what the world is like. Sight helps out here. When you see, you know something of what the world is like, and this provides security. But since your sight is getting worse all the time and the therapy is ending, perhaps you are in a hurry to get clarity and security. Maybe that's why you ask questions.*

Peter replies, "I remember the last operation. I was still under the anaesthetic when a machine began beeping, a machine that was connected to the drops. I just wanted to sleep and was boiling mad because the machine woke me up. I just wanted to sleep, for after the operation I couldn't see anything. I just wanted to sleep until my sight began to come back." I say that perhaps he feels now as he did after the operation: he doesn't want to wake up to the feeling of losing his sight. He just wants to sleep.

Peter tries to remember what has happened in the therapy and asks about it. "What did I previously ask about? What did I ask about at the start?" I say that perhaps he feels as though he will lose both memory and sight now that he is going to leave. He may be afraid that he won't remember me either. So I ask if he remembers what he told me about the most recent operation. Yes, he remembers how he just wanted to sleep, and adds that it is often like this in the mornings, too. He just wants to sleep. "Everyone else is in a bad mood and I don't want to wake up to that." And Peter cries a minute about this.

A few sessions later Peter asks me a question that I don't answer. When it becomes clear to him that I am not going to reply he tells me that he is under much stress. He has so many school assignments that he doesn't know how he can do them all. "This is too much. I think about saying to them, 'How do you expect me to find time for this?' They don't help me at all. They just sit drinking coffee—the teachers." Peter cries, and I say that perhaps he feels this way because I don't answer his questions and because the therapy is about to end. He may be thinking, "Henrik doesn't help me at all." And that I am leaving Peter with too many tasks that are much too difficult.

During the final weeks Peter began each session by telling me how many session we had left. He started to explore the therapy room again and was surprised by some things he had not previously discovered. He asked a great many questions about the details of the room. I tell him I think that now, before he leaves, he is trying to get a stronger "grasp" of the room where we work. Peter says that he woke up the night before coughing and couldn't go back to sleep. "I'd like some sleeping pills." Then he begins to question me exhaustively about various sleeping pill brands. When I don't reply and succeed in taking up the question of how he feels when I don't reply, Peter answers, "It's like there is something on a shelf but you can't get it. Like when you know that what you want is there, but you can't reach high enough to get it into your hand." The next session Peter exclaims, "I want to know, too!"

At the final session Peter tells me that for the first time he is going to a meeting arranged by an organization for visually impaired youth. *Hmm. Now you're starting this kind of thing.* Peter goes on to say that today he just wanted to go on sleeping when the alarm clock rang. I say that he didn't want to wake up to the day of the last session. *Maybe it's like it was after the operation?* Peter says that then he just wanted to sleep until his sight came back. I state that perhaps this might be the case on this day: "I don't want to wake up to the end of the therapy." Next comes, "What did I ask about at the start of the therapy?" I speak of memory and sight and say that Peter may now feel as though he is about to lose both. He replies, "I often don't want to wake up because there's nothing to wake up to." *Maybe you feel like that now.* "When I leave Henrik, I won't wake up to anything that's any fun." Peter cries a bit, and I say that of course he feels sad about this. I thank him for our time together. Peter thanks me in return.

DISCUSSION

In the introduction to this paper I said that the requirements of the object world could be found in two primary sense modalities, and that opportunity for the visually impaired to build up a primary sense matrix—which can function as a basis for the other sense modalities as well—is limited. Basic sense warp is a prerequisite for constituting objects.

Peter was born blind but got fairly good sight at the age of six months. After this, his sight had steadily worsened although repeated operations had postponed the inevitable loss of sight. Thus, even though fairly good sight had been established at six months, it is conceivable that blindness during the first half year had been significant for Peter's later development. His congenital blindness may have led to a sense warp with a built-in weakness, and this weakness may have brought with it a basic risk—a risk of losing objects.

It may nevertheless be supposed that Peter might have built up a primary sense matrix that made the object world meaningful to him. The basic risk mentioned above was probably actualized by the progressive illness. *His slowly worsening sight probably represented a distinct threat for Peter, and this may be seen as crucial to how he behaved in the therapy.* Peter was a very active boy—and this is unusual among children with visual impairment—and this activity may be interpreted as a reflection of the existing psychic base, but also as a reflection of the continuing loss of sight. One might say that Peter was trying through activity to retain the object world he was on the point of losing. Losing his sight was probably close to the experience of losing objects, and much of what one sees in the therapy probably tells this story.

In order to tie the material from the therapy to the blind child's special difficulties presented earlier in this paper, I will take up four themes I discerned in my work with Peter: (1) the wish to get into the "other room," (2) questioning and its functions, (3) control of excitement, and (4) concretization of experiences and concreteness in identification.

"THE OTHER ROOM"

Very early in the therapy it became clear that Peter had a distinct feeling that he was an outsider when it came to certain aspects of me. These can be summarized as the "other room"—the space behind the locked door, the message on my answering machine, the room behind the curtain, the contents of the refrigerator. These were aspects of my world Peter did not have direct knowledge of. That such hidden spaces existed was very difficult for Peter to handle, and he tried by all the means at his disposal to break through the obstacles blocking direct "insight" into them.

The "other room" that plagued Peter seemed to be related to my person. These hidden spaces were concrete to Peter, and he often asked about things that might populate them. I am inclined to think that the "other room" is a concrete metaphor for my mind—something Peter felt a compelling need to get hold of. Accordingly, then, Peter's wish to get at the hidden spaces was a reflection of his wish to get at those parts of my mind he had no direct knowledge of.

In his work on the therapeutic alliance Bollas (1998) says that the patient creates an alliance with the analytical *process,* not with the therapist. The patient sees himself as thrust into a reality controlled by an organizing intelligence, just as the child sees himself as living in a world controlled by his mother. The more important the object is, the more it is sensed as controlling the perceived reality. Bollas says that breaches in the therapeutic alliance can be explained with this as a starting point. The patient wants to get at what directs the perceived reality—what is "behind" it. In this way he can assertively try to get a concrete grasp of the therapy and the therapist. What the patient himself can be thought to experience is not interesting any more but only what the therapist, for example, "really" thinks.

Peter evinced a great interest in royalty, associating me with the royal family. He thought not only that I knew most things—for example, what he had imagined we would do in the session—but also that I could exert an influence on his circumstances—for example, by being a member of the school board. Thus Peter saw me as a powerful person. This probably reflected the fact that he perceived himself as being controlled by the importance he attached to me. In order to get a grip on what he perceived as controlling reality, he tried to get hold of what was "behind"—i.e., the aspects of me he did not have in his hand. Trying to get into the "other room" may be said to be an effort to grasp what he sensed as directing his perceptions beyond the obvious. Peter wanted to have my mind completely in his grasp since his perceived reality appeared to be controlled by it.

In the introduction I referred to a case Fraiberg (1968) described. Kathy clung tightly to her mother while she was learning to walk. Similarly, it might be said that Peter expressed an evident hunger for objects and that his wish to get into what lay on the "other side of the door" was a manifestation of that hunger. Considering that his sight was getting worse all the time, one can understand that this hunger was extreme—getting an absolutely firm hold on the object is important when you are afraid of losing it—and this probably was the case with both Kathy and Peter.

In order to get rid of this disturbing hunger Peter at first tried to break down the door, but then he cut off contact with me. I noticed that a more stringent restraint on my part caused Peter to cease utilizing his relationship to me. This came to involve a technical problem. Telling him about myself could on the one hand be seen as a compensation for his lack of sight, but on the other hand it was obvious that it might lead to an ever more unmanageable hunger. My solution was to tell him some of what lay "on the other side"—what he did not have immediate awareness of—but at the same time I tried to interject work with how Peter experienced this hunger. By this means I hoped that Peter could develop his own approach independent of sight, which could more successfully manage his object hunger.

PERSISTENT QUESTIONING

Peter's persistent questioning was one of the things that had led his parents to seek therapy for him. I have not been able to do justice to how repetitive and how exhausting the questioning often was in the therapy. At times I felt like an answering machine, particularly when the questioning seemed automatic and empty. Sometimes Peter demanded an answer but had already forgotten what he had asked about. At these moments it was evident that the content of the question at hand was not very important in itself. I discern two important functions this questioning may have had for Peter.

For the sighted child his mother's concrete presence is obvious—he just has to have a look. The same thing is true of his mother's psychic accessibility. Through sight it is eminently possible to decide how psychically present his mother is and so to decide to what extent she shares his own experiences. For the visually impaired the situation is different, and I think that Peter's questioning was connected to this.

By constantly asking questions—and constantly getting answers—Peter could be assured that I was concretely present. What he heard might in this way compensate for the lack of visual impressions. But by asking questions—and constantly getting answers—Peter could be assured that I was concretely present. What he heard might in this way compensate for the lack of visual impressions. But by asking questions Peter could also assure himself that I was psychically available to him. When he asked a question I was forced to think about the same thing that concerned him. By questioning Peter could thus be assured that I was both putting my mind at his disposal and sharing what he was thinking about. I think this was related to the second function of his questioning.

That Peter had previously had relatively good sight had established the importance of this sense modality to him. One can well imagine that Peter was trying to compensate for his slowly worsening sight by using others, among them me, as "eyes." When Peter asked questions he could get me to tell him about what I saw and knew, and in this way he could retain a feeling of himself possessing sight. In other words, he could preserve a feeling of having usable eyes. It was probably this functional aspect of the questioning that was exhausting for me.

This reasoning can also explain the escalation of the questions at the end of the sessions, especially at the end of the therapy. When Peter was on the point of losing me it became particularly important to reassure himself of my presence and also to use me as his eyes as long as this was still possible. Peter coupled his approaching loss of me with his loss of sight during a previous operation: ending his therapy was like waking up without sight. This could probably be interpreted as awakening to an objectless state as well as to a life without usable eyes.

When I spoke to Peter about how he might be feeling at the moment, I was often interrupted by questions, frequently concerning the nature of the outside world. Most likely this was connected with a feeling of uncertainty, which Peter perceived as dangerous. Feeling threatened by his awareness of more problematic experiences, Peter probably tried to transform this uncertainty into something that applied to the outside world. This uncertainty could then be conquered by questioning me. My answers about the outside world enabled him to feel that it was possible for him to configure the nature of material reality, and this calmed him down. Interrupting me with questions accordingly transformed an internal danger to an external one and gave him the feeling of having this external danger under control.

CONTROL OF EXCITEMENT

It must be apparent how excited Peter often was. This excitement was sometimes in evidence even before Peter came in—he might call from the stairs or through the mail slot. Peter's excitement was channeled, for example, through his going to the bathroom fairly often, and sometimes standing up to jump on both feet. Burlingham (1965) has described how blind children have to make great efforts to restrain their eagerness. In their excitement sighted children run around, but blind children can't do this; they associate overeagerness with the risk of injuring themselves. Blind children therefore bind their excitement into repetitive action patterns. Thus Peter channeled his excitement by jumping on both feet, but he also made use of his relation to me to control it.

Peter went into my kitchen for the first time when he did not get an answer to his question about whom I had been speaking to on the answering machine. This was probably a substitution for the opportunity to get into another variant of my "other room." In the kitchen Peter became extremely preoccupied by the refrigerator and stove. He tested how fast the refrigerator could freeze water and tried to find out how it could keep food cold. This can probably be seen as an effort to get a grasp on my ability to "freeze" what was far too exciting.

The stove, and especially the oven, were still more exciting. Peter was absorbed by the chance to regulate the heat himself, testing repeatedly how fast he could get the oven up to the highest temperature. At the same time he asked a lot of questions about what could be done at different temperatures.

I think that by capturing the kitchen Peter was trying to get a grasp on my ability to control excitement. By freezing and heating up the oven he was trying to acquaint himself with the apparatuses I had to accomplish this. Perhaps he felt that he was getting into the hidden room where I was doing the same with my excitement.

The sketch we enacted may also be regarded as Peter's use of me in an effort to get his own excitement under control. In the sketch Peter was a boy who insisted on staying up to watch TV and who became "boiling mad" when his father told him to turn off the apparatus and go to bed. The boy wanted to stay up to "look," but his father forced him to give up this idea. Peter always commanded me to be very strict, seeming to enjoy the antagonism this created between us. The game was probably an attempt to restrain his strong wish to "see" and an effort—through his relationship to me—to get some of his excitement over "seeing" under control.

During the course of the treatment some transformation of what might be termed instinctual dangers could be observed. At the beginning of the treatment, when I talked about the approaching eye operation Peter began to ask about various dangerous animals. How dangerous were they really? An eye operation involves a real risk of sight deterioration. For Peter losing his sight may have aroused a fear of not only losing the object but also of becoming a helpless victim of instinctual impulses. These may then have been transformed into dangerous animals. One interpretation is that this was an expression of castration anxiety. Losing sight involves the risk of being subjected to unmanagable instinctual dangers, analogous to castration, and these dangers are externalized. The end result was that the dangerous thing came from outside, and such danger is difficult to integrate; rather, it must be avoided.

Instinctual dangers were also kept in check by Peter's recurring visits to the bathroom. After one of these he asked me how phlegm comes up when you cough, and I showed him this by trying to configure the physical process tactilely.

It is possible that this latter configuration also involves a configuration of anal processes, and through that a configuration of anal impulses. By talking about dangerous animals Peter straightforwardly expressed in words an instinctual fear—a fear which was externalized—but through our conversation about coughing and phlegm this fear was probably represented in a way that did not disavow the origin of the impulses. As Salonen (2000) has explained in a work on the conditions for affect representation, one can here see how instinctual impulses take on an affective meaning; bodily sensations are integrated with an idea-content. From talking about dangerous animals Peter went to wanting a configuration of what was happening in his own body. By so doing he could make the impulses more his own, so that they would take on their own affective meaning.

CONCRETIZING EXPERIENCES AND IDENTIFICATION

Various sense functions are employed if they offer a functional benefit. Psychic mechanisms always have a motive. In Peter's case there was obviously a motive for finding out about factual realities, but—at least at the beginning of the therapy—he lacked a motive for imagining things. Peter could work out an alternative for how I had furnished my bedroom but he did not understand, so to speak, the point of doing this. Peter wanted concrete information.

The visually impaired person is mercilessly exposed to reality. External perils often crowd in unexpectedly and without any warning. The result is often a constant readiness for disaster. The visually impaired person must be ready at any time to be beset by something he is not prepared for, and this brings with it a tendency to adhere to concrete reality, without defenses. If he is so prepared, the external dangers will not be too surprising.

Something similar may be said about internal dangers. The visually impaired child relies on what is within reach. The sighted child can rely on the fact that his mother will soon relieve him from, for example, hunger if he sees her preparing food, but the visually impaired child has no chance to use this kind of reassurance. What is concretely present is reliable, but nothing else.

Because of this it is understandable that Peter did not download ideas that were not concretely anchored in external reality. As he once said, he had no use for such ideas. Imagining something that was later inaccessible would be much too uncertain—unusable—and could only lead to excitement bordering on panic. A world of imagination without external support might lead to excitement that was not relieved—and Peter wanted reliable information that could inform him of possible relief possibilities.

Perhaps the impression of concretization is due partly to the fact that the sighted person is simply alien to the experiential world of the visually impaired. The visually impaired individual naturally constructs his world in his own way, and the building stones of this world consist largely of concrete details. Peter often wanted to know about technical details, and this may be interpreted as an effort to build up a world with the means at hand. If meaningful impressions are concrete, then a world can be constructed by combining just exactly these. I tried to explain this to Peter by drawing on his hand when he asked about details of my life. I was trying in this way to show how he was building up an image of me.

If Peter's object representations were built up of concrete details, his identifications followed a similar pattern. Peter wrote doctor's certificates, like me, and at times he wanted to sit in my chair. He wanted to know what I did in various dangerous situations in order to know how he would manage them himself. By carrying out some concrete actions he could be like me. It is conceivable that for the visually impaired it is not so much a matter of looking like the identification object as of carrying out the actions that person carries out.

Conclusion

Compared to other visually impaired children Peter had some advantages. For a time his vision had been fairly good, so that he had constituted an object world. It is true that he was now about to lose the sight he still had and that he seemed to regard this at least partly as a loss of his object world. Through his intensive extroversion and activity he seemed, however, to be handling this situation relatively well. With great frenzy, Peter learned to use various aids for the visually impaired, and he didn't hesitate to try to learn new skills—sometimes dangerously, as when, for example, he tried to ride a bicycle. This activity, sometimes somewhat contraphobically tinged, contributed to the fact that Peter's world was relatively comprehensive.

Besides the direct alleviation of symptoms, some development within the therapy could be observed. Peter became less controlling vis-à-vis me, and his behavior during the sessions was less hectic. It was also obvious that Peter had gotten a grasp of the fact that he was experiencing and thinking various things and he began to show a willingness to share them with me. What is called episodic memory (Clyman, 1991) also developed. All this indicates that his psychic ability to elaborate became more developed during the course of the therapy.

When we ended the therapy both his parents and his teachers were satisfied with Peter's situation. Even though toward the close of the therapy he reverted to an earlier behavior pattern, this regression was limited to the therapy. At the end of the treatment the general view was that he was among the best students in his boarding school for the visually impaired, and he was appreciated for his willingness and ability to take care of more helpless students, even though one could see an effort to control others in this behavior. A similar helpfulness was in evidence at home where Peter was now able to be by himself for long periods—listening to novels on audiotapes and playing Nintendo. Some conflicts of an adolescent nature began to appear just at the time of the end of the treatment. What adolescence could bring with it on the whole I did not find out about since I lost contact with Peter when I moved to another country.

BIBLIOGRAPHY

Bollas, C. (1998). Origins of the therapeutic alliance. *Scand. Psychoanal. Rev.*, 21:24–36.

BURLINGHAM, D. (1965). Some problems of ego development in blind children. *Psychoanal. Study Child*, 20:194–208.

CLYMAN, R. (1991). The procedural organization of emotions: A contribution from cognitive science to the psychoanalytic theory of therapeutic action. *J. Amer. Psychoanal. Assn.*, 39 (suppl.):349–382.

CURSON, A. (1979). The blind nursery school child. *Psychoanal. Study Child*, 34:51–83.

FRAIBERG, S. (1968). Parallel and divergent patterns in blind and sighted infants. *Psychoanal. Study Child*, 23:264–300.

FRAIBERG, S., SIEGEL, B., ET AL. (1966). The role of sound in the search behavior of a blind infant. *Psychoanal. Study Child*, 21:327–357.

GRUBRICH-SIMITIS, I. (1984). From concretism to metaphor—thoughts on some theoretical and technical aspects of the psychoanalytic work with children of Holocaust survivors. *Psychoanal. Study Child*, 39:301–319.

KARLSSON, G. (1999). *Leva som blind; fenomenologisk-psykologiska undersökningar* (*Living as Blind; Phenomenological-psychological Investigations*). Stockholm: Carlssons.

KLEIN, G. (1962). Blindness and isolation. *Psychoanal. Study Child*, 17:82–93.

NAGERA, H. & COLONNA, A. (1965). Aspects of the contribution of sight to ego and drive development. *Psychoanal. Study Child*, 20:267–287.

OMWAKE, E., & SOLNIT, A. (1961). "It isn't fair"—the treatment of a blind child. *Psychoanal. Study Child*, 16:352–404.

PIHA, H. (1998). Binding auditory flow to imagery. Paper presented to the Finnish Psychoanalytical Society, Helsinki.

SALONEN, S. (2000). Recovery of affect and structural conflict. *Scand. Psychoanal. Rev.*, 23:50–64.

SANDLER, A.-M. (1963). Aspects of passivity and ego development in the blind infant. *Psychoanal. Study Child*, 18:343–360.

SEGAL, A., & STONE, F. (1961). The six-year-old who began to see—emotional sequelae of operation for congenital bilateral cataract. *Psychoanal. Study Child*, 16:481–505.

TÄHKÄ, V. (1993). *Mind and Its Treatment: A Psychoanalytic Approach*. New York: International Universities Press.

WILLS, D. (1965). Some observations on blind nursery school children's understanding of their world. *Psychoanal. Study Child*, 20:344–364.

——— (1970). Vulnerable periods in the early development of blind children. *Psychoanal. Study Child*, 25:461–480.

——— (1979). "The ordinary devoted mother" and her blind baby. *Psychoanal. Study Child*, 34:51–83.

APPLICATIONS

Father and Son

The Origins of *Strange Case of Dr Jekyll and Mr Hyde*

HILARY J. BEATTIE, Ph.D.

In Strange Case of Dr Jekyll and Mr Hyde *Robert Louis Stevenson created, out of one of his own dreams, the most famous pre-Freudian case study of the divided self. The present essay explores the roots of that work in Stevenson's lifelong difficulty in separating from his moody, conflicted, and passionately possessive father. Out of a matrix of religious guilt and social conformity, Stevenson struggled to create and define his own identity as a writer, a struggle that ran counter to many of his beloved father's deepest needs and led to sharp clashes, accompanied by periods of severe depressive and physical illness in both. Stevenson's creative block during his father's final depression and dementia was broken only by the nightmare that became* Jekyll and Hyde, *which enabled him to give enduring literary expression to the disavowed rage, guilt, and sense of deformity and fractured identity endemic to their internalized relationship. It may also have functioned as an act of exorcism and expiation that helped him recover rapidly from his father's death and exploit more productively the few years that were left to him.*

"... something unusual and great was lost to the
world in Thomas Stevenson. One could almost see

Faculty of the Columbia University Center for Psychoanalytic Training and Research, and in private practice in psychotherapy and psychoanalysis in New York City.

I am grateful to Ernest Mehew, the doyen of Stevenson scholars, for patient and detailed criticism of an earlier version of this paper. Rajendra Jutagir was extremely helpful in the matter of Thomas Stevenson's illness and dementia.

The Psychoanalytic Study of the Child 56, ed. Albert J. Solnit, Peter B. Neubauer, Samuel Abrams, and A. Scott Dowling (Yale University Press, copyright © 2001 by Albert J. Solnit, Peter B. Neubauer, Samuel Abrams, and A. Scott Dowling).

the struggle between the creature of cramped hered-
itary conventions and environment and the man nature had intended him to be."

(F. Stevenson, 1923, p. xx).

STRANGE CASE OF DR JEKYLL AND MR HYDE, THE SINISTER STORY OF ONE
man's doomed efforts to isolate, enjoy, and yet control the unacceptable aspects of his own nature, remains one of the most powerful examples of Gothic fiction ever written. Published in 1886, it brought
immediate and lasting fame to its author, Robert Louis Stevenson
(1850–1894), and has survived later critical fluctuations in his reputation to enter popular folklore, gaining a hold in the imaginations
even of those who have never read it or seen one of the many films
it has inspired. Each successive generation has read it in the light of
its own preoccupations, over everything from religion and ethics to
sexuality and gender. Critics, however, have always noted the relative
exclusion of women from the tale and the greater prominence of
power struggles with paternal figures (James, 1888, p. 1252; Maixner,
1981, p. 223; Veeder, 1988a).

While rebellion against patriarchal authority is a frequent theme
of the nineteenth-century *Doppelgänger* story, a genre to which *Jekyll
and Hyde* certainly belongs (cf. Miller, 1987), exclusion of the romantic, sexual element and the basic oedipal triangle is highly unusual
(and has forced the cinematographers to supply it). It is not, however, unusual in the early work of Stevenson, in which his friend
Henry James noted a striking "absence of care for things feminine"
and a preference for male camaraderie and adventure (1888, pp. 1233,
1238). The father figures in this male world tend, however, to be
absent, ineffectual, duplicitous, or controlling (cf. Eigner, 1966,
pp. 212–213). These features of Stevenson's earlier work reached
their nightmarish epiphany in *Jekyll and Hyde,* which was inspired by
an actual nightmare, dreamed in the early autumn of 1885, during
one of the darkest periods of his life; when his own ambivalently
loved father was suffering from depression and dementia in what
proved to be his final illness, and Stevenson himself was laid low by
devastating pulmonary complaints.

Most critics have recognized that Stevenson's preoccupation with
the double life and the struggle between good and evil derived
largely from his early upbringing in a strictly Calvinist environment,
and many have also noted the role played by his struggles to free
himself from the domination of his controlling and deeply religious
father. Thomas Stevenson (1818–1887) was no conventionally dis-

tant and autocratic Victorian patriarch, however, and the intense bond between him and his only child was hardly typical of Victorian fathers and sons. Yet no one to date has given an account of their close, mutually overidentified and passionate relationship that adequately explains its role in Stevenson's work, even though it is possible (especially because of the publication of Stevenson's *Letters,* 1994–5) to document that relationship in remarkable detail. Admittedly, the nature of the maternal tie must have contributed to the strength of Stevenson's bond with his father and the neglect of romantic, heterosexual themes in his work, but I shall address that theme in another paper (see also Beattie, 1998). Here the focus will be on the development of Stevenson's relationship with his father, both actual and internalized, and in particular on how it contributed to the birth of his uncanny masterpiece of the double life and personality.

STRANGE CASE OF DR JEKYLL AND MR HYDE

Stevenson's account of how he came to write *Jekyll and Hyde* is contained in a remarkable essay, "A Chapter on Dreams" (1888a), in which he outlined the role of his dreams in his formation as a writer. The essay begins with an extended meditation on the subjective nature of memory, fantasy, and dream, which, although retrospectively almost indistinguishable and unverifiable, are yet essential to an individual's sense of his own identity. Stevenson was long haunted by the nightmares of his childhood, in which he was powerless to find "some form of words" that would deliver him from the looming terrors of Hell and damnation, or from the sense of uncanny horror lurking in his dreams at the heart of innocuous seeming things. Only when he became a writer did he find a way to master these unspeakable anxieties and turn them to profitable account, by using the scenes presented nightly by "the little people" in the "internal theatre" of his mind as the basis of publishable tales. Since his unseen helpers, the "Brownies," had "not a rudiment of what we call a conscience" (1888a, p. 208), Stevenson's reworking of this material required conscious censorship, including the outright suppression of one dreamed tale in which the estranged son of a "very rich and wicked man" returned to England, accidentally killed his father in a quarrel, and lived in terror that his crime would be detected by his young and beautiful stepmother, only to find with delight at the end that the lady was in love with him!

Jekyll and Hyde, according to Stevenson, emerged as the outcome of prolonged efforts to "find a body, a vehicle, for that strong sense of man's double being which must at times come in upon and over-whelm the mind of every thinking creature" (1888a, p. 208). Indeed, earlier in the essay he outlined an eruption of this preoccupation during his student days, in the form of a recurrent nightmare so vivid that he actually had the sense of leading a "double life," with no means of proving the night-time one to be false. In his dream life he was a medical student, condemned to watch "monstrous malforma-tions and the abhorred dexterity of surgeons" by day, and endlessly, in wet clothes, to climb the stairs of his lodgings, brushing past a dreary procession of weary, ill-dressed men and women coming down, at night. This dream so clouded his days that he was at last driven to seek medical help, in the form of a "simple draught" that restored him to "the common lot of man" (1888a, pp. 200–201). Here already are some themes—the sinister medical operations, the transforming but in his case healing draught, and the implied alien-ation from fellow-beings as well as, perhaps, the impossibility of ac-knowledging sexual desire—that were also to surface in his later work.

The nightmare that became *Jekyll and Hyde* had no such organized narrative. Its author dreamed merely three scenes and "the central idea of a voluntary change becoming involuntary," as well as the mechanism by which the change is effected, namely, "the business of the powders," which in the book are mixed with a "blood-red liquor" to form the fateful draught (1888a, p. 208; Stevenson, 1886, pp. 55, 58). Out of these materials Stevenson created a tale of terror that un-folds gradually and insidiously through the eyes of a seemingly disin-terested observer, Gabriel Utterson. Utterson, a dry, dispassionate lawyer, suspects that his old friend and client, the respected Dr. Henry Jekyll, is being blackmailed by a sinister young acquaintance, Edward Hyde. Hyde disappears for a time, after murdering a distin-guished older man, but is eventually found poisoned, in Jekyll's study, dressed in Jekyll's clothes, after Utterson has broken down the door in a misguided attempt to save the mysteriously secluded and evidently terrified doctor. Only through posthumous statements left by Jekyll and his estranged colleague, Dr. Lanyon, is it revealed at the end that Jekyll and Hyde, though utterly different in appearance and personality, are one and the same individual. Hyde is the disavowed, pleasure-seeking alter ego released by the ambitious but hyper re-spectable Jekyll in the course of his researches into his own divided nature and the "perennial war among [his] members" (1886, p. 60). He becomes increasingly uncontrollable as his evil nature grows stronger and the change becomes harder to reverse. When the supply of the original powder used to produce the change runs out, Jekyll remains forever trapped in the by-now-abhorred persona of Hyde, with no recourse but discovery or death.

All the innumerable readings of *Jekyll and Hyde* have had to take into account the centrality of male relationships in the tale. The important characters are professional, childless bachelors who lack any history of passionate attachments. The few females are marginal (albeit in significant ways), and the only formative relations are those between father and son. The scenes dreamed by Stevenson included Hyde's flight after the commission of "some crime" and his self-transformation, by means of the powders, in the presence of his pursuers (1888a, p. 208). This was expanded into the vicious, pleasurable killing of an eminent, "innocent," older man and, later, the effectual murder of a disapproving, white-haired contemporary and rival. Another dreamed scene ("the scene at the window") represented Jekyll's involuntary transformation back into Hyde, in which Jekyll's vaunted intellectual triumph becomes the means of his undoing. Attitudes toward the father range from idealization to execration. It is the childhood memory of Jekyll's father that checks Hyde's frenzy of delight after the murder of Carew (1886, p. 70), but at the end the frantic Hyde turns on his progenitor, scrawling "startling blasphemies" in the pages of Jekyll's "pious books" and "burning the letters and destroying the portrait" of his father before, in despair, killing them both (1886, p. 75).

THE STEVENSON FAMILY: EARLY LOVE AND TERROR

If knowledge of a writer's life can in no way explain the secret of his artistry (cf. Freud, 1928 [1927], p. 177), it still may go a long way to elucidate his choice, timing, and handling of key themes and the relative freedom or inhibition with which he used his gifts. Stevenson had precocious verbal talents, and his infantile productions were written down by his nurse and his adoring parents long before he himself learned to write. At the same time his joyous use of fantasy was checked by the anxieties and prejudices of these same adults, whose own conflicts, and those of the milieu in which they lived, go far to explain Stevenson's enduring preoccupation with doubling and the nature of evil in human life. Of these adults, the most powerful was his father, Thomas Stevenson, a talented, mercurial, melancholic, and deeply religious man who profoundly invested himself in the physical survival, spiritual development, and later career of his only child, and was doomed to a lifelong mixture of pride, joy, fury, and disappointment in consequence. Stevenson the son was to be torn between his love and need for his father and his equally imperative need to pursue his chosen literary career in freedom. The story of their relationship, with its phases of revolt and outward reconciliation, illness, guilt, and lastingly incomplete separation, is vital to understanding the startling eruption of *Jekyll and Hyde,* in many ways the pivotal work of Stevenson's career.

Thomas Stevenson was himself the son of a formidable and domineering father, Robert Stevenson (1772–1850), the founder of the renowned engineering dynasty that built the great lighthouses of Scotland. The youngest of thirteen children, Thomas grew up in an exceedingly religious household, shadowed by the loss of eight of his older siblings to disease and stillbirth, and under the care of an understandably anxious and hypochondriacal mother. In early life he was exuberant and wayward, an indifferent scholar who was fond of practical jokes and storytelling and toyed with thoughts of publishing or bookselling as a career. After some early attempts at fiction writing were discovered and denounced by his enraged father, however, he vanquished his romantic inclinations and followed his two older brothers into the family profession of engineering (Calder, 1980, p. 26; Bathurst, 1999, pp. 131–134, 187–188). Always closely tied to his father, Thomas was deeply affected by his death in 1850, and four months later named his only son after him (G. Balfour, 1901, Vol. 1, p. 7).

As he grew older Thomas evidently became subject to mood swings. All accounts emphasize his "freakish," playful, and changeable temperament, in which "humourous geniality" masked a "profound essential melancholy of disposition" (Stevenson, 1887a, pp. 69–70). There is actually evidence of mental instability in the Stevenson family. Thomas's oldest brother, Alan (1807–1865), an aspiring classical scholar who had been coerced by their father into a successful engineering career, succumbed in 1852 after years of poor health to "a severe nervous affliction" that left him a recluse, obsessed with morbid religious guilt, for the remaining 13 years of his life (Hammerton, 1907, p. 5; Bathurst, 1999, pp. 195–97, 201–202, 215–216). Another brother, David (1815–1886), also a distinguished engineer, apparently suffered from mental illness in the early 1880s (Stevenson, *Letters,* Vol. 4, pp. 94n, 95). Stevenson himself, late in his life, admitted that the male Stevensons, from his grandfather's generation to his own, were oppressed by bleak pessimism, an "acute and unbroken" sense of "the tragedy of life" (*Letters,* Vol. 8, p. 304; Furnas, 1951, p. 231).

It has been suggested that one reason that the thirty-year-old Thomas Stevenson in 1848 married Margaret Isabella Balfour (1829–1897), and the nineteen-year-old daughter of the minister of Colinton, was that in her brightly optimistic disposition he unconsciously sought an antidote to his own depression (Calder, 1980, p. 28). His bride had her own history of sibling and maternal loss, however, and some of her optimism was evidently the result of her "peculiar gift of disguising all facts at all unpleasant whether from others or herself" (M. Balfour, 1981, p. 43). In her youth she was beset by both pulmonary and "nerve troubles" (Guthrie, 1924, p. 25) and took advantage of medical advice to stay in bed every day until lunchtime, throughout most of her son's boyhood (G. Balfour, 1901, Vol. 1, p. 26; G. W. Balfour, 1903, p. xvii). The nature of her "nerve troubles" is unclear, but an element of hysteria along with a tendency to somatize seems likely (cf. LeBris, 1994, p. 59). Why she had only one child is also unknown, but, given her youth and fondness for infants, it is possible that this was a deliberate choice, perhaps motivated by Thomas's fears of illness or loss. All accounts agree that Thomas adored and babied her and that he was preoccupied with her poor health and that of their son.

Thomas Stevenson's worries about his son were certainly justified. Assailed from infancy by attacks of croup, bronchitis, and pneumonia that left him slight and delicate, young Louis (as he was known) survived through the devoted care of his nurse, Alison Cunningham, who shared his room and sat up with him through many nights of illness. "Cummy" herself embodied many of the contradictions of his early life. The daughter of a Fife fisherman, she was a lively and fun-loving woman whose patience, tenderness, and selfless devotion were later to earn her the moving dedication of *A Child's Garden of Verses:* "My second Mother, my first Wife, The angel of my infant life." On the other hand, with her extreme religiosity and fiercely Calvinist morality she fostered such a fear of sin and worldliness in her charge that he was tormented by dreams of Hell, to the point where he was afraid to fall asleep lest he die and fall into "eternal ruin." Yet her teachings also "put a point on lust," leading him to experiment with supposedly sinful acts to see if God would really strike him dead (Stevenson, 1880a, pp. 154, 157). In a defiant, Whitmanesque ode written in his twenties, entitled "Stormy Nights," Stevenson described these torments in a way that also suggests a nightly struggle with mas-

turbation, "an itching mystery to meward," concealed and condemned by "the comely secrecies of education," never relieved by the
pardon that was "ever shut from passage" (1971, p. 87).

Stevenson later admitted that he had little joy in remembering his
early years and that he had been "lovingly, but not always wisely
treated." It was easier to ascribe the blame to Cummy, in her "over-
haste to make [him] a religious pattern," than to the parents who
gave her such a free hand and, in his mother's case, remained oblivi-
ous to his religious torments (1880a, pp. 157, 154). The constant
threat of damnation for the slightest fault must have contrasted
strangely with the hothouse care that surrounded him and the sedulous efforts made to shield him from knowledge of the harsh realities
of the world outside (Osbourne, 1923, p. xvi). He grew up, in his own
words, to be "sentimental, snivelling, goody, morbidly religious," apt
to lie "unconsciously" out of his "feverish desire for consideration,"
and often to be wrongfully punished for it (1880a, p. 157), even "repeatedly thrashed" (*Letters*, Vol. 5, p. 83).

Although such miseries were not unusual in Victorian childhoods
(Houghton, 1957, pp. 63–64), Stevenson seems to have been rendered particularly vulnerable through his innate hypersensitivity,
precocious imagination, and very real fear of imminent death. His
frequent fevers could have further attenuated a sometimes shaky
grasp of the boundary between reality and fantasy. When, in his delir-
ium, "the room swelled and shrank" and common objects "now
loomed up instant to the bigness of a church, and now drew away
into a horror of infinite distance and infinite littleness," he himself
seems to have swelled and shrunk inversely, so that he was either "a
poor little devil" standing "before the Great White Throne" or else
was called on "to swallow the populous world, and awoke screaming
with the horror of the thought" (1888a, p. 199). Evidently, any retal-
iatory aggression against the seemingly unpredictable and irrational,
yet constantly rationalized, threats of the object world would be
swiftly met with annihilation and endless torment. Such repeated
confusions must surely have contributed to a fragility in Stevenson's
sense of self, to a profound mistrust of appearances, and a resulting
lifelong sense of uncanny duality (cf. Bach, 1975). "I seem to have
been born with a sentiment of something moving in things, of an infinite attraction and horror coupled" (G. Balfour, 1901, vol. 1, p. 51).
Not surprisingly, the future author appears to have resorted early to
the use of his phenomenal imaginative gifts in the service of escape
and self-consolation. Once, when put in the corner for some mis-
deed, he "never came out" when the time was up, and when asked by

Cummy to explain, he replied, "I was just telling myself a story!" (Guthrie, 1913, p. 23).

In different ways all three parental adults fostered Stevenson's precocious literary talent. His mother recorded many curious sayings of his infancy and when he was six wrote down to his dictation a history of Moses that won a family prize (G. Balfour, 1901, vol. 1, p. 39). Thomas Stevenson, who largely shared Cummy's religious views, recorded with approval at least one of the religious "songstries" that his son would chant to himself before falling asleep at night, a proto-double story about the angel who turned into the Devil and thereby caused the Fall of Man (1880a, p. 153; G. Balfour, 1901, vol. 1, p. 32). He was also the only one who could calm his son's night terrors "by means of childish talk and reproducing aimless conversations with the guard or driver of a mail coach, until he had my mind disengaged from the causes of my panic" (1880a, p. 150). Thomas Stevenson all his life had eased his own sleepless nights by making up tales of adventure (1894, p. 196), and his son adopted the same method. When not in the grip of religious fervor, the boy at night told himself "romances" of "journeys and Homeric battles" in which he played the hero, tales that always bore some ambivalent relation to women but always ended in his own death (1880a, p. 155). This guilty atonement for Oedipal wishes was reinforced by religious strictures on the spiritual perils of romance.

Cummy too had nurtured the young Stevenson's literary gift through her command of Scots dialect and her spirited readings of the Bible and the stories of the covenanting martyrs, but her approach to secular literature was ambivalent. When he was five she read him a serial about a Crimean war soldier but feared that "from some superfluity of love affairs" it would "turn out 'a regular novel.'" That night, after pain in his side and a clear vision of Hell, he concluded it must be a punishment for worldliness and resolved to read no more of *The Soldier of Fortune* (1880a, p. 154).

One might speculate that the young Stevenson found the bond with his outwardly reassuring, masculine father to be a bulwark against the confusions aroused in him by his two mothers, the one in denial of evil, the other seductively insistent on it. Thomas Stevenson was often absent on business trips, however, leaving his son at the mercy of these two adoring adult women, one of whom at least was passionate, sexually deprived and perhaps unconsciously seeking her major emotional gratification from her fragile charge. The boy's need for his father to calm his night terrors sounds akin to what has been described as father hunger, invoked as a defense against precocious oedipal longings and sadistic conflicts (Herzog, 1980). Thomas, for his part, may well have found in his imaginative offspring an irresistible echo of his own youthful, prank-playing, and romantic self, as well as the frightening specter of his eight lost siblings. Weighed down by intermittent gloom, anxiety, and self-doubt, and passionate in his attachments, he needed his son to reassure him against further object loss and to fulfill all sides of his own divided nature: family and religious duty, professional accomplishment and, possibly less consciously, crushed literary aspirations.

The loneliness that Stevenson felt growing up with these three powerful adults was not relieved by much sustained peer contact. Because of his frequent illnesses he was educated more at home than at school, and even when he went to school his father was always ready to withdraw him in order to send him with his mother for lengthy periods to various health resorts. Perhaps because of his overprotection, Stevenson did not enjoy his school experiences, which were sometimes marred by cruel teasing from other pupils. His best times were the idyllic summers he spent playing with his numerous maternal cousins at his grandfather's manse in Colinton, with its river, woods, and mills, where he was able to take the lead in endless games of make-believe (1880a, pp. 151–53; 1887b). His own need for dominance sometimes verged on the sadistic, as when, in trading small "curiosities" with his cousins, he insisted on inflicting "whacks" on the hand with a strap or cane in exchange. He also terrified his younger cousins by shutting them up in a dark room with a magic lantern (worked by strings pulled under the door) and making them see "ghosts" (Hammerton, 1907, pp. 12–13; Furnas, 1951, pp. 17–19). This actually resembled a scary game he played with himself, when he would parade in front of the mirror in the dark drawing room with a white towel over his head and a taper in his hand, intoning the dirge from Scott's *Ivanhoe,* until the sight of his own face would make him flee in terror to the gaslit lobby (*Letters,* Vol. 3, p. 199; Scott, 1820, p. 468).

Stevenson's childish imagination was fed in a happier way by his older, paternal cousin, Robert Alan Mowbray Stevenson, the son of his reclusive uncle Alan, who introduced him to the joys of coloring the cutout figures of Skelt's toy theaters (Stevenson, 1884a). "Bob" proved to be his first dependable ally against the adult world of guilt and gloom, and a major prototype of the more positive male double figures who populate his fiction.

Stevenson appears to have enjoyed increasing closeness with his father in early puberty, starting with extended family trips abroad in

1862 and 1863, necessitated this time by Thomas's allegedly poor health as well as that of his wife (*Letters,* Vol. 1, p. 86; Calder, 1980, p. 43). (It seems likely, however, given Thomas's solid physique and depressive tendencies, that his ailments had an emotional origin, perhaps related to greatly increased responsibilities and worries about his brother Alan's relentless decline.) In 1863 Thomas also introduced his son to his future professional realm when they went alone together on a tour of the Fife lighthouses. For Stevenson the trip was enthralling because it was his "first journey . . . without the help of petticoats" (1888b, p. 10), and also because it enabled him to see the sites of some memorable and bloody chapters in the history of the Covenanting movement of the seventeenth century. He was already writing with a passion, mostly adventures and Scott-like romances, but when he attempted a novel about the rebellious Covenanters his father requested him instead to write a brief history of the movement and had it published anonymously, in 1866, as *The Pentland Rising* (Furnas, 1951, p. 33). Thomas soon tried to remove the work from circulation, however, by buying up as many copies as possible (G. Balfour, 1901, Vol. 1, pp. 67–68). This puzzling episode seems evidence of both pride and ambivalence over his son's literary efforts, as well as a need to control them.

Adolescence: The First Rift

When Stevenson entered Edinburgh University in 1867, at the age of almost 17, it was assumed that he would study for the family profession, a decision that was reinforced in the summer of 1868 when he was sent to gain first-hand experience of the engineer's life at the harbor works at Wick, in the bleak far north of Scotland. This marked a subtle turning point in the relationship between father and son. Thomas Stevenson was then just 50, at the height of his powers, and embarked upon the major project of his career, the lighthouse of Dhu Heartach, whose successful completion in 1872 would finally put him on a par with his two older brothers. At Wick he had undertaken a no less herculean but ultimately doomed struggle to erect a massive harbor and breakwater (Stevenson, 1887a, p. 66; Bathurst, 1999, pp. 223–233). Although the young Stevenson was exhilarated by the rough outdoor life, he showed no aspiration to take up his father's lifelong fight against the elements. On the contrary, he spent his solitary nights scribbling frantically in verse and prose, in a "morbid frame of mind" stemming from "an insane lust after human approbation," as he confided shamefacedly to Bob in Cambridge (*Let-*

ters, Vol. 1, p. 151). Back in Edinburgh his depression continued, as it became apparent from the half-hearted and erratic manner in which he pursued his studies, that his desire for literary fame was bound to collide with his father's wishes. His daily life, he claimed, was one of "repression from beginning to end," enlivened only by his taking refuge in literature (including the iconoclastic verse of Swinburne and Whitman) and in sedulous efforts to learn from the authors he admired (*Letters,* Vol. 1, p. 169; Stevenson, 1884b, p. 21; 1887c, p. 29).

Stevenson's "attacks of morbid melancholy" (*Letters,* Vol. 1, p. 192) seem to have been relieved somewhat in 1871 after he obtained the momentous concession from his father that he might give up engineering for a degree in law. They were lightened even more by Bob's return from Cambridge and by the acquisition of a group of lively and like-minded friends. Living at home and kept very short of cash by his father, Stevenson increasingly led two lives, one of respectable dinner and tea parties organized by his parents; the other, in the guise of an awkward, shabbily dressed, somewhat affected Bohemian, of high-spirited practical jokes and lowlife dissipations among the sordid public houses and prostitutes of the city. His nightmare of the double life (1888a, pp. 200–201) must reflect the guilty conflicts that these experiences engendered, conflicts that were aggravated, following much reading and discussion of authors like Herbert Spencer, by his increasing independent-mindedness in matters of religion.

The famous quarrel of father and son over religious belief is usually portrayed as if it erupted spontaneously in late January 1873 on Thomas Stevenson's discovery of the mysterious society founded by Stevenson and a few of his closest friends, among whose tenets was that its members were not to be bound by the doctrines of the Established Church (*Letters,* Vol. 1, p. 225n). A close reading of his letters in the period immediately before this suggests, however, that Stevenson, in his desperate longing to be honest about his aims in life, may have semi-consciously provoked the confrontation. To Bob in October 1872 he wrote: "kind and even sympathetic as my father has shown himself, the limits of his tolerance are so near to me, that I am always lingering about the landmark to pass which is to sour his half-hearted patience into petty persecution" (pp. 254–255). By the end of 1872 he was severely depressed, describing himself as "in a hell of a state—nerves, mind and body" (p. 262). On a dismal trip to Great Malvern with his mother in January 1873, he wrote to a friend of his utter demoralization and misery, compounded by an impotence to think and write that he jokingly ascribed to the rain: "My brain is just like a wet sponge: soft, pulpy, and lying spread out, flat and flaccid, over my eyes" (pp. 270–271).

This misery seems to have made Stevenson feel that he had nothing to lose by speaking out about his agnosticism when his father finally questioned him about his beliefs, but the consequences were incalculable. "I really hate all lying so much now—a new-found honesty that has somehow come out of my late illness—that I could not so much as hesitate at the time; but if I had foreseen the real Hell of everything since, I think I should have lied as I have done so often before" (*Letters,* Vol. 1, p. 273). In his childhood he had been punished for actual or presumed lying; now he was to be tortured for telling the truth. Clearly the conflict was about more than religion. Only the previous month, Thomas Stevenson's illusion of victory in his prolonged battles with the sea had been shattered by the tremendous storm that washed away the entire harbor of Wick and invalidated a lifetime's study of the force of waves (Bathurst, 1999, p. 231). Now, when he declared to his son, "You have rendered my whole life a failure," it appears that even the remnants of his self-regard were washed away by this further blow to his hopes for his heir, no longer an engineer and now not even a Christian. Stevenson's own illusions were likewise shattered. Not only was his kindly if melancholy father suddenly unmasked as the most terrifying of ogres, but, to his amazement, his adored mother compounded the blow by siding unhesitatingly with his father. Both parents were "ill," silent, and grim, and the house was hushed as if in mourning (*Letters,* Vol. 1, pp. 273–274).

This tense and miserable situation continued throughout the year, in spite of Thomas's subsequent efforts to displace the blame for his son's beliefs onto the corrupting influence of Bob. The father, in a state of rageful depression, overwhelmed his son with threats and reproaches. He even regretted that he had ever married and begotten a child and wished his son dead sooner than live as a threat to the faith of other young men and to the ruin of other families. But just as the father was too needy of his son to be able to carry out his menaces, the son was too overwhelmed with guilt for having "damned the happiness" of his parents, and by his fundamental attachment to his father, to be capable of whole-hearted revolt. "If I could only cease to like him, I could pull through with a good heart; but it is really insupportable to see his emotion—an impotent emotion . . . his sort of half threats of turning me out" (*Letters,* Vol. 1, p. 312). While the mother blew intermittently warm and cold, the stalemate told on both father and son: "this is just a mere trial of nervous strength between us. The weakest will die first, that is all. And I don't know whether to wish for the one alternative or the other. Both seem horrible" (p. 316). Stevenson's only recourse was cautious but futile attempts at "rational" discussion (p. 312), or else tearful placation (p. 345). Yet he resisted Bob's urgings that he break with his parents with the feeble excuse that they had just given him a better room for a study (p. 329). Even during calmer moments it was always like "a pic-nic on a volcano" (p. 325). As the year wore on, Stevenson's depression increased, as did his worries about his father's health (p. 341). His weight, never adequate for his 5'10" height, had dropped to 118 pounds (p. 301), and he was prey to weakness, neuralgia, and nervous tics (pp. 341–343).

That Stevenson survived and eventually escaped this protracted agony was probably due to his having formed (during a visit to England that summer) a powerful attachment to a married woman. Frances (Fanny) Sitwell was twelve years older than Stevenson, with an estranged husband, a young son, and a discreet and patient admirer, the art historian Sidney Colvin, whom she much later married. Despite her sexual unavailability, she readily entered into a romantically tinged friendship with Stevenson, who, back in Edinburgh, poured out his troubles to her in long, revealing, and often impassioned letters. Their correspondence seems to have functioned rather like psychotherapy, giving him the courage to endure the conflict and to find a partial way out. In late October 1873 he left secretly for London, with some thought of taking the preliminary exams for the English Bar. He arrived in such a state of "nervous exhaustion" that Mrs. Sitwell and Colvin (by now his close friend and mentor) sent him to the fashionable physician, Dr. Andrew Clark, who was perceptive about the relationship between depression and illness (as shown by his successful treatment of Charles Darwin [Bowlby, 1990, p. 413]). Dr. Clark ordered his patient to the south of France for a rest cure and, to Stevenson's relief, absolutely forbade his mother to accompany him.

In the more congenial climate of Menton, Stevenson slowly recovered from his physical prostration and emotional misery. To his uncomprehending father he wrote an impassioned plea for greater liberty, especially in financial matters, yet he remained incapable of acknowledging the depths of his own anger. To Fanny Sitwell he noted: "It is strange how perfectly I have got over all my feelings of anger to them; no, I never did feel angry . . . now I am away. I keep perhaps a little corner of anger against my mother for having been rude to you" (*Letters*, Vol. 1, p. 379). To another correspondent he blamed himself for his father's "illness" during that time and excused his parents' behavior by saying that they had no idea how ill he himself was (pp. 426–427). Evidently he saved himself through his "own favourite gospel of cheerfulness" (p. 369), verging as it did on denial, through his correspondence with Mrs. Sitwell, and through another romantic friendship with an older woman, a Russian, Mme. Garschine (who also had a young child and an estranged husband).

Stevenson resisted parental pleas to return home and even hatched a plan to go to Göttingen to study law, which was aborted not by his parents' direct prohibition but by the guilty "objections" of his own body (*Letters,* Vol. 1, p. 504). On falling ill in Paris, he concluded in April 1874 that he "must give up the game for the present" and "crawl very cautiously home," albeit with a face contorted by a nervous "tic" into a "hideous damned-soul mask of bitterness and pain" (p. 501). His only consolation was: "Going home not very well is an astonishing good hold for me; I shall simply be a prince" (p. 504). Thus he crawled back to finish his legal studies in Edinburgh and to a seeming reconciliation with his parents, including some financial concessions. Beneath this remained deep rifts and a shifting balance of power.

To assuage his misery in captivity Stevenson threw himself into writing and fostering his literary connections in London. To Fanny Sitwell he wrote repeatedly of his unhappiness and his ambivalence towards his parents, who now sought to win him with kindness: "each parent is one wing of the infernal portals and . . . with smiling faces, they are closing fatally upon my future happiness. That's a lie, of course" (*Letters,* Vol. 2, pp. 8–9). His inability to achieve any inner emancipation from them is dramatized in a brief and bitter fable, "The House of Eld" (1896), probably written that summer. Its hero runs away in a quest to get rid of the customary fetter that has been riveted to his ulcerated right ankle since infancy. After he uses a magical heathen sword to slay an evil enchanter in the guises of his pious but friendly uncle, his angry father, and his reproachful mother, the gyve falls off his leg. He then returns home with foreboding, only to find all his fellow-countrymen now wearing their fetters on the left leg instead of the right, and his family slain, "his father pierced through the heart, and his mother cloven through the midst." Bereft and weeping, he is deprived, unlike Oedipus, of even the brief semblance of a victory. To Stevenson's own surprise, his anger seeped into his fiction writing of this period. He did not understand why his stories were "always so nasty," one of them, about a nurse, "almost a crime against humanity" (*Letters,* Vol. 2, pp. 51, 53). In the following years we also hear of sudden rages that earned him the family nickname "The Old Man Virulent." These outbursts, such as slapping a Frenchman who was verbally abusing the British, were usually directed against anonymous strangers or authority figures (Furnas, 1951, p. 116).

His parents by now feared more than ever that they were losing him (witness his mother's hysterics when he made even a short trip to London [*Letters*, Vol. 2, pp. 3, 30]). Thomas Stevenson by the end of 1874 was suffering severe mood swings, between irritability and elation, that worsened into "a miserable state of depression and nervousness" and led his son to "fear some of the family ailments" (pp. 50, 53, 95). Although his doctor said there was "no fear of anything permanent or organic," Thomas's enraged threats to disinherit his son and his abuse of his wife before the servants shook Stevenson badly. He had never felt "so utterly adrift" in his life, at a loss until his father should "recover or die" (pp. 97–98). To make matters worse, his relationship with Fanny Sitwell was changing, on her initiative, from quasi lovers to that of mother and son. Stevenson consoled himself with the reflection that she could now be more of a mother to him than his own had been, with her unswerving loyalty to his father: "For my mother is my father's wife . . . the children of lovers are orphans" (p. 103).

Stevenson's adolescent conflict continued through his twenties, not merely because of financial dependence, but because of his inability to negotiate the process of internal separation from primary objects. The confusing and often smothering presence of his two mothers in childhood left him overly dependent on a defensive, quasi maternal bonding with his pre-oedipal father, which he was unable to surmount in his teens in part perhaps because of his father's own repressed father hunger and desperate fear of object loss (cf. Blos, 1984), as well as a narcissistic need for mirroring from his son. Thus Stevenson's natural moves towards separation were checked by his father's ensuing depression and illness (in which his possessive mother offered him little real support) and led to severe depressive episodes and further illnesses of his own. In order to preserve his increasingly unstable father as a good object Stevenson had to repress his own aggression (tabooed in any case by the strictures of his religious upbringing) and evade the normal work of adolescent de-idealization. It was easy for him to find companionship and even surrogate fathers in his relations with other males (like Colvin, or the poet and later editor, W. E. Henley, or his engineering professor, Fleeming Jenkin). But Stevenson evidently had difficulty attaching to women of his own age and class. The older, ambiguously married, mothers he was drawn to offered both the comforts of adoption and the illusion of oedipal victory. Significantly, Stevenson very early renounced the idea of having children of his own, despite his professed longing for them. Like his father, he felt vulnerable to their physical or emotional loss (even their hatred), and also evidenced some resentment of them as rivals (*Letters*, Vol. 2, pp. 116, 330; Vol. 3, p. 62).

THE SECOND RIFT: FLIGHT, MARRIAGE AND RECONCILIATION

The later 1870s found Stevenson at an impasse. Despite his rapid abandonment of the legal profession and his intense devotion to his writing, he still lacked clear direction in both work and life. This started to change only after the summer of 1876, which he spent at the artists' colony in Grez, France. There he met, through Bob, the *femme fatale* of his life. This was Frances (Fanny) Osbourne, a 36-year-old American woman with a teenage daughter and a young son. This second Fanny, after an adventurous life, had left her philandering husband in California in order to study art in France. She was short, dark, intense, dogmatic, and fiercely possessive, and the 25-year-old Stevenson soon fell in love with her, spending time with her in both France and London. His parents seem not to have been greatly worried by the attachment, given her age and marital status, but Stevenson was wretched after her return to California in August 1878. His desperation and his increasing sense of guilty alienation from his parents (cf. *Letters*, Vol. 2, p. 312) led him in August 1879 to stage another secret escape, this time on an emigrant ship bound for New York. The hardships of the trip, especially the long train journey to the West Coast, left him physically and mentally exhausted, in a state of death-like identity confusion: "I had no idea how easy it was to commit suicide. There seems nothing left of me; I died a while ago; I do not know who it is that is travelling" (*Letters*, Vol. 3, p. 8). Equally hard were his anguish and uncertainty, imagining his parents' reactions, and his painful awareness, "for the first time," of how much he loved his father, more than anyone except Fanny (p. 14).

Thomas Stevenson reacted with the same uncomprehending rage with which he had greeted his son's apostasy in 1873. Again, it may have been compounded by a sense of failure in his own career, for in 1877 his defiant efforts to rebuild the harbor at Wick had been annihilated, finally, by another apocalyptic storm (Bathurst, 1999, p. 231). Again he took his son's bid for independence as a personal rejection: "Is it fair that we should be half murdered by his conduct? . . . this sinful, mad business" (*Letters*, Vol. 3, p. 23). Threatening letters and telegrams poured out, using his own alleged illness to try to compel his son's return and even claiming that he would have to move to England in order to escape the disgrace (pp. 25, 38). To outside observers it was not clear "whether father or son is nearer lunacy" (p. 41). Meanwhile, his son, weak, depressed, starved of funds, and uncertain of the prospects of his suit with Fanny Osbourne, had come close to death while rashly camping out in the hills near Monterey. His carelessness of his own life and his immense, unacknowledged anger may be seen in a casual experiment wherein he set light to a dry pine tree to see how it would burn and started a serious forest fire. He had to run for his life, to escape detection and lynching. Shortly afterwards he had another near-escape when shooting a revolver that repeatedly jammed and could have exploded (p. 22; Stevenson, 1880b, pp. 131–133).

Although Stevenson did convince Fanny to divorce her husband and marry him, and his distraught parents ultimately relented and assured him of an income, the hardships of a dreadful, lonely, impoverished winter in San Francisco permanently damaged his health. That his ailment was "consumption" has been assumed but never proven (another possibility is bronchiectasis, consequent on chronic lung disease exacerbated by lifelong chain-smoking [Daiches, 1973, p. 49]). Stevenson's subsequent, lifelong physical fragility was a heavy price to pay for this latest bid for psychological freedom, however. At least this time he had acquired a permanent ally, for his wife, on their return to Scotland in 1880, got along well with his parents, particularly his father, whose tendency to dramatization, depression and doomsaying she shared (cf. *Letters,* Vol. 4, p. 47n).

One by-product of Stevenson's state of health was an inability to tolerate the rigors of Scottish weather, necessitating a retreat to Davos, in Switzerland, for the next two winters. The summer of 1881, however, he spent with his parents, wife, and stepson in the Highlands, in pouring rain but perhaps a more favorable climate in terms of his relationship with his father than at any time in the previous ten years, a climate that fostered the beginning of his most productive period of writing. Thomas was still deeply depressed over his son's abandonment of law and his commitment to literature, but he had evidently resigned himself so as not to lose him (Japp, 1905, pp. 23–24).

Stevenson by now had produced a number of well-regarded essays and short stories, plus two travel books (he suppressed the harrowing record of his journey to America in order to please his father) but nothing of major significance. This summer he worked on a number of fine short stories with Scottish settings but then, partly to amuse his twelve-year-old-stepson, Samuel Lloyd Osbourne, he began to elaborate a series of pirate adventures based on a map he had drawn and colored with Lloyd's paints. This suddenly proved the key to unlock his father's heart. Thomas Stevenson "caught fire at once with all the romance and childishness of his original nature" and, recognizing "something kindred to his own imagination," "set himself actively to collaborate" (Stevenson, 1894, p. xxvii). The tale, which "flowed . . . with singular ease" (p. xxix), was destined to become *Treasure Island.* Women were deliberately excluded from the story, although allusions to a less overt search for hidden sexual treasure may certainly be detected (cf. Kanzer, 1951). The essential theme is a boy's quest for adventure, self-knowledge, and maturity in the wake of his father's death, a quest that takes place in an all-male world of good and bad surrogate fathers whose true characters are not immediately apparent. Jim's survival depends on his ability to learn to read these men, above all the original hero and dominant paternal figure of the book, the powerful, mutilated, charming, cruel, utterly hypocritical Long John Silver. Silver was consciously based on Stevenson's rambunctious young literary friend, W. E. Henley, who had lost a leg to tuberculosis, but he is described as a large, suave, clean-shaven man of 50 whose dearest aspiration is to retire and become a gentleman (Stevenson, 1883, pp. 48, 67). His ambiguity and attractiveness, as well as his and Jim's mutual fondness, which survives Silver's murderous designs, may reflect something of Stevenson's own struggles to preserve his mercurial yet socially conventional father as a good object through all his outbursts of murderous-seeming rage (cf. Fowler, 1979, pp. 110–115).

From October 1882 there followed a period which Stevenson was later to call the one happy time of his life, when he and Fanny settled, again on doctor's orders, in his beloved south of France (*Letters,* Vol. 4, p. 79). Here he was safe from parental intrusion (although relying on parental support), and his health gradually improved. In the spirit of relief and reconciliation that evidently resulted, he worked on the collection of poetry that was to become *A Child's Garden of Verses.* This he dedicated to Cummy, "My second Mother, my first Wife, the angel of my infant life," in idealized gratitude for her devoted efforts to make his childhood happy (p. 76). In writing it he deliberately ignored the more painful aspects of his childhood, "that other 'land of counterpane,'" on the theory that it was fruitless to "renew these sorrows" (*Letters,* Vol. 5, p. 97). This was far from the spirit in which (in San Francisco during his estrangement from his parents) he had written the memoir (1880a) that gives the frankest account of his childhood torments, which in 1885 he ordered should never be published, lest it "be a shame" to him (*Letters*, Vol. 5, p. 131).

FATHER AND SON: ILLNESS AND DECLINE

This state of relative equilibrium and tranquility was soon upset, however. A major factor was certainly the insidious, progressive decline that began to be apparent in Thomas Stevenson from around early 1883. He had been preoccupied with the problems of his surviving brother, David, who was "subject to absurd mental hallucinations" and was causing trouble in the firm (*Letters*, Vol. 4, p. 48n), but he himself was increasingly depressed (pp. 85–86). Stevenson worried that the machinations of David and his two sons might force his father to retire. At the alarming prospect of having to become self-supporting, he resolved to be less of a financial burden (difficult, in view of his spendthrift habits and the modest returns from his writing), and, above all, not to return to England until he had recovered his health (pp. 94–95, 100). Thomas, meanwhile, was driven to consult Dr. Andrew Clark in London, who prescribed a dietary regimen, including a reduction in whisky consumption, but apparently to no avail (pp. 103n, 122, 134). By the summer of 1883, when he and his wife visited Stevenson and Fanny in France, his mind seemed (in retrospect) to be failing. He was apt to launch into wild monologues on "religion, death and eternity" that infected everyone with his gloom, although he could pull himself together when his son appeared and start making jokes or even suggestions for his current work (F. Stevenson, 1924a, p. x). He also began to manifest difficulties in word finding, a serious blow to a man who had always prided himself on his apt use of language (Stevenson, 1887a, p. 70).

At this distance of time, and given the family's reticence, it is impossible to diagnose exactly what ailed him. It has been assumed that it was a case of "progressive cerebral hemorrhage" (Furnas, 1951, p. 235) or "a gradual decline into senility" (Mehew, 1999). Another possibility, given the extreme mood and (later) behavioral aberrations, as well as language impairment with no initial mention of memory deficit, is frontal lobe dementia (Jutagir, 1998, p. 772; 1999). Thomas's own awareness of his cognitive problems very likely exacerbated his existing vulnerability to severe depression, but the dementia itself would have accelerated a process of ego disintegration and breakdown of defenses. What is not clear is how soon the family, and especially Stevenson himself (who was not in daily contact with his father, and whose mother tended to denial) recognized that Thomas's condition represented, not just an exacerbation of the problems of the previous ten years, but the beginning of an altogether different kind of decline.

Throughout 1883 Stevenson anxiously monitored his father's state of health, snatching eagerly at any report of improvement and concealing setbacks in his own health out of concern for the effect on his father (*Letters,* Vol. 4, pp. 185, 205). By the end of the year a tone of reproach crept in, as he lectured his father on his duty to count his blessings and be as happy as possible for the sake of others (pp. 221, 224). Thomas evidently refused to be consoled, evoking an exasperated if still humorous protest from Stevenson to his mother, over his father's "gallowsworthy" gloom: "I give my father up . . . I don't want no such a parent. This is not the man for my money" (p. 225). Behind these protests one may sense a profound unease, probably reflecting the fact that Stevenson's own physical and emotional health (manifested all too often in an inability to work) had long been linked to his father's. The worst crises of his adult life had paralleled their conflicts and his father's breakdowns; witness his feeling of terror and despair in the winter of 1874–75, when his father seemed "really *mad*" and he himself felt "utterly adrift" (*Letters,* Vol. 2, p. 97). His case is actually reminiscent of that of Dr. Clark's other famous patient, Charles Darwin, whose severe illness and depression in the late 1840s seem to have been directly related to the terminal illness and death of Darwin *père* (Bowlby, 1990, pp. 280–283).

In fact, Stevenson's physical health was beginning to decline again. Early in 1884 he caught a cold which turned to serious pulmonary illness, with fever and hemorrhage. Throughout the spring he was ill and unable to work much and was also plagued by eye infections that at times prevented him from reading or writing. He fought off severe depression as he contemplated the renewed prospect of a premature demise that would cheat him of his writing, which he recognized as more essential to him that anything else in life, even his relationship with his wife: "I am unready for death, because I hate to leave [my art]. . . . I *am* not but in my art: it is me; I am the body of it merely" (*Letters,* Vol. 4, pp. 252–253). His wife too feared for his life and agonized over how to deal with his parents, resentful of their initial dismissal of their son's problems as nerves, then of their hysterical reactions and attempted interference with his treatment. Above all, she feared the emotional impact of all three on each other, worrying at first that "if Louis died it would kill his father" (pp. 236–237), then that his mother would come and kill him with "excitement" or that his father would upset him by "worry[ing] himself ill" (pp. 289–294). By the summer of 1884 Stevenson was driven back to England to seek medical advice, which was preponderantly in favor of his returning to Switzerland (*Letters,* Vol. 5, pp. 1–3). Now, however, his father's health gave him a reason to break his earlier resolve not to return to live in England, and he chose to settle in the south coast health resort of Bournemouth (p. 14; Furnas, 1951, pp. 234–235).

The three years he spent there were the worst in Stevenson's life, physically and emotionally. He felt under immense pressure, both from his illness (which by November left him "nearly smashed altogether; fever and chills, with really very considerable suffering") and its effects on his ability to work (*Letters,* Vol. 5, p. 23). Stevenson was never able to live economically, and his financial anxieties were augmented, whether rationally or not, by his worries about his father, leading him to renew his never very successful efforts to earn money through theatrical collaboration with the ambitious and impecunious Henley. His wife, on whom he so depended, was herself apt to fall ill as a result of her anxieties about him (pp. 25, 29), and his father, though still working, continued to be depressed, ill, and argumentative. He upset Stevenson by criticizing his and Henley's latest play, Admiral Guinea, on religious and moral grounds, asserting that the "storm of indignant criticism" it would arouse on performance would be more than he could bear in his current state of poor health (ibid., pp. 19–20). Throughout this period Stevenson seems to have made heroic efforts to encourage and sustain his father, whose frequent visits could be trying (p. 120). Some denial is evident in his insistence that Thomas stand for election as president of the Royal Society of Edinburgh, an office that his father was reluctant to assume out of a well-justified fear that he would be incapable of doing the work (pp. 29, 68–69). In the spring of 1885 Stevenson attempted to stimulate his father's interest in a new project, another story of a boy's quest following his father's death, which was eventually to become *Kidnapped* (p. 94). Perhaps he hoped that it would revive his father's spirits as *Treasure Island* had done, but to no avail. At the same time, Stevenson's own illness and constant need for money reinforced his sense of dependence, both material and emotional, on his father. In March 1885, he wrote: "It is fortunate for me I have a father, or I should long ago have died; but the opportunity of the aid makes the necessity none the more welcome" (p. 91). Later he said: "I fall on my feet; but . . . the best part of my legs seems to be my father" (p. 109).

Throughout 1885 it must have been apparent that Thomas Stevenson was getting worse, much as the family might struggle to deny it. As late as November his wife, grasping at the doctor's reassurances, was insisting that there was nothing wrong with him but "*brain fag* and *hypochondria*" (*Letters*, Vol. 5, p. 145n). Stevenson's own physical and emotional state was likewise under constant siege. In June that year he was shocked by the sudden, premature death of his former engineering professor, Fleeming Jenkin, who had long been a good friend and mentor to him. Then, in September he fell extremely ill, with severe hemorrhage, after a visit to Thomas Hardy. Although he made desperate efforts to remain cheerful, his persistent difficulty in working made him fear that "his brain was in a condition of dry rot" and would never produce again (Masson, 1922, p. 213). His grim jokes, as when he once signed himself "The pale wreck, The spectral phantom, The abhorred miscarriage" (*Letters*, Vol. 5, p. 37), began to have the ring of unconscious truth. The strains of this double life must have been extreme. Sidney Colvin was one of the few who ever saw him drop the mask. One day when Colvin came upon him unexpectedly in the garden, Stevenson "turned round upon me a face such as I never saw on him save that once—a face of utter despondency, nay tragedy, upon which seemed stamped for one concentrated moment the expression of all he had ever had, or might yet have, in life to suffer or to renounce" (Colvin, 1921, p. 143).

It was in this context, around the beginning of October 1885, that Stevenson, consumed with the idea of writing a "shilling shocker" that might relieve his financial worries, dreamed the nightmare that was to become *Jekyll and Hyde* (Stevenson, 1888a, p. 208; Masson, 1922, p. 213). This sudden eruption from the unconscious evidently broke through the "strange condition of collapse" that had smothered him for months "like the vast, vague feather-bed of an obsession" (*Letters*, Vol. 5, p. 136), and had semi-paralyzed his efforts to work. Fanny described him as "possessed" by the story and intolerant of any interruptions (p. 128n), and though her claim that he wrote two complete, separate drafts in six days during a period of serious illness may be exaggerated, we have Stevenson's own word that it was "conceived, re-written, re-re-written, and printed inside ten weeks" in "white hot haste" (p. 216; Swearingen, 1980, pp. 98–100). He attributed the haste to the need to get the story on the market in time for the Christmas season, but his excitement surely had some deeper cause, related to the sudden sense of relief and release it gave him. To Colvin he wrote of it with almost manic glee, in doggerel verse reminiscent of a music hall song: "I am pouring forth a penny (12 penny) dreadful; it is dam dreadful . . . they call it Dr Jekyll, but they also call it Mr Hyde, Mr Hyde. I seem to bloom by nature—oh, by nature into song; but for all my tale is silly it shall not be very long." (*Letters,* Vol. 5, pp. 128–129).

Stevenson's state of exhilaration and happiness on finishing the work was intense enough to impress observers like his stepson (Osbourne, 1924, p. xi). It may not have lasted, but some sense of creative freedom did, resulting in the rapid production of another double story, "Olalla" (also based on a dream), and the revision and publication of an earlier one, "Markheim" (seemingly influenced by Dostoevsky's *Crime and Punishment*). Why he was so overtly preoccupied with the double theme at this time in his life is something that Stevenson never explained. His wife later claimed that he had been thinking of the career of the notorious Deacon Brodie, a respected Edinburgh cabinet maker who was hanged for burglary, and about whom he and Henley had written their first play, *Deacon Brodie, or, The Double Life* (1879–80). She also noted that he had been "deeply impressed by a paper in a French scientific journal that he read on sub-consciousness" (F. Stevenson, 1924b, p. xvi). Beyond this, it is likely that his own "sub-consciousness" was increasingly overwhelmed by the anxiety of his own and his father's illnesses. Their shared fears, perhaps not yet admitted, that there was some more sinister process at work both undermining and disintegrating the personality of Thomas Stevenson, must have stirred up in the son conflicts that were still close to the surface and only precariously resolved. Interestingly, in a letter to his father written at the point when the manuscript version of *Jekyll and Hyde* was finished and sent to the printers, Stevenson was for once able to acknowledge directly, albeit in a humorous way, his ambivalence toward his father. Responding to his wife's criticisms of his conduct as a son, he admitted to "a most unkind reticence, which hung on me then, and I confess still hangs on me now, when I try to assure you that I do love you. Ever your bad son Robert Louis Stevenson" (*Letters,* Vol. 5, p. 145).

"POLAR TWINS" STRUGGLING IN "THE AGONIZED WOMB OF CONSCIOUSNESS"

On its publication, in January 1886, *Jekyll and Hyde* rapidly made its author famous. If it touched a nerve in the public, with its exploration of "the recesses of human nature" (Maixner, 1981, p. 204), it was also of profound emotional significance to Stevenson himself. As he explained to his friend Will Low, this "gothic gnome . . . came out of a deep mine, where he guards the fountain of tears" (*Letters,* Vol. 5,

p. 163). By the time of the nightmare it must have been at least sub-liminally apparent to Stevenson that his father, long subject to alarm-ing mood swings that at times could seem like the eruption of an alien personality, was now in the grip of something much more seri-ous. Whatever the underlying brain pathology, it must further have undermined Thomas Stevenson's rigid but precarious defenses and made him seem even more uncannily "other." (It is striking how of-ten Stevenson in his letters refers to his father, with relief or dismay, as being "like" or "unlike" himself.) That Henry Jekyll is described as having started to go "wrong in mind" more than ten years before Ut-terson's first encounter with Hyde (1886, p. 15) may not be casual, given that Thomas's severe depressions started in 1873, ten years before the initial onset of his dementia. As Feigelson (1993) has pointed out, a brain-injured individual whose familiar personality is intermittently dying tends to challenge object constancy in his closest relatives, giving the uncanny impression of being increasingly haunted by a ghostly—and ghastly—revenant.

At the outset Jekyll is portrayed as healthy and prosperous, "a large, well-made, smooth-faced man of fifty, with something of a sly-ish cast perhaps, but every mark of capacity and kindness" (1886, p. 22). (The description echoes that of Long John Silver, also fifty, and might also, except for the slyness, fit Thomas Stevenson, who at fifty was at the high watermark of his career and of his relationship with his son.) Jekyll's problem appears to be an external one: he is being persecuted by a younger man, possibly an illegitimate son or former homosexual lover, who gives an indefinably unpleasant im-pression: "something wrong . . . something displeasing . . . downright detestable . . . giving a strong feeling of deformity" (p. 12). As time wears on, however, Jekyll appears sick and depressed. Only at the end, through his posthumous confession, is it learned that the ill-favored stranger, with his irrational rages and "malign and villainous acts," is actually an inextricable and ever more dominant part of Jekyll himself: "an insurgent horror . . . knit to him closer than a wife, . . . caged in his flesh." Hyde, for all his "energy of life," has become for Jekyll something dead and shapeless, which shockingly "usurp[s] the offices of life" (pp. 74–75). The change is no longer temporary and voluntary but increasingly out of Jekyll's control, so that by the end there is a dizzying confusion of "I" and "he" as the two personali-ties merge, even as they struggle for separate survival. Finally, Jekyll disappears, subsumed by Hyde, who can escape only in death.

If the portrait of Jekyll reflects Stevenson's horror at witnessing his father's gradual possession and deathly transformation by a malign and sinister Other, the multiple doublings of the story (especially the intermittently checked but ever more violent growth of Hyde) may have to do, in a more profound way, with an unconscious regression and feared loss of control in Stevenson himself. This was more than the regression typical of survivors of the brain-injured, who often project their anger and guilty wishes for the victim's death on to a monstrous, persecutory Doppelgänger (Feigelson, 1993). Stevenson since adolescence was trapped by his unconscious need to maintain an ideal, internalized father image in the face of all disconfirmation and to protect his father from any direct expression of his own rage (his fictional portrayals of father figures as absent, ineffectual, treacherous, or outright murderous may have been his only outlet). When these defenses were challenged by his developmental needs and by his father's inability to understand or accept them, one recourse was to fall ill, mentally or physically; another was actual flight, but that option was foreclosed during the prolonged crisis of the mid-1880s. His father's mounting loss of control must have evoked in Stevenson not only the terror of their earlier conflicts, but also a corresponding rage that he had always been forced to deny and to control in himself.

In mid-1885, as Stevenson struggled to hold himself together (avoiding, unlike in 1873, any open allusion to the possibility of his father's death), his defenses were further weakened, first by the sudden death of Fleeming Jenkin, then by the severe hemorrhage he suffered in September. His "mad" and irrational behavior during this episode was attributed by Fanny to his treatment with ergotine (*Letters*, Vol. 5, p. 126), but one wonders if it was also an expression of intolerable mental conflict, as indeed his prolonged sense of creative sterility and at times terrifying incapacity to work must have been. Unconsciously, it may have seemed to Stevenson that his overpowering need to develop his gift as a writer had been the agent of his father's insidious decline over the previous thirteen years. Thus, any further creative spurt that risked expressing the conflicts that gripped him (as in "The House of Eld"), might result in, or require, his father's death and, with it, his own.

It is Stevenson's ambivalence toward his own ruthless, irrepressible genius and the unconscious rage that its frustration engendered that must be emphasized in any reading of *Jekyll and Hyde*. Henry Jekyll's real sin lies not in his youthful "gaiety" and harmless "irregularities" (which "many a man would have even blazoned" [1886, p. 60]), nor even in his wish to enjoy them without endangering his social position, but in his overweening intellectual pride in his "mystic and transcendental" scientific studies and the self-interested "ambition" that corrupts the outcome of his experiment (pp. 60, 64). (One may recall the adolescent Stevenson, in his father's fiftieth summer, lusting "insane[ly]" and guiltily after "human approbation"). With reckless confidence, Jekyll pursues his Faustian quest to dissociate the "polar twins" of his divided nature and find an escape from the "more upright" one, unaware that his discoveries are fatally incomplete and that a terrible price will be exacted (1886, pp. 61–62).

Jekyll at first welcomes, in the mirror, his "younger," "livelier," more "natural and human" self, which enables him at any moment to shed his respectability and "like a schoolboy . . . spring headlong into the sea of liberty" (pp. 63, 65). But it is through the mirror of others' disgust that Jekyll is reminded of the "pure evil" of this liberated self (p. 63), much as Stevenson in his childhood and adolescence was made to mistrust his most natural impulses, including his single-minded drive to fulfill his literary gift. We also catch an echo of his despairing sense, during the quarrels of his early twenties, of always being "nasty," "worse than myself," with his parents: "I am always bad with them, because they always seem to expect me to be not very good; and I am never good because they never seem to see when I am good" (*Letters,* Vol. 2, p. 56). This despair must surely have been exacerbated in the mid-1880s by his father's increasingly rigid intolerance of religious or social impropriety in his work and his wife's insistence that he publish nothing that did not meet his father's standards (*Letters,* Vol. 5, pp. 20, 71). Hyde's behavior at the outset is portrayed not so much as deliberately vicious but as ruthlessly indifferent to anything that might get in his way, like the little girl whom he tramples "calmly over . . . like some damned Juggernaut" (1886, p. 9). Any rage and loathing are engendered in the others who witness his seemingly inhuman acts and conspire to check and punish them. Hyde is likewise indifferent to the "father's interest" shown in him by Jekyll (p. 68), whereas Jekyll fails to understand that it is his own selfish readiness to reject and repudiate his "son," when his own respectable self-image is threatened, that actually fuels Hyde's mounting resentment and cruelty (pp. 65, 68–69). Thus, when "accosted" by a seemingly innocent, "beautiful," self-satisfied old man (the eminent M. P., Sir Danvers Carew), Hyde suddenly breaks out "in a great flame of anger," which is fanned past all control by his victim's hurt reaction, leading him to commit a violently orgiastic and pleasurable murder (pp. 25–26, 69). (The metaphor, like the earlier characterization of Jekyll/Hyde's back street as shining out "like a fire in a forest," recalls the author's fire-setting exploit in California.)

Hyde breaks Carew as "a sick child may break a plaything" (1886, p. 69), but lest this be read too simply as an expression of hostility toward a controlling and disappointing father, it should be noted that the murder victim in Stevenson's original draft was a young man named Lemsome, an "incurable cad" with "suffering eyes" under blue spectacles, who comes to Utterson to inform on Hyde (Veeder 1988b, p. 8; 1988c, p. 24; 1988a, pp. 112–113). This may represent Stevenson's identification with the aggressor against himself as a weak, disappointing, vicious son, who, interestingly, is portrayed with some of the physical characteristics of his own weak sighted, bespectacled, by now adolescent stepson, Lloyd Osbourne. The odiousness and implied hypocrisy of Lemsome, however, are but reflections of the hypocrisy of Henry Jekyll, which Stevenson later described as Jekyll's worst trait (*Letters,* Vol. 6, p. 56), but of which he may have felt himself to be more guilty, with his history of self-protective lying and dissembling, than was the painfully sincere Thomas Stevenson. Hyde's ruthless murder of the patriarchal but seductively mild mannered Carew (who had also, literally, got in his way), is followed by ecstatic triumph and then tearful remorse and self-loathing, as he becomes Jekyll once more and is recalled to the memory of God and his own father.

Hyde's next victim is his prematurely white-haired, erstwhile friend Hastie Lanyon, who has angered Jekyll by condemning his use of his scientific gifts but who brings about his own doom (rapid aging and death) by accepting Hyde's challenge to witness the transformation and with it the proof of Jekyll's genius. A crime (and the gradual cutting off of the means of escape from it) was the essence of Stevenson's original nightmare and perhaps reflects his unconscious fear (or guilty wish) that the full, unfettered use of his powers constituted an aggression that could only destroy his rapidly deteriorating father (as his father had indeed insinuated in his complaining letter of November, 1884 [*Letters,* Vol. 5, p. 20]). Again, Jekyll's moment of ecstatic, reckless, phallic triumph, at the one point in the book where his and Hyde's personalities are clearly united, is followed by remorse and tearful confession. Significantly, Stevenson removed from the printer's copy the description of Jekyll kneeling at Lanyon's feet and covering his hands with caresses, which perhaps sounded too painfully like his own tearful placation of his father in the year of their religious quarrels (Veeder, 1988c, p. 34; *Letters,* Vol. 1, p. 345).

From this point on there is a change. Jekyll is no longer afraid of the gallows, but is "racked by the horror of being Hyde." The transformation possesses him ever more frequently as he leaps from a weak, feverish state "into the possession of a fancy brimming with images of terror, a soul boiling with causeless hatreds, and a body that seemed not strong enough to contain the raging energies of life" (1886, pp. 73–74). Hyde resents Jekyll's hatred of him and retaliates by scrawling blasphemies on his pious books and burning the letters and destroying the portrait of his father. At the same time, bound to Jekyll for survival, "his terror of the gallows drove him continually to commit temporary suicide, and return to his subordinate station of a part instead of a person" (p. 75). A better description of an acute separation conflict would be hard to imagine. But this time, unlike in the double-life nightmare of Stevenson's adolescence, there is no "simple draught" that will restore the protagonist "to the common lot of man" (Stevenson, 1888a, p. 201). The original, perhaps "impure," supply of the salt from which Jekyll's draught is compounded runs out, and the new supply does not work. Jekyll's personality dies (as that of Thomas Stevenson was actually dying), but Hyde's guilt leaves him incapable of profiting from his victory, so that his only recourse is actual suicide. The ultimate, implied victor is Jekyll/Hyde's other double, the seemingly dispassionate, asexual Utterson, the "utter son" who survives to utter the tale and to inherit the doctor's wealth, but who has in fact contributed to his demise through his ruthless attempts to expose the secret and who directly provokes Hyde's death by his violent assault on the cabinet door.

If the effectively castrated Utter-son is seen as representing the emotional price Stevenson felt he had to pay in order to write without losing his father's love (as well as the creative sterility that resulted when he could not), it becomes easier to understand the early preoccupation with male relationships in his work and the lack of interest in overtly oedipal, heterosexual themes. I am obviously not claiming that oedipal conflict did not play a significant role in his life, only that his creative life was so defensively bound up with the mutual identification of father and son and his struggle to extricate himself from it that overtly oedipal material (like the dream of the parricidal son and his beautiful young stepmother) remained for much of his career beyond his artistic ability to deal with.

The true passion in *Jekyll and Hyde* is between men, and it is primal and pregenital. Hyde is "knit to [Jekyll] closer than a wife" (1886, p. 75), and together they form an ambiguously sexed couple who repeatedly give birth, one to the other, in an orally induced, orgiastic transformation that results at first in an anal delivery (Hyde emerges from and returns to the "sinister," "distained" back door whose "story" forms the first chapter). The "smooth-faced" Jekyll, with his "white and comely hands," is at first described in feminized terms, whereas the swarthy, hairy, muscular, "apelike" Hyde is defensively masculine. Later, as their personalities begin to merge, this distinction starts to break down. Hyde, when first pleading with Lanyon, wrestles "against the approaches of the hysteria" and at the end is heard to weep pitifully "like a woman or a lost soul" (pp. 57, 48). (Stevenson was himself prone to fits of hysterical weeping even in adulthood [*Letters,* Vol. 2, p. 186].) Indeed, "the last night," when Utterson and the butler listen with bafflement and horror to the noises from behind the locked door, suggests a perverse, intensely arousing primal-scene fantasy in which one party is finally swallowed up by the other. It induces the simultaneous paroxysm in which Utterson has Poole repeatedly axe the resistant door, just as the panicked Hyde, swamped in Jekyll's clothing, drinks his final draught and is convulsed by death.

If the dynamics are those of a struggle for release from a sexualized, identificatory bond with a quasi-maternal, pre-oedipal father, then it is not surprising that women are relegated to a subordinate role in the story. The few female characters are split into the weak, naïve, innocent, or virginal (like the little girl Hyde tramples on or the sentimental maidservant who faints away at the sight of sexualized violence) or else the older, evil, or vindictive (the "harpies" who try to attack Hyde after he tramples the girl, or Hyde's evil-faced, hypocritical landlady). Here, surely, are some characteristics of the important women in Stevenson's early life: his mother's hysteria and obliviousness to all unpleasantness, and his nurse's relishing of sin in the guise of piety. No help is to be expected of them, for they are all ready to ally with male authority in order to betray and attack the deviant Hyde. (Even Stevenson's wife sided with his father when it came to the propriety of his writings.) The one sexually available woman Hyde meets in his desperate roaming of the city before his meeting with Lanyon, the probable prostitute who offers him a "box of lights" (an obvious sexual metaphor), is struck and repulsed by him as an irrelevant distraction.

It is clear from surviving earlier versions of the text that Stevenson steadily toned down the overtly sexual references in *Jekyll and Hyde,* particularly Jekyll's descriptions of his early moral turpitude, which hinted at masturbation (Veeder, 1988b, p. 11). Critics (like Elwin, 1950, pp. 201–202) have speculated that he was being deferential to his wife's censorship and, through her, his father's, but perhaps he intuitively understood that any mundane listing of sexual aberrations would detract from the uncanny horror and violence of the book and its underlying theme. As Henry James perceptively remarked about Stevenson's "ladies," "they must have played an important part in [Mr Hyde's] development" but the "gruesome tone of the tale is, no doubt, deepened by their absence" (James, 1888, p. 1252). In the sinister world of Jekyll and Hyde, women are irrelevant; they offer no significant attraction and no support. At a deeply unconscious level, they may represent an all-pervasive temptation and overwhelming threat, as represented in the powders supplied by Messrs. Maw, a name with unmistakeably oral and maternal connotations. The crucial salt at first provides the means to release desire but then runs out, entrapping the hapless experimenter (cf. Veeder, 1988a, pp. 128–129; Beattie, 1998, p. 209). Only other men can offer protection against them, but that in turn leads to entrapment in a world of sterile ambition, hypocrisy and sadistic cruelty (cf. Heath, 1986). Stevenson himself, in a letter of 1887, took pains to downplay a purely (hetero) sexual interpretation of the story and focused on the corruption of integrity that results from social conformity (as he evidently felt his own character had been corrupted when young under the pressure of parental needs): "The harm was in Jekyll, because he was a hypocrite—not because he was fond of women. . . . The Hypocrite let out the beast Hyde—who is no more sexual than another, but who is the essence of cruelty and malice, and selfishness and cowardice: and these are the diabolic in man—not this poor wish to have a woman, that they make such a cry about" (*Letters*, Vol. 6, p. 56).

THE RETURN OF THE REPRESSED

The official birth of *Jekyll and Hyde* coincided with a further stage in Thomas Stevenson's decline. On January 16, 1886, Thomas was ordered by his doctors to take three months' rest, which then turned into his permanent retirement from the family business (*Letters*, Vol. 5, p. 183n). This severing of his life's major interest, along with everything it represented in the way of stabilizing routine, may have aggravated both his depression and his cognitive decay. Two days later Stevenson, in an encouraging letters, made the first unmistakable reference to his father's memory lapses (p. 179), and by March he was able to admit openly that the case was desperate: "My father is an old man . . . He has many marks of age, some of childhood; . . . the change (to my eyes) is thoroughly begun; and a very beautiful, simple, honourable, high-spirited and childlike (and childish) man is now in process of deserting us piecemeal" (*Letters*, Vol. 5, p. 236).

Thomas's mood and behavior evidently became more and more

erratic at this time and took a severe toll on his son. One can only speculate as to whether the very success of *Jekyll and Hyde* and the instantaneous fame it brought him could have exacerbated any unconscious guilt Stevenson felt over his father's worsening condition. He certainly made a self-sacrificing effort to take care of Thomas single-handedly during a visit they made together to a spa in Derbyshire in April, but he soon collapsed under the strain. Unable to work, he wrote despairingly to his mother in terms that showed that he now consciously identified his father's increasingly violent extremes with the "polar twins" of his horror story and that he was unable to insulate himself from them:

> My father, I am sorry to say, gave me a full dose of Hyde this morning. . . . He is certainly hard to manage. . . . my father has one form of attack, that of accusing me of being down myself, for which I have found no answer, as it instantly justifies itself and sends me down to zero. . . . I suppose I am gloomy today, because I could not sleep last night, and the dose of Hyde at breakfast finished me (Jekyll has been in the ascendant till now) . . . (*Letters,* Vol. 5, pp. 245–246)

Two days later, in relief and, no doubt, guilt at having escaped, he signed himself to his mother: "Yours—(I think) Hyde—(I wish) Jekyll" (ibid., p. 247).

Indirect evidence that *Jekyll and Hyde* may have relieved Stevenson by expressing his torment over his conflicted attachment to his dying father is afforded by the fact that his creative energies revived somewhat afterwards. In the first few months of 1886 he found the resources to finish *Kidnapped,* with its moving portrayal of comradeship and conflict between a younger and an older man. But he found it hard to tackle the memoir of his old friend and mentor, Fleeming Jenkin, which perhaps evoked too many memories of the time of his worst troubles with his father and made him aware of forbidden wishes for an end to Thomas's suffering. Around May he wrote apologetically to Jenkin's widow: "It is difficult for any one to believe how much my mind is impaired in these times. . . . That there may be in this some fault of unconscious compliance on my part, I have often thought myself; but . . . the impotence was real. In the last thirteen months, I have only worked . . . not quite five months" (*Letters,* Vol. 5, p. 249). Stevenson was diagnosed with "brain exhaustion," and his self-description sounds, not for the first time, like an identification with his father's condition: "I cannot tell you how empty, weak and rebellious are my poor brains; I can do, and remember, nothing" (p. 255).

As the year wore on, the strain seems to have told on Stevenson more and more and led to occasional attempts at emotional escape. In June 1886, with the connivance of his old friend and lawyer Charles Baxter, he indulged in a spate of bizarre hoaxes designed in part to harass seemingly dishonest newspaper advertisers, a regression to adolescent pranks that also recalls his father's youth (*Letters*, Vol. 5, pp. 264–268). In May he had rented a piano, and in the second half of the year he threw himself into playing it with a feverish intensity (pp. 278, 298–99). In August he claimed he was too ill to join his parents in Scotland, but he recovered his health and spirits miraculously during a holiday in Paris (pp. 297, 301). The respite was brief, however, as his father steadily deteriorated. In December Stevenson wrote sadly to Colvin: "He—my father—is very changeable; at times, he seems only a slow, quiet edition of himself; again, he will be very heavy and blank; but never so violent as last spring; and therefore, to my mind, better on the whole" (p. 336).

By the spring of 1887 the end seemed to be approaching. Thomas Stevenson was continually ill with jaundice and seemed to be regressing to earlier, happier times: ". . . yesterday he seemed happier, and smiled, and followed what was said; even laughed, I think. When he came away, he said to me, 'Take care of yourself, my dearie,' which had a strange sound of childish days, and will not leave my mind" (pp. 383–384). Shortly afterwards Stevenson (under the influence of Tolstoyan Christianity) hatched a bizarre scheme to defy the current Fenian violence in Ireland by moving in with the family of a murdered Irish farmer and allowing himself to be murdered in turn (pp. 389–392; Furnas, 1951, pp. 259–261). Whatever the rationalization, it was clearly a guilty attempt to escape from, and atone for, the agonizing reality of his father's impending death.

The Irish plan vanished abruptly in May, when Thomas Stevenson returned home to Edinburgh to die. Stevenson hurried after him and was shocked that his father, although outwardly conscious, died without recognizing him. In a way curiously prefigured by the ending of his son's novella, Thomas Stevenson's old personality had been replaced by that of a sinister stranger in his outward garb. The son later expressed his feelings in a poem, "The Last Sight":

> Once more I saw him. In the lofty room,
> Where oft with lights and company his tongue
> Was trump to honest laughter, sate attired
> A something in his likeness. 'Look!' said one,
> Unkindly kind, 'look up, it is your boy!'
> And the dread changeling gazed on me in vain.
> (Stevenson, 1971, p. 282)

Soon afterwards Stevenson was finally able to admit to Colvin his relief at his father's death, and the horror of his personality change: "About the death, . . . I was long before I could tell my mind; and now I know it and can but say that I am glad. If we could have had my father, that would have been a different thing. But to keep that changeling—suffering changeling, any longer, could better none and nothing. Now he rests; it is more significant, it is more like himself; he will begin to return to us in the course of time as he was and as we loved him" (*Letters,* Vol. 5, p. 411).

Perhaps not surprisingly, Stevenson fell so ill on his arrival in Edinburgh that he was forbidden to attend his father's funeral. During his stay there he wrote a brief obituary essay, the reserved tone of which gives the impression of an immense effort to be evenhanded and to vanquish painful feelings. The greater part is devoted to his father's professional achievements and his modesty, honesty, and integrity in public life. Of that life, the "chief disaster" was the ruin of the harbor at Wick, where the forces of nature "proved too strong" (as, perhaps, the force of his son's expressive needs ultimately shattered his attempts to contain them). Stevenson nowhere makes direct mention of their personal relationship. Rather, he focuses on the baffling inconsistencies of his father's character and his public versus private persona, "the most humourous geniality" that masked a "profound essential melancholy of disposition" and a "morbid" conviction of his own unworthiness. Although his father was "a wise adviser" to others, it is implied that he could be difficult for those closest to him to deal with: "passionately attached, passionately prejudiced; a man of many extremes, many faults of temper, and no very stable foothold for himself among life's troubles." Above all, he was a man divided, for "he had never accepted the conditions of man's life or of his own character." Stevenson concludes by praising an attribute of his father's that he wholeheartedly valued, namely his "just and picturesque" use of language, whose inexorable waning was one sign of his impending end (Stevenson, 1887a, pp. 66, 68–70). The memoir reflects Stevenson's effort to subdue his resentment over the suffering inflicted on him by Thomas's steadfast mortification of his own character and to emerge with the somewhat bleak consolation that his father's life was on the whole happy, and that death came to him at the last "unaware."

THE FINAL ESCAPE

Just as, in the story, Utterson's Pyrrhic victory and pecuniary enrichment are brought about by the death of his old friend, together with his unassimilable alter ego, so the death of Stevenson's ambivalently loved father became inextricably linked with the beginnings of his own fame and financial success as a writer. It also marked the end of the worst period, in terms of physical and mental health, of his entire life. Soon afterwards, in August 1887, Stevenson joyfully took advantage of his doctors' advice to leave the British Isles and seek health, first in America and then in the South Seas. That he was also thereby escaping the depression engendered by his father's decline and death there can be no doubt. Already on the ship taking them to New York he was in immensely high spirits, despite terrible weather and discomfort, and wrote in October that "the dreadful depression and collapse of last summer has quite passed away" (*Letters*, Vol. 6, p. 18). In the bracing climate of Saranac Lake, in the Adirondacks, his physical condition likewise started to improve, to the point where Dr. Trudeau, founder of the famous tuberculosis sanatorium there, pronounced that he had no active symptoms of the disease (*Letters*, Vol. 6, pp. 59, 115n). With all this came a renewed ability to work, notably on *The Master of Ballantrae* (1889), the story of two contrasted Scottish brothers and their struggles for their father's affections and inheritance, which in uncanny ways echoes some of the underlying structure and themes of *Jekyll and Hyde*.

If *The Master* embodies in a general way Stevenson's preoccupations with doubling and the father-son relationship, another work from the period right after his father's death reveals more specific traces of his conflict and grief and of his efforts to banish the horrifying memories. This is *The Wrong Box*, a darkly comic novel begun by Lloyd Osbourne when the family was at Saranac at the end of 1887. The basic plot was Lloyd's, but it struck Stevenson so powerfully that he dropped work on *The Master of Ballantrae* in order to help Lloyd revise it. Perhaps, less consciously, it recalled the pleasures of the three-way collaboration on *Treasure Island* that had temporarily revived Thomas Stevenson's spirits more than six years before. Stevenson found it a "real lark" and ended up almost entirely rewriting it, supplying most of the characterization and style and the narrative flair of the finished work (*Letters*, Vol. 6, p. 247; Stevenson & Osbourne, 1889, pp. xx–xxii).

The Wrong Box is a black comedy of ghoulishly mistaken identities, doublings, disguises, and practical jokes perpetrated by two rival cousins, as one of them tries to conceal the presumed death (in a railway accident between Bournemouth and London) of his elderly uncle Joseph, whose preservation to become the one remaining subscriber of a tontine is essential to his nephew's enrichment. (The other surviving subscriber, Joseph's brother, Masterman, lives in

seclusion and is rumored to be dead.) The barrel containing the disfigured and unrecognizable body of the anonymous elderly gentleman who is assumed to be Uncle Joseph is first switched with a packing case that turns out to contain a huge marble statue of Hercules.
Later, the unwanted body, an embarrassment to everyone who inher-
its it, is concealed in a grand piano which has been stripped of its in-
nards and is palmed off on an idealistic young lawyer and aspiring
writer. After he in turn tries to get rid of it, it eventually disappears,
stolen in error by a luckless thief.

Whatever its literary merits, this entertaining farrago does seem
to reflect Stevenson's continuing struggle, in the more exhilarated
mood that followed his flight from Britain, to come to terms with the
horror of his father's decline and death (and his own guilt over profiting from it). This time the grim story is transposed into a light and
cheerful key, in an attempt to laugh it off in the manner of the irrev-
erent practical jokes of his own (and his father's) youth. The story
has unmistakable echoes of the miserable years in Bournemouth,
whither both Stevenson and his father had repaired for reasons of
health, and where Stevenson had, for a time, attempted to dispose of
his own sorrows in the piano. The reluctant lawyer and would-be
writer of thrillers, Gideon Forsyth, has elements of satiric self-portrai-
ture, and one of the few moments when uncanny horror breaks
through the determinedly facetious tone of the narrative is when the
piano containing the corpse utters no sound to his touch. Gideon's
shocked exclamation must echo both Stevenson and the father
whose words failed him and who failed to recognize his son: "'Is
there anything wrong with me?' he thought . . . 'I am stark staring
mad,' he cried aloud, 'and no one knows it but myself. God's worst
curse has fallen on me.' . . . 'My mind has quitted me forever'"
(Stevenson & Osbourne, 1889, p. 118).

The central theme is the relentless struggle to keep alive one of
two rival old men and to dispose of another one, dead and unwanted. Although the tone is hectic and absurd, an underlying parricidal anger breaks through in the mangling of the corpse's head and
the decapitation and smashing of the gigantic Hercules. In the end,
younger and older generations are reconciled, along with their financial disputes; Gideon gets the young lady he loves, the unwanted
old man in the piano disappears, and the irrepressible, verbally
adroit Uncle Joseph merges unscathed. The remaining mystery, the
fate of his contrasted brother, Masterman, the other survivor of the
tontine, is solved at the very end when his son says: "'In one sense
[he] is dead, and has been so long; but not in the sense of the ton-

tine. . . . he still lives, but his mind is in abeyance'"—to the point where he does not recognize his own brother (Stevenson & Osbourne, 1889, p. 178). In other words, although the dead body is disposed of, a living corpse remains. One critic called the book "a strange funeral procession" which is "attended by shouts of glee at each of its stages, and finally melts into space" (Raleigh, 1924, p. 16). Yet the repressed refuses to stay repressed, and the specter of the once masterful Thomas Stevenson is never quite exorcised, even if the impact of his presence is denied.

In the remaining years of his short life Stevenson was able to regain some measure of health and strength and to live out his romantic fantasies through travel in the more hospitable climate of the South Seas. He finally established himself in Samoa as patriarch of his own island domain (perhaps rivaling the rocky islets that bore the lighthouses of his forefathers), surrounded by all the women of the family (his mother, wife, and stepdaughter) and by Samoan retainers whom he likened to Scottish clansmen owing loyalty to their chief. Although this symbolic conquest of the oedipal father was never complete (Stevenson voiced regrets to the end of his life that he could not have been a man of action as well as a writer), some beginning of conflict resolution is evidenced by the fact that themes of adult heterosexual relationships gradually began to appear in his fiction, from *The Master of Ballantrae* onward, and especially in his last novel, *Weir of Hermiston,* which he left unfinished at his death. But to the end, he seems to have struggled to rebuild his internalized relationship with his lost father and to overcome any lingering bitterness and guilt (cf. *Letters,* Vol. 7, p. 108). By the summer of 1894, just five months before his own death (from a cerebral hemorrhage), he could write to console an English friend on the death of her mother:

> You remember perhaps, when my father died, you told me those ugly images of sickness, decline and impaired reason, which then haunted me day and night, would pass away and be succeeded by things more happily characteristic. I have found it so; he now haunts me, strangely enough, in two guises: as a man of fifty, lying on a hillside and carving mottoes on a stick, strong and well—and as a younger man running down the sands into the sea near North Berwick, myself—*aetat.* eleven—somewhat horrified at finding him so beautiful when stripped! (*Letters,* Vol. 8, p. 327).

The paternal image is still split, but projected back in time so as to predate the period of their acute conflict during Stevenson's adolescence and to recapture the positive elements of Thomas Stevenson that were most deeply embedded in his own personality. First is the oedipal father, in his prime (fifty again, the age of Henry Jekyll and Long John Silver), strong, successful, phallic, opinionated; then, further back, the more alluring, seductive, negative oedipal father of infancy, springing, like Edward Hyde, "headlong into the sea of liberty."

DISCUSSION

It may be dangerous to make inferences about a writer's life from his fiction, but perhaps less so in the case of Stevenson, for whom life and fiction, fantasy and reality, were from his earliest days inextricably intertwined. As he noted in the dream essay, for him the sense of self and of the past was an unstable and evanescent one, based, like dreams, merely on "some incontinuous images and an echo in the chamber of the brain" (1888a, p. 198). The ego fragility that resulted from the contradictions of his upbringing and early experiences was reflected in an oppressive sense of the uncanny unpredictability of good and evil in the object world, the "sentiment of something moving in things, of an infinite attraction and horror coupled." Yet, with astonishing toughness, Stevenson set himself the lifelong task of repeatedly evoking and exorcising his terrors, of creating and defining himself, through the use of his immense imaginative gifts.

The themes of danger, illness, death, doubling, and mastery run like a leitmotiv throughout his life and work, from the childhood games and stories and propitiatory nighttime incantations to the romantic adventures of his adult writings. They are perhaps epitomized by the mirror game that he repeatedly played with himself in childhood, reciting the dirge from that supremely romantic adventure, *Ivanhoe*, to his own ghostly, candle-lit image in the darkened drawing room. The dirge, sung by the novel's heroine over her husband's supposed corpse, begs for the soul's release from the torments of purgatory, in the hope that prayer and penance will eventually "set the captive free" (Scott, 1820, p. 468). One might see this repeated creation of a mirrored double, guiltily craving pardon, as an attempt to ward off fears of both ego dissolution and object loss (cf. Bach, 1975; Feigelson, 1975), a defensive manoeuvre that repeatedly failed as the ghostly double turned into a menacing harbinger of death and the young Stevenson fled to the reassuring lights of the lobby (cf. Rank, 1971, ch. 5). But at the same time it represented narcissistic satisfaction in an artistic performance whose terrors could immediately be relieved (like those of his young cousins at the "ghosts" he created with the magic lantern) through flooding with light.

The constant juxtaposition of darkness and light in Stevenson's images of his younger self is striking. One thinks of the family lighthouses, beaming safety in the night, and of his longing for the nightly appearance of Leerie, the lamplighter, in *A Child's Garden of Verses*, as well as for the light and sounds of dawn after sleepless nights of illness. But light represented, not only safety, but the joy of the creative enterprise itself, as symbolized in the bull's-eye lanterns carried secretly, and blissfully, by the young Stevenson and his boyhood companions on dark nights at the end of the summer holidays (1888c). This imagery reaches its apogee in the dream essay, written, we must remember, as a kind of explanation of the genesis of *Jekyll and Hyde*. By positing the creative collaboration of his "Brownies" he was able to tame and control the dark, unconscious forces of his own personality, disclaim responsibility for their excesses, and thereby finally substitute the bright lights of the theater for the lurid shadows of Hell.

This story of creative endeavor was shaped by the successive conflicts of fathers (aided and abetted by mothers) and sons. Thomas Stevenson remained in thrall to his own fathers, actual and religious. Having "never accepted the conditions . . . of his own character," he attempted to tame his creative urges and fears of loss through his fateful battles with the sea and with his wayward son. Robert Louis Stevenson was evidently forced to resort early to what W. R. D. Fairbairn (a fellow Scot, also burdened with a Calvinist upbringing) was later to term "the moral defense," an unconscious identification with the badness of the object in order to preserve its outward goodness. For the young Stevenson to admit his bad internal objects to awareness, and with them his own destructive wishes, would have been to court intolerable loss of both other and self. Better to be a "poor little devil" cowering "before the great white Throne" than risk living, in Fairbairn's words (1943, pp. 666–67), "in a world ruled by the Devil." The resulting anguished sense of inner deformity and depression was, in adolescence, tempered by the joyous discovery of literature as a vocation (Stevenson, 1884b, p. 21), as well as by a conscious identification with his mother's relentless optimism. This "hard hopeful strain" was to bolster the defiance of convention, duty, and death manifested in such youthful essays as "An Apology for Idlers" (1877) and "Aes Triplex" (1878), even if it did not save Stevenson from the depression of his male forebears toward the end of his life (*Letters*, Vol. 8, p. 304).

In his young manhood, when the clash became overt, Stevenson survived, precariously, through evasion, persuasion, accommodation, and the help of new allies. But these makeshift solutions had to be paid for with immense physical and mental suffering on both sides and finally were tested to the breaking point in the prolonged crisis of Thomas's progressive dementia, coming as it did after years of depressive illness. The disintegration of Thomas's personality and his increasing loss of control must have deeply shaken his son at a time when he was beginning to experience greater success and confidence in his literary powers. As Fairbairn saw it, when the bad objects by which the individual feels "possessed" are released from the unconscious (whether by analytic work or by the occurrence of some psychic catastrophe), the world around him becomes "peopled with devils which are too terrifying for him to face" (Fairbairn, 1943, pp. 62, 67, 69). To put it another way, the terrifying, unpredictable emergence into consciousness of the split between good and bad objects can give rise to the sense of uncanny horror that Freud (1919) described so well, a challenge to adult reality testing, and a blurring of the boundaries between fantasy and reality that Stevenson had tried to master all his life. As Thomas's demons reemerged and took over, they must have threatened his son's ego with regression and disintegration, as he struggled against the emergence of the kind of primitive rage and guilty fear that he had experienced in his childhood nightmares and recapitulated in his account of Henry Jekyll's last, frenzied days. This time, the possibility of his father's death as the one release from their torments could not even be mentioned because of the intensity of his guilt and fear of loss. A partial solution was his own, penitential illness and creative stalemate. On a deeper level, an unconscious process of doubling and splitting must have been taking place, allowing repudiation and distancing of both the bad self and the bad other, which had remained so inextricably intertwined.

The nightmare that burst from the unconscious to become *Jekyll and Hyde* expressed the germs of this conflict: the crime, pursuit, and loss of control over the means of transformation and escape. It was Stevenson's genius to transform it, not into a simple allegory of pure good and evil, but into a profound study of a deeply flawed man's struggle with the complexities of his own nature. In the book, the only solution was annihilation of both parties to the conflict, leaving as survivor and heir the sterile, unconsciously destructive figure of Utterson. In life, the outcome was less grim in that Stevenson survived his father's death to enjoy seven more adventurous, productive, and relatively healthy years, albeit years marred by depression and homesickness toward the end. But one may also speculate that the intense release of writing *Jekyll and Hyde,* with its exposure of the "deep mine" of conflict within its author and the public debate on morality and character it evoked, may in itself have served a function of exorcism and expiation that helped Stevenson to escape the depression surrounding his father's death and to spring himself, literally and metaphorically, into the seas of liberty.

BIBLIOGRAPHY

Note: References in the text to *"Letters"* are to Stevenson (1994–1995), below. "Tusitala," below, refers to *The Works of Robert Louis Stevenson,* Tusitala Edition, published in London by William Heinemann, Ltd., 1923–1924.

BACH, S. (1975). Narcissism, continuity and the uncanny. *Int. J. Psychoanal.* 56:77–86.

BALFOUR, G. (1901). *The Life of Robert Louis Stevenson.* 2 vols. London: Methuen.

BALFOUR, G. W. (1903). Introduction to *From Saranac to the Marquesas and Beyond,* by M. I. Stevenson. London: Methuen, pp. ix–xx.

BALFOUR, M. (1981). The first biography. In *Stevenson and Victorian Scotland,* ed. J. Calder. Edinburgh: Edinburgh University Press, pp. 33–47.

BATHURST, B. (1999). *The Lighthouse Stevensons.* London: Harper Collins.

BEATTIE, H. J. (1998). A Fairbairnian analysis of Robert Louis Stevenson's *Strange Case of Dr Jekyll and Mr Hyde.* In *Fairbairn, Then and Now,* ed. N. J. Skolnick & D. E. Scharff. Hillsdale, N.J.: Analytic Press, pp. 197–211.

BLOS, P. (1984). Son and father. *J. Am. Psychoanal. Assoc.,* 32:301–324.

BOWLBY, J. (1990). *Charles Darwin: A New Life.* New York: W. W. Norton.

CALDER, J. (1980). *Robert Louis Stevenson: A Life Study.* New York: Oxford University Press.

COLVIN, S. (1921). *Memories and Notes of Persons and Places, 1852–1912.* London: Edward Arnold & Co.

DAICHES, D. (1973). *Robert Louis Stevenson and His World.* London: Thames & Hudson.

EIGNER, E. M. (1966). *Robert Louis Stevenson and Romantic Tradition.* Princeton: Princeton University Press.

ELWIN, M. (1950). *The Strange Case of Robert Louis Stevenson.* London: Macdonald & Co. Ltd.

FAIRBAIRN, W. R. D. (1943). The repression and the return of bad objects (with special reference to the 'war neuroses'). In *Psychoanalytic Studies of the Personality.* London: Routledge & Kegan Paul, 1952, pp. 59–81.

FEIGELSON, CAROLYN (1993). Personality death, object loss and the uncanny. *Int. J. Psychoanal.,* 74:331–345.

FEIGELSON, CHARLES (1975). The mirror dream. *Psychoanal. Study Child,* 30:341–355.

FOWLER, A. (1979). Parables of adventure: The debatable novels of Robert Louis Stevenson. In *Nineteenth-century Scottish Fiction: Critical Essays,* ed. I. Campbell. Manchester: Carcanet Press.

FREUD, S. (1928 [1927]). Dostoevsky and parricide. S.E. 21:173–196.

—— (1919). The 'Uncanny'. S.E. 17:217–256.

FURNAS, J. C. (1951). *Voyage to Windward: The Life of Robert Louis Stevenson.* New York: William Sloane Associates, 1951.

GUTHRIE, C. (1913). *"Cummy" the Nurse of Robert Louis Stevenson: A Tribute to the Memory of Alison Cunningham.* Edinburgh: Otto Schulze & Co.

—— (1924). *Robert Louis Stevenson: Some Personal Recollections.* Edinburgh: W. Green & Son Ltd.

HAMMERTON, J. A., ed. (1907). *Stevensoniana: An Anecdotal Life of Robert Louis Stevenson.* Edinburgh: John Grant.

HEATH, S. (1986). Psychopathia sexualis: Stevenson's *Strange Case. Critical Quarterly,* 28, 1/2:93–108.

HERZOG, J. M. (1980). Sleep disturbance and father hunger in 18- to 24-month-old boys: The Erlkonig syndrome. *Psychoanal. Study Child,* 35:219–233.

HOUGHTON, W. E. (1957). *The Victorian Frame of Mind, 1830–1870.* New Haven: Yale University Press.

JAMES, H. (1888). Robert Louis Stevenson. In *Literary Criticism: Essays on Literature, American Writers, English Writers.* new York: Library of America, 1984, pp. 1231–1255.

JAPP, A. H. (1905). *Robert Louis Stevenson: A Record, an Estimate and a Memorial.* London: T. Werner Laurie.

JUTAGIR, R. (1998). Psychology in the diagnosis and treatment of the dementias. In *Brocklehurst's Textbook of Geriatric Medicine and Gerontology,* 5th Ed., ed. R. C. Tallis, H. M. Fillit & J. C. Brocklehurst. Edinburgh: Churchill Livingston, pp. 765–782.

—— (1999). Personal communication.

KANZER, M. (1951). The self-analytic literature of Robert Louis Stevenson. In *Psychoanalysis and Culture: Essays in Honor of Géza Róheim,* ed. G. B. Wilbur & W. Muensterberger. New York: International Universities Press, pp. 425–435.

LEBRIS, M. (1994). *R. L. Stevenson: Les années bohémiennes 1850–1880.* Paris: NiL/Seuil.

MAIXNER, P., ed. (1981). *Robert Louis Stevenson: The Critical Heritage.* London: Routledge & Kegan Paul.

MASSON, R., ed. (1922). *I Can Remember Robert Louis Stevenson.* Edinburgh: W. R. Chambers, Ltd.

MEHEW, E. (1999). Personal communication.

MILLER, K. (1987). *Doubles: Studies in Literary History.* Oxford: Oxford University Press.

OSBOURNE, L. (1923). Preface to *Treasure Island:* Stevenson at Thirty-two. Tusitala, 2:xi–xvi.

———— (1924). Preface to *The Strange Case of Dr Jekyll and Mr Hyde:* Stevenson at Thirty-seven. Tusitala, 5:vii–xiv.

RALEIGH, W. (1924). *Robert Louis Stevenson.* London: Edward Arnold.

RANK, O. (1971). *The Double,* trans. & ed., H. Tucker, Jr. Chapel Hill: University of North Carolina Press.

SCOTT, W. (1820). *Ivanhoe.* Oxford: Oxford University Press, 1996.

STEVENSON, F. (1923). Prefatory Note to *Treasure Island.* Tusitala, 2:xix–xxii.

———— (1924a). Prefatory Note to *The Black Arrow.* Tusitala, 9:vii–x.

———— (1924b). Prefatory Note to *Dr. Jekyll and Mr. Hyde.* Tusitala, 5:xv–xviii.

STEVENSON, R. L. (1877). An Apology for Idlers. In *Virginibus Puerisque,* 1881. Tusitala, 25:51–60.

———— (1878). Aes Triplex. In *Virginibus Puerisque,* 1881. Tusitala, 25:73–81.

———— (1880a). Memoirs of Himself. Tusitala, 29:147–168.

———— (1880b). The Old Pacific Capital: Monterey. Tusitala, 18:127–142.

———— (1883). *Treasure Island.* Tusitala, 2.

———— (1884a). "A Penny Plain and Twopence Coloured". In *Memories and Portraits,* Tusitala, 29:103–109.

———— (1884b). Old Mortality. In *Memories and Portraits,* 1887. Tusitala, 29:19–27.

———— (1886). *Strange Case of Dr Jekyll and Mr Hyde.* Oxford: Oxford University Press, 1987.

———— (1887a). Thomas Stevenson: Civil engineer. In *Memories and Portraits,* 1887. Tusitala, 29:65–70.

———— (1887b). The Manse. In *Memories and Portraits,* 1887. Tusitala, 29:52–58.

———— (1887c). A College Magazine. In *Memories and Portraits,* 1887. Tusitala, 29:28–36.

———— (1888a). A Chapter on Dreams. Appendix B in *Strange Case of Dr Jekyll and Mr Hyde.* Oxford: Oxford University Press, 1987, pp. 198–209.

———— (1888b). The Coast of Fife. In *Random Memories.* Tusitala, 30:9–28.

———— (1888c). The Lantern Bearers. In *Random Memories.* Tusitala, 30:29–40.

———— (1889). *The Master of Ballantrae.* Oxford: Oxford University Press, 1983.

———— (1894). My First Book: *Treasure Island.* Tusitala, 2:xxiii–xxi.

———— (1896). The House of Eld. In *Fables.* Tusitala, 5:86–92.

———— (1971). *Collected Poems,* ed. J. A. Smith. New York: The Viking Press.

———— (1994, 1995). *The Letters of Robert Louis Stevenson,* ed. B. A. Booth & E. Mehew. 8 vols. New Haven: Yale University Press.

STEVENSON, R. L. & OSBOURNE, L. (1889). *The Wrong Box,* ed. E. Mehew. London: The Nonesuch Press, 1989.

SWEARINGEN, R. G. (1980). *The Prose Writings of Robert Louis Stevenson.* Hamden, Ct.: Archon Books.

VEEDER, W. (1988a). Children of the night: Stevenson and patriarchy. In *Dr*

Jekyll and Mr Hyde after One Hundred Years, ed. W. Veeder & G. Hirsch. Chicago: The University of Chicago Press, pp. 107–160.

—— (1988b). The texts in question. In *Dr Jekyll and Mr Hyde after One Hundred Years,* ed. W. Veeder & G. Hirsch. Chicago: The University of Chicago Press, pp. 3–13.

—— (1988c). Collated fractions of the manuscript drafts of *Strange Case of Dr Jekyll and Mr Hyde.* In *Dr Jekyll and Mr Hyde after One Hundred Years,* ed. W. Veeder & G. Hirsch. Chicago: The University of Chicago Press, pp. 14–56.

Robert Frost's "The Road Not Taken"

Childhood, Psychoanalytic Symbolism, and Creativity

JULES GLENN, M.D.

Robert Frost, often regarded as a folksy farmer-poet, was also a more profound, even terrifying, creator. His poem "The Road Not Taken" reveals his delight in multiple meanings, his ambivalence, and his penchant for misleading his readers. He denied that the poem proclaimed his striving for the unconventional and asserted that it was meant to tease his friend Edward Thomas for his compulsive indecisiveness. This essay also notes the unconscious meanings of the poem, including Frost's reactions to losing his close friend, his own indecisiveness, his conflict between heterosexual and homosexual object choices, his need for a "secret sharer," and his attachments.

ROBERT FROST, DESPITE HIS SURFACE SIMPLICITY, DOWN-HOME CASU-alness, and the colloquial quality of his poetry, was a complex thinker and writer. In view of his efforts to portray himself as a folksy farmer-poet, he was shocked when Lionel Trilling (1959) at a celebration of

Clinical professor of psychiatry, New York University Medical Center. Training and supervising analyst emeritus, The Psychoanalytic Institute at N.Y.U. Medical Center.

I thank the members of the following discussion groups for their comments on this paper, which I presented as a work in progress: The Great Neck Study Group; The Interdisciplinary Colloquium at New York University; CAPS Group #1. An earlier version was preserved as The Melitta Sperling Lecture of the Psychoanalytic Association of New York, November 6, 2000.

The Psychoanalytic Study of the Child 56, ed. Albert J. Solnit, Peter B. Neubauer, Samuel Abrams, and A. Scott Dowling (Yale University Press, copyright © 2001 by Albert J. Solnit, Peter B. Neubauer, Samuel Abrams, and A. Scott Dowling).

Frost's eighty-fifth birthday, declared him not only a "mythical" poet but also a "terrifying" writer, "radical" and "tragic" (p. 448, 451). When Frost more or less recovered from what he said felt like a "surprise" (Thompson, 1964, p. 583) and an assault, he recognized the truth of Trilling's assertion. Trilling was in fact complimenting Frost.

Trilling was not the first to alert the world to the deeper, darker, and frightening aspects of the poet. Leithauser credits Randall Jarrell with providing startling insight into the man as early as 1953: "The 'other' Frost that Jarrell discovered behind the genial homespun New England rustic—the 'dark' Frost who was desperate, frightened, and brave—has become the Frost we all recognize" (Jarrell, 1999, p. xviii). There is also the Frost who sought and wrote the truth about people, their relationships with one another, and the world about them. There is the generous Frost, the encouraging Frost, who sympathetically, tenderly, and sensitively identified with others and loved to teach and parent, the loving, sexual man who also fought for what he wanted, who competed, sometimes childishly, and raged. There is the mischievous, joking, ironic, sometimes sarcastic Frost who teased and tormented while adhering to those people and the world of nature he adored; the adventurous and unconventional man who clung to those from whom he feared separation and loss, and the sad Frost, who fought depression.

Many of these multiple frosts appear in the latent content of his poem "The Road Not Taken," a powerful synthesis of diverse yet integrated traits. In this paper I shall address a number of these elements and allude to others.

Frost glorified in multiple meanings and basked in the power of irony. He loved to pun in his speech and poetry. He despised those who imputed simple statements to him and did not disavow the interpretations of others who found a variety of meanings in his writing. Rather, he declared, "I am entitled to every meaning" (Meyers, 1997, p. 152). He belonged neither to the school that attributes a poem's significance largely to the reader nor to the group of scholars that, emphasizing conscious content, ascribe everything to the author (Eagleton, 1983).

We are on safe ground when we examine "The Road Not Taken" to ascertain Frost's unconscious motives and meanings as well as the audience responses. The poem is especially appropriate to psychoanalytic investigation in that it involves the classical image of the trifurcation of the road at which Oedipus encountered and unknowingly killed his father, Laius, after which he married his mother, Jocasta, again without realizing their relationship. Abraham (1923) asserted that the trifurcation unconsciously represented a woman's genital area. Weinberger and Glenn (1977) affirmed this in two analytic cases while observing (as did Abraham) other meanings as well. They stated that a fork in the road is an ego symbol of uncertainty (doubt and indecision), and that in one of their cases a Y-shaped crossroad represented the conflict between heterosexual and homosexual desires. There is evidence that Frost's poem harbored these meanings. I shall also dwell on Frost's concern with duality, the role of the double and the "secret sharer" in Frost's creativity, and his influence on another author, Edward Thomas.

THE POEM

The Road Not Taken
Two roads diverged in a yellow wood.
And sorry I could not travel both
And be one traveler, long I stood
And looked down one as far as I could
To where it bent in the undergrowth;

Then took the other, as just as fair,
And having perhaps the better claim,
Because it was grassy and wanted wear;
Though as for that the passing there
Has worn them really about the same,

And both that morning equally lay
In leaves no step had trodden black
Oh, I kept the first for another day!
Yet knowing how way leads on to way,
I doubted if I should ever come back.

I shall be telling this with a sigh
Somewhere ages and ages hence:
Two roads diverged in a wood, and I—
I took the one less traveled by,
And that has made all the difference.

A SUMMARY OF FROST'S LIFE[1]

Before discussing "The Road Not Taken," I want to summarize Frost's life in order to put the poem and its meanings in perspective,

1. The sources of this summary include: Hall (1977), Meyers (1996), Parini (1999), Pairier (1977), Pritchard (1984), Sergeant (1960), Thompson (1966, 1970), Thompson and Winnick (1976, 1981), and Walsh (1988).

in the context of the poet's entire life. In examining the poem I shall first discuss Frost's conscious ideas about the poem at the time he wrote it and then gradually assess fantasies and defenses that he was less aware of but that appeared in his ideation. Eventually I shall tackle the more repressed sexual and aggressive aspects of the symbol of the fork in the road, including the unconscious conflicts involved.

Robert Frost was born on March 26, 1874, in San Francisco, the first child of a couple that had great difficulties. His father, William Prescott Frost, graduated from Harvard and became a teacher and then a school principal. He later became a newspaper writer and editor. He failed in his aspirations to attain public office, losing an election to a minor post. Despite his intellect and education, William was an aggressive man who engaged in verbal and physical fights. He even brandished a gun as he threatened to shoot the doctor caring for his wife as she was about to give birth to Robert if the delivery resulted in a death. An alcoholic, he developed tuberculosis, which killed him on May 5, 1895, when his son was 11.

Robert's mother (née Isabelle Moodie and called Belle), much to her shame, was born to unmarried parents. Her father was a seaman, her mother a dissolute woman, sometimes said to be a prostitute, who did not properly care for her daughter. Belle eventually was sent from her native Scotland to the United States, where relatives of her father's parents raised her strictly and religiously. She reacted to her feelings of disgrace by becoming a paragon of religious virtue. As an adult she changed denominations several times—from Presbyterian to Unitarian to Swedenborgian. She met William when she taught in a small school in New England where he was principal.

Shortly after the wedding, Mr. Frost moved to San Francisco, where he established himself in the newspaper business. Belle then joined him in California. She proved to be inefficient and disorganized. Her husband indulged her by moving into a hotel periodically so she could avoid keeping house.

After William died, Belle returned to the East, where she held a series of low-paying jobs to support herself, Robert, and his younger sister, Jeanie. She was very close to Robert, whom she allowed to sleep in her room when he was afraid. She, a poet herself, influenced him by reading to him. A somewhat cantankerous child, Robert got into fights with other boys and became a belligerent grownup.

Frost's school career was checkered. His mother allowed him to stay home from school when he was fearful of leaving her. Instead she taught him herself. Once he entered high school he became an excellent student, sharing the valedictorian honor with his future wife, Elinor White. He engaged in athletics as well. He attended Dartmouth and Harvard, but quit both colleges and never did receive a degree (except for numerous honorary degrees later in his life). He started to compose and publish poems in his school publications (which he also edited), and as an adult became a serious poet. He also ran several New England farms with relatively little success. He cultivated and could project the persona of a down-to-earth folksy farmer who wrote poetry.

When Robert fell in love with Elinor White, she turned down his marriage proposal. She even refused a small but precious book of poems he prepared for her. After Robert threatened suicide by travelling through the dangerous Dismal Swamp near Kitty Hawk, Elinor changed her mind and decided to marry him. The Frosts led a hard life. Elinor became pregnant eight times and suffered several miscarriages. She bore six children. Eliot died at four years of age of an intestinal disorder. An infant named Elinor after her mother lived only two days. Margaret, who survived into young adulthood, died of puerperal fever after giving birth. In addition, two of the Frost children succumbed to psychoses as adults: Irma required hospitalization until the end of her life, and Carroll committed suicide. Lesley, the sole healthy survivor, was a bitter woman who blamed her father for her unhappiness (Meyers, 1996, p. 232).

Robert never recovered from the pain that Elinor's early rejection of him produced. The illnesses and deaths of the children accentuated the tension between the Frosts, furthering distance, recrimination and bitterness in a couple whose mutual love was tainted by suspicion, depression, and fear of rejection.

In 1912 the Frost family moved to England, where Robert was able to find a publisher and establish a reputation as a poet. When World War I erupted, Frost took his family home. Back in the United States, he completed "The Road Not Taken" and sent it to Edward Thomas, a close English friend for whom he had written it. He continued to write poetry while he tried to find other means of earning money. An inheritance from his grandfather helped, as did the farming he engaged in. He supported the family mainly as a university teacher and poet-in-residence. Later he received money for lecturing and, when he had become a true icon, stipends connected with honorary posts like Poetry Consultant at the Library of Congress.

Starting in 1917, Frost taught at Amherst, Dartmouth, the University of Michigan, and the New School for Social Research in New York. He moved frequently, usually when he was offered more money and/or a less demanding schedule. Lesley later complained that the frequent changes in location created problems for the children, who had trouble making friends.

Elinor Frost was a frail and fragile person who was diagnosed as having heart disease in childhood. In 1925, she suffered a "nervous breakdown." She developed a breast malignancy requiring surgery in 1937 and died in March 1938 of a "severe heart attack." Frost was 64 at the time of her death.

Frost's mourning was intense and desperate. Depressed and "crazy," he did not know what he was doing. He took to bed, leaving his daughter Lesley to arrange the funeral. Chaos reigned. He could not even attend Elinor's cremation ceremony.

He was saved by Kathleen Morrison, the young wife of Theodore Morrison, a poet and the director of the Breadloaf Conference. Kathleen was infatuated with Frost, a successful and esteemed man whose power and prestige she could share and use. She refused his proposal of marriage but became his secretary, organizing much of his work, and his mistress.

As he achieved greater fame and power Frost recovered from his loss and became reasonably content despite his constant battle with depression. He became a good-will ambassador to Israel and Russia. A devoted conservative (who was also a Democrat and a friend of President John F. Kennedy and even Henry Wallace), he was largely responsible for the release of Ezra Pound from St. Elizabeth's Hospital during Eisenhower's administration.

Frost received many honors, including four Pulitzer prizes and the Presidential Medal of Honor. He was appointed Poetry Consultant of the Library of Congress, a position he hoped to use to influence legislation by introducing the impact of art. President Kennedy invited him to write and deliver a poem of appreciation at his inauguration in 1961.

Frost died at 88 on January 29, 1963 of pulmonary emboli resulting from thrombophlebitis of his left leg, a complication of treatment for a prostate carcinoma. His body was cremated, and memorial services were held at Harvard and Amherst.

Sadly, after the poet's death Thompson (Thompson, 1966, 1970; Thompson and Winnick, 1976) sullied his sterling reputation in a biography that emphasized unsavory traits: Frost's pretentious posing as a simple farmer, his sometimes infantile behavior, his puerile competitiveness, and his temper. Others have placed Thompson's perceptions in perspective, often without denying Frost's many ungracious traits.

INTERPRETATIONS OF "THE ROAD NOT TAKEN"

THE AUDIENCE RESPONSE AND FROST'S CONSCIOUS INTENT

"The Road Not Taken" has frequently been understood as a proclamation favoring an unconventional life style and experiences that most people shun. In fact Frost himself supported this view of the poem while at other times asserting that he was promulgating no philosophy.

The circumstances during the composition of the poem cast significant light on the poem and demonstrate a greater complexity. "The Road Not Taken" contains several different meanings to Frost, some contradictory.

In his late thirties, Frost, who had never published a book of his verses, decided in 1912 to take his family to England, where he hoped for recognition and publication. There, supported by such well known poets as William Butler Yeats, who praised his work, *A Boy's Will* (1913) and *North of Boston* (1914) were published, to general acclaim. Favorable commentary in the United States fortified his reputation. The subsequent publication of a number of other volumes in England and America brought him further fame as one of America's most beloved poets.

In England Frost struck up an intimate relationship with Edward Thomas, a neighbor who wrote commendatory reviews of Frost's poems. The two men were similar. In a poem written for Thomas, Frost referred to him as a "brother," and Thomas in turn emphasized their sharing of ideas and feelings. Not only were both men writers; they held similar convictions about poetry and were similarly knowledgeable about nature, even naturalists. Further, they had personality traits in common. Each had a troubled marriage, each had threatened suicide, and each tended to obsess, Thomas more intensely and openly than Frost. When they took walks together, Thomas often selected a path along which they might find a rare plant or special view and then regretted "with a sigh" that he had chosen a less rewarding path than he might have (Thompson, 1964, pp. xiv–xv). Frost greatly influenced his friend, encouraging him to expand his literary vistas and compose poems. Thomas became a well known poet, although a minor one compared to Frost.

With the advent of World War I the Frosts left England on February 13, 1915, to return to the United States. The two friends maintained contact through the mail. Thomas was tempted to move to America, where he could live near Frost. But he also thought he should join the British Army, in part to prove his manliness, a characteristic both men valued. Another possible choice was to remain at home with his family. Thomas was indecisive in his letters as he mulled over the possibilities. At this point Frost completed an earlier version of "The Road Not Taken," which he had started to write while in England. He sent the poem to Thomas, most likely in April 1915. The final version was made public in a reading to the Phi Beta Kappa at Tufts College.

Thomas hailed the poem as a salute to the unconventional mode. Frost, on reading his friend's interpretation, was chagrined. He explained that he had been making fun of Thomas when he wrote "The Road Not Taken." The difficulty of selecting the road to traverse alluded to Thomas's difficulty in making choices. The sigh replicated Thomas's frequent sighs as he tried to arrive at a decision. The final line ("And that has made all the difference") was intended to be ironic; actually, Frost said, it makes no difference at all which road one takes. But one must decide!

The manifest content of "The Road Not Taken" contains contradictions, as do other poems of Frost—"Mending Walls" for instance. On the one hand, the two roads were different: One of them had "perhaps the better claim because it was grassy and wanted wear"; that road "was less traveled by." On the other hand, the two roads were essentially the same: "both [paths] that morning lay in leaves no step had trodden black"; the second road was "just as fair."

We may surmise that the contradiction in the manifest content of the poem reflects a contradiction in the poet's mind—i.e., in the latent content, to borrow a term from the study of dreams (Freud, 1900). Frost implied the presence of latent thoughts when he said that in poetry one says one thing but means another. This statement may refer to metaphors, but the contradictions in Frost's work involve more than figures of speech. Frost, at times mischievously and humorously, misled his readers while at the same time palpably stating several concurrent meanings.

Despite his statements to the contrary, Frost believed that the less traveled road was the better one. He wrote that he "had always been right to choose the less practical and more poetical way" and stated that "I've been pulled two ways and torn in two all my life. . . . Every time I have taken the way it almost seemed I ought not to take, I have been justified by the results" (quoted in Meyers, 1996, p. 142). Frost could make up his mind, but he also shared the quality of indecisiveness with Thomas, with whom he identified. Frost once said that he decided to go to England by tossing a coin, a neat remedy for indecision.

The fork in the road served as an ego symbol for the uncertainty, doubt, and indecision the two men held in common. The uncertainty included Thomas's conflict about whether to stay in England with his wife, a heterosexual object choice, or move close to Frost (a latent homosexual choice) as well as with his (Thomas's) wife.

Frost recognized that Thomas was but one of many who "misinterpreted" the poem. Although he tried "to make it obvious that I was fooling" at the Phi Beta Kappa reading, the audience took it seriously (Walsh, 1988, p. 213). Frost knew he was teasing his audience, including Thomas, and enjoyed the mischievous playful aggression.

THE ROADS AND THE DOUBLE

Another significant psychological determinant of the content of the poem is suggested by a letter Frost wrote to Susan Ward, an editor and publisher to whom Frost often confided. (She and her brother Edward published "My Butterfly," Frost's first professionally submitted poem.) On February 10, 1912, six months before he went to England, Frost described an experience which, as several authors (Pritchard, 1984, Meyers, 1996) have noted, contains many of the elements that later appeared in "The Road Not Taken."

Frost described walking on one of "two lonely cross-roads that themselves cross each other" and seeing "a man, who . . . looked for all the world like myself, coming down the other. . . . I felt as if I was going to meet my own image in a slanting mirror . . . as we slowly converged . . . at the same point as if we were two images about to float together. . . . I verily expected to take up or absorb this other self and feel the stronger by the addition. . . . But I didn't go forward to the touch. I stood still in wonderment and let him pass by" (Thompson, 1964, p. 45). Both Pritchard (1984) and Meyers (1996) identify the figure as a "double," and Pritchard underlines the strength Frost felt he achieved from the virtual but not actual contact or merger. Clinically, in the course of analyses, we find that such fantasies of fusion or merger depict a wished-for or defensive union with a powerful maternal or paternal figure of childhood (Glenn, 1993).

Pritchard (1984) says the poem is "interestingly predictive" (p. 67). We can conclude that the two roads of "The Road Not Taken" represent Frost and his double. The imagery here is the reverse of the roads diverging in that the two arms of the Y join to form one road.

Meyers (1996) suggests that the two persons who merge are Frost and Thomas "to produce in the poem the impossible desire to 'travel both [roads] and be one traveler'" (p. 141), thus transforming the original fantasy to signify the relationship between Frost and Thomas. More accurately, we may say that Frost had a strong wish for merger with a powerful figure, a double, a wish he held before he met Thomas, and expressed in "The Road Not Taken" and one he ultimately did satisfy in his relationship with Thomas.

SEPARATION AND UNION

A related meaning of the fork in the road has to do with the fact that the two men, symbolized as roads, reacted to their parting by an accentuation of their desire to be together. Frost had left his close friend but wanted contact with him. The appearance of the double symbolized by the roads that came together signified a wish to remain close; I suggest that Frost wanted to join with his friend in order to avoid the sadness and anger that separation entails. Frost, who was similar to Thomas to begin with, wanted to maintain intimacy, to converge rather than diverge, just as Edward ambivalently wanted to be close to Robert.

The defensive attempt at union did not altogether succeed in stemming the anger. The teasing quality of the poem, in which Frost pokes fun at Thomas (and other readers who "misinterpret" the poem), expresses antagonism toward the separating object. Sensitivity to desertion, real and fantasized, characterized Frost. He never recovered from Elinor's rejection of his initial proposal. Even as she lay dying he felt she was spurning him and sulked as he waited for her to invite him to enter her room and forgive him. Frost also provoked rebuff by Kay Morrison after Elinor's death by proposing marriage to her, despite the fact that she was a married woman with close ties to her children and husband; he thus justified a sustained feeling of being rejected. Such sensitivity to rejection suggests a childhood origin, and indeed he did cling to his mother to such a degree that he had to sleep in her room and avoid school to stay with her. Her allowing him to remain unusually close to her may have facilitated his fear of separation and certainly fortified his use of fantasized union as a defense.

THE DOUBLE AND THE "SECRET SHARER"

Frost and Thomas were like the "secret sharers" of Joseph Conrad's story, a pair of similar-looking doubles. (The protagonist of Conrad's story sees what appears to be his reflection in the water as he looks over the side of his boat. Actually he observes an escaped criminal, whom he rescues from the authorities.) Basing his concepts and terminology on Conrad's tale, Meyer (1967, 1972) (and following him Coltrera, 1981 and Glenn, 1995) has described the relationship between two creative people in which one influences the other; they write for each other and share an unconscious fantasy of creating together in a sublimated (neutralized—Hartmann, 1964) sexual act. Meyer (1967) found that Conrad and Ford Madox Ford comprised such a couple. Extremely close and similar in many ways, they even wrote several books together. After the two broke up, Conrad's writing deteriorated. Although generally two creative individuals make up the duo, only one of the pair need be creative. It is not unusual for one to maintain the fantasy of the creative "secret sharer."

Although Meyer's use of the borrowed phrase "secret sharer" was appropriate in regard to Conrad and contained poetic appeal, the sharing is often quite overt and not secret. Insofar as the fantasies behind the relationship are unconscious, the sharing may be considered secret.

The "secret sharer" fantasy is a narcissistic one in which the double often represents the mother of early infancy with whom one merges and creates. It is also oedipal in that in fantasy the relationship spawns a product—unconsciously a baby. The oedipal attachment may be of the positive or negative type.

I have already mentioned Frost's and Thomas's similarities, which the two men recognized. In addition, Frost stated in a letter to Amy Lowell on October 22, 1917: "[T]he closest I ever came in friendship to anyone in England or anywhere else . . . was with Edward Thomas. He more than anyone else was accessory to what I had done and was doing. We were together to the exclusion of every other person and interest all through 1914—1914 was our year. I never had and never shall have another such year of friendship" (Thompson, 1964, p. 220). So close were they that Frost considered Thomas his sole male sibling.

In a poem "To E.T.," Frost declared: "I meant, you meant, that nothing should remain/Unsaid between us, brother." And in a letter to Edward Gannett, Frost wrote: "Edward Thomas was the only brother I ever had. I fail to see how we can have been so much to each other . . . I hadn't a plan for the future that didn't include him" (Thompson, 1964, p. 217).

On his part, Thomas admired and praised Frost. They spent many "comradely" and intimate hours discussing poetry, nature, the war, and courage as well as the intricacies of Thomas's marriage and his longing for solitude (Meyers, 1996, p. 119). His laudatory reviews of Frost's work fostered Frost's acceptance as a poet akin to Wordsworth and Whitman.

The outward evidence indicates that Edward Thomas got more from his "secret sharer" relationship than Frost did, but the poem indicates that Frost acquired a great deal too. Thomas became a poet under Frost's influence. Frost's wife also greatly influenced Frost's creativity. She too served as his "secret sharer." As we have seen, the poet stated that he wrote all his poems with Elinor in mind. Although through much of her life Elinor had verbally opposed his composition of verse and attended few of his readings, he felt her support anyway, especially since she opposed his sharing his work with his readers. She wanted him to write exclusively for her. Early in his career Elinor read and transcribed a great deal of his work (Meyers, 1996, p. 279). Later Kay Morrison replaced Elinor as his inspiration and helper.

The theme of the double had great significance for Frost. Not only did it appear in the letter to Susan Ward which adumbrated "The Road Not Taken." It also appeared in a short play, "A Way Out," written in 1917 (Meyers, 1996, p. 279), the year Frost left England. In the drama a criminal trying to elude the law kills a hermit, apparently his identical twin brother, and then pretends to be the man he has killed. The story highlights the trickiness of twins who fool others by assuming each other's identity. It also underlines aggressive feelings toward the double.

SEXUALITY, THE OEDIPUS COMPLEX, AND THE FORK IN THE ROAD

Freud (1900) asserted that it is best to interpret dreams through the patient's associations. However, when there are too few associations one can use psychoanalytic symbols (which possess more or less universal meanings) to understand a dream. The trifurcation of the road is a psychoanalytic symbol whose oedipal significance has been documented (Abraham, 1923; Weinberger and Glenn, 1977). We can apply Freud's principle to our work on applied analysis. The appearance of this symbol in "The Road Not Taken" leads us to suspect an oedipal valence to the poem which supplements the uncertainty, doubt, anger, and desire for closeness the poem depicts. Perhaps his ambivalence toward Thomas derived from his relationship with his father, whose strength and temper were impressive, and his love for his mother. Frost left England and Thomas with his wife and family in America. Perhaps the move back to America represented for Frost a repetition of his family's return to New England after his father's death. (Parenthetically, Eugene Halpert (personal communication) has suggested that Frost's move to England to establish himself is reminiscent of his father's move to San Francisco.)

There is indeed an abundance of evidence pointing to Frost's aggressive and libidinal oedipal involvement, particularly through his reactions after Elinor's death. Sheehy (1990) summed up the libidinal aspects in his remarks about Frost's attachment to his wife and, after her death, to Kathleen Morrison: "The two women were as temperamentally different as were the forms of the two relationships. In each, however, Frost found beyond all vicissitude the inspiration to make poetry of life and the faith necessary to make life of poetry. . . . The career of the poet could be in itself a figure for love" (pp. 230–231). Sheehy was referring to an aspect of what we have called Frost's need for a "secret sharer."

Frost's attachment to his wife was intense and fraught with fears that she would reject him. She was cold, distant, and critical, and he clung to her as he had, when a phobic child, clung to his mother. Like his mother, Elinor was disorganized and inefficient. All his poems referred to Elinor, he said, but particular poems were more obviously about her. "Kitty Hawk" described his reaction to Elinor's refusing to marry him. "The Subverted Flower" referred to a forbidden and failed love; he wrote it before 1913 about his attempted seduction of Elinor prior to their marriage. Elinor would not permit him to publish it during her lifetime. Meyers (1996) suggested that even though the Frosts had many children, Elinor was a reluctant sexual partner and that Frost had to suppress his sexuality. Possibly repression occurred as well.

Things changed after Elinor died. Following a period of profound grief, Frost turned to Kay Morrison, with whom he had an intense love affair. She refused his proposal that she divorce her husband and marry him but continued, as his secretary, to organize his life. How long their overt sexual relationship lasted is not known. Sheehy (1990) assessed the importance of the affair after he learned of it in Thompson's notes for his biography of Frost, and Meyers (1996) assumed that the affair continued for a long time. Parini (1999) acknowledged its occurrence but downplayed its duration and significance. Thompson omitted the affair from his biography even though Frost wanted the whole story told (Meyers 1996, p. 256).

Kay Morrison was a passionate and uninhibited lover, quite different from Elinor. Not only was she a source of direct sexual gratification for Frost, but she replaced Elinor as a source of poetic inspiration. He started to write "The Silken Tent" while Elinor was alive and with her in mind, but he completed it after her death and dedicated it to Kay.

Both women reminded Frost of his mother. Not only did he picture them as rejecting gratifiers. They were also objects of his attacks. Frost said that his relationship with them showed that no woman could mother him with impunity. More specifically, although Kay was, unlike his mother Belle, organized and orderly, she shared Belle's Scottish ancestry and her auburn hair. In addition Kay was actually promiscuous (she had affairs with a number of her husband's and Frost's friends including Thompson, Frost's biographer) while Frost's mother was sexually illicit only in his fantasy; Frost imagined incorrectly that his mother had become pregnant with him prior to her marriage. Having heard that Belle's mother had been a prostitute, he fantasized that Belle too was sinful.

Early indications of the aggressive aspects of Frost's Oedipus complex include his intense competitiveness with fellow poets. Although he encouraged younger authors, he attacked his peers and was known for his fits of temper and his vindictiveness. When Carl Sandburg planned to attend one of his readings, Frost feared that the poet would steal the limelight and, for a while, refused to go on with the performance. On another occasion Frost distracted the audience during an Archibald MacLeish reading by crackling and then burning paper!

More direct proof of Frost's triangular rivalrous relationships occurred when he expressed his jealousy of Ted Morrison by banning him from vacationing with Kay and him. Previously he had vacationed with the Morrisons. He continued to spend a great deal of time with them and their children as if he were a part of the family. Frost thus enacted his oedipal wishes in a variety of forms, including both positive and negative configurations.

DEATH AND THE FORK IN THE ROAD

Knowing that Robert Frost, in common with Edward Thomas, entertained suicidal thoughts and feelings, one would surmise that the trifurcation, a symbol of identification with the other poet, referred to death. And indeed the oedipal interpretation does involve death— hostility toward and the murder of the father or father surrogate. There is another poem which for me (and others) evokes a visual picture of three roads converging as well as associations to death: "Stopping By Woods on a Snowy Evening." In that poem Frost experiences a temptation to enter woods as he stops his buggy along a road. As I picture it, the protagonist of the poem is tempted to turn left (or right) to enter the woods, thus conjuring up an imaginary path into the woods. The poet restrains himself and instead moves on because "I have promises to keep/And miles to go before I sleep."

Frost rejected suggestions that entering the woods, which are "lovely, dark and deep," indicates a wish to die, even through suicide, against which Frost struggled. The poet and teacher W. D. Snodgrass recalled that after years of denial Frost said he had reread the poem and agreed that it sounded that way. "Well, now," he said, "that does have a good deal of the ultimate about it" (Meyers, 1996, p. 184).

Another poem, written much later than "Stopping By Woods," carries a similar imagery but emphasizes aggression. In "The Draft Horse" a madman springs out of the woods and stabs the horse pulling a couple's tram along a road. The couple looks on helplessly as the killer races away. The imagery is that of a road intercepted by the murderer's path out of the woods.

That the juncture represents a place of death does not preclude it from also being a site of love. "The woods are lovely, dark, and deep" suggests a forbidden entry into a warm and cozy woman. Frequently imagery of intimate fusion depicts not only mature intercourse but also union with a fantasized preoedipal mother (Isakower, 1937; Glenn, 1993). Freud suggested that wooded areas may represent the female genitals (1905) and that representations of mother and earth are intimately related to each other and to death (1913).

SOME DETERMINANTS OF FROST'S DUALITY

Some authors have characterized Frost's emotions as ambivalent. They certainly were. Duality, as it appears in double entendres, punning, presenting opposite ideas, and ambivalence, is so common that it appears in most people's personalities. However, Frost employed this complex of traits so frequently and so skillfully that his poetry often depended on it. To understand "The Road Not Taken" requires that the duality be studied.

On a relatively conscious level we may note Frost's admiration for Ralph Waldo Emerson, a man who considered contradiction a virtue. Emerson (1844) proclaimed that "a foolish consistency is the hobgoblin of little minds, adored by little statesmen and philosophers and divines. With consistency a great soul has simply nothing to do"

(p. 145). Frost described his love for contradictory statements and the importance of Emerson to him in interviews with Poirier (1963, 1977).

There also appear to be personal historical motives for Frost's duality. Thompson (Thompson, 1966, 1970; Thompson and Winnick, 1976, 1981) suggests a developmental origin. Frost's mother attempted to instill the "fundamentals of religious truth" in her children by telling them stories "that involve pairs of opposites—evil and good, chaos and order, darkness and light—until Robbie developed a habit of thinking in terms of paired images." He added: "Throughout his life he was inclined to build his thinking and his poetry around these pairs" (p. 13).

An analyst might emphasize the conflict between morality and forbidden wishes as well as note Frost's identification with his parents. He identified with his mother in his superego formation and cognitive style. Frost's identification with his father also facilitated his thinking in dualities. William Frost was a man of contradictions. An intellectual and a thinker, a Harvard graduate, an educator and a newspaper man, he was also a playboy who drank heavily and a fiend with a horrible temper. He was unable to live up to his vow to his wife to reform. At the same time he loved his family very much.

Frost not only identified with both parents, who were opposites in many ways. Their characteristics evoked a displaced ambivalence to others that haunted him. He loved and clung to his mother, who pampered him and at whom he most likely became furious when he felt separated from her. He admired his father for his manliness and aggression but must have feared his anger and responded to him with anger. Biological factors should be included in assessing Frost's ambivalence.

At the same time certain similarities of his parents reinforced each other and influenced Frost as a poet. Both were literary people and educators. His mother's reading to him affected him favorably and probably gave rise to his emphasis on the sound the poet produces.

Summary

Robert Frost, a serious and dedicated poet, admired in America and throughout the world, created an image of himself as a farmer philosopher who wrote in folksy colloquial language. Behind this superficial exterior lay a surfeit of complex, dark, and frightening thoughts and feelings. Frost reveled in dualities: double entendres, puns, and contradictory statements. Ambivalence characterized his emotional life.

Frost asserted that "The Road Not Taken," often interpreted as a plea for an unconventional life, was intended to make fun of his friend Edward Thomas, an obsessive man who could not make up his mind. The poem contains numerous meanings, some conscious to the author, others unknown to him. It reveals the author's (and the subject's) indecision, ambivalence, and his interest in a fantasized double, in part a bulwark against separation anxiety. His need to be a "secret sharer" is evident in his encouraging Thomas, his alter ego, to write poetry. Other "sharers" who inspired him and for whom he wrote were his wife and, after she died, Kathleen Morrison. Oedipal and preoedipal determinants of the symbol of the fork in the road and of Frost's creativity can be seen. The use of the more or less universal symbol was also determined by Frost's personal history and personality.

BIBLIOGRAPHY

ABRAHAM, K. (1923). Two contributions to the Study of Symbols. In: *Clinical Papers and Essays on Psychoanalysis.* New York: Basic Books, 1955. Pp. 81–85.

COLTRERA, J., ed. (1981). *Lives, Events and Other Players: Directions in Psychobiography.* New York: Aronson.

EAGLETON, T. (1983). *Literary Theory.* Minneapolis: University of Minnesota Press.

EMERSON, R. W. (1844). Self-Reliance. In: *The Portable Emerson.* Edited by C. Bode and M. Crowley. New York: Penguin Books, 1946.

FREUD, S. (1900). The Interpretation of Dreams. S.E. 4.

——— (1905). Fragment of An Analysis of a Case of Hysteria. *S.E.* 7.

——— (1913). The Theme of the Three Caskets. *S.E.* 12:289–301.

FROST, R. (1995). *Collected Poems, Prose and Plays.* New York: Classics of the United States.

GLENN, J. (1995). *Psychoanalytic Study of the Child* 50:383–397.

——— (1993). Developmental Transformations. The Isakower Phenomenon as an Example. *J. Amer. Psychoan. Assoc.* 41:1113–1134.

——— (1995). The Child Is Father of the Man. Wordsworth's "Ode" Intimations of Immortality" and His Secret Sharers. In *Psychoanalytic Study of the Child.* New Haven: Yale University Press, pp. 383–397.

HALL, D. (1977). *Remembering Poets.* New York: Harper and Row.

HARTMANN, H. (1964). *Essays on Ego Psychology.* New York: International Universities Press.

ISAKOWER, O. (1938). A Contribution to the Psychopathology of Phenomena Associated with Falling Asleep. *Intl. J. Psychoanalysis* 19:331–345.

JARRELL, R. (1953). *Poetry and the Age.* New York: Knopf.

———— (1999). *No Other Book. Selected Essays.* Ed. and with an Introduction by B. Leithauser. HarperCollins.

MEYER, B. C. (1967). *Joseph Conrad. A Psychoanalytic Biography.* Princeton, N.J.: Princeton University Press.

———— (1972). Some Reflections on the Contribution of Psychoanalysis to Biography. In: *Psychoanalysis and Contemporary Science.* Volume 1. Eds. by R. R. Holt and E. Peterfreund. New York: Macmillan. pp. 373–391.

MEYERS, J. (1996). *Robert Frost. A Biography.* Boston and New York: Houghton Mifflin.

PARINI, J. (1999). *Robert Frost. A Life.* New York: Henry Holt.

POIRIER, R. (1963). Robert Frost. In: *Writers at Work. The Paris Review Interviews.* Second Series. Introduction by Van Wyck Brooks. New York: Viking Press. pp. 7–34.

———— (1977). *Robert Frost. The Work of Knowing.* New York: Oxford University Press.

PRITCHARD, W. H. (1984). *Frost. A Literary Life Reconsidered.* New York: Oxford: Oxford University Press.

SERGEANT, E. S. (1960). *Robert Frost. The Trial By Existence.* New York: Holt, Rinehart and Winston.

SHEEHY, D. G. (1990). (Re) *Figuring Love: Robert Frost in Crisis, 1938–1942.* New England Quarterly. Pp. 179–231.

THOMPSON, L. Ed. (1964). *Selected Letters of Robert Frost.* New York: Holt, Rinehart and Winston.

———— (1966). Robert Frost. *The Early Years. 1874–1915.* New York: Holt, Rinehart and Winston.

———— (1970). Robert Frost. *The Years of Triumph, 1915–1938.* New York: Holt, Rinehart and Winston.

———— AND WINNICK, R. H. (1976). *Robert Frost. The Later Years, 1938–1963.* New York: Holt, Rinehart and Winston.

———— (1981). *Robert Frost. A Biography.* Condensed Single Volume. New York: Holt, Rinehart and Winston.

TRILLING, L. (1959). A Speech on Robert Frost. A Cultural Episode. *Partisan Review* 26:445–522.

WALSH, J. (1988). *Into My Own: The English years of Robert Frost.* New York: Grove Press.

WEINBERGER, J. L. AND GLENN, J. (1977). The Significance of the Trifurcation of the Road; Clinical Confirmation and Illumination. *J. Amer. Psychoan. Assoc.* 25:655–667.

Hamlet's Delay

ERROL B. DENDY, M.D.

This paper raises a question about Freud's understanding of Hamlet *and offers a fresh psychoanalytic perspective on the play, emphasizing the psychological use made of Hamlet by the audience. It suggests Hamlet and Claudius both serve as sacrificial objects, scapegoats, for the audience, embodying, through a mechanism of both identification and disidentification, the fulfillment, punishment, and renunciation of the audience's forbidden (i.e. Oedipal) wishes. The play is thus seen to represent unconsciously a rite of sacrifice in which both Claudius and Hamlet, both the father and the son, are led, albeit circuitously, to the slaughter. The need for delay on the part of Hamlet is thus seen to arise not merely from Hamlet's psychology, whatever the audience may project onto it, but ultimately from the function (both sadistic and defensive) that the sacrificial spectacle, the play as a whole, serves for the audience. The paper also speculates somewhat on the role of tragic heroes and heroines in general, and points to the unconscious collusion that permits author and audience to make use of them. Finally, in an addendum, the paper discusses the work of René Girard, a nonpsychoanalytic thinker whose ideas nonetheless are somewhat similar to those presented here.*

FREUD'S FOOTNOTE ON *HAMLET* IN *THE INTERPRETATION OF DREAMS* (1900, pp. 264–266) (which later editions include in the main body of the text) may be the most famous and influential footnote in psychoanalysis. Ernest Jones (1910) elaborated on it in an erudite and

---

Psychiatrist in private practice in Roslyn, New York; voluntary attending on the staff of the Hillside Division of Long Island Jewish Medical Center in Glen Oaks, New York.

My thanks to Dr. Alan Jacobs for his suggestion that I write this paper and for his indispensable help with it.

The Psychoanalytic Study of the Child 56, ed. Albert J. Solnit, Peter B. Neubauer, Samuel Abrams, and A. Scott Dowling (Yale University Press, copyright © 2001 by Albert J. Solnit, Peter B. Neubauer, Samuel Abrams, and A. Scott Dowling).

thoughtful essay. Numerous critical papers have focused on it. The ideas put forward in it have worked their way successfully into the general world of psychoanalytic awareness.

The insight it contains—that Hamlet, in general a man of craft and action, could not kill Claudius because Claudius's crime merely mirrored his own in unconscious fantasy—seems to fit Hamlet's nature as revealed by the play and human nature in general as revealed by psychoanalysis. Thus it appears to explain the central enigma of the play and its universal appeal so well that it would appear little more needs to be said. To the psychoanalytic observer Hamlet seems clearly to be a man under the sway of the Oedipus complex, and psychoanalytic experience shows repeatedly how that complex, when its influence remains too strong, can lead to paralysis and illness.

Nonetheless, something has always bothered me about Freud's explanation; namely: although the conscious recognition of similarity between one's own crime and another's ordinarily tends to inhibit punitive aggression ("He that is without sin among you, let him first cast a stone"—*John*, King James Version, 8:7), the *un*conscious identification of the two crimes typically does not, at least, not in the fashion of Hamlet's paralyzed rage. (A vicariously gratifying indulgence of the criminal might be more likely.) To the contrary, such an identification often promotes aggression. Over the course of history, the projection of one's own unconscious evil onto others and then the merciless persecution and destruction of those others have, in fact, proved to be among mankind's favorite preoccupations. The inhibiting power of Christ's injunction "He that is without sin . . ." comes, I would suggest, not from making a new connection, but from making an existing one conscious. Moreover, Maloney and Rockelein (1943) make the point specifically with regard to Hamlet's situation. Commenting on Ernest Jones's restatement of Freud's hypothesis, they note, "The major premise that Hamlet's own repressed urge to have killed his father links him so closely to Claudius that he cannot act, is not in keeping with psycho-analytical experience" (p. 93). Rather, they infer, "His unconscious feeling of guilt would have spurred him to kill Claudius," "to display how he, the stout-hearted prince, would have saved the King had he been present at the murder," "to deny to himself his own unconscious desire to have killed the King," and "to pose as the vindicated man, to flaunt his innocence before the world" (p. 94). Whether or not one accepts their arguments, it is clear that while Freud's invoking of the Oedipus complex and oedipal guilt to explain Hamlet's hesitation seem on the mark, his narrower explanation that Hamlet cannot act because Claudius represents the prince's own repressed oedipal impulses leaves at least room for question.

If Hamlet were a patient in psychoanalysis or psychoanalytic psychotherapy, unable to take the recourse appropriate in his world for an injustice done to himself or a loved one, we should expect (as, of course, would Freud) to find multiple determinants of his inhibition. Accordingly, after repeating Freud's explanation, Ernest Jones (1910) adds: "There is a second reason why the call of duty to kill his stepfather cannot be obeyed, and that is because it links itself with the unconscious call of his nature to kill his mother's husband, whether this is the first or the second; the absolute 'repression' of the former impulse involves the inner prohibition of the latter also. It is no chance that Hamlet says of himself that he is prompted to his revenge 'by heaven and hell'" (p. 58).

Other perspectives within the oedipal domain also come readily to mind. For instance, if Hamlet were to kill Claudius, the sexual tension of his mother's new availability might become unbearable. Thus, as long as Hamlet lives, Claudius must live. Maloney and Rockelein (1910) observe that much of Hamlet's speech and behavior suggests a fear of growing up, of the dangers and losses that fulfillment of the oedipal destiny would bring. Seeing Hamlet not so much as essentially childlike or immature, as do Maloney and Rockelein, and Kurt Eissler (1953) as well, Lora and Abraham Heller (1960) "consider him as having *regressed* to the period of oedipal conflict under the stress of three awful shocks: his father's sudden death, his mother's hasty remarriage a month later to his uncle, and the Ghost's revelation of his father's foul murder" (pp. 413–14). Ernest Jones, in a later paper (1948), points to the homosexual, or negative, side of the oedipal complex and says, "According to Freud Hamlet was inhibited ultimately by his repressed hatred of his father. We have to add to this the homosexual aspect of his attitude so that Love and Hate, as so often, both play their part" (p. 176). Mark Kanzer (1951) says, "The central theme of Shakespeare's works is the problem of the fidelity of the heroine" (p. 15), and this aspect of the oedipal dilemma clearly plays a great role in *Hamlet* and in Hamlet's conflicted psychology.

In addition to oedipal explanations, some authors (Wertham, 1941; Rubin, 1970–1; Kanzer, 1951; and Maloney and Rockelein, in a

---

1. Janet Adelman (1992) has offered a rich and insightful interpretation of *Hamlet* from a "preoedipal" point of view. However, I think her most telling observations regarding the psychology of Hamlet can be best seen, given the material of the play, as revealing the preoedipal regressions and nostalgia of an oedipally traumatized child. Along a somewhat similar vein, Avi Erlich's (1977) interpretation of Hamlet's delay as arising from his search for a "strong father" and his flight from heterosexual dangers could, given again the actual material of the play, be most persuasively construed in terms of the Oedipus complex.

1949 addendum to their 1910 paper, emphasize the matricidal and pre-oedipal conflict evident in *Hamlet,* and these might be construed to contribute to Hamlet's inability to kill Claudius.[1] Thanks, one might note, to Hamlet's delay, Gertrude and her younger incarnation, Ophelia, are also destroyed.

Theories from nonpsychoanalytic sources also have merit and have had great influence. A. C. Bradley (1904) attributes Hamlet's inaction to his "exquisite [moral] sensibility," shocked and aroused, in particular, by his disillusionment in his mother (p. 111). A number of theories have also followed Goethe's that, as Freud (1900) summarized it, Hamlet "is paralyzed by an excessive development of his intellect" (p. 265). Today, we might consider an excessively developed intellect of Hamlet's ruminative sort as pointing to an obsessional disorder. Or, just as Bradley (p. 120) considered Hamlet "melancholic," we might attribute his paralysis to some form of depressive disorder.

Granted, with elaborations of the oedipal theme rife throughout the play, most psychoanalytic observers will, I believe, find oedipal explanations for Hamlet's behavior the most powerful, especially if these include an understanding of the Oedipus complex in its various aspects, as pointed to by the authors cited above. Nevertheless, even in this realm, it should be clear that wide differences in emphasis can occur. Kurt Eissler (1953) says, "To exhaust the possible interpretations it would be necessary to write a study of *Hamlet* comparable to the one Freud wrote of dreams (he showed that almost all prior theories and speculations about dreams, with only a few exceptions, were valid as far as they went, although the full claims of their authors had, of course, to be disputed). I anticipate that such a study of all the interpretations which *Hamlet* has had in the past may show the partial validity of almost all of them" (p. 95). Some might argue that since Hamlet is a fictional creation, we are free to project onto his character whatever explanation for his behavior has the most meaning to us. In this vein, Norman Holland (1975) entitles his paper on the play's hero "Hamlet, My Greatest Creation."

When all these explanations are considered, however, something seems to me most unsatisfying and unfinished. Although the central drama of the play lies in the tension between Hamlet's call to kill the usurper king, Claudius, and his inability to do so, I still have the feeling that something beyond Hamlet's character, or psychology, as revealed by the play or projected onto him by the audience, is required to explain his delay. That something would reside in the unconscious meaning and function of the play itself, in its entirety. Thus, from the standpoint of *his* psychology, Hamlet's behavior could never be fully explained. For the rest of the answer, we must look to the psychology of the author and audience for whom he exists, to see what purpose the play as a whole serves for them. This purpose, I believe, would be that unconsciously the play represents to both author and audience a rite of sacrifice—the inevitable sacrifice of the totem animal, the murder of the father, the king. All the artifice of the play would serve to draw out that sacrifice, to disguise it, and to permit the audience to participate fully in it. Hamlet is given good reason by the play to commit the ordained murder, but he cannot do so because (all the argument and art of the play to the contrary) the author and the audience know unconsciously that the play's pretext is a sham. That is, the Ghost is but an artful device to deceive (the necessary "lie" on which the play is built): Claudius and his predecessor are the same (in the Unconscious, one king, or one lover of one's mother, merges with another); and the murder of the father thus occurs not prior to the play but rather, at the end. And it occurs only after the play has put Hamlet through endless, self-torturing ruminations, punished him with a wound that spells certain death, and interposed a whirlwind of activity and death that makes the murder seem almost peripheral. For only thus can it be allowed.

"The Ghost," says John Dover Wilson (1935), "is the linchpin of *Hamlet;* remove it and the play falls to pieces" (p. 52). But the play, like any great work of art, like a dream, with condensations, reversals, displacements, and so forth, arises from the need for both expression and disguise. And so, to move as quickly as possible to the psychological essence of the play, we must remove that linchpin. Then the underlying meaning starts to emerge. Curiously, even within the manifest presentation of the play, an ambiguity crops up as to the Ghost's real existence. In the bedroom scene, where it appears for the last time, only Hamlet, not Gertrude, can see or hear it (a departure from its previous behavior, but one consistent with that of Hamlet, who cannot forget his father, and of Gertrude, who has forgotten him). Even if we take note, as Bradley (p. 136) reminds us, that "a ghost, in Shakespeare's day, was able for any sufficient reason to confine its manifestation to a single person in a company," I think the viewer, if only unconsciously or subliminally, must experience a moment of doubt regarding this figure, which, as Wilson (p. 59) observes, Shakespeare has previously employed "all his cunning" to make "dramatically convincing," and which has set the play in motion.

Throughout *Hamlet,* Shakespeare plays upon the audience with ambiguities and enigmas, the chief of these, of course, being that which Freud addressed. The perplexing enigma of Hamlet's motivation and behavior serves, interestingly and, one might say, craftily (and *Hamlet* at times seems all about craft, does it not?), to distract the viewer from the true nature of what is going on. As Bradley notes, "the whole story turns upon the peculiar character of the hero. For without this character the story would appear sensational and horrible" (p. 93).

Given the "horrible" nature of what the play depicts, the forces of defense must make their claim. The audience must endure repeated postponements; Hamlet, the hero/executioner, must endure worse. And the eventual murder of the king/father must not only be fully justified and already punished; it must, as noted, become almost peripheral, so as not to evoke too much overt pleasure. But the delays themselves paradoxically serve the purpose of pleasure. For one thing, they permit ultimately a carnage of far greater scope than originally envisioned—with hated father figures, unfaithful or distrusted mother figures, challenging rivals, and betrayers of various kinds (Claudius, Polonius, Gertrude, Ophelia, Laertes, and Rosencrantz and Guildenstern) all destroyed. This is a bloodbath whose totality matches the tantrum-like rage of the hero and, in some dark corner of the soul, that of each member of the audience. Moreover, something further occurs. In his essay "On the Universal Tendency to Debasement in the Sphere of Love," Freud (1912) asserts, "An obstacle is required to heighten libido; and where natural resistances to satisfaction have not been sufficient men have at all times erected conventional ones so as to be able to enjoy love." The principle he applies to the erotic impulse can also apply to a murderous one. Obstacles and delays serve to add meaning and value to the impulse's eventual fulfillment.

In Act III of *Hamlet,* Shakespeare achieves a sort of crescendo of delay. After Hamlet's embittered games of madness and his melancholy soliloquizing, when the play within the play has come and gone and the time for the murder of Claudius has clearly arrived, Hamlet promises, "Now could I drink hot blood/And do such bitter business as the day/Would quake to look on." But when, on his way to his mother's bedroom, he happens upon Claudius, defenseless and kneeling in prayer, he lets the golden opportunity pass. And then, in the bedroom scene, just as he has called Claudius, in front of his mother, "a murderer and a villain" and seems about to share with her the terrible truth, the Ghost appears to interrupt him in his purpose. Although it claims that its visitation "is but to whet thy almost blunted purpose," it serves, in fact, to keep Hamlet from revealing everything to Gertrude—a revelation that, once made, we might expect would have begun a chain of events leading quickly to the end of Claudius' reign. Hamlet would have crossed the line, and the die would have been cast. But instead Hamlet is distracted, and the scene ends with him ready to be carted off to England, like an Oedipal child exiled from the parental bedroom, his rage having been partially displaced and spent in the murder of Polonius.

Of course, we know that Hamlet will return to accomplish the deed that now, more than ever, we yearn for him to do. Our repeated frustrations have made us all the readier to see the play achieve its goal.

The long-awaited deed that the play has promised us from the start is the murder of the father. And so, what Jones describes as "the second reason why the call of duty to kill his step-father cannot be obeyed" is really primary. However, stepfather = father is not merely the key to Hamlet's unconscious thinking. The equation of the one man, loathed and despised, with the other, loved and revered (which Hamlet attempts to deny with all his might), is, in fact, key to the meaning of the play for all who share in the fundamental experience of it. Conveniently, as befits our own ambivalence, the play splits the imago of the father in two, the original father presented as all good, the current one all bad ("Hyperion to a Satyr," says Hamlet). Yet it is only from the unconscious equation of the two fathers that arises for the spectators, for all who partake of the drama, the full need to see the predestined execution accomplished, as well as to see it impeded and delayed.

Natalie Shainess (1975) offers a curiously unempathic interpretation of *Hamlet*. Yet it is a rather intriguing one as well. She sees Hamlet as a psychopath, not neurotically inhibited but biding his time, waiting for the right moment to strike, his self-serving speeches brimming with rage and accusation. There is a kernel of truth, I believe, in this explanation, except that it is not Hamlet who is the psychopath but we, the audience. Poor Hamlet tortures himself with doubt and hesitation; and he dies. *We* are eager for him to proceed (our eagerness heightened by his excessive self-doubt), enjoy ultimately the completion of his mission, and escape unharmed as he pays the price for it. In this sense, Hamlet is like Christ: he is the son who dies for our sins.

Earlier, I referred to the "manifest presentation," or content, of the play. One might, of course, question this analogy to the dream and ask, "What is the latent, or hidden, content?" But this I have defined already. Now, we can define it even more precisely. Whatever other meanings Hamlet's behavior and *Hamlet* the play may take on for members of the audience idiosyncratically or in general, the play as a whole, at its core, presents to them a rite of sacrifice in which both Claudius and Hamlet, both the father and the son, are led, albeit circuitously, to the slaughter.

To add a further note: the story of Hamlet actually derives from a number of earlier tales in which the prince's murder of his stepfather king is delayed by external obstacles; thus, the *Hamlet* we know may be said to enjoy a collective authorship. By relocating the cause of the delay to Hamlet's psychology, Shakespeare has made the drama more interesting and more meaningful to the modern audience. But if the need for delay lies ultimately in the nature of the spectacle itself—the spectacle of the torture and sacrifice of father and son— this raises for me two questions, both of which could take us beyond the range of the present paper. One concerns the origin of the play as an art form in general. To what extent does the lay derive from theatrical rituals of sacrifice and, even more specifically, of the hunt? (Cf. Burkert, 1972; also Muller, 1956, and Weisinger, 1953.) And what rules generally apply to the relationship between audience and protagonist? To what extent do we use the protagonist not merely as a vehicle, through identification, to fulfill our unconscious wishes, but also for other purposes—for instance, as in Hamlet's case, to stand in for us, like a sacrificial animal, to receive the punishment that, because of those wishes, we know we ourselves deserve? Of course, the presentation of such a sacrificial stand-in could be said to fulfill a basic unconscious wish in itself. In such a case, the unfortunate protagonist would serve the wish-fulfilling purpose we have assigned him by our initially identifying ourselves with him and then ultimately disidentifying, discarding him, to face alone his tragic ending.[2]

---

2. In his paper "The Puberty Rites of Savages" (1915), speaking of early Greek tragedy, Theodor Reik observes, "Dionysus redeems guilt-laden humanity (i.e., the spectators) by the blood he sheds at his death. He takes upon himself the whole guilt; he is the really guilt-laden one; the spectators have no longer to fear punishment." He notes that the spectators have "'empathized' with," "identified themselves with," the suffering hero and that, "In his punishment they complete the self-punishment of their own unconscious hostile and incestuous tendencies, and condemn those wishes." He notes also the "identification of the spectators with the hero, as well as their psychical differentiation from him" and regards catharsis "as a means of objectivization," by which he means, I believe, the transfer or relocation of the spectators' crimes, together with the terror and pity they entail (as per Aristotle's concept of catharsis), onto the tragic object. (See also Aristotle, trans. Sinclaire, 1962, and Else, 1970.)

To speak in the very broadest terms, we would expect the ill-starred heroes and heroines of tragic dramas of all sorts to offer the audience a means to resolve temporarily various issues of unconscious impulse and defense. In *Hamlet,* I believe, the central impulse, gratified in a sadistically extended manner (i.e., Claudius is teased and toyed with before being killed), is that of patricide; the central defense, also sadistically drawn out (i.e., Hamlet is held in shackles of thought before being killed), is the shifting of blame and punishment to the sacrificial hero, Hamlet. Works of tragedy also typically allow the audience to indulge vicariously, through the hero or heroine, in emotions of self-glorification (hubris) and self-pity that are ordinarily not acceptable. Here again, a mechanism of both identification with and distancing from the tragic object would come into play. It is only through a deep identification with and then disconnection from the tragic figure that the process we call "catharsis" could successfully occur, only through a resonance of these two opposing forces that the tragic figure could linger in our mind, retaining its full meaning and serving its full purpose.

Thus could the memory of the tragic figure symbolize in our unconscious the fantasy of simultaneously gratifying, punishing, and renouncing our forbidden inclinations. We would have our cake and eat it, too, our darkest wishes fulfilled, our sense of safety and moral order preserved. No surprise, then, that we should love our tragic heroes and heroines, who (again, in a sense, like Christ) for us have lived, and for us have suffered and died. We blame "cruel fate" or their intrinsic flaws or the perfidy of others for their ordeal, an ordeal made spectacle for our benefit and entertainment.

To be sure, I cannot in the confines of this paper examine the array of forbidden unconscious wishes for which tragic art attempts a solution and for which a tragic hero or heroine must be sacrificed. We might expect that in many plays the hero's critical transgression would be preoedipal rather than oedipal, as, for instance, perhaps, in *The Bacchae* (cf. Arvanitakis, 1998). Nor can I attempt to consider the characteristics that separate successful tragic art, such as *Hamlet,* from unsuccessful examples. The reader might consult Freud's "Creative Writers and Daydreaming" (1908) or Hanns Sachs's *The Creative Unconscious* (1942). In the latter work, Sachs discusses the need in tragic art for disguise, inasmuch as "Anything which would threaten to uncover the secrets of the Unconscious would produce the strongest revulsion in the creator and violent repugnance in his audience" (p. 39). He adds: "The most effective method of disarming the resistance against the introduction of the repressed contents is the downright opposite of the happy end. We have seen it used in a class of rather exceptional daydreams, in which suffering takes the place of pleasure. The wish-fantasy leads to doom and death, the triumph turns into catastrophe. This is the method chosen by the tragic Muse" (p. 40). He refers here to unconscious wishes vicariously fulfilled through the hero or heroine. I have pointed to what I believe to be the central unconscious wish and defense that the tragedy as a whole can represent, with the hero or heroine serving merely as the leading and ultimately disposable prop. The unacknowledged sacrificial function and sadistic potential of tragic art, concealed in our sorrow would be hinted at by its very name—for the word *tragedy* is widely believed to derive from the Greek word *tragōidia*, or "goat song."

In *Totem and Taboo* (1913), though proceeding on a highly suspect premise, Freud nonetheless makes an intriguing remark with regard to early Greek tragedy. On the basis of his notion of inherited memories of the primal horde and the primal crime of patricide, he accuses the Greek Chorus of "a refined hypocrisy," for it laments the suffering of the Hero while (as Freud understands it) it has ultimately caused that suffering and committed the very crime of rebelliousness for which the Hero is being punished. I have suggested that in *Hamlet*, and perhaps in tragedy in general, hypocrisy of the sort Freud attributes to the Greek Chorus extends to the unconsciously colluding author and audience. Out of this hypocrisy, this shared sense of innocent participation in the sacrifice, would, to expand a concept of Sachs, arise in the audience a sense of "community (37)."

Finally, during the play within the play in *Hamlet*, Shakespeare places in the audience the actual murderers: Claudius, who has murdered the previous king, and Hamlet, presenter and partial author of the play within the play, who, we know, will murder the current king. In this scene, author, audience, actors, and perpetrators all merge. The particular crime Hamlet unmasks in the play he presents is the pouring of a lethal potion by Claudius into King Hamlet's ear. The primal-scene implications of this imagery have been pointed out by Harry Trosman (1987), among others. (Gertrude, of course, must be punished with death for her unfaithfulness to Hamlet with the first as well as the second father; homosexual themes in the relationship between Hamlet and his fathers are clearly implied in the imagery, too.) Trosman has also noted that in *Hamlet* Shakespeare refers to the ear 24 times. Might Shakespeare, who pours the potion of his words into our ears, be revealing another side of the author-audience relationship, with the audience unconsciously representing victim as well as accomplice?

ADDENDUM

Since I wrote this paper, the work of René Girard has been called to my attention. Girard puts forth what is by his own understanding a nonpsychoanalytic (one might say anthropologic) theory of sacrifice. As summarized by John Vignaux Smyth (1989), in his introduction of Girard to an audience at Bennington College, Girard's two major concepts are (1) that our desires tend to derive "not directly from the value of their objects, but from imitation of the desires of others" (imitative or mimetic desires) and (2) "that all human societies—their languages, rituals, and social orders—were originally founded on collective violence against an arbitrary scapegoat." (The notion of the scapegoat as "arbitrary" is certainly nonpsychoanalytic.) "According to Girard," adds Smyth, "all sacred myths and religions are founded on this principle." Furthermore, this principle extends also to tragic art. Girard has written a paper on *Hamlet* (1986) in which he interprets *Hamlet* and Hamlet's delay as a Shakespearean critique of the theatrical genre and the entire ethos of sacrificial revenge. He wonders that "it never occurs to most critics that Shakespeare himself could question the legitimacy of revenge," and considers that Hamlet's hesitation might thus be deemed something other than an enigma or evidence of psychological disorder. "*Hamlet* against revenge," he dubs his idea. Yet he recognizes that the play derives theatrical power from its ritualized representation of sacrifice (and recognizes as well the essential identity, or twinship, of Old Hamlet and Claudius). More generally, he observes, "The theater still relies on imperfectly detected [he eschews the term "unconscious" (see Girard, 1972, pp. 169–192)] scapegoat processes for its cathartic effects, much attenuated, of course, but structurally identical to the rituals of primitive religion." And, he adds, "It may well be that traditional cultural forms, such as the theater, can never dispense entirely with victimage." Later, in a presentation on *Julius Caesar* to the audience at Bennington (1989), he repeats, "Tragedy is a by-product of sacrifice; it is sacrifice without the immolation of the victim, an attenuated form of ritual sacrifice." So, while he comes from a very different discipline (and reaches some different conclusions), his thinking, nonetheless, includes and emphasizes some ideas that are quite similar to ones I am presenting here.

The psychoanalytic path of inquiry must always approach a work of art from the standpoint of wish and defense. This is the way I have attempted to look at our most famous work of tragic art, *Hamlet*. From this endeavor, a general sense of tragic theater has suggested itself to me. Outside the theater, members of the audience know that they face real terrors, inescapable losses, and certain (from their point of view, tragic), death. Unconsciously, I believe, they blame their evil wishes for their predicament. Whatever larger social purposes tragic theater may serve, from the intrapsychic or psychoanalytic perspective, this form of spectacle, with its magnetic but flawed heroes, suitable for identification, and its sacrificial culminations, I believe offers the audience a way to gratify their evil wishes and at the same time enjoy the temporary illusion of purification and escape. And, while the experience of watching tragic theater, thus described, includes an unconsciously exploitative and sadistic attitude toward the hero or heroine, it also includes, as the word *purification* implies, the need for the audience to suffer empathically to some extent, along with the play's hero or heroine.

Preferring his own theories of "mimesis" and "foundational violence" (1972, 1986, 1989), Girard, for the most part, rejects the psychoanalytic perspective (including the "Oedipus complex" (see 1972, pp. 169–192);[3] indeed, at times he seems hostile to psychoanalysis. In his paper on *Hamlet* (1986), he says of Ernest Jones, "Like Polonius before him, he is absolutely certain Hamlet's problem can be reduced to sex." Then he expounds, "The only difference is the shift from the daughter of the analyst to the mother of the patient. That shift makes everything more interesting and modern. Our time being the more disjointed of the two, it should and does produce the more sophisticated Poloniuses it so richly deserves." And "If the psychoanalysts could only get the contemporary Hamlet on their couch, if they could only straighten out his Oedipus complex, his *specific aboulia* would vanish; he would stop shilly-shallying and push that nuclear button like a real man." Perhaps, one might say, Girard has found *his* scapegoat.

As for Girard's interpretation of *Hamlet* as self-critique—that is, a critique of the ethos and literature of violent revenge—I do not know. But I do know that a crucial discovery of psychoanalysis is the durability of the unconscious. Accordingly, we must expect that primitive unconscious impulses—such as that to find substitute objects of

---

3. It is not unusual, I might note, for creative thinkers to use one insight to deny another.

revenge for crimes against oneself long since consciously forgotten, or to find sacrificial representations of the bad or inadequate self— will always play a role in human relations, on both the small and the large scale. Through activities such as festivals or sports or (I have suggested), in an even more disguised fashion, tragic theater, society can at least allow nondestructive channels for these impulses. But they will always remain, and that is something we should not forget.

BIBLIOGRAPHY

ADELMAN, J. (1992). "Man and Wife is One Flesh: *Hamlet* and the Confrontation with the Maternal Body," in *Suffocating Mothers,* ed. Janet Adelman, London and [New York and London] Routledge, Chapman, and Hall.

ARISTOTLE. (1962). *Politics.* Translated by T. A. Sinclair, London and New York: Penguin.

——— (1970). *Poetics.* Translated by Gerald F. Else, Ann Arbor: University of Michigan Press.

ARVANITAKIS, K. I. (1998). "Some Thoughts on the Essence of the Tragic," *International Journal of Psycho-Analysis,* 79:955–964.

BRADLEY, A. C. (1904). *Shakespearean Tragedy,* Penguin Books.

BURKERT, WALTER (1983) [1972]. *Homo Necans.* Berkeley: University of California Press.

EISSLER, K. R. (1953). On *Hamlet. Samiksa,* 7:85–132.

ERLICH, A. (1977). *Hamlet's Absent Father,* Princeton, N.J.: Princeton University Press.

FREUD, SIGMUND (1908). Creative writers and daydreaming. *S.E.* IX:141–153.

——— (1900). *The Interpretation of Dreams. S.E.* IV.

——— (1912). "On the Universal Tendency to Debasement in the Sphere of Love," *SE* XI:187.

——— (1913). *Totem and Taboo. SE* XIII:155–156.

GIRARD, RENÉ 1977 [1972]. *Violence and the Sacred,* Baltimore, MD: Johns Hopkins University Press.

———. 1986. "Hamlet's Dull Revenge," in *Literary Theory/Renaissance Texts,* eds. Patricia Parker and David Quint, Baltimore, MD: Johns Hopkins University Press.

——— (1989). "Collective Violence and Sacrifice in Shakespeare's *Julius Caesar,*" The Belitt/Troy Chapbooks, 1989.

HELLER, LORA, & HELLER, ABRAHAM (1960). "Hamlet Parents: The Dynamic Formulation of a Tragedy," *American Imago,* 17:13–421.

HOLLAND, NORMAN (1975). "Hamlet, my Greatest Creation," *Journal of the Academy of Psychoanalysis,* 3(4):419–427.

JONES, ERNEST (1910). "A Psychoanalytic Study of *Hamlet,*" *Essays in Applied Psychoanalysis.* London: International Psychoanalytic Press.

——— (1948). "The Death of Hamlet's Father," *International Journal of Psycho-Analysis*, 29:174–176.

KANZER, MARK (1951). "The Central Theme in Shakespeare's Works," *Psychoanalytic Review*, 38:1–16.

MALONEY, JAMES CLARK, & ROCKELEIN, LAURENCE. "A New Interpretation of *Hamlet*," *International Journal of Psycho-Analysis*, 30:92–107.

MULLER, HERBERT J. (1956). *The Spirit of Tragedy*. New York: Alfred A. Knopf.

REIK, THEODOR 1946 [1915–16]. "The Puberty Rites of Savages." In Reik, *Ritual: Psychoanalytic Studies*. New York: International Universities Press.

RUBIN, SAMUEL S. (1970–1971). *Hamlet*, "A Psychoanalytic Reinterpretation," *Psychoanalytic Review*, 57(4):660–670.

SACHS, HANNS (1942). *The Creative Unconscious*. Cambridge, MA: Sci-Art Publishers.

SHAINESS, NATALIE (1975). "The Coup That Failed," *Journal of the Academy of Psychoanalysis*, 3(4):383–403.

SHAKESPEARE, WILLIAM. *Hamlet Prince of Denmark*. The Pelican Shakespeare, ed. Willard Farnham, Baltimore, 1957.

SMYTH, JOHN VIGNAUX (1989). Introduction to René Girard, "Collective Violence and Sacrifice in Shakespeare's *Julius Caesar*," "The Belitt/Troy Chapbooks.

TROSMAN, HARRY (1987). Panel on "Unconscious Fantasy." American Psychoanalytic Association, New York, Dec. 16–20.

WEISINGER, HERBERT (1953). *Tragedy and the Paradox of the Fortunate Fall*. Michigan State College Press. London.

WERTHAM, FREDERIC (1941). "The Matricidal Impulse," *Journal of Criminal Psychopathology*, 2:455–464.

WILSON, JOHN DOVER (1935). *What Happens in Hamlet*. Cambridge: Cambridge University Press.

Psychological Insights in Shakespeare's Final Play, *The Two Noble Kinsmen*

EUGENE J. MAHON, M.D.

Shakespeare's final play, The Two Noble Kinsmen, *contains profound psychological insights. Like all of Shakespeare's reworkings of old material, the result is not merely a variation on a theme but a psychological statement in and of itself, which respects and revisits the past even as it presents a new and original statement. In this paper I argue that the transformation of the Chaucerian into the Shakespearean has a premonition of the Freudian in it also: Shakespeare not only delivers insights on development and sexuality, he anticipates an important Freudian concept in his introduction of the theme of the jailer's daughter whose "love-sickness" requires an understanding of transference before sense can be made of it!*

THIS PROFOUND WORK OF ART, WHETHER WRITTEN IN ITS ENTIRETY BY Shakespeare, as Paul Bertram (1965) has argued, or in collaboration with John Fletcher, as perhaps most commentators believe, is a neglected classic. Shakespeare's final poetic and dramatic statement, it contains remarkable insights about development, sexuality, and object relations. There may even be a premonitory intuition, a poet's anticipation, if you will, of the concept of transference. There is no way of knowing if Freud, a great lover of Shakespeare, had ever read *The Two Noble Kinsmen;* in his time it was not so firmly considered part

---

Supervising and training analyst, Columbia College of Physicians and Surgeons, Psychoanalytic Center for Training and Research; private practitioner of adult and child psychoanalysis.

The Psychoanalytic Study of the Child 56, ed. Albert J. Solnit, Peter B. Neubauer, Samuel Abrams, and A. Scott Dowling (Yale University Press, copyright © 2001 by Albert J. Solnit, Peter B. Neubauer, Samuel Abrams, and A. Scott Dowling).

of the Shakespeare canon, although De Quincey, Coleridge, and Lamb had argued very convincingly that at least some of the text bore the unmistakable stamp of Shakespeare's style and genius. If indeed Freud had read this play, one wonders what he would have made of the notion that Shakespeare may have had an intuition about transference as early as 1613!

Whereas Frank Kermode (2000) finds Shakespeare's late writing style complicated, convoluted, and unclear, Harold Bloom (1998) believes that *The Two Noble Kinsmen* shows evidence, in its maturity, of the great legacy that preceded it (*Hamlet, King Lear, Macbeth, Anthony and Cleopatra, The Winter's Tale, The Tempest*). Bloom does not deny that, from *Coriolanus* on, a psychological sea-change shifted Shakespeare's literary agenda away from the complex, conflicted characters of the great tragedies to the fantastic, cynical, dark motifs of the late Romances. This is not the place to take up the issue of whether Shakespeare had a nervous breakdown at the time of writing *Timon of Athens* or *Coriolanus* (as Dover Wilson [1960] and Empson [1986] have implied, respectively). I suggest, rather, that Shakespeare probably wrote himself out of whatever psychological troubles he was experiencing and that history is the great benefactor of his literary self-analysis. While the profound cynicism of *Troilus and Cressida* may have found further expression in some of the darkness of *The Two Noble Kinsmen,* there is more than darkness in this final project, as I will attempt to show in this paper.

Since we can assume that this play does not enjoy the readership of the better known tragedies, comedies, histories, and romances, a summary is in order to orient the reader and place my commentary in a context that will allow critical evaluation.

The Two Noble Kinsmen, as the self-conscious, even self-derogatory prologue makes clear, is a retelling of Chaucer's "The Knight's Tale," but with an additional and original subplot about the love and madness of a jailer's daughter. At the beginning of the play, Theseus, Duke of Athens, is about to marry Hippolyta, Queen of the Amazons. The ceremony is interrupted by the arrival of three queens, who beg Theseus to postpone his wedding and to help them in their dispute with Creon, King of Thebes, who had forbidden the burial of those enemies who died in the unsuccessful War of the Seven against Thebes. The husbands of the three queens were among the dead. Theseus, at first reluctant to interrupt his marriage ceremony, is finally persuaded to do so by his bride-to-be, Hippolyta, her sister, Emilia, and his friend, Pirithous. This sets the stage for the involvement of the cousins Palamon and Arcite, the two noble kinsmen, in the ensuing drama. Nephews of Creon, they dislike him but nevertheless fight on his side and end up captured and imprisoned by Theseus. From their prison, they spot Emilia, and the plot begins to thicken. Up to this point they have professed great love for each other, extolling the uniqueness and durability of their kinship. Now that Palamon has laid eyes on Emilia first, he summons Arcite to take note of her too. Palamon feeling immediate and intense love tells Arcite, "Never till now I was in prison, Arcite." Arcite has not noticed Emilia yet. Palamon, pointing, says, "Behold and wonder. By heaven she is a goddess."

Arcite also falls in love instantly, and the cousins' prior insistence that only death can sever the bonds of love between them is forgotten. Now each insists on his claim to Emilia, even if it means the death of the other. When Pirithous intercedes on Arcite's behalf, the young knight is freed but banished. He doesn't want to leave Athens, imagining that Palamon, even in prison, will have some access to Emilia that he, banished, would be denied. He disguises himself and wins the admiration of Theseus and Emilia for his prowess. But not for long. The jailer's daughter, who has fallen in love with Palamon, frees her prisoner. Still shackled, he meets Arcite in the woods. They quarrel. Arcite, the epitome of knighthood and chivalry, agrees to procure a file to remove Palamon's bonds so that the two cousins can fight to the finish on equal terms. As they begin to fight, Theseus happens upon them, and they are apprehended again. Both profess love for Emilia. Convinced that banishment would not work in view of their love for Emilia, Theseus arranges that they will return within a month, with three knights each, to fight a contest: Theseus will place a pyramid in the ground, and the cousin who forces the other "by fair and knightly strength to touch the pillar" will win Emilia. The defeated warrior and his knights will be executed. Emilia reluctantly agrees to this plan even though she is deeply affected by the realization that her plight has no good solution since her happiness with one cousin means the death of the other.

In the meantime, the subplot is brewing. The jailer's daughter who freed Palamon, hoping to rejoin him eventually, goes mad as a consequence of unrequited love and perhaps also of the fear/wish that her father, the jailer, may get into trouble because of her actions. A doctor summoned by the jailer believes he can exploit "the lover's malady" the girl suffers by redirecting it away from Palamon onto another object. By the play's end, the doctor's treatment has been successful.

Things are not going quite so well for Emilia. The contest between Palamon and Arcite begins but she can't bear to watch it. At first Palamon seems to be winning, but eventually it is Arcite who is victorious. Palamon and his knights are about to be executed when news reaches them that Arcite has been thrown from his horse and is near death. Palamon is reprieved by this intervention of fate. The two kinsmen revive their mutual affection, however briefly. Arcite kisses Emilia before he dies. Emilia and Palamon are united. Theseus reveals that Arcite had acknowledged to him that since Palamon had seen Emilia first, it was only fair that he should have her. The play ends with Theseus's admission that fate is more powerful than he. "The gods my justice Take from my hand, and they themselves become the executioners."

This sketch of the plot in no way conveys the rich and profound awareness of human psychology that pervades many aspects of the play. The chivalrous Chaucerian motif, which Shakespeare bends to his own purposes, can nevertheless prevent a full appreciation of the philosophical maturity of the bard at this stage of his life. It is not without relevance, perhaps, to consider, or attempt to consider, the psychology of the author as he approaches the writing of this, his final work (he died a few years later at the age of 52). It has been suggested that *The Tempest* was his final dramatic statement and that Prospero's vow to "drown his book" was an allusion to Shakespeare's own retirement from the stage. Since he subsequently wrote *Henry VIII* and *The Two Noble Kinsmen* (both presumably in collaboration with John Fletcher) it would seem that his retirement to Stratford did not completely erase the memory and allure of the theatre from his mind. Given the depth and intuitive creativity of *The Two Noble Kinsmen,* I believe it is reasonable to argue in hindsight that his genius and its timeless unconscious inventiveness had a final statement to make and that in this final statement he reviewed, with remarkable prescience, a fair portion of human developmental psychology. He even threw in a precursory prefiguration of transference for good measure. Let me begin to spell out the details.

From a symbolic point of view, the arrival of the three queens at the beginning of the play and their interruption of the marriage ceremony of Theseus and Hippolyta can be considered a dramatic statement about the conflict between the forces of fate (the three sisters, the Parcae, one of whom represents Death[1]) and the forces of life (a

---

1. Ideas proposed by Freud in his comments on the themes of three caskets in *The Merchant of Venice* and the three daughters in *King Lear.*

marriage ceremony). As mentioned earlier, the play ends with Theseus' acknowledgment that the gods are in control, not he. If fate has the first word and the last word, the whole conflicted drama of the human condition is wedged between their powerful presences. From this perspective, we can say that Shakespeare is asking us to consider Emilia's hesitations as she considers her sexuality and development and the jailer's daughter's madness as reminders of the great risks involved in falling in love. If we consider Emilia and the jailer's daughter as two aspects of a Shakespearean statement about female sexuality, careful scrutiny of the text reveals the depth of the insights. In Act I, Scene 3, there is a remarkable exchange between Hippolyta and Emilia. Emilia has noticed the close relationship between Theseus and Pirithous, and Hippolyta tells her that the two men have an extraordinary friendship. She even wonders whether, if forced to make a choice, Theseus would be able to decide between them. Emilia immediately chides Hippolyta, insisting that of course Theseus would choose her over Pirithous. Then Emilia reminisces about her own closeness as a child to a "playfellow," Flavina, who died "when our count/was each eleven." This passage is especially beautiful, and I quote it at some length.

> You talk of Pirithous' and Theseus' love,
> Theirs has more ground, is more maturely seasoned,
> More buckled with strong judgement, and their needs
> The one of th'other may be said to water
> Their intertangled roots of love. But I
> And she I sigh and spoke of were things innocent,
> *Loved for we did,* and like the elements
> That know not what, nor why, yet do effect
> Rare issues by their operance, our souls
> Did so to one another. What she liked
> Was then of me approved, what not, condemned,
> No more arraignment. The flower that I would pluck
> And then put between my breasts—O, then but beginning
> To swell about the blossom—she would long
> Till she had such another, and commit it
> To the like innocent cradle, where phoenix-like
> They died in perfume; on my head no toy
> But was her pattern; her affections—pretty
> Though happily her careless wear—I followed
> For my most serious decking; had mine ear
> Stolen some new air, or at adventure hummed one
> From musical coinage, why, it was a note
> Whereon her spirits would sojourn—rather dwell on
> And sing it in her slumbers.

This is as beautiful a description as one can imagine of the homosexual intimacy between two eleven-year-olds. Shakespeare has astutely captured the phenomenology of young love: the dawn of adolescent sexuality, the heterosexual avoided at first perhaps for defensive reasons, the regressive turning toward the pre-oedipal mother and its attendant anxieties, leading to a first expression of homosexual intimacy, symbiotic almost in its imitative lack of differentiation between the two parties. Innocence is insisted upon, guilt denied, as the love is viewed as "like the elements that know not what nor why, yet do effect rate issues by their operance."

Emilia ends her speech saying that this reminiscence of a long-ago love, while imperfectly remembered perhaps, still suggests "that the true love 'tween maid and maid may be more than in sex dividual!" All that a psychoanalyst can add to this extraordinary description would be the suggestion that Emilia's love for Flavina may antedate her experience at age eleven and may owe some, if not all, of its emotional urgency to her relationship with her mother in the first year of life. Hippolyta notices that Emilia is out of breath at the fast-paced telling of her memory. She comments:

> You're out of breath,
> And this high-speeded pace is but to say
> That you shall never—like the maid Flavina—
> love any that's called man.

"I am sure I shall not," says Emilia, her identification with the dead eleven-year-old shaping her convictions at this stage of her development. Since we know that Shakespeare's only son, Hamnet, a twin, died at age eleven, it is tempting to suggest that Emilia's deep sentiments for the loss of an eleven-year-old must echo the anguish of Shakespeare himself, still grieving perhaps, in a sublimated form to be sure, for the loss of his son some twenty years earlier. In fact, one could argue cautiously that the whole subsequent play, which deals with Emilia's agonizing choice between Palamon and Arcite, could be a reflection of Shakespeare's own fateful dilemma and mandate that he must continue to love Judith (the other twin) even while grieving Hamnet! Since it is known that Judith lived to the age of seventy-seven, surviving her own children, we can surmise that the Shakespeares, William and Anne, did not neglect Judith's development while mourning Hamnet. It goes without saying that Emilia could echo not only Shakespeare's grief but his empathic understanding of Judith's psychology as well. But I have gotten ahead of myself. Let us return to the text and continue to examine it closely.

In many ways, the play can be considered a reflection on the nature of sexuality, which is life-long, as Palamon suggests in Act V Scene 1, as he addresses the goddess: "O thou that from eleven to ninety reign'st/In mortal bosoms, whose chase is this world/And we in herds thy game." Earlier in the same scene, Palamon, prior to his fight with Arcite for Emilia's hand, acknowledges the great power of Venus to stoke the fires of sexuality in old age.

> I knew a man
> Of eighty winters . . . who
> A lass of fourteen brided, 'twas thy power
> To put life into dust. The aged cramp
> Had screwed his square foot round;
> The gout had knit his fingers into knots;
> Torturing convulsions from his globy eyes
> Had almost drawn their spheres, that what was life
> In him seemed torture. This anatomy
> Had by his young fair fere a boy, and I
> Believed it was his, for she swore it was,
> And who would not believe her?

If sexuality for Shakespeare spans the period between age eleven and ninety, he would not seem to have anticipated the infantile sexuality of the first five years of life. That remarkable insight would have to await the genius of Sigmund Freud for its explication. (In his "Seven Ages of Man" [in *As You Like It*], a kind of developmental profile of human life from infancy to old age, Shakespeare does skip from phase I, "at first the infant mewling and puking in the nurse's arms," to phase II, "and then the school boy with his satchel and shining mornin' face, creeping/like a snail unwillingly to school," as if infantile sexual development between infancy and latency didn't exist.) However, what Shakespeare did intuit between eleven and ninety is nothing short of extraordinary.

If Emilia is Shakespeare's depiction of a young woman still trapped in the psychology of an eleven-year-old, yearning for pre-oedipal symbiotic union with the maternal imago, reluctant to embrace heterosexual strivings, Hippolyta is a mature woman who is able to chide Emilia's homosexual fixation, saying in effect that if she allowed Emilia to influence her she would end up thinking that Theseus loved Pirithous more than he loved her, that Pirithous rather than she "possessed the high throne in his heart." Throughout the play, in fact, Emilia seems to make comments that betray her maternal preoccupations with Hippolyta serving as a psychological corrective to this unidimensionality, stressing the paternal. For instance, in Act II

Scene 5, where Emilia, praising Arcite, says

> His mother was a wondrous handsome woman;
> His face, methinks, goes that way.

Hippolyta counters with

> But his body
> And fiery mind illustrate a brave father.

By Act IV Scene 2, Emilia's development has matured. She enters the stage alone with two pictures, one of Arcite, one of Palamon, trying to decide between them. At first she finds Arcite more to her liking, exclaiming:

> Here love himself sits smiling
> while Palamon is but his foil, to him a mere dull shadow;
> He's smart and meagre, of an eye as heavy
> As if he had lost his mother. . . .

Still harping on the mother, it would seem; yet a few lines later, she has changed her mind about Palamon

> On my knees
> I ask thy pardon; Palamon, thou art alone
> And only beautiful and . . .
> What a bold gravity, and yet inviting
> Has this grown manly face! O love, this only
> From this hour is complexion.

This wavering between homosexual leanings and the heterosexual is well captured by Shakespeare: Emilia, asked by her brother what her choice is, names Arcite; but if asked by her sister, she says Palamon. If Arcite is symbolic of the masculine and Palamon of the feminine, at this stage of the play, Shakespeare is suggesting that maturity demands that they be integrated. Describing the knights that attend Arcite and Palamon, Shakespeare suggests that a mixture of male and female characteristics seems to make them even more heroic: of one it is said

> in his face
> The livery of the warlike maid appears,
> Pure red and white, for yet no beard has blessed him;
> His red lips, after fights, are fit for ladies.

Of another

> His arms are brawny
> Lined with strong sinews—to the shoulder-piece
> Gently they swell, like women new-conceived

> Which speaks him prone to labour, never fainting
> Under the weight of arms; . . . .
>   He's grey-eyed,

Which yields compassion where he conquers. Since grey eyes were considered to be a sign of compassion and to be marks of beauty in a woman, this description of a male warrior with swollen muscles that evoke pregnancies and labor (a pun on hard work and childbearing) does seem to extol the integration of masculine and feminine features in the ideal male.

There is also a subtle suggestion by play's end that Emilia possesses an unconscious and that *it* chose Palamon. Whereas at the beginning of the play, Emilia implies that her love for Flavina at age eleven was innocent, "like the elements that know not what nor why," at the end of the play it is clear that Emilia *knows* guilt and conflict. She cannot watch the fight between Arcite and Palamon because if either glanced at her and suffered injury because of the momentary lapse of attention to the fray she would be guilty:

> O better never to have been born
> Than minister to such harm.

She also acknowledges that she kept Palamon's picture on her left side, where "the heart lies"; Palamon therefore had the best-boding chance." "Why so I know not," she declares, dismissing conscious cognizance of the act, but Shakespeare would appear to understand the mysterious workings of the unconscious in this instance. Later, when Arcite is declared victorious, Emilia again betrays an unconscious superstitious line of thought when she says:

> I did think
> Good Palamon would miscarry, yet I knew not
> Why I did think so. Our reasons are not prophets
> When oft our fancies are.

Shakespeare suggests that the primary processes of imagination are more prophetic than the secondary processes of "reason." The language is poetic, but is there a finer way of describing the unconscious at work? There is one other piece of suggestive unconscious ambiguity or irony that Shakespeare deploys to deepen the character of Emilia with a final tragic nuance: Arcite is thrown from the horse that Emilia "did first bestow on him," a black horse "owing not a hair-worth of white." Shakespeare insists that if Emilia claimed innocence at first, an eleven-year-old's abdication of psychological responsibility, maturity allows no such escape from the complexity of human conflict as the twin emotions, love and hatred, are engaged and the psychology of choice, rejection, and differentiation cannot be avoided.

Finally, in this psychology-laden play, if we turn to the subplot that deals with the jailer's daughter, I believe we will discover that Shakespeare has an ultimate dramatic ace up his sleeve. As mentioned earlier, it is possible to think of Emilia and the jailer's daughter as a composite character, Shakespeare exploiting both to explore the complexities of female sexuality. In fact I think one could argue that the psychology of both these women is more deeply probed than that of the anonymous knights. The two major changes Shakespeare makes in retelling Chaucer's "The Knights' Tale" are in the dramatic ending, whereby the loser of the contest must die (Chaucer's rendition did not demand the death of Palamon) and the addition of the jailer's daughter (in Chaucer the knight is freed by the intervention of a friend). Clearly the introduction of the jailer's daughter (who, incidentally, has more soliloquies than any other female character in Shakespeare's plays) is the major emendation.

The jailer's daughter is tragically affected by her love of Palamon. She wanders in the forest distracted, unrequited. "I am mop'd," she says.

> Food took I none these two days.
> Sipped some water, I have not closed mine eyes
> Save when my lids scowrd off their brine; alas
> Dissolve, my life, let not my sense unsettle
> Lest I should drown, or stab or hang myself.

When she next appears she is mad. She sings songs and talks a seeming nonsense about flowers, love, and Palamon.

When her father, concerned about his daughter's behavior, asks the doctor, "What thinks you of her, sir?" the doctor replies, "I think she has a perturbed mind which I cannot minister to." This exchange sounds very similar to Macbeth's dialogue with Lady MacBeth's physician in Act V, Scene 3, of *Macbeth*.

> *Macbeth:* How does your patient, doctor?
> *Doctor:*   Not so sick, my lord,
> As she is troubled with thick coming fancies,
> That keep her from her rest.
> *Macbeth:*   Cure her of that.
> Canst thou not minister to a mind diseased,
> Pluck from the memory a rooted sorrow,
> Raze out the written troubles of the brain
> And with some sweet oblivious antidote
> Cleanse the stuff'd bosom of that perilous stuff

Which weighs upon the heart?
Doctor: Therein the patient
Must minister to himself.

The doctor in *The Two Noble Kinsmen,* however, is not so dismissive: he has a novel plan of intervention which he believes can cure the patient (by Act V, Scene 4, the cure has in fact been accomplished), and this treatment plan in some features resembles the exploitation of transference and transference neurosis in modern Freudian psychoanalyses.

The doctor also says, by way of diagnosis: "'Tis not an engraffed madness but a most thick and profound melancholy." This would seem to be the Elizabethan equivalent of what Lawrence Babb (1951) has called "lover's malady." The doctor, on learning that the jailer's daughter was attracted to another man prior to falling in love with Palamon, suggests that she be confined to a place "where the light may rather seem to steal in that be permitted." The young man who preceded Palamon in her affection—called "the wooer" in the text—should now pretend that he is Palamon. "This will catch her attention, for this her mind beats upon." The doctor's diagnosis, couched in pompous, verbose language that was no doubt meant to make audiences groan or snicker, nevertheless reveals Shakespeare's thinking about the nature of mental illness. He implies that excessive gazing upon Palamon has unhinged the girl's other senses: "The intemp'rate surfeit of her eye hath distempered the other senses; they may return and settle again to execute their preordained faculties, but they are now in a most extravagant vagary." The doctor, in my opinion, is suggesting that the wooer, by becoming an object of transference, will draw her attention back from Palamon and the other objects to which it has been displaced. While Shakespeare seems to be on to the concept of "displacement," which after all is the essential economic "vector" in transference, there is no intuition about the "genetic" origin of the process, the early maternal or parental relationship that sets it in motion. However, Shakespeare does seem to sense that rerouting of libido and its exclusive new focus on the wooer will provide a cure for the girl's madness. He describes the displacement referred to above in the following manner: "Other objects that are inserted 'tween her mind and her eye become the pranks and friskins of her madness." The doctor advises the wooer that, once he has captured her attention by this subterfuge, he should "sing to her such green songs of love as she says Palamon has sung in prison; come to her stuck in as sweet flowers as the season is mistress of, and thereto make an addition of some other compounded odours which are grateful to the sense . . . Learn what maids have been her companions and playferes, and let them repair to her with Palamon in their mouths and appear with tokens as if they suggested for him. It is a falsehood she is in, which is with falsehoods to be combated."

Shakespeare seems to have had an inkling of "the false connection" between one object and another; its full explication would have to wait a few centuries, of course, for Sigmund Freud. The doctor suggests that this treatment "will bring forth comfort" and "may bring her to eat, to sleep and reduce what's now out of square in her into their former law and regiment." As for his own role in the treatment plan, the doctor says, "I will, between the passages of this project, come in with my appliance." Since appliance means "treatment," this is a reference to what the doctor's activity will be while "the falsehoods" are being expressed by the doctor's assistant, the "wooer." Shakespeare and Fletcher do not spell out how the doctor might have "ministered to a mind diseased" or planned to re-integrate the various aspects of his treatment plan into a coherent whole that would "hasten the success, which doubt not will bring forth comfort."

The Elizabethan doctor would approach the lover and his other malady with a variety of therapeutic strategies. If the object of the patient's love could be identified and satisfaction "arranged," this could result in cure. The doctor would be on the alert, trying to identify the object, which could prove to be an arduous task at times. Recording a rapid pulse rate when the love object came into view or even when the name of the beloved was mentioned would be on the right track, so to speak, in pursuit of his diagnosis. If the desired object could not be procured for the patient, for whatever reason, and cure by satisfaction could not be arranged, then alternate methods would have to be considered: for example, bloodletting, distraction of the lover toward religious ideas, etc. The sufferer would be told to avoid wine, stimulating foods, and dark, depressing environments. By suggesting a dimly lit environment, the doctor in *The Two Noble Kinsmen* is not following the conventional (Elizabethan) wisdom, suggesting that Shakespeare was contemplating a new, revolutionary approach to cure. (The commentator who remarks that this is an example of a crude cure by love is missing the subtlety of the cure by transference that Shakespeare is hinting at here, in a precocious prefiguration of a central Freudian concept.)

The idea of curing a falsehood with a falsehood, for instance, invites comparison with the Freudian concept of transference. Transference can be viewed as a false connection that the analysand makes unwittingly between a current object (the analyst) and a genetic one from the past. When the false connection is pointed out to the analysand, the insight thus gained into the workings of the unconscious is, as Freud remarked, one of the most convincing aspects of psychoanalytic process. Truth is rescued from distortion as past is sifted from present through the interpretation of transference. Current reality is no longer confused with the realities or even unrealities (phantasies) of childhood when exposure of transference distortion reveals the false theories of childhood that insinuate themselves into adult perception. This is a roundabout way of arriving at the truth, to be sure, but it *is* the way of psychoanalytic process. "By indirection find direction out," as Shakespeare once put it in a totally different context. The analyst, mistaken for a childhood revenant, eventually, through the interpretation of psychoanalytic process, becomes himself again, and the analysand becomes himself again, only more so, armed as he now is with an expanded consciousness. The transference neurosis, a kind of post-Elizabethan lover's malady, uses the falsehood of transference to arrive at a more abiding and compelling version of truth.

When the doctor in *The Two Noble Kinsmen* says, "I will between the passages of this project come in with my appliance," Shakespeare, who never spells out any details of the treatment the doctor planned, nevertheless seemed to be uncannily hinting at what Elizabethan medicine might have done with the transference had it known how to understand and exploit it. Three hundred years would pass before Sigmund Freud would recognize its power and use it therapeutically. Surely it diminishes Freud's monumental discovery not a whit to acknowledge Shakespeare's remarkable psychoanalytic intuition in Stratford three centuries before the discovery of the unconscious in Vienna. In fact, one could argue that science, literature, and the history of ideas thrive on these associative connections between two such noble kinsmen of the mind.

I have been emphasizing Shakespeare's intuition about transference, which I think is particularly interesting from a psychoanalytic point of view. But of course the jailer's daughter is important for other reasons too. It is suggested that she goes mad not only because of her unrequited love for Palamon but also for fear of the trouble her actions may cause for her father. She speaks generically at one point, saying that if her father had more prisoners like Palamon and more daughters like her, he would soon have an empty prison to watch over. Surely Shakespeare is alluding here to the adolescent's mandate to fly the coop and all the psychological complexities that have to be negotiated so that maturity rather than madness is the outcome.

If Shakespeare is thinking developmentally, is he suggesting that it is understandable for Emilia at age eleven to be regressive, tentative, symbiotic, and homosexual since becoming a young woman means dealing with adolescent infatuations and conflicts with parents?

From a further developmental point of view, Theseus and Hippolyta would seem to be symbolic of heterosexual maturity; yet Theseus in his final statement senses that maturity does not mean mastery over all of life's contingencies. Wisdom in a sense is a mature acceptance of all we cannot know or control. In *Hamlet,* Shakespeare contended that "readiness is all" and in Lear that "ripeness is all." In *The Two Noble Kinsmen,* in his last serious poetic utterance, he seems to be restating his definition of maturity, implying ironically that there may always be an element of childhood in it:

> O you heavenly charmers,
> What things you make of us! For what we lack
> We laugh; for what we have we are sorry; still
> Are children in some kind. Let us be thankful
> For that which is, and with you leave dispute
> That are above our question. Let's go off,
> And bear us like the time.

Theseus' parting shot at the capricious "heavenly charmers" would seem to be his identification with them, or rather his refusal to identify with them, as he goes off to bear himself "like the time." This does not seem to be akin to Emilia's plea for innocence in Act I, when she imagines herself like the elements, but rather an identification with time, which by definition takes change in stride. Shakespeare seems to be suggesting that maturity lies not in resistance to or rejection of developmental change but in actively embracing it, the "existential" becoming the "personal" as life rings its many changes from age eleven to ninety.

A psychoanalyst's definition of time obviously would not exclude the first ten years of life, and one senses that the Shakespeare who could write "still are children in some kind" was not without certain intuitions about our earliest years. This is what gives Shakespeare's last words their extraordinary poignancy as child and man join forces in a complex definition of psychological maturity. "No concluding lines elsewhere in Shakespeare seem to me nearly as comforting," writes Harold Bloom in his deeply moving, deeply insightful chapter on *The Two Noble Kinsmen.* Bloom's reading of "bearing us like the time" suggests that Shakespeare, "saying goodbye to us forever," implies that maturity lies not in sustaining the mere here-and-nowness of existence but in a sober if not exuberant embrace of whatever time remains to us. This is not just Shakespearean wisdom but Freudian wisdom also, two noble kinsmen of the mind complementing each other across the ages.

BIBLIOGRAPHY

BABB, L. (1951). *The Elizabethan Malady.* East Lansing: Michigan State University Press.

BERTRAM, P. (1965). *Shakespeare and* The Two Noble Kinsmen. New Brunswick, N.J.

BLOOM, H. (1998). *Shakespeare: The Invention of the Human.* New York: Riverhead Books.

EMPSON, WILLIAM (1986). "Essays on Shakespeare." Cambridge University Press, 1986.

FREUD, S. [1913]. The Theme of The Three Caskets. S.E. Vol. 12, p. 291.

KERMODE, F. (2000). *Shakespearean Language.* New York: Farrar, Straus and Giroux.

SHAKESPEARE, W. (1613). *Two Noble Kinsmen,* E. Waith, ed. (1994). New York: Oxford University Press.

WILSON, J. (1960). *The Essential Shakespeare.* London: Cambridge University Press.

Index